Bar Wars

Contesting the Night in
Contemporary British Cities

PHIL HADFIELD

OXFORD
UNIVERSITY PRESS

OXFORD

UNIVERSITY PRESS

Great Clarendon Street, Oxford OX2 6DP

Oxford University Press is a department of the University of Oxford.
It furthers the University's objective of excellence in research, scholarship,
and education by publishing worldwide in

Oxford New York

Auckland Cape Town Dar es Salaam Hong Kong Karachi
Kuala Lumpur Madrid Melbourne Mexico City Nairobi
New Delhi Shanghai Taipei Toronto

With offices in

Argentina Austria Brazil Chile Czech Republic France Greece
Guatemala Hungary Italy Japan Poland Portugal Singapore
South Korea Switzerland Thailand Turkey Ukraine Vietnam

Oxford is a registered trade mark of Oxford University Press
in the UK and in certain other countries

Published in the United States
by Oxford University Press Inc., New York

British Library Cataloguing in Publication Data
Data available

Library of Congress Cataloging in Publication Data
Hadfield, Phil.
Bar wars: contesting the night in contemporary British cities / Phil Hadfield.
p.cm.
Includes bibliographical references and index.
ISBN-10: 0–19–929785–1 ISBN-13: 978–0–19–929785–6 (hardback: alk. paper)
ISBN-10: 0–19–929786–X ISBN-13: 978–0–19–929786–3 (pbk.: alk. paper)
1. Sociology, Urban—Great Britain. 2. Great Britain—Social life and customs. 3. Central business districts—Great Britain 4. Bars (Drinking establishments)—Law and legislation—Great Britian. 5. Public spaces—Great Britain. I. Title.
HT133.H285 2006
307.760941—dc22   2006008570

Typeset by Newgen Imaging Systems (P) Ltd., Chennai, India
Printed in Great Britain
on acid-free paper by
Biddles Ltd., King's Lynn

ISBN 0–19–929785–1 (Hbk.)   978–0–19–929785–6 (Hbk.)
ISBN 0–19–929786–X (Pbk.)   978–0–19–929786–3 (Pbk.)

10 9 8 7 6 5 4 3 2 1

General Editor's Introduction

Clarendon Studies in Criminology aims to provide a forum for outstanding empirical and theoretical work in all aspects of criminology, criminal justice, penology and the wider field of deviant behaviour. The Editors welcome excellent Ph.D. work, as well as submissions from established scholars. The *Series* was inaugurated in 1994, with Roger Hood as its first General Editor, following energetic discussions between Oxford University Press and three Criminology Centres. It is edited under the auspices of these three Criminological Centres: the Cambridge Institute of Criminology, the Mannheim Centre for Criminology at the London School of Economics, and the Oxford Centre for Criminology. Each supplies members of the Editorial Board.

Phil Hadfield's highly original book, *Bar Wars: Contesting the Night in Contemporary British Cities*, continues a longstanding tradition of key sociological studies of urban life. He documents the longstanding tensions between freedom and control in nightlife settings, showing how the night's economic potential is successfully exploited by powerful private interests. Regulatory constraints which once held the alcohol industry in check have been reduced as increasing numbers of night-time 'consumption zones' appear in our neo-liberal cities. The author provides a fascinating account of the 'core consumers of nightlife' and of the roles of the DJ and others in manufacturing just the right atmosphere in these venues. Clubs should be boisterous, intoxicating, but moderately controlled—settings in which maximum profits can be secured. Harms caused by increasing supplies of popular spots are sidelined in official construction of the night-time economy and its risks. In an account reminiscent of the best classical studies of criminal courts, licensing trials are shown to be dominated by commercially directed and political interests. Ordinary residents of urban communities, and evidence-based research, play minor and heavily constrained roles in the decision making about new premises. A democratic deficit exists in the 'governance of the night'. This is a first rate ethnography of the contemporary night in British cities and a carefully critical account of the deregulation of its control, and the powerful role of the leisure industry in this process.

The editors welcome this important addition to the *Series*.

Alison Liebling
University of Cambridge,
March 2006

Council (R42200034167) and I remain grateful to the Council for its support.

Last, but not least, I would like to thank all the people who gave freely of their time in helping me conduct this research. Assurances of anonymity prevent me from naming those from whom I learned everything, from the meaning of *de novo* to 'the best thing about vomits (*sic*)...'.

Acknowledgements

Firstly, I would like to thank everyone who accompanied me on my night-time forays. The various reprobates know who they are and shall remain nameless. I simply couldn't have done this stuff without you guys and hope you all had a few laughs along the way.

Safely back in daylight, my examiners, Paul Rock and Robin Williams, aided me immeasurably with their incisive comments on early drafts. Both offered me invaluable advice and I found their work inspirational. I am also indebted to Martin Elvins, James Hardie-Bick, Stuart Lister, Ian Loader, Kate O'Brien, Nigel South, Richard Sparks and Tank Waddington, and to OUP's anonymous reviewers for their curiosity, insight, and constructive criticism. Philip Kolvin was always supportive and helped me unravel some of the regulatory process's many mysteries. Thanks also to my editor, Gwen Booth, and to the series editor, Alison Liebling, for their assistance in navigating the publication process. The cover image was crafted by Becky Hutley and many thanks go to her and to Graham Warren at *North* bar, Newcastle. My greatest academic acknowledgement must go to Dick Hobbs, who supervised the original thesis. His wisdom and, most of all, his wit, continues to inspire. The book's undoubted flaws are of my making.

I owe a great debt to my family for supporting me in what has been an unavoidably protracted process. Latterly, the nature of the task meant that I often had to immerse myself in work to the extent that other things which should have been done were not. My parents Sam and Una Hadfield were always there to tie up some of those loose ends. Sarah brightened my days and I am grateful for that. Thanks to Lily for her smile.

Small sections of Chapter 4 previously appeared, in a different form, in a paper I wrote for P. Kolvin (ed.) (2004) *Licensed Premises: Law and Practice* (Haywards Heath: Tottel) and are used here with the permission of Tottel Publishing. The research for this book was initially funded by a three-year studentship award from the Economic and Social Research

Contents

Acknowledgements ix

Introduction

1 'Couldn't Give a XXXX for Last Orders?':
   The Politics of the Night   1

Part I: Nights Past

2 The Uses of Darkness   21
3 Paradise Lost: The Rise of the Night-time High Street   39

Part II: The Contemporary Environment

4 Behind Bars: Social Control in Licensed Premises   81
5 Contesting Public Space   123

Part III: Contemporary Contestations

6 The Combatants   159
7 Rose-coloured Spectacles Versus the Prophecies of
   Doom (the Shaping of Trial Discourse)   175
8 Notes from the Frontline: Licensing and the Courts   215

Conclusions

9 Contesting the Night   259
10 Shadowing the Night People: A Methodological
   Postscript   273

Glossary   283

References   285

Index   317

1

'Couldn't Give a XXXX for Last Orders?': The Politics of the Night

If you're in the business of fighting crime, then you have to be in the business of dealing with the alcohol issue.

Britain's 'violent crime tsar' (Paul Evans, Home Office Police Standards Unit, *The Observer* 21 November 2004: 15).

Each side musters what power it can exert to its own advantage, or at least to block the other side and force a compromise . . . The night group fights harder because its jobs and profits are at stake (Melbin 1987: 70–71).

The night-time economy (NTE) arguably poses the greatest threat to public order in Britain today. Certain forms of violent crime, criminal damage and anti-social behaviour have long been concentrated in and around nightlife areas (Bromley and Nelson 2002, Budd 2003, Hobbs et al. 2003, Hope 1985, Nelson et al. 2001, Tuck 1989) with the majority of incidents occurring on the streets rather than within licensed premises themselves (Nelson et al. 2001, Tuck 1989, Warburton and Shepherd 2004). Similarly, analyses of temporal patterning have shown violent and disorderly incidents to peak between 11pm and 3am on Friday nights/Saturday mornings and Saturday nights/Sunday mornings; periods in which pedestrian activity is at its height (Budd 2003, Hope 1985, Maguire and Nettleton 2003, Nelson et al. 2001, Shepherd 1990, Tuck 1989). Environmental criminologists are unlikely to be surprised by such trends. It is often noted that crime events are concentrated in space and time and considerable progress has been made in explaining why this might be so (Bottoms and Wiles 2002, Brantingham and Brantingham 1993, Ekblom 2001, Felson and Clarke 1998).

This book is the first study to look in detail at that most salient and criminogenic component of the NTE, the night-time high street. The term 'night-time high street' will be used to describe those central areas of our towns and cities in which licensed premises are most densely concentrated. A further defining feature of this environment is the proliferation of themed and branded venues operated by major corporate players. These night-time zones of consumption therefore mirror the day-time shopping environment to the extent that each high street increasingly resembles another, local idiosyncrasies having been replaced by a more standardized and homogenous range of products and services. The form of nightlife available to consumers in such areas is thoroughly populist, as constituted by mainstream options relating to music, dress, social comportment and cultural norms; it is a leisure experience fuelled by recreational drugs, principally alcohol.

In drawing conclusions from a previous study,[1] my colleagues and I argued that one should not fear bouncers or other inhabitants of the night-time city quite so much as the market forces that have shaped the human ecology in which all participants must now swim.[2] This book attempts to answer a number of urgent questions arising from that statement: how might market forces be said to create such criminogenic environments? What type of political and economic conditions may encourage corporate interests to colonize the night and ensure that such development proceeds largely unchecked by regulatory constraint? What forms of social control, street life and public sociability are fostered by the new leisure environment, and what impact might they have upon modes of public and private policing? How do central government and the leisure and drinks corporations act to protect and consolidate their interests against external threats?

The following chapters chart the rise of the high street leisure market during a period of rapid political, economic and regulatory change. As urban stakeholders, local government, central government, nightlife operators, the police, local residents, and consumers, all have various, and often competing,

---

[1] Economic and Social Research Council (ESRC) Violence Research Programme award no. L133251050, culminating in the book, *Bouncers: Violence and Governance in the Night-time Economy* (Hobbs, Hadfield, Lister and Winlow 2003).

[2] See introduction and conclusion to Hobbs et al. (2003), especially pages 11 and 277.

conceptions of social order in relation to what is seen as the 'appropriate' usage and meaning of night-time public and private space. This book seeks to highlight the resulting struggles within and between such groups.

The shifting terrain

Since the publication of *Bouncers*, policy debate regarding the NTE has moved on and the political situation has become more heated. Much of this controversy has been stimulated by the Licensing Act (2003) (henceforth referred to as 'the Act'). On the night before the 2001 General Election, a quarter of a million young people received a text message which read: 'Cldnt give a XXXX 4 last ordrs? Thn vte Lbr on thrsday 4 xtra time.' This, then popular, manifesto promise translated into the policy of a government which saw the extension of licensing hours as an economic boost for a drinks and leisure sector that had been lobbying hard for de-regulation of their business interests. Although the Act received Royal Assent in July 2003, a lengthy process of transition ensued and the new licensing system did not become fully operable until November 2005.

Having decided upon its course of action, the government had to 'find a system of justification that explained exactly why it was the right and proper thing to do' (Chomsky 1992: 127). Licensing policy had historically been developed by the Home Office. In 2001, this changed following the transfer of licensing jurisdiction to the Department for Culture, Media and Sport (DCMS), Tourism Division. Having gained responsibility for licensing, this 'ministry of fun', as it is sometimes known, was tasked with drafting and implementing the Act. The DCMS outlined a number of key policy aims for the legislation, including:

- The removal of 'obstacles to the further development of the tourism, retail, hospitality and leisure industries';
- The 'slashing' of regulatory 'red tape' for businesses;
- 'Relaxed trading hours' that will 'provide greater choice for consumers . . . allowing England and Wales' NTEs to rival their European (*sic*) counterparts';
- The introduction of a 'crucial mechanism for the regeneration of areas that need the increased investment and employment opportunities that a thriving NTE can bring' (DCMS 2004a: 4)

The government also argued that the Act—through its removal of 'fixed' closing times and the introduction of a range of enhanced powers for the police and local authorities (Clarke and Findlay 2004, Kolvin 2004)—should be seen as a crime reduction measure. These aspects of the system were, it was claimed, sufficient to ensure that the new age of 'choice and prosperity' would not be marred by increases in alcohol-related crime and anti-social behaviour. One might have assumed that in an era of 'evidence-based' policymaking, these opinions would have been formed on the basis of criminological research and the evaluation of limited trials. Instead, the *Time for Reform* White Paper (Home Office 2000a) chose to rely upon an aged report of consultants to the drinks industry (Marsh and Fox-Kibby 1992) which argued that extended hours might reduce 'binge drinking' and associated violence around closing time (see Chapter 3). The House of Commons All-Party Parliamentary Beer Group and trade organizations such as the *British Beer and Pub Association* (BBPA); *The Portman Group*; the *Association of Licensed Multiple Retailers* (ALMR); and the *Bar, Entertainment and Dance Association* (BEDA) appeared to be exerting strong influence over the alcohol policy agenda. Such groups had the resources to participate in politics, apply pressure, lobby, and build platforms with government.

Throughout the development of the Act, one consistent problem for government was that no independent commentators from the academic and medical communities were prepared to endorse or confirm its assumed benefits. In particular, little, if any, empirical support could be found for the libertarian view that the so-called 'British disease' of alcohol-related disorder had been fermented by temperance traditions, or a history of restrictive licensing; drink being regarded as some form of 'forbidden fruit'. This type of argument was simply not borne out by international research literature and experience concerning the de-regulation of licensing hours; the introduction of extended drinking hours appearing to have, at best, neutral effects upon crime rates across a range of cultural contexts (Chikritzhs and Stockwell 2002, Glen 2000, Isle of Man Constabulary 2002, Republic of Ireland Commission on Liquor Licensing 2003, Ragnarsdottir et al. 2002, Raistrick, et al. 1999, Smith 1989). Indeed, as discussed in Chapter 7, scientific opinion increasingly ran contrary to the precepts of the Act (Academy of Medical Sciences

2004, Babor et al. 2003, Edwards et al. 1994, Room 2004a, Warburton and Shepherd 2004). Expert advisers warned that in order to stem the tide of social harms associated with alcohol, it would be necessary to reduce overall levels of consumption by imposing greater supply-side controls:

> I had watched British drinking levels rise throughout the 1990s with increasing alarm . . . I was very keen to have a scientific discussion about alcohol. But the most extraordinary process evolved . . . It didn't matter where we pointed or how we said it, the civil servants were deaf . . . They were not able to be impartial. It was like being in secret service meetings. All they wanted to do was keep the drinks industry happy and excise levels stable. (Griffith Edwards, lead author of *Alcohol and the Public Good* (Edwards et al. 1994), cited in Levy and Scott-Clark 2004: 21–22).

Thus, as Campbell (2005: 758) notes, 'that there was a risk of deplorable consequences was known, but the government undertook to manage those consequences when deciding to run that risk'.[3] In order to maintain the 'necessary illusions' (Chomsky 1989: 20) which surrounded the Act, the government chose to suppress or discard any knowledge 'inconvenient' to their purposes (see Chapter 7). As Home Office Minister Hazel Blears candidly admitted:

> I respect the scientific view, but it wasn't for us. We needed practical measures . . . Alcohol is a legal product and it is a huge part of our economy. Companies are beginning to adopt a much more socially acceptable approach . . . If there is glass on the table and vomit on the floor, places will close down (Levy and Scott-Clark 2004: 27).

In the light of their close affinities with industry, it was perhaps unsurprising that the government intended the new local 'licensing authorities' to have no power to control growth in the number of licensed premises. Yet, dissenters—drawn most prominently from the police and municipal government—pointed to ways in which expansion of the high street had generated chronic public order issues. Chapter 3 describes how in 2002–2003, as the *Alcohol and Entertainment Licensing Bill* gradually

---

[3] Interesting parallels may be drawn with the government's initial refusal to impose an outright ban on smoking in licensed premises, a decision that ran contrary to public opinion and the advice of the scientific and health care community, including one Chief Medical Officer, Sir Liam Donaldson.

mutated into the Act, the government remained enshrined in the industry camp, leaving their critics out in the cold. The Act itself was to make no reference to the 'cumulative impact' of licensed premises; market intervention being the sole prerogative of planning departments. The issue was to resurface as a major theme of contestation as the memoranda of guidance issued by the DCMS to explain how the government expected the system to be administered (DCMS 2004b, henceforth referred to as 'the Guidance') passed through the House of Lords. As Chapter 3 explains, calls for the Guidance to acknowledge cumulative impact had garnered broad and influential support and the government were ultimately forced to concede (Coulson 2003). By July 2004, when the document was finally approved, a begrudgingly tentative set of provisions had been inserted.

As scepticism also began to mount regarding the case for extended hours (see Chapter 3), the government's defeat gave renewed hope and impetus to the efforts of those councils and police forces that were seeking to exercise licensing restraint. Widespread expressions of concern regarding the possible implications of the Act similarly buoyed the cause of campaigners anxious to ensure that, despite the power of the corporate bar chains, what they regarded as the destruction of residential life and public space in urban centres would no longer become a creeping inevitability (Flanagan 2005). The political mood swing gathered pace in 2003 and 2004, being reflected in newspaper commentary on the issue (for example, Harrington and Halstead 2004, Hetherington 2003b; Kettle 2003, Levy and Scott-Clark 2004, McCurry 2003, Parker 2003) and a string of television documentaries (including a special investigation by the BBC's *Panorama* programme and a series entitled *Drunk and Dangerous* which provided weekly visceral footage from high streets across the UK).

In politics, perception becomes reality. Debate no longer surrounded the question of whether or not the 'problems' were real and, if they were, what was to be done about them. The government's new public stance was that the problems were real and something *had* to be done about them. As the pre-General Election campaign machine stirred into action again, that 'something' emerged as a pledge to 'take a stand against anti-social behaviour'; a slogan which formed the subtitle of a Home Office White Paper in which the government's defeat over cumulative impact was re-packaged as a triumph for urban citizens (!) in their fight for 'safer and cleaner public spaces' (Home Office 2003a: 10). More importantly, a new target for governmental intervention had emerged: the errant consumer. The young city centre 'binge drinker' had become emblematic of so much: the decline of civility, individual responsibility, and self-respect. In 2004, Steven Green, the Chief Constable of Nottinghamshire, was appointed as the Association of Chief Police Officers' (ACPO) spokesperson on alcohol-related crime. Green was more forthright than his predecessors in publicly highlighting the role of the police as 'mop-and-bucket' (Green 2004) of the corporate high street. During the summer and Christmas periods of 2004, the Home Office Police Standards Unit instigated high profile policing campaigns in urban centres across England and Wales.

By January 2005, the government's attempts to bound public debate regarding licensing policy were being forced into meltdown. Criticism of the Act emerged from three prominent sources: Sir John Stevens, then Commissioner of the Metropolitan Police; the Royal College of Physicians; and the parliamentary Home Affairs Select Committee on anti-social behaviour. Soon after, internal documents revealing an apparent rift between the Home Office—alarmed at increased public concern over alcohol-related crime and binge drinking—and the DCMS, were leaked to the press. The tensions arising between these very different arms of government were perhaps unsurprising when one considers the way in which policy had been formulated: the national Guidance and other matters to do with the Act being the responsibility of a department which aimed to promote Britain's leisure and tourism industries, sitting uneasily alongside a set of official licensing objectives at the core of the legislation (see Chapter 3) relating to crime control and the prevention of harm.

These various controversies combined to provide front page news and plentiful ammunition for the government's more opportunist political opponents, notably the *Daily Mail*, who launched a campaign entitled '24-Hour Drinking: The Great Rebellion' (12 January 2005). The Labour Party's woes were compounded by opinion polls commissioned by national newspapers (*Guardian/ICM*, Travis 2005, *The Times/Populus*, Riddell and Ford 2005) indicating strong public opposition to the Act. The struggle for the night had been drawn to the very epicentre of crime and disorder policy discourse.

These factors, especially the need to appease police opinion during a sensitive political period, led to the publication of a hurriedly prepared consultation document entitled *Drinking Responsibly* (DCMS, Home Office and ODPM 2005). The document announced a range of proposals, including the designation of 'Alcohol Disorder Zones' (ADZs)—a 'polluter-pays' initiative, which, for the first time, proposed a *compulsory* levy on pubs and clubs to pay for extra policing in areas where a voluntary self-regulation approach had failed. The political storm subdued, only to resurface in August 2005 when responses by ACPO and the Council of Her Majesty's Circuit Judges[4] sought to link the extension of licensing hours under the Act to a predicted escalation in violence and sexual assault; Judge Charles Harris QC commenting that 'continental-style drinking requires continental-style people'.[5] In October 2005, opposition MPs launched a final bid to delay implementation of the Act on 24 November of that year. A House of Commons motion to that effect received strong support, being rejected by 293 votes to 218. The challenge was met by an immediate assurance by ministers that the police would be encouraged to use their 'tough new powers' and that there would be a £5-million public education campaign warning against the perils of binge drinking. This campaign was to be timed to coincide with the early months of the new licensing regime, and specifically the Christmas period of 2005.

---

[4] A body representing approximately 600 practising judges from across England and Wales.

[5] Responses to the *Drinking Responsibly* consultation, published in August 2005, were predominately critical. The Local Government Association, for example, described the proposals as 'short term' and 'reactive', fearing that the designation of an ADZ may have 'a negative impact upon an area's reputation'. ACPO expressed their concern that the schemes would be repeatedly challenged in the courts at 'considerable cost to the public sector, in terms of time and money' (Turney 2005: 1). ACPO's response appeared especially pertinent in the light of Campbell's (2005: 760) concern that it may be both 'unjust and unjustifiable' to levy further taxes upon an industry whose development had been enormously encouraged by a government acting in the full knowledge that such investments may generate additional crime risk.

Critics saw such moves as an overdue admission by government that the new era of licensing really would be a step in the dark. Temperance campaigners, the Institute of Alcohol Studies (IAS), summarized the feelings of many in stating: 'so far as we know, this is the first time any British government has been forced to mitigate the worst effects of a piece of legislation before it has even come into force' (IAS 2005: para 1.1).

Having explained the book's rationale and the political context in which it was written, it is now necessary to describe its intellectual heritage, the research process from which it derives, and its contribution to an emergent literature on the NTE.

The origins of the book

My own biography was of key importance to the genesis of this book. Between 1991 and 2002, I spent over 1,000 nights in paid employment as a disc jockey (DJ) working at approximately 250 different locations, mostly in the North West and West Midlands of England. For much of this period, DJing and nightclub promoting was my chief recreation and source of income. The bright lights, intensity and glamour of the NTE were my workplace and it was a social world that was familiar and seductive to me. My long-standing interest in criminogenic aspects of the NTE was given added impetus by my involvement in the aforementioned research project. Like Armstrong who studied his home town's football hooligans: 'I knew a little, but sensed that there was a lot more to know' (1993: 12). I became drawn into a stimulating research process, one which encompassed and drew upon my personal experiences and interests whilst presenting an intellectual challenge—the demystification of a particular sphere of social life.

The book started life as a study of night-workers. My fieldwork during 2000 focused upon issues of work-related risk within a nightlife context. This proved to be a rewarding and fruitful topic of investigation. However, I found that many of my informants had other, more pressing, concerns. By 2001, it became apparent that two sets of issues were of particular salience to the licensed trade and gatekeeper agencies such as the police, local authorities and the NHS: firstly, the need to understand the rapid transformations in political, economic and regulatory governance that were shaping the NTE; and secondly, the need to conceptualize, measure, record and prevent what appeared to be an associated tide of alcohol-related violence.

Correspondingly, the dissemination of research findings from the bouncer project had begun to attract the attention of crime prevention practitioners from across the UK. Police, local authorities and leisure corporations began to approach members of the research team with requests for assistance in the form of consultancy work. I responded positively to these requests in order to broaden my contextual knowledge, establish valuable links with key gatekeepers and take advantage of the numerous associated fieldwork opportunities. Small-scale projects were conducted, the most significant of which involved my management of a nine-month study in the West End of London concerned with the auditing of policy-relevant data (Elvins and Hadfield 2003). However, the vast majority of enquiries involved requests for me to appear as an expert witness in licensing trials.

Participatory engagement in the courtroom was not, therefore, initially sought or planned, but rather, was something that was thrust upon me as the price to be paid for an otherwise unattainable quantity and quality of research access. Introductions from my consultancy clients were invaluable in helping me to gain the trust and co-operation of new informants within their own organizations and beyond. As my insight deepened, it became increasingly apparent that something very important was going on. Licensing litigation was playing a quite fundamental role in shaping not only the high street and its related crime patterns, but also the wider public life and economic development of Britain's towns and cities. Moreover, some people were getting rather upset about this. Open conflict had broken out between those sections of the drinks and leisure industry who wanted to open up the night to further development and a number of police forces, residential communities, and local authorities who were seeking to adopt an increasingly restrictive approach to licensing. Feelings were running high on all sides. Local skirmishes fuelled and mirrored the broader battles occurring at a national level in the debates that raged over impending legislation widely understood to be ushering in a new era of '24-hour drinking'. The theme of conflict therefore emerged as a major focus of my research. My consultancy work—conducted during the last years of the 'old' licensing system (see Chapter 3)—provided access to key protagonists; social actors who occupied centre stage in the contestation of the night at a time of radical upheaval and transformation.

The analyses I present are mostly derived from participant observation. As described in the methodological postscript to this book, the study may therefore be situated within a long tradition of sociological work on the construction of urban order and disorder, most notably that of the Chicago School and symbolic interactionism (Downes and Rock 2003, Lindner 1996). Like many others working in this tradition, I have sought to trace the conditions of action that shape process within the discrete social settings I explore. The study therefore combines thick description (Geertz 1973) of various milieux with contextualizing analyses of regulation, political economy, and the propagation of knowledge and discourse. In order to protect the interests of informants and others, pseudonyms have been used when referring to specific places, people and organizations. Names appear unadulterated only where persons have given their express permission to be named, or where the story being told has previously entered the public domain.

It is necessary to acknowledge that many of the social mores and regulatory concerns discussed in this book are likely to be quite specific to Britain. Although reference to evidence from other countries is made above, and in Chapters 2 and 5, readers should note that all of the primary data was collected in British towns and cities. In the alcohol field, cross-cultural comparisons have tended to focus on trends in consumption and public health, rather than urban disorder (Babor et al. 2003, Edwards et al. 1994, Raistrick et al. 1999) and, with regard to the latter, it is necessary to acknowledge the paucity of systematic evidence. This realization, combined with my relatively limited understanding of other cultures and the dearth of secondary literature, has encouraged me to adopt a cautious approach to cross-cultural comparison. Thus, the book remains, first and foremost, an *empirical* study of the *British* condition; as such, it cannot, and does not, make claims to wider resonance. The discovery of omission, however, may be regarded as a finding in itself, and prompts me to add my voice to the long-standing demand for independent and comprehensive programmes of comparative research.

Existing literature on the night-time economy

Sociological literature on the NTE is dominated by accounts of urban lifestyles and regeneration,[6] club and drug cultures,[7] governance,[8] alcohol-related violence,[9] and the role of bouncers.[10] An overarching analysis of these themes is provided in Hobbs et al. (2003) and it is not my intention to revisit them. My colleagues and I also briefly alluded to matters of contestation (ibid.: 258–259, 269–270). However, the evolving political, economic and moral conflicts over night-time entertainment that form the central concerns of this book are more extensively discussed in Ekirch (2005); Erenberg (1981); Melbin (1987); Schlör (1998) and Weightman (1992). These authors examine various periods of European and North American cultural history and their numerous contributions to our understanding of night-life contestation are explored in Chapter 2.

The only researchers to address issues of contemporary struggle are Chatterton and Hollands (Chatterton 2002, Chatterton and Hollands 2002, 2003). In his fullest exposition of the theme, Chatterton (2002: 28) identifies a number of tensions between stakeholders regarding issues such as creativity, culture, escapism, quality of life, regulation, crime, and economic development. Chatterton's analysis of these conflicts is thin and accorded secondary importance to the formation of a 'consensus':

. . . for how the NTE should develop which is largely based around meeting the needs of large and highly acquisitive property developers and

[6] (Bianchini 1995, Bromley et al. 2000, Comedia 1991, Hadfield et al. 2001, Heath and Stickland 1997, Kreitzman 1999, Lovatt 1996, Lovatt et al. 1994, Melbin 1987, Montgomery 1995, 1997, Montgomery and Owens 1997, Moran et al. 2003, Thomas and Bromley 2000, Worpole 1992, 2003).

[7] (Brain 2000, Collin 1997, Cressey 1932, Hammersley et al. 2002, Haslam 1999, Hollands 2002, Jackson 2004, Malbon 1999, Redhead et al. 1998, Rietveld 1993, Thornton 1995).

[8] (Chatterton 2002, Chatterton and Hollands 2002, 2003, Hobbs et al. 2000, 2005, Valverde 2003, Valverde and Cirak 2003).

[9] (Bromley and Nelson 2002, Burns 1980, Chikritzhs and Stockwell 2002, Dyck 1980, Felson et al. 1997, Gofton 1990, Graham and Wells 2003, Hollands 2000, Nelson et al. 2001, Tomsen 1997, Wikström 1995).

[10] (Calvey 2000, Hobbs et al. 2002, Lister et al. 2000, 2001, McVeigh 1997, Monaghan 2002a, b, c, Wells et al. 1998, Winlow 2001), Berkley and Thayer's (2000) study of US cities being one of the few papers to describe the role of the public police.

entertainment conglomerates, profit generation and selling the city through upmarket, exclusive leisure aimed at highly mobile cash-rich groups (ibid.: 23).

Although Chatterton accurately identifies local government, police, licensing magistrates, residents, door security firms, night-life operators, consumers, and workers as key protagonists, in highlighting an emerging consensus, he fails to comprehend the depth of oppositional feeling and activity within and between such groups. Blind to the means through which the ascendancy of a pro-business entrepreneurial agenda has occurred, his analysis confuses consensus with domination. One gets no sense, for example, of the importance of licensing litigation and the way in which corporate interests are pitted against local community groups and public sector agencies; courtroom trials of strength which have far-reaching implications for the development of the NTE at a local, regional and national level. Such analytical slip-pages are understandable as social scientists have rarely concerned themselves with the operation of administrative technologies of governance such as licensing law (Valverde 2003). My analysis regards consensus as closely, but problematically, linked to the notion of 'partnership'; the salience of both concepts arising from their use as rhetorical devices in an official discourse which serves to obscure material inequalities of power and the realities of conflicting interest and contestation. By offering an empirically-based exposition of these technologies in action, this study will aim to show how any superficial appearances of consensus are likely to have been bought at a price, resulting from struggles in which dissenting voices are not merely overlooked, but actively silenced and subordinated.

New directions

Building upon these literatures, this study aims to explore a number of largely uncharted terrains. This introductory chapter explains the book's central themes of investigation and the social and political context from which it stems. The book is then organized into three sections. Part I—'Nights Past' (Chapters 2 and 3)—traces the contestation of the night in Western cities. This is not a general history of nightlife, nor a history of alcohol licensing.[11] My aim is more modest and partial in exploring the night-time hours as a period of release, control, resistance, economic opportunity and struggle. Inspired by the work of those who note night's liminal character (Alvarez 1995, Bourdieu 1977, Melbin 1987, Williams and Bendelow 1998), Chapter 2 describes how the street had for centuries (and probably, since the very birth of the city) been a primary arena of contestation. In Medieval and early-industrial society, both the state and municipal authorities associated nocturnal movement with nocturnal mischief. The chapter examines how street lighting and public police forces initially emerged as expressions of feudal and state power over the night, a power that was gradually relinquished as leisure capital increased its ability to shape the trajectory of urban development and control. In mid-nineteenth century Britain, high profile contestations over the mass public entertainment/alcohol nexus were already beginning to occur in politicized and quasi-legal settings. In a bitter trade protection war mirroring the contemporary struggle between long-established late-night operators and the pub chains (see Chapter 3), London's theatre owners fought for greater regulation of their more lucrative rivals, the music halls, which, they claimed, were little more than 'glorified pubs' (Weightman 1992: 25–28, 96–97). Nightlife entrepreneurs also faced legal challenge from without, in the shape of moralists and social reformers. Part I demonstrates that—although the moralist agenda was to be largely replaced by more sober social policy and 'quality of life' themes—it is to the Victorian city that many of today's litigious preoccupations may be traced.

Chapter 3 develops the book's historical thread by focusing upon a period of rapid politico-regulatory change in British cities between the early 1990s and implementation of the Act in 2005. More specifically, the chapter describes how commercial investors—aided and abetted by central (and in some cases, local) government—were able successfully to circumvent the remnants of a decades-old regulatory system. The chapter shows how evolution of the contemporary night-time high street corresponded

---

[11] For a general history of nightlife, see A. Roger Ekirch's masterful *At Day's Close* (2005). The lengthy history of liquor licensing in England and Wales is comprehensively recorded by Kolvin (2004) and Mehigan et al. (2004).

with the rise of corporate branding, the atrophy and suppression of less profitable forms of nightlife, and the triumph of a largely homogenous alcohol-led entertainment model. These various political, commercial and regulatory shifts served to shape the social context of criminal opportunity and allowed industry players to colonize ever greater portions of space and time in order to supply their product more efficiently to an increasingly restless nocturnal city.

Part II (Chapters 4 and 5) examines the demarcation of the high street as a principal context for nightlife and the ways in which forms of social control, involving both enablement and constraint, may be woven into the organization of human activity. Both chapters draw extensively upon ethnographic fieldwork and interview data to explore the peculiarly criminogenic features of these settings and the challenges created for formal and informal 'policing'. Chapter 4 looks in detail at high street premises themselves and their specificity as interaction settings. The chapter departs from previous studies by adopting a more holistic understanding of the ways in which nightlife operators seek to control patron behaviour. In particular, the traditional focus upon the application of force and guile by dedicated security staff is eschewed in favour of an analysis which highlights the cooperative work of all members of staff in the constitution and maintenance of social order. These methods are often informal, conducted in the course of other diverse work tasks, and may permeate every aspect of operational practice, from music policy through to the design and décor of the building.

These notions of control contrast sharply with the forms of public sociability to be found in surrounding streets where formal and informal constraints are relatively weak and large intoxicated crowds converge. Chapter 5 contrasts the mores of the high street with liberal ideals of 'disorderly', but democratic, urban public space. The chapter goes on to explore the role of the police in managing crowd behaviour and attempting to apply normative rules of constraint within peculiar, bounded interaction settings in which such social norms are largely eschewed. The penultimate section of the chapter goes on to explore the experiences of those who live in close proximity to the high street. The chapter concludes with a discussion of recent official responses to negative public perceptions of night-time public space. This analysis highlights the state's collusion with industry in promoting campaigns of education, policing and enforcement premised upon individualized notions of personal responsibility and the identification and blaming of errant consumers and suppliers of alcohol.

Part III (Chapters 6–8) explores licensing litigation, the licensing trial, and concrete themes which form the foci of court-room discourse. The court of law is the single most important arena of contemporary contestation, for it is there that far-reaching decisions regarding the development of the night are taken. Yet, in highlighting the role of legal process, it is not my intention to suggest that all, or even most, contested licensing applications come before the courts. Many cases are settled out of court through negotiation and the striking of regulatory deals (see Chapter 3). These negotiations are analogous to those of 'plea bargaining' in the criminal courts. Yet, the courtroom casts a long shadow. The *threat* of court action and its financial, personal and organizational consequences may often be a spur to agreement and concession, even where outcomes do little to assuage a party's concerns. These spurs are felt most sharply, I contend, by local residents and public sector agencies.

This theme is developed in Chapter 6 by profiling various social actors within the licensing field. Chapter 7 then identifies and dissects what is termed an 'argument pool'—a set of arguments and counter-arguments that are repeatedly submitted to the courts. As indicated above, licensing trials, despite their import, are not the *only* sites of conflict. Broader struggles occur at a national level in political and media discourse. Accordingly, Chapter 7 points to ways in which licensing deliberations may become infused by a dominant governmental ideology that acts to suppress and belittle alternative opinion. This point is illustrated explicitly by reference to the selective suppression of scientific knowledge regarding the aetiology of alcohol-related harm.

Chapter 8 focuses upon the trial itself as a legal process, within and through which the corporate will is exercised and challenged. Previous ethnographies of *criminal* procedure have tended to rely, to varying degree, upon observation of the organization and workings of the courts (Atkinson and Drew 1979, Bottoms and McClean 1976, Carlen 1976, Darbyshire 1984, Emerson 1969, McBarnet 1981, Rock 1993). Although my analysis draws extensively upon ethnographic engagement in the preparation and execution of trials, I do not attempt to provide a broad and detailed account of the licensing court as a social world. Rather, in accordance with the book's focus upon contestation, emphasis is placed more narrowly upon the construction and presentation of *arguments* and the social and economic context within which trials occur. By extension, I do not *analyse* the entire range of interactions that occur within the trial. I attend primarily to the experience of witnesses, the delivery of live oral testimony, and cross-examination.

As Baldwin (2000: 245) notes, a serious problem facing those conducting observational research is that 'open court proceedings present only the public face of justice'. In equal measure, the observation of administrative trials reveals only the public face of regulation. What non-participant observers cannot see is the way in which the evidence and arguments of the parties are shaped in preparation for trial. As the postscript to this book explains, my role as a direct participant afforded access to the hidden processes through which opposing parties sought strategically to construct their own competing and malleable accounts. Chapter 8 explores the peculiar forms of strategic interaction adopted by protagonists in their efforts to present their own arguments in a favourable light, whilst, at the same time, attempting to discredit the counter-arguments of their adversaries. In the chapter's concluding paragraphs, it is argued that ethnography can provide a rarely glimpsed view of differentially and asymmetrically assigned skills, resources and capacities and the ability of actors to deploy them in interaction. These factors, I suggest, may be understood as vital elements in the constitution and exercise of power.

The study concludes in Chapter 9, where the central threads of its analysis are summarized and extended. In its final paragraphs, the book calls for the development of a more fully democratic approach to the adjudication of night-time conflict.

Part I
Nights Past

2

The Uses of Darkness

The best prophet of the future is the past (Lord Byron).

The work of fang and claw: contesting the 'natural' night

Deep night, dark night, the silent of the night, the time of night when Troy was set on fire, the time when screech-owls cry and ban-dogs howl and spirits walk and ghosts break up their graves (William Shakespeare *Henry VI, Part 2, Act 1, Scene 4*).

It's 2.30am on a warm, wet morning in late August and I'm driving home from work through the largely deserted streets of Cheshire towns and villages—in the headlights of oncoming cars I see something that looks like a ball stuck to the bonnet of my car. As I look more closely, to my amazement, I see the ball moving—a large snail with horns fully extended is moving effortlessly across the bonnet despite the fact that I'm driving at over 50 miles per hour. The snail stays on for the full 20-mile journey and as I park the vehicle my path is blocked by other creatures: two toads and a large earthworm. I stop the car and carefully remove the animals, placing them in the warm moist grass of the garden. I like these creatures. They are, more so than we can ever be, of the night. We fear them because we cannot see them—they represent fear of the rural night, the wilderness, the primeval night, a night without lights, of unseen eyes which see us even though we don't see them, and eerie, mysterious sounds: the howl of the wolf; the screeching cry of the barn owl; the soft patter of bats in flight.

The physiological limitations of the human senses have fuelled our fear of the night and the creatures that populate it. Starved of vision, our principal sense, human imagination and culture have filled the void our eyes cannot penetrate. Penny (1993) argues that humanity's fear of the dark arises, in part, in relation to feelings of vulnerability in comparison with the ability of nocturnal animals to move freely and precisely in darkness. Often these animals have sensory abilities which far surpass our own. As Urry (2000: 388) notes, in the 'sensuous geography' of Rodaway (1994), for example: 'each sense contributes to people's orientation in space; to their awareness of spatial relationships; and to the appreciation of the qualities of particular micro- and macro-spatial environments'. Loss of vision equates with loss of control. What cannot be seen cannot easily be avoided, ordered or understood and may therefore elicit conjecture and superstition. Throughout history, nocturnal animals have been feared and persecuted, with tales of horror casting them as icons of evil. Following Douglas, one sees the biblical texts of Leviticus and Deuteronomy classify certain animals as abominable by dint of their failure to 'conform fully to their class . . . or whose class itself confounds the general scheme of the world' (1966: 56). Interestingly, the biblical list of animals 'not to be eaten' includes many nocturnal species, including the owl and the bat (Lev. 11: 13–19). Animals identified by scripture as unclean were often those whose physical features, capacities or behaviours rendered them in some way anomalous. Douglas finds similar interpretation in the treatment of persons of indefinable status who, in many societies, may be ascribed as deviant, rendering them susceptible to accusations of witchcraft and sorcery (ibid.; Palmer 2000). As Muchembled (1985: 85–6) notes of witchcraft in Medieval France, women abroad at night were 'charged with the morbidity of the hour'.

'The newer a culture is the more it fears nightfall' (Schivelbusch 1995: 81)

Throughout much of human history, nightfall has brought a period of mysterious recess to which people ascribe 'forces very different from those that rule the day. In the symbols and myths of most cultures, night is chaos, the realm of dreams, teeming with ghosts and demons as the oceans teem with fish and sea monsters . . . it holds both repose and terror' (Schivelbusch, ibid.). The night is feared as much (and in most of the contemporary world, undoubtedly more), for the darker deeds of humanity than the 'work of fang and claw' (Milne and Milne 1956: 7). Yet, the archaic association of darkness with mystery, defilement and evil remains, filling the pages of Western theology and literature (Boyd 2001, DeLamotte 1990, Link 1995, Palmer 2000) from

Shakespeare through to Shelley, Stoker, Dickens,[1] and Joyce, it continues as an instantly recognizable motif for poets, film makers[2] and musicians:

I can't sleep. Something's all over me, greasy insomnia please release me and let me dream about making mad love on the heath, tearing off tights with my teeth.

But there's no relief. I'm wide awake in my kitchen, it's dark and I'm lonely. Oh, if I could only get some sleep! Creaky noises make my skin creep. I need to get some sleep. I can't get no sleep (Rap, written and performed by Maxi Jazz of *Faithless*, from their 1995 club anthem, 'Insomnia').[3]

The uses of darkness

Historian A. Roger Ekirch's (2001, 2005) studies of the social life of night in pre-industrial Western society from the late Middle Ages to the early-nineteenth century reveal that, for the most part, only the wealthiest people could afford candles:

Nights were dark, and accidents were extraordinarily common. People fell into ditches, ponds and rivers and off bridges; they were thrown by horses unfamiliar with dark paths. Accidents were especially common when alcohol was involved, and people were most inclined to drink at night (Ekirch, quoted in Wolkomir and Wolkomir 2001: 40).

Moreover, 'to be out at night was to court danger, for night was often a time to settle scores' (Palmer 2000: 32). Notions of the night as a time of surreptitious sexual activity, deviant cultural innovation and crime underlined suspicion of those who populated the darkness, with the innocent pedestrian of the day magically recast as night prowler (Alvarez 1995: 254–255, Aubert and White 1959). Before the advent of effective artificial light, the concealing darkness provided ample opportunity for crime (Ekirch 2005: Chapters 2, 9, O'Dea 1958: 94–95), generating fear and stringent precautionary action. People 'prepared for bed as if girding for

---

[1] The novels and journalism of Dickens are replete with images of the nineteenth-century London night, see for example, Dickens (1934, 1977, 1996).

[2] In addition to the most obvious examples of the horror genre and film noir, consider the salience of the night-time cityscape in mainstream cinematic classics such as Martin Scorsese's *Taxi Driver* or the archaic and quasi-religious motifs of light and darkness employed in the film adaptations of Tolkien's *Lord of the Rings*.

[3] Used here with the permission of *Champion Music*.

an impending siege. 'Barricaded', 'bolted' and 'barred . . . backside and foreside, top and bottom' (Ekirch 2001: 353, Muchembled 1985: 25–26). In densely packed urban areas, fire was an even greater peril than crime due to the combination of naked flames from hearth and candle and the combustibility of building materials. O'Dea (1958: 94) describes how, in sixteenth-century Paris, the population were terrorized by 'bands of incendiaries who set fire to houses to pillage them and their fleeing inhabitants'.

Yet, as well as being a time of danger and vulnerability, the night was also, on occasion, a time of revelry and celebration. Public holidays and religious festivals involved the lighting of great bonfires. Festivals of light were features of the religious calendar from midnight mass to the pagan rituals of midsummer solstice (Alvarez 1995). On some nights, pagan and Christian traditions intertwined. The night before All Saints' Day, known as Halloween, was said to provide 'the final opportunity for unplacated spirits to run about on errands of mischief' (Milne and Milne 1956: 5). Now highly commercialized and largely shorn of its spiritual significance, Halloween continues to fire the imagination of children, whilst serving temporarily to legitimize otherwise unacceptable acts (Jeffries 2004).

Of tricks and treats

In contemporary Britain, suburban teenagers sometimes use the fall of darkness for pranks and hauntings. Spaces such as neighbours' gardens that are guarded by adults and thus out of bounds in daylight become open to youthful appropriation once the curtains are drawn and the adult world withdraws for a night in front of the television. When darkness falls, the street is used as a meeting place; the phone booth, grit box and bus shelter take on new meanings as sites of sociability and conflict; territories that can be claimed, fought over and marked with graffiti. Sometimes the teenage night-world meets the adult one. On Halloween, custom allows the recess of the adult night to be shattered by a confident knock on the door. In 'trick or treat'—a deviant form of play which can border on intimidation—horrific costumes are worn and options dictated. To treat is normative, to rebuff is defiant—*a dare* that can invite mischievous retribution. An egg attack on the windows, acts of vandalism, nocturnal noises, practical jokes with sometimes unnerving or sinister overtones, the leaving of animal bones on the doorstep. Trick or treat can get out of hand, especially in rural areas where tricksters work under cover of darkness and don't always offer the option to treat.

Other, relatively innocuous activities such as camping and night-fishing, still offer excitement for lovers of the 'natural night', adults and children alike. Young adult groups may create their own alternative and surreptitious forms of nightlife which subvert commercial values: free and relatively spontaneous parties in urban (warehouses, motorway service stations, housing blocks, etc.) and rural (beaches, caves, woods, etc.) locations, or more intimate fireside gatherings in the wilderness. These activities can be understood as attempts to recapture something of the nights we have lost.

Night in the medieval city

Compared to Paris, the darkest and loneliest forest is a safe retreat (Boileau, cited in Schivelbusch 1995: 84).

Up until the nineteenth century, the night was still regarded as anomalous, a different 'season' (Ekirch 2005) in which there lurked danger, opportunities for transgression (Burke 1941, Cresswell 1999, Jacobs 1992, Palmer 2000), a rest from toil, and an often uneasy sleep. Although the Medieval city afforded its citizens some sense of protection against the unseen terrors of the rural night, people's activities after dark remained restricted by both fear and official sanction. The issue of who controlled and used the night was of great salience (Burke 1941, Ekirch 2005: Part 2). Ruler and citizen, rich and poor, all were vulnerable in sleep and sought protection of their property and persons. Schivelbusch (1995: 81) describes how:

Each evening, the Medieval community prepared itself for dark like a ship's crew preparing to face a storm. At sunset, people began a retreat indoors, locking and bolting everything behind them. First the city gates, which had been opened at sunrise, were closed. The same thing happened in individual houses. They were locked and often the city authorities took the keys for safekeeping overnight.

In Medieval France, as in England:

The cities slept early . . . In the streets there were few if any passers-by and almost never were there fixed lights; nothing could be seen but an occasional torch leading the hesitant steps of the few who ventured out (Muchembled 1985: 25).

Throughout much of Medieval Europe, after-dark activity in urban areas was suppressed by the hours of curfew[4] from sunset to sunrise, within which, 'night closed officially upon the community' (Salusbury-Jones 1938: 197). Curfew was enforced by armed, torch-bearing watch patrols.[5] In England, enactments of 1252 and 1285 decreed that 'six men were to be stationed at each city gate, twelve men were to guard each borough, and smaller groups were to be summoned according to the size of the population' (Langmead, cited in Salusbury-Jones 1938: 135). These regulations were intended to prevent all contact with the world beyond city walls whilst also suppressing nocturnal movements within. For men, serving on the watch was a mandatory civic duty and considered by many, an onerous one. In larger towns and cities, the watch was assembled at ward-level by constables and beadles who had the power to select and summon its constituents and fine absentees (ibid.). Whilst some watchmen kept static guard at key entrances, junctions and vantage points, others formed into armed and torch-led foot patrols, apprehending and questioning persons found beyond doors.

The Medieval curfew can be understood as a very stringent mechanism of order-maintenance, premised upon the maxim of 'the less movement, the less mischief'—a principle embodied in the wording of numerous local prohibitions against 'night-walking'. Burke describes how, in England, most people observed the curfew because it was 'in harmony with their own habits' of

---

[4] The word 'curfew' derives from the Norman-French *covre-le-feu*, 'douse the fire' (Alvarez 1995: 14). Curfew periods were often announced by the sounding of a bell. The time at which curfews came into force varied for different areas and seasons. For example, 'In summer time in London, it was sometimes allowable to walk abroad until ten o'clock, but this was the latest hour ever permitted' (Salusbury-Jones 1938: 139). By the eighteenth century, English watchmen performed a number of civic functions. In addition to the suppression of crime and insurgency, the watch might be involved in 'crying the hour after the chimes, taking precautions for the prevention of fire, proclaiming tidings of foul or fair weather, and awakening at daybreak all those intending to set out on a journey' (Sidney 1892: 17, cited in Schivelbusch 1995: 88). At daybreak the bell would sound again to signal the watch's dispersal.
[5] Watch patrols were the forerunners of the public police (Ekirch 2005: 332–333, Emsley 1996).

'early to bed, early to rise'. This meant that 'in summer . . . town as well as country was up and doing at five in the morning; in winter at seven' (1941: 1–2, O'Dea 1958: Chapter 1). Citizens were required to provide strong justification for their nocturnal errands in order to avoid fines or incarceration. In London, a statute of Edward I (1272–1307) read:

None be so hardy as to be found going or wandering the streets of the city after curfew tolls at St. Martins-le-Grand, with sword or buckler, or other arms for doing mischief, or whereof evil suspicion might arrive, nor in any other manner, unless he is a great man, or other lawful person of good repute, or their certain passengers having their warrants to go from one to another, with lanthorn in hand (quoted in O'Dea 1958: 94).

Similarly, a Parisian decree of 1380 required that: 'At night, all houses . . . are to be locked and the keys deposited with the magistrate. Nobody may then enter or leave a house unless he can give the magistrate a good reason for doing so' (Schivelbusch 1995: 81). A Leicester ordinance of 1467 stated that 'no man walke after IX of the belle be streken in the nyght withoute lyght or withoute cause resonable in payne of impresonment' (Salusbury-Jones 1938: 139). Those who bore arms and/or did not identify themselves by carrying a light were regarded with particular suspicion and might be subject to immediate arrest and imprisonment, 'like someone without papers' (Schivelbusch 1995: 82, Alvarez 1995: 17). In some cities, torch-bearing 'linksmen' were employed as escorts-for-hire to guide officially-sanctioned travellers through the streets (Bellan 1971, Ekirch 2005: 125–127, O'Dea 1958).

The curfew was often difficult to enforce, particularly in larger cities, where the streets and other 'places of public concourse' remained the domain of 'evilly disposed persons' (O'Dea, ibid.: 94). This criminogenic night of the Medieval and Early-Modern periods is depicted in a famous engraving by William Hogarth entitled *Night*. Hogarth shows the anarchic environment of a gloomy London street replete with illicit fires, night watchmen, prostitutes, lurching drunks and the emptying of a chamber pot from a bedroom window (Hogarth 1973). Crimes committed at night were generally judged more harshly than similar offences during daylight hours (Muchembled 1985: 117) and suspects risked arrest from unanticipated raids (Aubert and White 1959). The cloak of darkness and respite therefore presented danger as well as opportunity for the criminal. Arrestees were held in a prison or at an inn until the morning when they were brought before a mayor or bailiff (Salusbury-Jones 1938: 140).

The imposition of light

. . . lanterns showed who lit the streets and who ruled them (Schivelbusch 1995: 87).

In *Disenchanted Night* (1995), Schivelbusch traces the development of public lighting in European cities and its intimate relationship with state power and the attempt to impose police-defined notions of order on the urban night. Schivelbusch argues that from as early as the sixteenth century, it was recognized that permanent public lighting could play a vital role in the suppression of disorder and political dissent by ensuring that processes of on-street surveillance and identification were reciprocal: in order to maintain the desired 'balance of power', both police and the citizenry should see and be seen.[6]

Muchembled (1985: 25) describes how in fifteenth-century Burgundy, citizens were ordered to place a torch before the door of every house before night-time visits by the Duke. Whilst in sixteenth-century Paris, every house was required to identify itself by lantern light (Schivelbusch 1995: 82). As Schivelbusch notes, such regulations were intended to render the streets more navigable after dark, thus imposing structure and order on the night-time city. However, 'this was not yet street lighting, but simply an extension of the old duty to carry a torch after dark' (ibid.). More comprehensive illumination, consisting of lanterns attached to cables strung across the street, was introduced by royal decree in 1667 (ibid.: 86). In London, public street lighting in the form of oil lamps was not introduced until 1736; here again, the core rationale for illumination was the suppression of crime and disorder (Alvarez 1995: 18, Melbin 1987: 12, O'Dea 1958: 97). The new lighting was restricted to the main thoroughfares and most densely populated streets and much of the city remained in darkness. Early Parisian street lighting fell under police jurisdiction, becoming the subject of 'minute, arbitrary and draconian' decree (ibid.). Thus, although ostensibly of benefit to all, the new light was regarded by

---

[6] The use of light and darkness as technologies of concealment and surprise is discussed in both Schivelbusch (ibid.) and O'Dea (1958: 74–75).

many as an imposition, exposing citizens to the panoptic gaze of the police and their spies.

Schivelbusch explains how, in the tense pre-revolutionary context of late eighteenth-century Paris, the new street lanterns attracted hostility and resentment. Street lighting was a governmental technology which represented the power of a despised absolutist regime. The political sensitivity of street illumination explains, at least in part, the popularity of lantern smashing during this period and the severity of punishment such acts inspired:

. . . the darkness that prevailed after the light had gone out stood for disorder and freedom . . . Every attack on a street lantern was a small act of rebellion against the order it embodied . . . destroying lanterns was not treated as (merely) disorderly conduct but as a criminal offence not far short of lese-majesty (ibid.: 98).

In the early weeks of the 1789 Revolution, lantern-fixtures were used as gallows from which officials of the *ancien régime* were strung, whilst in the July Revolution of 1830, the rebels used the darkness imposed by their wholesale destruction of street lanterns to assist their guerrilla war against royal troops (ibid.: 100–106). As Schivelbusch notes, such 'revolutionary acts reversed the order that absolutism had imposed on the street 150 years earlier' (ibid.: 106).

The development of public nightlife

Night-time leisure had long been regarded as an indicator of social privilege and conspicuous consumption (Alvarez 1995, Burke 1941, Ekirch 2005, O'Dea 1958), betokening the lifestyle of the upper and 'dangerous' classes, people who might take to their beds at a time when the day for workers was just beginning. As Burke (ibid.: 5) notes, in Medieval England there was 'no public amusement at night: no public play, dance, concert, assembly, or illuminated garden. These things came later . . .'. When night-time entertainment did take place, it was usually only in the great houses of the noble and wealthy.

Schivelbusch locates the origins of public night-time leisure in the cities of eighteenth-century Europe, which, in addition to benefiting from advances in the technology of light, were experiencing great social and political change. Up until the late eighteenth century there had been little significant improvement in lighting technology for a thousand years (O'Dea 1958).

As Melbin (1987) argues, spread of the new gas and then electric lighting and the increasing social acceptability of nocturnal wakefulness, permitted Western society to colonize the hours of darkness in a way which resembled its settlement of the globe. Yet, in parallel with exploration of the land frontier, the spread of artificial light and human activity beyond (and within) the central loci of political and economic power was slow and uneven (O'Dea, ibid.).

Even in the world's greatest cities, it was not until the mid nineteenth century that commercial leisure truly began to flourish in the wake of industrial revolution (Alvarez 1995, Burke 1941, Ekirch 2005, Melbin ibid., O'Dea ibid., Weightman 1992).

Over time, ancient traditions such as the celebratory bonfire were supplemented by festive illuminations. In late eighteenth- to early nineteenth-century pleasure gardens such as London's Vauxhall, outdoor illuminations and firework displays lit up the night sky before crowds of awestruck spectators. Nineteenth-century towns and cities featured a growing array of entertainment for the bourgeois and worker alike, ranging from masquerades and assemblies to theatre, opera, music halls, brothels, gin shops and nighthouses[7] (Burke ibid., Ekirch ibid., Schlör 1998, Weightman ibid.). As Giddens (1984: 119) notes, 'the invention of powerful, regularized modes of artificial lighting . . . dramatically expanded the potentialities of interaction settings in night hours', displacing a sense of time grounded in the natural rhythms of the diurnal cycle. The night was increasingly regarded as a time of commerce, entertainment and escape from the dark, squalid and dreary living conditions endured by much of the urban population. Compared to the working class home, even the gin shop was a 'palace' of warmth and glitter (Weightman, ibid.: 12–13).

The uses of light

In his work *Nights in the Big City* (1998), a cultural history of Paris, Berlin and London from 1840 to 1930, Joachim Schlör traces the struggle between two emblems of night:

. . . on the one hand the nocturnal city as celebration, as the place of pleasure and entertainment and on the other the nocturnal city as the

---

[7] The name given to all-night taverns.

place of terror, of threatening danger . . . Both images present nocturnal reality, but they awaken totally different feelings: temptation, desire and fascination on the one hand; intimidation, fear and terror on the other (p.10).

In 1840, Schlör writes, the night was still seen as 'a time of retreat . . . from the street to the house, a time for sleep, rest and regeneration—and also a time for ghost stories' (p.21). Yet, opportunities for a more active nightlife were rapidly developing as population growth and new industrial technologies began to render the fortified night and the remnants of its curfew system archaic. With darkness partially conquered by artificial light, night-time activities outside the home became increasingly associated with notions of social, economic and technological progress. Participation in new, specifically *urban*, night-time activities became a mark of modernity and social mobility. Yet, as Schlör reminds us, not all the 'ghosts' were vanquished by more effective street lighting: 'in the years after 1880, the debate about the danger, insecurity and immorality of the nocturnal city gained in intensity . . . New themes emerge: the criminal underworld, prostitution, the closing time for taverns, bars and restaurants' (ibid.: 86–88).

In England and Wales these concerns were to inform legislation governing 'public dancing, music or other entertainment of the like kind' (Disorderly Houses Act 1751, s 2). This Act required places of entertainment to be licensed,[8] whilst the Sunday Observance Act 1780 made the 'sale' of entertainment (charging admission fees) unlawful on Sundays (Manchester 1999: Chapters 1, 10). Licensing became a tool of control exercised by the justices in their role as keepers of the peace, 'simultaneously representative of central government and the focus of local power' (Moir 1969: 210). Licensing's prominence as a tool of urban governance

---

[8] *Alcohol* licensing in England and Wales has a much longer history, dating back to the fifteenth century. Those wishing to explore this history are referred to core texts on the subject (Kolvin 2005, Mehigan and Philips 2003, Webb and Webb 1903, Wilson 1940). The struggles which raged between temperance campaigners and the drinks industry throughout much of the nineteenth century receive comprehensive analysis in the work of Harrison (1967, 1973, 1994), whilst Dorn (1983, Ch. 2) assesses the impact of those struggles upon Britain's political economy. My colleagues and I described the development of alcohol licensing and the regulation of nightlife during the early nineteenth to late twentieth century (with particular reference to Manchester), in Hobbs et al., (2003: Chs 2–3).

increased greatly with the rise of the industrial city in the eighteenth and nineteenth centuries. The title of 'licensing authority' became consonant with that of the 'guardians of order' (Valverde 2003: 238) wherever threats were perceived in the nocturnal restlessness of a newly urbanised poor (Vogler 1991).

Whilst the police and magistracy attempted to (re)impose the security and order of a 'sleeping city' by restricting the trading hours of night-time businesses and imposing codes of public behaviour, various religious philanthropists, temperance campaigners and other moral entrepreneurs struggled to defend a 'nightly threatened morality' (Schlör 1998:15, Weightman 1992). Many of those who opposed nightlife were, Schlör argues, anti-urban reactionaries who sought to combat the 'moral degeneracy' of the city by evoking ancient anxieties and superstitions in which the night was cast as a 'realm of constantly threatening danger' (p.144).

An urban night associated with the loosening of restraints regarding leisure, pleasure, and sexuality, could, especially for women, be experienced as a hazardous and fearful environment of public sexual harassment requiring the development of precautionary strategies of avoidance and self-regulation (Stanko 1997, Valentine 1989). As Walkowitz (1992) argues in her study of late Victorian London, women were forced to confront and negotiate powerfully restraining narratives of sexual danger in order to assert their presence within the heterogeneous public spaces of the city. The increasing participation of women in urban public nightlife during the late nineteenth century can be understood as part of a wider democratization of the night (Erenberg 1981). The primeval fears were beginning to lose their potency. The new urban industrialists and their workforce demanded freedom of movement to incorporate an ever greater portion of the night-time hours within the temporal rhythms of social and economic life (Ekirch 2005: 324–339, Marx 1976: 367–374, Melbin 1987: 14–15, Palmer 2000: Chapter 7, Rosenzweig 1983: Chapter 2). Following the abolition of watch patrols and curfew, night walkers and revellers were able to leave their homes without having to provide account of themselves. Yet, those who sought to open up the night for work and play continued to experience the security measures of the authorities as restrictive. Schlör describes how confrontation mounted in the mid nineteenth century as European cities entered an era of rapid social and technological change:

Different views about how the hours of the night are best to be organized and fitted into the daily routine almost inevitably come into conflict. Public struggles break out between those who see the night as a closed-off time of retreat and those who want to open it up for life—for pleasure and work; a fight develops between the representatives of a strict nocturnal order and those who question it (1998: 21).

As Burke (1941: 94–95) describes, in certain districts of early nineteenth-century London, watchmen had been instructed by the churchwardens of the parish to stand on street corners holding placards bearing the legend 'beware bad houses'. These boards, which were intended to protect 'respectable' people from unwanted encounter with the environs of a disreputable tavern, also 'had the effect of a free advertisement' (ibid.), attracting revellers to such areas. Tavern goers expressed their resistance in popular song:

We're jovial, happy and gay, boys!
We rise with the moon, which is surely full soon,
Sing with the owl, our tutelar fowl,
Laugh and joke at your go-to-bed folk
Never think but what we shall drink,
Never care but on what we shall fare—
Turning the night into day, boys! (ibid.)

As Melbin notes, with increasing urbanization and technological progress, the growth of round-the-clock activity became an issue of contestation. Regulatory struggles broke out between those who, for personal pleasure or economic reasons, promoted incessancy, and those who wished to conserve a period of nightly respite in the interests of good order, daylight industriousness and the enjoyment of a peaceful night's sleep (1987: 68–71).[9] The night owls began to learn that 'a large, drowsy population wanted them to keep their noise down' and interest groups formed to argue over whose rights would prevail (ibid.: 8, 69–71).

In 1857, open-air dancing at Chelsea's Cremorne Gardens was '. . . indicted as a nuisance because of the hullabaloo that went on after midnight, the shouting and singing, and disputing of cab fares,

---

[9] These pressures toward incessancy have, of course, continued to mount over the decades with the development of a vast array of new technologies permitting global business transactions, travel and communication across continents and time zones (Kreitzman 1999, Moore-Ede 1993).

and sometimes fights. There was much controversy for and against closing the Gardens at eleven o'clock, but the summons, when heard, was dismissed' (Burke 1941: 111). *Punch* magazine argued in favour of later hours, claiming that 'respectable people . . . would not be in the Gardens after midnight, and should not be prevented from enjoying an evening there because of the behaviour at later hours of a rowdy few' (ibid.). Burke describes how 'turning the night into day' became popular among all social classes and catering to the entertainment needs of the urban populace became big business. As Weightman notes of London's theatreland:

What distinguished London in the Victorian and Edwardian periods was not so much a genius for creating new forms of entertainment, nor artistic inspiration, but the fact that it was a huge market place. It was the sheer size of its audience, with their growing spending power and increased leisure time that gave rise to new forms of commercial showbusiness. For those who got the formula right, huge profits could be made out of amusing Londoners (1992: 6).

Graham's observations of 'Saturday midnight at Piccadilly Circus' and the café bars and nightclubs of Soho during the 1920s are reminiscent of even the contemporary scene; with the key exception that, by 1.30am, 'all life was emptied of the place' (1929: 199). Yet, nightlife *was* expanding temporally as well as spatially. Entrepreneurs sought to extend their business activities into the night for the same reasons that people strove to conquer new lands and migrate geographically—'to exploit the region for economic gain' (Melbin 1987: 15). As Melbin points out, 'production takes time, consumption takes time . . . The chance to exploit facilities that are left idle . . . arouses our initiative to use more of the night. Using the same space more of the time is a way to multiply its capacity' and improve returns on one's investment (ibid.: 4, Palmer 2000). In Berlin, from the 1870s onwards, police demands for strict closing times were opposed not only by the entertainment industry, but also by the '(left-) liberal-inclined city council' (Schlör 1998: 78) who regarded the control agenda to be an out-dated irrelevance, impeding the city's emergence as a tourist destination and 'yardstick of modernity and progress' (ibid.: 108).[10]

---

[10] Here, the more recent tensions between police forces and local authorities in Britain offer a striking historical parallel (Chapter 3, Hobbs et al. 2003: Ch. 3).

In late nineteenth-century England there was a big extension in the number of theatres, music halls and public dance-halls, especially in larger towns and cities. Music halls and variety theatres were regarded as more proletarian and disreputable than the theatre due to the unsophisticated and populist nature of the acts, the lower social standing of their audiences, and the greater availability of alcohol. Indeed, 'music halls began as extensions to public houses and the sale of drink remained the mainstay of their profits' (Stedman Jones 1983: 204). *Nights in Town: A London Autobiography* by Thomas Burke (1915) provides a fascinating account of the music halls and the vivacious entertainment to be found within them.

During the Victorian and Edwardian eras, the 'respectability' of an establishment 'had a great deal to do with drink' (Weightman 1992: 13, 49) with temperance campaigners and other moralists calling for suppression of the music halls. Yet, their rise could not be halted and between 1850 and 1900 the number of halls increased dramatically.[11] Stedman Jones (1983: 198) notes how the 'popularity of music hall songs extolling the pleasures of drink and lampooning teetotalism was a general indication of antipathy towards the temperance cause'.

In the 1890s, London's Leicester Square became associated with this struggle for the night and its association with 'sex, drink, prostitutes, popular taste and the profits of show business' (Weightman 1992: 78). The *Empire Theatre* was especially emblematic of Victorian concerns. The *Empire* had opened as a theatre in 1884, but by 1887 had begun to offer variety shows, becoming a popular gathering place. Opponents of the *Empire* alleged that male patrons were purchasing alcohol, watching sexually stimulating shows and being solicited by prostitutes who worked in and around the theatre's bars and promenade. Controversy regarding calls for the venue's enforced closure raged in the pages of the *Daily Telegraph,* with pronouncements by vice campaigner, Mrs Ormiston Chant of the *Social Purity League,* being countered by the critic Clement Scott who famously labelled his opponents 'prudes on the prowl' (Burke 1941: 130). Mrs Chant gave evidence to the Music Halls and Theatres

---

[11] Rosenzweig (1983) describes similar struggles over working class leisure in late nineteenth- and early twentieth-century America, particularly in relation to drinking in 'saloons', the American equivalent of the tavern.

Committee of the London County Council (LCC) in objection to the *Empire*'s application for renewal of its licence. The LCC decided to renew the licence on condition that a screen was erected between the promenade and the back row of seating, and that no alcohol was to be served in the auditorium. Weightman (1992: 84) quotes a press report of November 1894 which describes how the theatre re-opened with a temporary screen in place, only for it to be ripped down by members of the audience.

In some instances, objectors and leisure entrepreneurs were able to reach a compromise. Moreover, public sensibilities also changed. By the early twentieth century, a mixture of commercial pressure, stringent regulation and criticism from reformers had led to the gradual sanitization and gentrification of the music hall repertoire (Burke 1915: 52, Stedman Jones 1983: 233–234, Weightman 1992).

Schlör and Weightman's accounts of the flourishing commercial nightlife of late nineteenth- to early twentieth- century European cities is mirrored in Erenberg's (1981) descriptions of New York and Rosenzweig's (1983) study of Worcester, Massachusetts, during this period. Each of the four authors', in many ways very different works, traces an opening up of the night in which popular recreation is linked to the formation of a new and progressive urban culture. The rise of after-dark entertainment is regarded as constitutive of the gradual dissolution of earlier rigid restraints and the heralding of a new age of public informality. All four historians identify the emergence of hitherto inaccessible outlets for self-expression, with greater intermingling of the sexes,[12] classes, and different ethnic and racial groups. These shifts were facilitated by the commercial appropriation of working class modes of vibrant public sociability.

This democratization of nightlife nurtured cosmopolitan sensibilities that were quite distinct from those of more peripheral areas in which the full opportunities of the night had yet to be exploited. It is interesting to note that, in Britain, this urban culture

---

[12] Night-time alcohol-based entertainment and its links to gendered notions of respectability and safety have continued to restrain opportunities for female participation. For example, as recently as the 1970s, it would often be deemed socially unacceptable in Britain for 'unaccompanied' women to drink in pubs (Hey 1986, Rogers 1988).

continued to flourish in the early twentieth century despite stringent controls on the availability of alcohol imposed during the First Word War (Shadwell 1923) and subsequent periods of austerity which saw alcohol consumption plummet in comparison with earlier and later periods (Weir 1984).

Discussion

This is where this brief examination of archaic nightlife in Western society must end. The purpose of this chapter has been to explore cultural aspects of the night and their contestation. As these themes develop through subsequent chapters, it may be seen that history has much to teach us about the origins and significance of our own public and regulatory discourse.

In their most hidebound manifestations, the tensions and conflicts of interest which exist between those who wish to claim the night-time hours for escapism and unfettered commerce, and those who would set the night aside as a time of tranquillity and order, remain intractable. Schlör's work in particular echoes in the multifarious shifts in regulation, public sentiment and technology that continue to shape the urban night, both materially and imaginatively. As Schlör notes, 'It isn't a matter of deciding who is right. What is much more interesting is the fact that the same phenomena, at the same time, in the same city, can be perceived in such different ways' (1998: 19). As subsequent chapters will demonstrate, Schlör's identification of the street as the primary site of contestation is particularly edifying:

Control of the city is in particular control of the street, because it is here rather than in the more easily supervised indoor spaces that the threat of disorder is greatest. What can be pressed into a rigid order there, the police fear, may break free and 'pour out' onto the street (ibid.: 33).

It is to the streets of contemporary Britain that we now turn.

3

Paradise Lost: The Rise of the Night-time High Street

... with the passing of the frontier, the bright-light areas or 'jungles' of the city become the *locus* of excitement and new experience (Burgess 1932: xiii).

Publicans, concerned to find sites that would attract the greatest number of passers-by, favoured street corners, railways stations, horse tram and bus termini, park entrances and any spot that attracted pleasure seekers (Weightman 1992: 16).

This chapter presents a history of the present. It recounts how the Act was anticipated by a decade of political and regulatory change. More specifically, it charts the commercial exploitation of the night through the rise of the high street leisure market. The chapter therefore sets the scene for Part II, which goes on to explore how these changes have shaped the night-time city as an enacted environment. Before this journey begins, it is necessary to explain briefly the regulatory frameworks which have governed the NTE.

Licensed development and the law: a basic framework

The old system

In England and Wales, the development of licensed premises has long been subject to three primary forms of municipal control: planning; public entertainment licensing; and liquor licensing. Let us assume that an operator is seeking to open a new late-night bar in a town or city centre, that the building currently has a non-leisure use—possibly a former bank or shop—and that liquor licensing is controlled by the provisions of the Licensing Act 1964 (the legislation pertaining during the course of this research). The developer would initially approach the local authority planning department in order to obtain planning permission[1] with no adverse restrictions on terminal hours. If permission was denied, the applicant could appeal and the matter would be decided by a specially appointed central government Planning Inspector.

Once planning permission had been obtained, the applicant would then apply to the local authority licensing department for a Public Entertainment Licence (PEL).[2] There were no restrictions on the hours that councils or the courts could permit for a PEL,

---

[1] The Town and Country Planning (Use Classes) Order 1987 (UCO) allocated standard planning classifications to a number of very broadly-related land uses. Thus, category A3, for example, was applied to all premises selling food or drink for consumption on the premises or hot food for consumption off the premises, whilst a D2 classification was assigned to 'assembly and leisure' uses as diverse as 'dance-halls' and gymnasia (DoE 1987). Introduction of the Use Class system had a significant de-regulatory effect, as once planning permission was granted to use a property for one purpose within a designated class, a developer would then assume 'the express right to use it for all other purposes in that class' (Rowley and Ravenscroft 1999: 124). The UCO has had important implications for the NTE, as it has allowed cafés and restaurants to turn into alcohol-led bars and quasi-nightclubs without requiring further planning consent. This has occurred regardless of the very different effects upon the urban environment that these uses may have. As Bromley et al. (2000: 92) note, whilst 'one type of A3 use may be beneficial to a particular street, another may not'. Licensed premises vary greatly in 'character and function . . . with obvious implications for the social characteristics of the market attracted'. Such problems have long been identified in research and consultation exercises (Baker Associates 2001, Central Westminster Police/ Community Consultative Group 1998, Delafons 1996, ODPM 2002).

The UCO was amended in 2005. Class A3 now covers restaurants and cafés (use for the sale of food and drink for consumption on the premises); a new Class A4 covers drinking establishments (use as a public house or wine bar, etc.); and Class A5 refers to hot food take-aways (use for the sale of hot food for consumption off the premises). Previously, all of these uses fell within Class A3, allowing premises to change into one of the other uses without planning permission. This is no longer the case. The changes have made it difficult to reconcile hybrid uses (i.e. emphasis on food during the day and drink at night—now a mix of A3 and A4 classes). 'Nightclubs' primarily used for entertainment and dancing remain within Class D2.

[2] PELs were required for all businesses offering 'music and dancing or other entertainment of a like kind' to the public (an exemption was made for private members' clubs). The licences were administered by local authorities on an annual renewal basis. In order to obtain a PEL, premises had to meet certain standards with regard to issues such as fire risk, air conditioning, air-filter changes and door staff. The operating conditions attached to PELs would allocate terminal trading hours and capacity limits for the premises and impose measures to control noise emission.

allowing, in principle, licences to cover the whole twenty four-hour period, seven days a week. PEL applications were considered by local authority licensing committees at quasi-judicial hearings. In the courts, PEL cases began as appeals against the denial of new licences or variations to existing licences. Appeals were brought before a district judge in the magistrates' courts; both parties then having a right of appeal by way of re-hearing in the crown court before a judge and at least two magistrates. Having obtained planning permission and a PEL, the applicant would then need to obtain a liquor licence.

Under the Licensing Act 1964, the standard permitted hours for the sale of alcohol terminated at 11pm from Monday to Saturday and at 10.30pm on Sundays. If a pub, bar or nightclub wished to extend those hours in order to sell alcohol after 11pm it had to obtain an s 77 Special Hours Certificate (SHC). The SHC effectively replaced the normal permitted hours[3] allowing alcohol sales up until a statutory limit of 2am (3am in Central London). In order to obtain a liquor licence or SHC one had to apply to the local licensing justices. Before granting an SHC the justices had to be satisfied that a PEL was in place[4] and that the sale of alcohol was to be ancillary to music and dancing and/or substantial refreshment (food). Thus, under the 1964 Act, it was, strictly speaking, illegal to sell alcohol after the end of normal permitted hours (except where a special occasions licence had been obtained, or to guests in a hotel or private members' clubs) unless drinking was ancillary to some other activity: normally, eating or dancing. Contested liquor applications were heard at the magistrates' court, usually following objections from the police and/or local residents and businesses. The parties could then appeal to a crown court, where a re-trial would be conducted in front of a judge and a panel of magistrates.

---

[3] *R v Stafford Crown Court, ex p Shipley [1998] 2 ER.465 162 JP 429, CA (1998) Licensing Review*: (Justices' Clerks' Society 1999: 6.19, Phillips 2002: 6.90.3).

[4] Industry commentators often pointed out that, as the Licensing Act 1964 s 77 permitted post-11pm drinking in pubs and clubs only where a PEL was in place, the law created a strange anomaly whereby one was obliged to 'make a noise' in order to serve late drinks. This, it was suggested, militated against the development of a more relaxed post-11pm drinking environment. The requirements of s 77 were therefore cited as one of the reasons why the late-night economy remained dominated by the young.

The new system

The licensing process described above has been radically transformed by the Act. Key provisions of the new system include:

- Replacement of statutorily 'fixed' permitted hours with a system in which the times of sale are agreed for each set of premises individually. This creates the *potential* for up to twenty-four-hour opening, seven days a week;
- The transfer of licensing powers from magistrates to local authorities. The Act requires each licensing authority to establish a licensing committee and that such a committee may create sub-committees consisting of three members to which it may delegate any of its functions (s 9). Local government therefore gains jurisdiction over all three primary forms of municipal control, allowing them to 'offer a comprehensive one-stop-shop on the range of regulatory requirements' (Haskins 1998: 216);
- The justices' liquor licence is replaced by two licences—the premises licence (pertaining to the venue) and the personal licence (held by qualified individuals);
- A simplified scheme for premises which sell alcohol, offer public entertainment, or provide late-night refreshment. This brings together a number of previously distinct licensing regimes, including PELs and SHCs, which are now incorporated within the single premises licence;
- The introduction of operating schedules in which applicants outline how their premises are to be run. These documents contain information such as proposed hours of trading, capacity limits, and crime prevention arrangements;
- The planning system continues as a distinct regulatory mechanism;
- Licensing authorities are required to promote four licensing objectives: the prevention of crime and disorder; public safety; prevention of public nuisance; and the protection of children from harm;
- The licensing authority must issue a 'Statement of Licensing Policy' which sets out how it intends to exercise its licensing functions and promote the licensing objectives. Licensing authorities are compelled to have regard to the Guidance in formulating these statements. The Guidance is framed in such a way as to allow for variations and different interpretations with each application considered on merit;

- The licensing authority *must* grant all premises applications unless an objection is received from the police, local residents, or one of the other statutorily defined 'interested parties' and 'responsible authorities'. If an objection is received, a hearing must be held in which both sides present their views to the licensing sub-committee. The panel is not permitted to raise its own objections and must act fairly and judicially in reaching its decision, while having regard to the Guidance and the authority's licensing statement;
- Conditions may be attached to the premises licence in an attempt to balance operators' requirements against the concerns of objectors;
- The Act provides that responsible authorities (such as the police, or the fire authority) and interested parties (such as residents living in the vicinity of the premises and local businesses) may, at any stage following the grant of a premises licence, request that the licensing authority review the licence because of problems arising at the premises in connection with any of the four licensing objectives (s 51–s 53). In reviewing a licence, the authority has a range of statutory powers at its disposal. These powers permit a graduated response, from modification of conditions through to revocation of the licence.
- The licensing authority cannot fix hours of sale, and in the absence of objections, must grant the hours requested. The Guidance rejects the curtailment of hours as a mechanism for preventing crime and disorder. It endorses restriction only on the grounds of public nuisance in residential areas. The Guidance recommends the limiting of hours as an action of last resort, appropriate only where, having heard both sides of the argument, the licensing authority deems the imposition of conditions to be inadequate (DCMS 2004b: 6.8);
- The licensing authority can adopt a Special Saturation Policy (SSP) where there are concerns regarding the cumulative impact of premises in a particular area. In drawing up an SSP, the authority must have regard to the Guidance and cannot include provision for a fixed terminal hour. The licensing authority cannot apply its SSP unless and until an objection is received, either from interested parties, or from one of the responsible authorities. A premises licence cannot be denied unless a representation to such effect is received. When objections are received, the SSP then creates a presumption against the grant. However, each application must be judged on merit and the presumption may be overturned if the

applicant can successfully argue that his or her premises will not add to the cumulative problems already experienced;
- If the applicant is dissatisfied with the decision of the licensing authority they have a right of appeal to the magistrates' court. The appeal is a re-hearing of the licensing authority's decision and is adjudicated by a panel of licensing justices who may decide on issues of both fact and law. There is, however, no further right of appeal to the crown courts as had been enjoyed under the old liquor and public entertainment licensing legislation;
- Following judgment by the magistrates, the parties have a further right of appeal to the High Court.[5]

The following paragraphs trace the development of both the Act and the contemporary night-time high street. Particular attention will be paid to the shifting forces of political economy which have facilitated the expansion of an alcohol-oriented leisure market through incremental processes of de-regulation and commercial consolidation.

Local politics, regeneration and the '24-hour city'

As discussed in Chapter 2, some people imagine cities at night to be particular kinds of social setting in which they may experience 'time out' from their daily lives. Lovatt (1996: 162) describes how the urban night may often be regarded as:

. . . a time in which the world of work is seen to lose its hold. A time for and of transgression, a time for spending, a time for trying to be something the day-time may not let you be, a time for meeting people you shouldn't, for doing things your parents told you not to, that your children are too young to understand.

---

[5] Two appeal mechanisms are available to aggrieved parties: appeal by way of case stated and judicial review. Appeal by way of case stated is brought where there is an allegation that the magistrates' or licensing authority's decision was wrong in law, in excess of jurisdiction, or reached upon an inadequate factual basis. Judicial review is an appeal mechanism which scrutinizes the *processes* through which the decision was reached. In judicial review, the Administrative Court will consider whether the public body acted reasonably and proportionately in accordance within its powers (*intra vires*), or whether it in some way abused, or acted outside its powers (*ultra vires*) (Light 2004a, Manchester et al. 2005, Ranatunga 2004).

These activities, Lovatt tells us, are 'now being promoted as vibrancy' (ibid.), a key pillar of the post-industrial leisure economy.

During the middle to late 1990s, many municipal authorities in Britain had political ambitions to create a '24-hour city'; an urban core populated by residents, workers and visitors around the clock (Bianchini and Schwengel 1991, Heath and Stickland 1997, Jones et al. 1999). Such initiatives focused upon 'bringing new dynamism to streets . . . previously deserted after 5pm' (Heath 1997: 193). This was to be achieved by 'extending the 'business day' and integrating it with an expanded evening and night-time economy' (Thomas and Bromley 2000: 1404), thereby stretching the 'vitality and viability' (DoE 1996)[6] of central urban areas across a longer time-span. Drawing upon established planning principles of compact (Rogers 1997) and mixed-use (Coupland 1997) development, it was envisaged that urban centres would be transformed into 'organic/holistic' locations for work, shopping, leisure and residence (Kreitzman 1999, O'Connor and Wynne 1996).[7] These ambitious and romantic visions looked forward to a time when British cities had shed their dour industrial pasts to be re-born as fully 'European'; relaxed, cosmopolitan and urbane. The NTE was regarded as the driver of this civic renewal, streets being brought to life by large numbers of visitors, or—more accurately—*consumers*.

Public safety via animation

Drawing upon the concept of 'natural surveillance', councillors, planners, architects, and academics argued that the '24-hour city' would not only be livelier and more prosperous, but also safer and more welcoming due to the creation of a diverse and inclusive mix of after-dark activity (Lovatt et al. 1994). Cultural development experts such as Montgomery (1995) and Worpole (1992) followed Jacobs in arguing that 'a well-used street is apt to be

---

[6] As Ravenscroft (2000: 2534) notes, these interrelated concepts are central to government planning policy guidance. The concept of 'vitality' refers to activity within urban centres at various times and locations, whilst 'viability' relates to the commercial life of an area and its ability to attract investment.

[7] Such policies were in accordance with land use planning guidance issued by the Department of the Environment (1996) which urged local authorities to promote a mixture of retail, leisure and residential usage in urban centres.

a safe street, a deserted street is apt to be unsafe' (1961: 44). Public spaces populated around the clock, would, it was anticipated, be safer due to the greater number of 'eyes upon the street' (ibid.: 45) allowing urban centres to police themselves to some degree. This 'increased safety through animation' approach received official endorsement from the Department of the Environment (DoE and Welsh Office 1994, DoE 1996), the DoE circular *Planning Out Crime* stating that:

One of the main reasons people give for shunning town centres at night is fear about their security and safety: one of the main reasons for that fear is the fact that there are very few people about. Breaking that vicious circle is a key to bringing life back to town centres . . . adopting planning policies that encourage a wide and varied range of uses . . . may well extend, for instance, to enabling arrangements that help promote the night economy (DoE and Welsh Office 1994: 14).

The temporal restrictions placed on the sale of alcohol by the Licensing Act 1964 proved an obstacle to these localized attempts to create or recapture the 'living street'[8] over a longer time-span. The importance of licensed trade investment prompted many civic entrepreneurs to identify this legislation, together with certain aspects of local regulatory practice, as a hindrance to the development of successful urban spaces (Jones et al 1999, Leeds City Council 1995). Montgomery (1997: 98) describes how in a report to Manchester City Council of 1992, his consultancy company, *Urban Cultures Ltd*, recommended a revision of the city's licensing policy with a presumption 'in favour of longer opening hours, more late licences and pavement seating'. In accordance with these recommendations, a letter was sent by the leader of the council to all existing licence holders in the city, encouraging them to apply for pavement licences and late-night extensions to their entertainment and liquor licences. As Montgomery notes, in Manchester, 'from late-1992 onwards, the softening of attitudes towards licensing, which was already in train, gathered momentum' (ibid.: 99). The linkage of economic re-generation with crime prevention had created what appeared to be a virtuous circle.

---

[8] See http://www.livingstreets.org.uk

In towns and cities across the UK, developers were welcomed with open arms:

In 1995, I was based in Reading where there were just a few pubs, old men, and nasty gangs of youths in the town centre. Many post offices, banks and building societies had closed down. Then *Bass* came offering to spend three to four million pounds knocking three empty buildings into one to create a new *O'Neill's*. We were delighted (Simon Quin, Chair of the Association of Town Centre Management, cited in Levy and Scott-Clark 2004: 17–19).

The new era of de-regulation dawned contemporaneously with rapid transitions in the leisure market.

(Cattle) market opportunities: the march of the brands

In recent years, a number of the major high street leisure corporations have announced plans to focus the future development of their businesses on branded outlets located within central nightlife areas. The rise of branded and themed licensed premises has been analysed by Chatterton and Hollands (2003) who note how large-scale operators have sought to rationalise production techniques, reduce costs and overheads, and tap into sacred consumer principles such as choice, quality through reputation, safety, convenience and reliability. They describe how such investment may be understood as a response to market opportunities arising as a result of major social changes such as women's increasing involvement in leisure, and young people's extended periods of lifestyle transition.

In contemporary marketing, the building of brand image and brand awareness is seen as essential in helping companies to make their products stand out in a crowded market-place (Klein 2001, Ries and Ries 1999). Brand names are themselves nothing more than words which lodge in the mind of the consumer, allowing, as with the ranch herd, one cow to be differentiated from another, 'even if all the cattle on the range look pretty much alike' (Ries and Ries 1999: 7). However, branding is much more than simply naming. Brands seek to evoke feelings of emotional attachment by linking the image of a product to aspects of the consumer's identity, lifestyle and aspirations (Elliott and Wattanasuwan 1998). Brand development thus involves the grouping of consumers into categories for purposes of identification and the nurturance of a specific market niche. Within a competitive arena, where consumer expectations are high, the creation of themed environments allows larger operators to develop several variations on the basic drink + sex + music = profit equation, targeted towards subtly different audiences. In particular, different brand identities allow companies to operate a number of venues in the same city without unduly duplicating their offer.

Branded outlets are of core importance to corporate players as they generate the highest proportion of turnover, profit and value for shareholders. For example, in October 2003, *Luminar Leisure*, the operators of over 200 sites across the UK, announced a major rationalization and restructuring programme involving plans to operate a completely branded estate. The company said it would be investing £100 million in the conversion of a large proportion of its unbranded sites into one of a number of brands—*Chicago Rock, Jumpin' Jaks, Liquid, Life Café, Lava/Ignite and Oceana*. The company's remaining unbranded outlets were to be operated separately under new management until suitable buyers could be found.

One of the central aims of branding is to develop consumer loyalty; however, customers can be fickle. As new premises open, the crowds move on, spending more of their Friday and Saturday nights (the vital peak trading hours) in one of the latest additions to the 'circuit'. Operators recognize that themed environments can soon become 'tired' and venues frequently have to be re-furbished, re-branded and re-launched in order to keep up-to-date with the latest trends. A fundamental problem for the chains is that, because their themed environments are replicated in urban centres across Britain (and in some cases internationally) they have little distinctiveness and few decipherable links to particular regions or localities. Large-scale investment by national chains has transformed Britain's night-time high streets into a series of homogenized 'brand-scapes'. As with the temples of day-time consumption, one high street can look much the same as another, each having its own predictable combination of market leaders, such as: *Yates's, J.D. Wetherspoon, Edwards, Hogshead, O'Neill's, Slug and Lettuce, Pitcher and Piano, All Bar One,* and *Walkabout*. For this reason, the high street brands are sometimes derided by consumers, the media, and industry insiders for their artificiality and 'soullessness'. One article in the *Manchester Evening News* bemoaned the development of an 'identikit café culture'. The corporate bar chains, it was said, had already made 'Castlefield akin to a tacky holiday resort at weekends' and were now threatening 'vogue-ish Deansgate Locks' with a similar fate (Press 2001: 30). The *Which? Pub Guide 2004* criticised chain operators for their:

... tendency to submerge the individual 'units' in conformity, make them all the same-same beers, same look (you can bulk buy that nice Irish green paint) and a series of managers who pass through. Such practices make sound business sense (economies of scale, etc.), but it doesn't make for a very interesting product (Turvil 2003: 23).

Unsurprisingly, articles in the trade press have expressed similar sentiments. Reporting on a night out in the small Cumbrian town of Penrith, Mirauer revels in the uniqueness of a nightlife still dominated by local independent operators, the diversity of which is:

... so much greater than the managed house drinking circuits of so many Northern towns with their depressing and loutish clientele, where the girls dress like Spanish whores, kiss with the chewing gum still in their mouths and eat their fish and chips while distractedly servicing the ardour of their nocturnal squires. It's dispiriting to think that the time warp will eventually be corrected and that Penrith, and towns like it, will become homogenized, carpeted by mediocrity and sameness, uniform and themed for the benefit of far off shareholders (Mirauer 2001: 106).

Objectionably sexist and regionalist as such comments may be, they reveal a fascinating degree of world-weary cynicism and self-loathing; a longing among certain sections of the industry to distance themselves culturally and aesthetically from their core consumers: to bite the hand that feeds.

To the critical eye, the chains thus provide the type of sanitized and predictable consumption environments that anthropologists and social theorists have identified as non-places (Augé 1995, Ritzer 2004). In Ritzer's terms, the rise of the branded night-time high street may be understood as part of a general shift within global capitalism from 'something' to 'nothing'. For Ritzer, the concept of 'something' implies a social form that is indigenously conceived, locally controlled, and generally rich in distinctive content. This something contrasts with 'nothing'—that which is centrally controlled and conceived and relatively devoid of distinctive content.

As one of Chatterton and Holland's informants succinctly notes in reference to one of the more 'aspirational' high street brands: 'what people don't realise is that it's actually *McDonalds* with a marble bar' (2003: 125).

The following paragraphs explore how the rise of the branded high street was facilitated by a paradigm shift in regulatory culture.

Controlling the use of urban space and time

Regulation of the night has long comprised two major components: control of time (when things can be done) and control of space (where things can be done). As we shall see, the Act was preceded by a decade or more of alcohol and entertainment licensing de-regulation. These processes afforded free reign to the market, providing the 'corporate nightlife machine' (Chatterton and Hollands 2003: 232) with ever greater opportunity to colonise our urban nightscapes.

Too much broth: the story of 'extended hours'

It has long been argued, principally by central government and the drinks industry, that extended night-time licensing hours might reduce violence and disorder by removing the incentive for people to consume large quantities of alcohol shortly before closure of the bar. This is said to promote a more relaxed atmosphere in which people drink the same amount, but over a longer period of time. It is concurrently suggested that the extension of licensing hours might facilitate the gradual dispersal of customers, thus reducing crowding, frustration, and tension at taxi ranks, fast food outlets and other congregation points.[9] As noted in Chapter 1, when formulating the Act, the government made no attempt to verify these assumptions through empirical research. The *Time for Reform*... White Paper (Home Office 2000a) justified its stance by referring to the recommendations of a then eight-year-old report which had been commissioned and published by drinks industry

---

[9] I have argued elsewhere that there is a need for theory and practice to develop a more complex awareness of the ways in which NTE-related crime and disorder may be associated with the spatial and temporal ebbs and flows of street life (Hadfield and contributors 2004b).

lobbyists, *The Portman Group* (Marsh and Fox-Kibby 1992). Despite the paucity of evidence, optimistic assumptions regarding the impact of extended hours attained the status of 'received wisdom' in the later half of the 1990s. Such views were often extolled by a liberal opinion-forming elite, who took their holidays in the sunnier climes of Southern Europe. Their ranks included many city councillors and senior police officers.

The most ambitious local authorities actively reinterpreted existing restrictions, removing 'time limits' on PELs and encouraging justices to adopt a similarly relaxed approach. In order for de-regulation to progress, 'permitted hours' legislation, and the strict criteria for extending those hours (Licensing Act 1964 s 77), needed to be circumvented. To obtain 11pm–2am (or up to 3am in Central London) closing times, it was necessary for applicants to prove that the sale of alcohol was going to be ancillary to dancing or serving food. Accordingly, the new branded chains blurred the distinction between pubs, clubs and restaurants. Industry legal teams deliberately pitched applications in such a way as to convince the justices that they were offering a new type of hybrid venue, something distinctly different from the 'pub' or 'discotheque'; something to which the old restrictions need not apply (see Chapter 7). As licensing lawyer Jeremy Allen explains:

> We were touring the country doing licences. Everyone wanted a chrome bar, white oak, flowers on the table . . . We would produce extensive market research, photographs and brochures. Hundreds of licences were approved that previously might have been refused (Levy and Scott-Clark 2004: 17, 19).

In some areas, the police were lobbied by local politicians and business leaders. When police did object to licence applications, they were castigated for 'needlessly obstructing city centre regeneration by adhering to a 'dated' and 'puritanical' control mandate' (Hobbs et al. 2003: 80). Stung by such criticism and carried along by the mood of optimism, many senior police officers embraced the 24-hour city agenda, instructing their licensing officers that the funds were 'no longer available to challenge applications for new late-licences. It was argued that it didn't really matter because the law was going to be changed anyway in the near future' (Allen 2003a: 12, Light 2000: 929). In many areas, police objections all but ceased, often being replaced by the attempt to engineer 'staggered' closing times through voluntary agreement with the trade.

These processes of back-door de-regulation resulted in a sharp increase in the number of licensed premises trading into the early hours.[10] In the centre of British cities, the impact of this transformation was dramatic. Even long-established entertainment areas such as London's West End experienced unprecedented growth. In 1992 there were 91 venues in the West End holding PELs, by 2000 this figure had risen to 278, an increase of 205% (Town Centres Limited 2001: 5.108).[11] There was, and remains, a general trend toward the development of larger entertainment premises with increased capacities in the area (ibid.: 5.20). Between 1992 and 2001 there was a 328 per cent increase in the capacity of PEL venues in the West End, whilst the number of such premises licensed to operate beyond 1am doubled between 1993 and 2001. As a raw total, the number of West End venues closing between 3am and 4am rose from 45 in 1982 to 199 in 2000 (City of Westminster 2002: 8.56d).

Whilst providing greater flexibility for business, these ad hoc experiments in extended hours did not deliver the anticipated public 'goods'. The leisure market's colonization of the early hours appeared to, at best, redistribute when criminal and disorderly events occurred, placing chronic and temporally-extended pressure on emergency and environmental services (Alcohol Harm Reduction Group 2003, Metropolitan Police 2004). In response, many local authorities and police forces began to reconsider their stance, returning to a more cautious and restrictive approach that utilized the proactive crime reduction opportunities afforded by their licensing function (GLA 2002a, Green 2003, Isle of Man Constabulary 2002, Maguire and Nettleton 2003). These regulatory u-turns placed local public sector practitioners on a collision course with central government. The state continued its love affair with business, clinging doggedly to its de-regulatory agenda

---

[10] For example, by 2003, market analysts *WestLB Panmure* had estimated that 61 per cent of the quoted high street bar market already traded beyond the normal permitted hours of 11pm (Neame 2003). See also the rise in the number of SHCs between 2001 and 2004 cited in Light (2004: 1342).

[11] Some trade commentators argue that local authorities were able to charge 'excessive fees' for PELs and therefore had a clear financial incentive to issue as many of them as possible (Neame 2003: 30).

despite mounting evidence from academic and practitioner communities that linked the increased availability of alcohol with corresponding rises in various forms of social harm (Academy of Medical Sciences 2004, Metropolitan Police 2004, Room 2004a). A parallel story had unfolded in relation to control over the spatial distribution of licensed premises.

Too many cooks: the story of 'cumulative impact'

As noted, from the early-1990s onwards, leisure companies began to compete with each other for development sites as nightlife brands were rolled out across the nation's high streets. By the later part of that decade, some local magistrates had begun to adopt a more cautious approach to licensing in locations they felt were already well served with pubs and clubs. In such circumstances, the justices might require applicants to prove the existence of a 'need, or unsatisfied demand, for the provision of an additional licensing outlet before they would consider the grant of a new licence' (Clowes 1998: 18). The concept of need had, since the inception of alcohol licensing circa 1495, given 'effect to the policy of controlling the number of drinking establishments by methods other than pure market forces. Justices and the Judges of Assize who supervised the system were given the authority to suppress alehouses which were in their view unnecessary' (Mehigan et al. 2003: 261: 2.2). More recently, the need criterion, largely shorn of its moral connotations, was often used by justices as a method of paying due regard to the functional character and possible exacerbation of crime and nuisance in an area (Light and Heenan 1999). However, the justices enjoyed complete discretion in applying this test, with some committees adopting a much more liberal approach than others. These 'inconsistencies' provoked leisure industry ire. One trade commentator notes how Tim Martin, Chair and founder of the major pub company, *J.D. Wetherspoon PLC*,[12] 'successfully challenged the concept of need head on, arguing that if he was prepared to invest, there must be a market' (Neame 2003: 28).

---

[12] Following over a decade of major expansion, Martin's company now has approximately 650 UK outlets. The company have regularly expressed their intention to open 100 new pubs per year, with a target of 1,500 premises across the UK. See also Macalister (2001).

As with extended hours, the police and magistracy were lobbied on the issue. One police Inspector from a Midlands city told me:

Some years ago, in response to comments made from politicians and business people, the Chief decided—as a policy—not to object to licensed premises on the basis of need; which we traditionally had done. People were saying; 'because you keep objecting on need, it's stifling the ability of our business to grow.

Trade criticism of the magistracy prompted a thorough appraisal of the licensing system by the Better Regulation Task Force.[13] In their final report of July 1998, the Task Force recommended that alcohol licensing jurisdiction be transferred to local authorities, with the role of the justices limited to the handling of appeals. Importantly, the report also specifically recommended that 'regulation should not be used to manage demand through judgments by licensing authorities over the need for additional providers' (Better Regulation Task Force 1998: 7).

The subsequent transfer of control to local authorities was strongly resisted by the Magistrates' Association (Magistrates' Association 2000) and Justices' Clerks' Society. In a bid to retain jurisdiction and demonstrate their members' ability to modernize and self-regulate, these bodies sought to adopt voluntarily many of the Task Force's recommendations. Publication of the *Good Practice Guide: Licensing* (Justices' Clerks' Society 1999) provided an opportunity to display their commitment to uniformity of practice across the 370 licensing committees in England and Wales. In their introduction to the *Guide*, senior officials explicitly warned their members that it was now necessary to 'demonstrate that the courts are the right place to adjudicate on licensing matters into the next century' (Fuller and Moore 2001, cited in Mehigan and Philips 2003: 912). Committees were urged to 'review, reflect and ultimately, to adopt many of the suggested practices' (ibid.).

The *Guide* clearly highlighted the need criterion as an issue of 'inconsistency' (Justices' Clerks' Society 1999: 3.25) and moreover,

---

[13] A commission appointed by the Chancellor of the Duchy of Lancaster in September 1997 to advise government on methods of improving the effectiveness of regulatory policy. The recommendations of the Task Force proved to be highly influential, informing the White Paper, *Time for Reform* (Home Office 2000a) and subsequently, many of the core provisions of the Act.

one that was now 'out of date and unnecessary' (3.23). In recommending the abolition of need, the *Guide* implicitly endorsed *laissez-faire* (government/trade) opinion which held that within a competitive market, economic forces and planning law alone might effectively regulate the number of licensed premises in an area.[14]

The *Guide* did not, however, entirely abandon the concept of market intervention. Committees were recommended to consider 'issues of public safety and the protection of the public against nuisance and disorder' by ensuring that 'premises in an area do not become so numerous as to produce problems' (3.26). The *Guide* put the onus 'squarely on the police to object should they have concerns about an application for a new licence' (Light 2000: 928). As the *Guide* stated, 'the police have an important role to play in licensing to ensure that where there is an identifiable risk of public disorder or to community safety it is drawn to the attention of the committee' (3.29). Moreover, the police were required to show that such risks were 'real rather than fanciful' (3.28).

Within the day-to-day proceedings of the courtroom, the sceptical tone of this recommendation gave rise to an increased burden on objectors (such as police officers, hospital consultants, local authority officials, and residents). Objecting witnesses were now expected to produce evidence *directly linking* crime and disorder within an area to nearby licensed premises. Police statistics showing hot spots of recorded crime within nightlife areas, together with assault data from Accident and Emergency Departments (AEDs) were the main evidential devices used in such objections. As described in Chapter 7, attempts to discredit such statistical evidence became an important focus for trade-commissioned lawyers tasked with securing licences for new high street premises. Furthermore, the technical difficulties faced by police in meeting the 'real rather than fanciful' test, served to discourage their objections at a time when the need to limit the high street's criminogenic growth had become most acute. In the absence of formal police objections, the case of other objectors was often fatally undermined. The argument could be put to the licensing committee that, as the police had raised no objections,

---

[14] Issues relating to planning law and its longstanding failure to perform this function were discussed in n25.

any crime risk could not be 'real, and that under the terms of the *Guide*, the licence should be granted' (Light 2000: 929).

The abolition of need served to transform the way in which applications were considered, leaving 'magistrates under the impression that they had to grant any new licence provided there wasn't anything wrong with the premises or the applicant' (Allen 2003b: 14). This approach was taken one step further during the development of the Act. Neither the White Paper (2000) nor the *Alcohol and Entertainment Licensing Bill* (2002) made reference to over-concentration as a potential crime risk, however fanciful, or indeed real. The draft legislation provided that where objections were received, a licence could be denied, or have conditions attached to it, in the interests of preventing crime, disorder, and public nuisance. However, such issues were to be addressed only in relation to operation of the premises itself. The individualized, good operator/good operation tests were to be the only admissible criteria.

Meanwhile, back on the high street, the abolition of need and discouragement of crime-related objections had begun to have a powerful de-regulatory effect, fuelling the market-led development of spatially concentrated drinking circuits. The exacerbation of crime, criminal damage and nuisance in these areas, often fuelled by the heavy discounting of alcohol, produced a backlash of public and practitioner opinion. Far from consigning issues of cumulative impact to history, the abolition of need—together with the government's apparent rejection of all such criteria—served to raise awareness and focus minds. The topic was set to become one of the most contentious and divisive issues in the contestation of the night.

By the autumn of 2002, there was widespread alarm among public sector practitioners and pressure groups regarding the government's apparent intention under the Bill to afford local authorities little or no power (outside of planning law) to control either the spatial agglomeration or terminal hours of licensed premises (Alcohol Alert 2002). Assistant Chief Constable Rob Taylor of Greater Manchester Police (GMP), formerly the ACPO spokesperson on licensing matters, explained his concerns:

One thing that's absolutely got to be writ large is that whatever group takes responsibility as licensing authority, they are given teeth. One issue is the question of saturation in an area. If you look into the way the legislation is cast at the moment, that doesn't appear as one of the measures that the licensing authority needs to take into account when it's making its judgment—and we're saying it *should*. The experience in big cities like this and in London, for example, is very much that there's almost a point at which the number of premises in an area precipitates violence no matter how well they are managed individually.

By contrast, there was increasing evidence of a concerted effort on the part of central government and elements of the trade to ensure that local authorities were stripped of the wide discretionary powers they had enjoyed in relation to PELs. Such concern intensified following the publication of a *Framework for Guidance* (DCMS 2002) to accompany the Bill—a document described, during a conference presentation by one prominent licensing lawyer, as reading 'like a piece of hate mail to local authorities'. The *Framework* appeared to confirm that local authorities were to be rendered impotent; lacking the necessary powers to strategically control the NTE and its dominant youth and alcohol-led trajectory, in particular (Hobbs et al. 2003: 263–267).

As noted, in response to the failure of earlier *laissez-faire* approaches, some councils, principally including the City of Westminster, had decided to adopt a more restrictive stance. Such policy shifts were met with displeasure by a government/trade alliance keen to press ahead with the de-regulatory agenda. The shift of licensing jurisdiction from the Home Office to the DCMS in 2001 had been symbolic. It had indicated the government's aim to portray the drinks industry as a benign and economically important player in the leisure and tourism sectors, whilst correspondingly 'sexing-down' the long-established links between alcohol policy and crime and disorder. During this period, Andrew Cunningham, the official in charge of licensing policy at the DCMS, became the subject of a complaint to the Cabinet Secretary for allegedly making partisan speeches. It was said that he had explicitly denounced critics of government policy as 'extremists' and 'nanny staters', assuring trade audiences that dissenting local authorities would be brought to book; the time had come, he told the delegates of one trade convention, to 'stop Westminster City Council's silly games'.

The power to regulate development with due regard to the needs and wishes of a broad range of urban stakeholders was seen by many as central to the effectiveness of the new local licensing authorities. Representations from a number of bodies supporting recognition of the 'cumulative impact criteria' were made to the National Guidance Sub-Group of the Bill Advisory Group. Advocates of the approach emerged from a broad range of interested parties including the Local Government Association (LGA); the Greater London Authority (GLA); the Civic Trust; Alcohol Concern; the Institute of Alcohol Studies (IAS); ACPO; and—to the surprise of many—from trade organization BEDA.[15] By the time the *Guidance* began its passage through the House of Lords, a powerful lobby had emerged. Stormy debate in the Lords resulted in a government u-turn, with cumulative impact considerations eventually receiving somewhat grudging accommodation[16] (Coulson 2003).

Sorting the competition: the story of 'rave'

Before the alcohol industry could really begin to exploit the urban leisure market it was necessary for them to address the problem that drinking had become less fashionable. Given more recent trends, it is perhaps surprising to recall that between 1987 and 1992 pub attendances fell by 11 per cent, with a further 20 per cent slump predicted over the following five years (Henley Centre, *Leisure Futures*, cited in Carey 1997: 21). The ascendant 'rave' culture had eschewed alcohol and licensed premises in favour of illegal drugs, soft drinks and spontaneous partying in warehouses, motorway service stations and the rural wilderness. This behaviour could not be tolerated (it was beginning to affect the bottom line).

Rave culture was an easy target for suppression by the alcohol industry's political allies, for three primary reasons: firstly, it

---

[15] BEDA had long been more critical of the government's proposals than other trade organizations, particularly those drawing their membership predominately from the 'normal permitted hours' pub trade. BEDA members had traditionally dominated the late-night market, prompting the organization's cautious and sceptical stance to be dismissed by trade and government commentators as 'protectionist'.

[16] The *Guidance* was re-drafted to include a number of lengthy and ambiguous clauses pertaining to the determination of cumulative impact. It stated, for example, that the problems generated by an over-concentration of licensed premises were 'unusual' (DCMS 2004b: 3.15). In other work, which focuses on the genesis of cumulative stressors within the urban environment, I have questioned both the accuracy and logic of this assertion (Hadfield and contributors 2004b).

involved the nocturnal movements of large numbers of young people and the furtive sequestration of private property, particularly rural agricultural land; secondly, it was driven by the 'buzz' of psychoactive consumption, principally, the Class A drug, ecstasy; and thirdly, it was associated with unlicensed, noisy and disruptive outdoor events. The Criminal Justice and Public Order Act 1994 was the most draconian of a number of laws enacted during the period 1990–1997, increasing police powers against promoters and free party organizers, as the alcohol lobby and its political allies consorted to kill rave in its original sub-cultural form (Carey 1997, Collin 1997). In introducing the Criminal Justice Bill, Home Secretary Michael Howard explained the government's intention that: 'local communities should not have to put up with, or even fear the prospect of, mass invasions by those who selfishly gather, regardless of the rights of others' (Hansard 11 January 1994). Sections 63–77 of the ensuing Act provided that the new powers were to apply in respect of gatherings, or even suspected gatherings, of people 'likely to cause serious distress to the inhabitants of the locality' (Manchester 1999: 7.22–7.27). Party organizers would, henceforth, be arrested and have their assets seized, notably including any sound systems capable of generating 'a succession of repetitive beats' (Collin 1997).

Dance culture was not humanely put to sleep in 1994, but rather, subjected to a lingering death. Once safely corralled within licensed premises, the scene was sanitized, commercialized, and infused with an alien alcohol-oriented aesthetic. This was achieved via the drinks industry sponsorship of club tours, specially targeted advertising campaigns, and most importantly, the development of products such as the RTD (ready-to-drink)—bottled and branded mixes of fruit juice, stimulants, and spirits; formerly known as 'alco-pops'—inspired by the popularity of soft drinks at dance events (Brain 2000, Carey 1997).[17]

It is instructive to compare the political suppression of rave with the subsequent defence of business interests in relation to extended hours and cumulative impact. The new night-time high

---

[17] RTDs particularly appealed to 18–35-year-old women and by 2002, market analysts *Mintel* estimated the alco-pop market to be worth £1.6 billion. In 2005, the market share had fallen to £1.2 billion. Fashion had shifted, with young female drinkers increasingly turning to more 'sophisticated' alternatives, such as cocktails (Carvel 2005).

streets also encouraged the 'mass invasion' of public and private space by large crowds of intoxicated young people; created noise and nuisance; attracted criminals; and generally caused distress to innocent residential communities. The difference was, of course, that, unlike rave, the proceeds of this particular form of psychoactive consumption could be channelled into the pockets of corporate investors and used to drive the economic renaissance of post-industrial cities. As we have seen, the legislative response could hardly have been more divergent, nor the political pronouncements of both Tory and Labour administrations more hypocritical. 'Stress-inducing mass invasions' were soon to become, in official eyes, not such a bad thing after all.

With the external competition defeated[18] and regulatory restraints removed, the trade could now pursue its ambitions for profit maximization, a course that would increasingly create division within its own ranks.

Location, location, location

Further insight into the industry's drive to colonize the night may be gained by examining the importance of spatial agglomeration. Why is the right location so important to operators? Why is it necessary to be located so close, or even next door, to one's competitors? Are there any commercial drawbacks to being so located? The following paragraphs will suggest some answers to these questions.

In an interview with trade newspaper *The Morning Advertiser,* Paul O'Reilly, managing director of the pub company *RTA,* expressed the opinion that business success within the leisure market was 'a question of location, location, location' (Ridout 2003: 38). O'Reilly also acknowledged the downside of this maxim in relation to the creation of compact urban environments which now contained 'too many operators, too many silly-priced drinks promos, and too many consumers' (ibid.). This over-saturation was brought about by the pursuit of profit. In O'Reilly's words, 'I think the problem we've got on the high street arose because a lot

---

[18] It was not only the rave scene that was squeezed out. In many towns and cities, the new branded outlets replaced other, less alcohol-oriented attractions such as high street cinemas, live music venues and even restaurants (Hadfield 2004, Chatterton and Hollands 2003).

of people looked at the market and thought it was easy to get into it. They thought: "if they (their competitors) can make a lot of money, so can we"' (ibid.).

In 2001, less than four years after they had first acquired a handful of rundown bars in Newcastle, North East-based *Ultimate Leisure* had expanded into a PLC worth more than £30 million. By May 2003, *Ultimate* were operating twenty-seven bars, restaurants and hotels across Tyneside and were moving into Nottingham, Leeds and Sheffield, with two new bars about to open and another three in the pipeline. In 2001, the company had a turnover of £16.6 million, an increase of 38 per cent from its financial results for 2000 and profits of £4.2 million, a 33 per cent increase over the same period. In an interview with the trade press, *Ultimate's*—now former—managing director, Bob Senior, commented:

We've done nothing more than anyone else could have. We simply spent the right kind of money on the right premises in the right location. We buy in the already established market . . . One of the reasons we're so successful is our ability to identify prime sites in the fulcrum position of established drinking circuits (Night 2001a: 18–19).

Senior's self-congratulatory tone contrasts with that of Myles Doran, marketing manager of *Mustard Entertainment Restaurants*, who, in an interview with the same journal, sought to explain a business failure in the following terms:

Night Magazine: This time last year we featured *Mustard* in Birmingham. What lessons have been learned from the problems you encountered there?

Doran: *Mustard* in Birmingham was a gorgeous venue, but is the best example I can think of in recent bar history of the old nutmeg 'location, location, location'. It is easy to talk in retrospect; however, if *Mustard* was positioned on a circuit/high street you would now be talking to me about what lies behind the success of the brand. There is a fine line between success and failure as the market-place becomes ever more saturated (Night 2001b: 33).

The 'out-of-town' expansion policies pursued in the 1980s and early 1990s by large corporate enterprises such as the *Rank Organization* and *First Leisure* had, by the mid 1990s, come to be regarded as fundamentally flawed. In 2000, *Rank's* recently constructed and commercially ailing, out-of-town nightclub and feeder bar development *Pulse, Vogue and Hotshots* in Sheffield was

sold to *Brook Leisure* for a knock-down price. Instead of
re-launching the site, which had originally cost *Rank* £8 million to
build, *Brook* immediately transferred its licence to the former
Odeon Cinema in Sheffield city centre. Commenting on the deal,
one of *Brook's* directors, Jason Brook, stated:

We've bought the most expensive purpose-build nightclub in Yorkshire
and we're shutting it down to transfer the licence . . . we now have a
50,000 sq. ft building down the road that we can convert to a non-leisure
use—a call centre or something of that nature.

By contrast, Brook described the *Odeon* site as:

So important to us that we stuck with it through thick and thin . . . we
think it's one of the best locations in the country. It's right between the
main drinking drag and the taxi rank. In fact, since we acquired the
building, the gap between the pub run and the club has been filled with
new bars like *RSVP* and *Lloyds* (*Night* 2000: 43).

Classified advertisements in the trade press confirm the
commercial primacy of a central, on-circuit location:

City centre nightclub for sale in the North of England's most rapidly
expanding leisure area. Close to *Chicago Rock, Varsity, J.D.
Wetherspoon, Edwards,* etc., 600 capacity, 3am PEL, open 7 nights
(Night 2001b: 94).

Northern Home Counties Town Centre. High Street night club on A3
Circuit 2am licence with 540 capacity (ibid.).

The commercial benefits of being located 'at the fulcrum of an
established drinking circuit' seem clear. One's potential market
and customer base is well-established and predictable. As long as
one can deliver the type of experience that customers are looking
for, at the right price, and provided there are enough customers to
go round, success seems assured.

Securing the site: trade tactics

Most chain operators have a dedicated Estates Manager, usually a
very senior person within the organization who deals with
operational expansion and the acquisition of new development sites.
Expanding chains are constantly seeking and targeting new
locations in towns and cities across the UK and beyond. The

following case notes permit insight into the methods employed by those who manage corporate estates:

A senior colleague and I are called to a mysterious meeting—the purposes of which remain unspecified—at the Head Office of a national leisure corporation. The company is located in a huge industrial estate containing a maze of non-descript warehouses and offices. We have not been given details of the exact location of the site and our taxi driver has difficulty finding it. We stop to look on a map showing the location of businesses on the estate. The company we are looking for is not listed. We ask at a local taxi office and finally obtain directions. We are dropped in a car park which contains rows of executive cars at the front of a large anonymous building with no signage, blacked-out windows, and extensive CCTV coverage. The exterior of the building offers no clue as to what goes on inside and we remain uncertain that we are in the right place. We enter a smoked glass and marble reception area. The female receptionist confirms our appointment and we are directed to wait on a black leather couch. After five minutes we are shown into the building; we pass through plush, design-conscious and ultra-modern office space. Fixtures and fittings are luxurious and of the highest quality. The building appears to be staffed almost entirely by attractive young women. The receptionist shows us to a meeting room, where 'Mr Big's' female secretary asks us to wait, before closing the door. We wait for around ten minutes and begin to feel as though we have entered a real life Bond movie and are about to be interrogated by some psychotic criminal mastermind.

Eventually, we are joined by Mr Big, a man in his late fifties in an immaculate pinstriped suit. He seems affable enough as he introduces himself as the Estates Manager of the company. We are offered tea and biscuits and the mood brightens. After a few minutes of small talk, Mr Big gets down to business. He explains that he has called this meeting because he has heard a lot about our research and thinks that we might be able to help him. He explains that what he wants us to do relates to two approaching licensing hearings regarding new clubs and bars in different cities. He asks his secretary to bring in some paperwork and proceeds to show us detailed radius maps of the city centres in question; both of which are around two-hundred miles away, in different regions of England. The scene resembles film footage of the World War Two Cabinet Office 'War Rooms', the maps being marked up to show the location of all the licensed premises in each city centre, accompanied by a key which details their names, trading details and capacities. Mr Big explains that his company already has a significant stake in these NTEs. He displays an intimate knowledge of the leisure market in each city, detailing issues such as the trading profile of premises, drinks discounting, policing constraints, and crime problems. Mr Big explains his company's strategy for each city, their role and stake in it, and future expansion plans.

Mr Big's concern is protectionism. His plan is to mount licensing objections in relation to the new competition his company's premises will face from the national chain operators seeking licensing approval in these cities. He sees major threats to his company's business in each city emanating from the two ventures in question. This protectionism is pitched to us as mutual concern regarding crime and the environmental impact of new premises within these cities. He explains that there will be no objections from the local authorities who are still 'promoting growth'. Similarly, there will be no residential objections, as the city centres in question are sparsely populated. Mr Big described the liberal approach of justices and police in one of the cities as having provided an 'open season' for development. This season had now drawn to a close. The police were opposing new licences, but did not, Mr Big assured us, have sufficient resources, experience or competence to mount effective legal objections. Mr Big explained that he would like us to visit these cities and to write reports that might be used in court in support of his company's objections. He requested that our meeting be treated as strictly confidential. We say we will consider his proposals and respond in due course.

As we leave, a call comes in for Mr Big from a leading licensing lawyer whose name I recognise. Mr Big asks me if I have given evidence before and the names of the barristers I have encountered. I begin to get the impression that licensing practice is a small world. Mr Big appears to know all the main legal practitioners and all the executives of the major companies. I feel I have gained a new degree of insight.

It seems little wonder that rapid expansion of the high street has taken place. Leisure companies such as this are well resourced and well connected—professionally, legally and politically. They have detailed market knowledge and a strategic vision which provides a clear idea of what they want and the various ways and means of getting it. Once they have what they want, they then seek vigorously to protect it. The scene contrasted sharply with my visits to police licensing offices, typically home to one beleaguered Licensing Sergeant struggling with limited resources against a mountain of paperwork. Police licensing officers often have little organization power or support, their work focusing on every-night local problems that are largely divorced from the broader, regional or national picture.

The protectionist agenda in licensing has been driven by the regulatory changes discussed above and especially by the increasing proportion of businesses seeking to trade after 11pm. Up until the mid 1990s, SHC holders would typically be night-club operators whose premises were purpose-built and operated in accordance with the requirements of a PEL and the Licensing Act 1964 s 77. As noted, during the period of de-regulation that preceded the Act, more and more PELs and SHCs were issued, very often to premises which had not been structurally adapted to the same degree, and which did not strictly meet the s 77 criteria of alcohol sales being ancillary to music/dancing and/or dining. This transformed the late-night market by opening it up to encroaching competition from the pub and bar chains. The new generation of late-night café bar/club hybrids gained popularity with consumers partly because—in comparison with the traditional nightclub—they offered free, or substantially reduced, admission charges, plus possible additional savings on the price of drinks. These highly competitive insertions into the late-night market threatened the profits of long-standing late-night operators. As the following case notes illustrate, some operators sought to uphold strict interpretations of s 77 in order to protect their established interests within the late-night market.

The cultural mores of the British high street dictate that, in pubs, bars and clubs after 9pm, drinking is hardly ever ancillary to eating, or even to dancing.[19] However, during the 1990s, post-11pm trading was increasingly encouraged for the reasons outlined above. Many justices were happy to provide a liberal interpretation of s 77 and although the police had powers under the 1964 Act to seek the revocation of a SHC on the grounds of s 77 non-compliance, in practice, these laws were very rarely enforced (Allen 2003:b, Asthana 2005). In the leading 'Schofield'

---

[19] My observations indicate that those consumers who choose to 'eat out' generally prefer to either dine in a dedicated restaurant before moving on to another venue for their drinking and dancing, or to visit a late-night restaurant (traditionally a 'curry house') or take-away at the end of their night out. Late-night café culture has yet to significantly penetrate the West End of London, let alone our provincial urban outposts. In British cities, alfresco eating in the early hours still consists principally of standing on the pavement shovelling sauce-drenched and dripping kebabs, saveloys and chips into one's mouth.

case,[20] the nightclub chain, *Northern Leisure* (now part of *Luminar Leisure*), challenged a magistrates' decision to grant an SHC to a competitor who was not intending to provide dancing throughout the whole of their opening hours. The applicants had also admitted that no more than 2 per cent of their total turnover would be from food. The High Court's judgment held that courts should consider the whole period of trading and not refuse a licence simply because during some periods, customers would be neither eating nor dancing. Furthermore, the court held that, although the facts of the case made it unlikely that drinking was going to be a merely ancillary activity, the magistrates had been entitled to believe that this was the applicant's intention.

Following this decision it became even more important for SHC applicants to demonstrate their intentions to provide food and entertainment. This was done by outlining the facilities and services that were to be provided, rather than the extent to which patrons might make use of them.[21] In a trial setting, this would typically involve the presentation of plans outlining the size and location of dance floors, kitchens and dining areas. It might also involve the submission of glossy menus and brochures providing detailed descriptions of the intended music policy and other forms of entertainment on offer. In this way, the law encouraged a somewhat cynical approach by applicants, who, in order to obtain the late-night trading hours they desired, had to vow to provide substantial food and entertainment facilities in the full knowledge that these facilities were likely to be little used.[22] This

---

[20] *Northern Leisure Plc v Schofield and Baxter* 164 JP (2000) 613, *Licensing Review* (43) 2000 (October).

[21] In the context of licence revocation proceedings brought against *existing* premises, courts might typically have been presented with evidence indicating that a premises was not s 77 compliant because customers had been observed to use the premises primarily to drink.

[22] It is not suggested that applicants were regularly committing perjury by promising to provide facilities and then simply failing to do so once a licence was obtained; in the vast majority of cases, the physical features such as kitchens and dance floors would be installed as outlined in court. Operators needed to comply with the basic requirements of s 77 in order to guard themselves against the possibility of its enforcement and the scurrilous whispers of competitors. In a worst case scenario this might involve licence revocation proceedings being mounted as a result of police investigations. The actual *use* of such facilities and the provision of services was a quite different matter. The disjuncture between the requirements of

gaping disjuncture between the requirements of the law and the commercial realities of the high street were an open secret among both operators and enforcement agencies. In abolishing permitted hours, the Act effectively swept away this anomaly, allowing, in principle, any style of operation to extend its late-night trading hours provided that certain individually negotiated conditions could be met. Impending reform did not, however, stop *Luminar* from continuing to question the criteria by which SHCs were granted.

Between 2000 and 2004, two bar brands, *J.D. Wetherspoon's Lloyds No. 1* and *Regent Inn's Walkabout*, made major insertions into the late-night market. Both brands were performing particularly well and expanding rapidly—both physically in terms of their 'rolling out' across the nation's high streets and temporally in terms of obtaining late-licences. Both forms of expansion met legal challenge from *Luminar*, a company which had become the UK's largest nightclub operator. *Luminar* continually sought to draw the attention of the courts to the open secret of s 77 non-compliance; in some cases employing private investigators to secretly video activities within their competitor's premises. A report in the trade paper, *The Morning Advertiser*, noted how:

The opening of nine *Lloyds No. 1* sites in the past year will help *J.D. Wetherspoon* turn over £100 million at its fifty *Lloyds* sites this financial year—a twenty-fold increase on the £5 million a year being achieved by the original ten sites. The success of the fifty *Lloyds No.1s*—thirty-four now have late licences with many applications pending—also sheds light on the legal challenge by nightclub and venue bar chain *Luminar* to *J.D. Wetherspoon's* attempts to obtain late licences for the brand (*The Morning Advertiser* 11 September 2003: 11).

In one case, *J.D. Wetherspoon* launched an appeal against the decision of the Norwich magistrates' court to deny them an SHC for *Lloyds* on the grounds of a predicted failure to comply with s 77.

s 77 and the dictates of the market produced quite farcical results as the Security and Licensing Manager of a major pub chain candidly admitted:

Our *Select* chain is fully fitted out with state-of-the-art kitchens, the vast majority of which are locked and gathering dust. They have to be opened and cleaned every so often to meet the environmental health (inspections). We have the food, but nobody wants to buy it. There's food in our nightclub freezers which stays there until it's out of date. I have to remind managers to throw it out and replace it every so often. It's just a loss that has to be written off.

Norwich Crown Court subsequently found that from 8pm onwards, the vast majority of the venue's customers were likely to be drinkers and concluded that the company's motivation for seeking an SHC was to compete in the city's late-night drinking market. In spite of this, the court followed the Schofield interpretation in finding that the applicants had met their legal duties by stating their intention to provide music, dancing and food, and that these were the key criteria, as opposed to whether customers would actually want or use such facilities. The judgment also expressed the view that times had changed and that late-night drinking was now part of contemporary life to the extent that s 77 should be interpreted more generously than in previous eras.

Luminar applied to the High Court for judicial review of this decision. In a letter to *The Morning Advertiser, Luminar's* Chief Executive Stephen Thomas defended his company's actions:

What we require is a clarification of the law. If pubs can turn into late-night venues by putting in a dance floor and claiming that this is the principal activity then we too will be happy to operate in this way. However, our understanding is that the drinking element of the activities must be ancillary at all times when the venue is open. We do not believe that the *Lloyd's No. 1* in Norwich meets this criterion, especially bearing in mind the critical time beyond normal licensing laws. Our opinion was supported by the local bench who refused the initial application (28 August 2003: 15).

In his judgment of October 2003, Mr Justice Stanley Burton found in *Luminar's* favour. The judge rejected the approach of Norwich crown court and the more generous interpretations of the law implied in the Schofield case. Burton reiterated that the facilities provided for customers were of vital importance. However, he stressed that the courts were entitled to assess whether or not the intentions of the operator were genuine and the likelihood that a sufficient number of customers would make use of the food and dance-related facilities, such as to render the sale of drink ancillary. The judge also made it clear that in making such assessments, it was legitimate to consider evidence relating to customer behaviour in similar premises run by the same operator in which SHCs were already in force.[23]

---

[23] In the case of an application from a new independent operator, one could, of course, only speculate as to the primary purpose for which people might resort to the premises.

J.D. Wetherspoon subsequently referred the case to the Court of Appeal, arguing that Burton had failed to draw an essential distinction between the bona fide provision of facilities by the licensee and the use to which such facilities were put. The test, it was argued, could only be applied retrospectively. If, at a later date, it could be found that the premises were not being used in an appropriate way, it was open to the police to seek remedial action (Allen 2004). In a landmark judgment,[24] the appeal judges upheld Burton's decision and made it clear that *facilities* for music, dancing and dining were necessary, but not sufficient; in order to comply with s 77, applicants must show that their customers would not use the premises primarily as a venue for late-night drinking.

This thoroughgoing review of s 77, arising as it did in the dying days of the Licensing Act 1964, arguably closed an important legal loophole. In short, the judges reiterated the law's intention that extended hours should not be obtained for the purpose of selling additional alcohol; the power to grant an SHC was not to be used to license a 'late-night pub' (Allen 2004, Clifton 2004).

As discussed, the licensing of what were effectively late-night pubs had defined the growth of the NTE in Britain for over a decade. These attempts to achieve 'reform through the back-door' were now judged to have been based upon fundamental misinterpretations of the law. Yet, the genie was out of the bottle. Failure to apply and enforce the maxim of 'ancillary drinking' had encouraged the development of an alcohol-oriented late-night leisure culture. As editorial comments in the trade press candidly admitted:

The logical extrapolation of this decision would see virtually every late-licence operation in the country close down. It's an obvious fact that customers go to nightclubs and late-licence bars, firstly, to enjoy a few drinks. A substantial number will have a bit of a bop at some stage. A handful will avail themselves of a meal (Charity 2004: 13).

To summarize, the growth of extended hours licensing in the years preceding the Act had provided lucrative commercial opportunities for those operators who could please a late-night audience. The most potent attempts to restrict such changes were

---

[24] *Norwich Crown Court v Luminar Leisure* [2004] 1 WLR 2512, LR [57]19.

driven by protectionists from within the trade's own ranks. These legal challenges highlighted a mundane failure by regulators and enforcement agencies to uphold the legislative intention that drinking should be ancillary to other specified activities occurring in licensed premises after 11pm. Trade objectors sought to attack their competitors by drawing the attention of the courts to specific instances of non-compliance. Protectionist litigation ultimately prompted a judicial review of case law that called into question the entire legal basis for extended hours de-regulation under the 1964 Licensing Act.

The following paragraphs examine a number of subtle methods for manipulating the regulatory system that were employed by the trade and its legal representatives when pursuing particular commercial goals. The discussion will begin by considering one popular method, known to police and local authority informants as the 'creeping' licence.

Creeping licences

In instances of 'creeping', applications for a new licence (or for variations to an existing one) were couched in terms suggestive of a conservative, up-market, or family-friendly trading format. This approach would be adopted in order to offset potential objections and gain the sympathy of the regulator (see Chapter 7). Once a licence had been granted, the operator would then seek to have conditions forbidding such attractions as disc jockeys, dance floors, or open-plan spaces, rescinded. The venue would then be re-branded to attract a younger, more profitable clientele. As one police licensing officer explained:

This has not just happened once, but four or five times. We received an application for a brand new public house which was bona fide and we met with the applicant and vetted the applicant and everything is really nice and rosy. We go to court and agree that we won't object to the granting of the licence, so long as certain conditions are applied. So then, when it is granted, they go away really happy, 'look at this, we have a licence with all these conditions on!' Two days later, we get an application for a change in those conditions. So why did they accept the conditions if they weren't happy with them? (Lister et al. 2001: 3).

Creeping strategies were particularly apparent in relation to PELs. Over a period of years, a local authority might receive a stream of variation applications pertaining to the same premises. These variations would often relate to the physical capacity of the premises or its terminal trading hour. Some venues became considerably larger and traded considerably later over time—transforming from a quiet café or pub to a bustling quasi-nightclub. Although the applicant's ultimate ambition may have been to obtain a 2am licence, a booming sound system and a large capacity venue, to have submitted such proposals all at once would have increased the likelihood of denial or extended litigation. Thus, the creeping approach was particularly favoured by smaller, independent operators who were less likely than their corporate competitors to have access to elite legal representation. Creeping could effectively reduce the risk of having one's application denied. Commercial goals were pursued incrementally, by achieving, for example, a midnight extension and a small capacity increase one year and a 1 am licence and further capacity, the next.

Special removals

Other tactics included the use of 'special removals', whereby operators were able to open new premises within an established drinking circuit by exploiting a loophole in the Licensing Act 1964 s 15 which rendered them practically immune from objections. In a number of cities, operators sought to purchase premises holding 'old on-licences' continuously in force since 15 August 1904. Unlike other types of licence, old on-licences could be transferred to any other premises within the same licensing district. These 'special removals' could be made on the grounds that 'the premises for which the licence was granted are, or are about to be, pulled down' or 'have been rendered unfit for use for the business carried on there under the licence by fire, tempest or other unforeseen and unavoidable calamity' (Mehigan and Philips 2003: 2.477). In considering the suitability of an application to transfer the licence to another premise, the licensing committee could 'consider only the suitability of the applicant . . . and may not take extraneous matters into account' (Philips 2002: 3.129).

Some operators sought to purchase and stockpile relevant premises in order to keep a reserve of transferable licences. If a particularly prime site within the same licensing district became available, the operator would then move to secure the new premises in the knowledge that a costly legal battle with objectors could probably be avoided. In order to apply for a special removal, it was necessary for the premises which held the old on-licence to be kept in a suitably dilapidated condition and in licensing circles, rumours of strangely enhanced fire risks at pre-1904 properties would abound. Once it became clear that the Act would make no provision for special removals, operators rushed to cash their stocks of old on-licences.

In Newcastle (the site of a number of special removals), licences from some of the city's smallest and oldest pubs were transferred to new premises some distance away. Big bars and even a nightclub in the prime Quayside area sprang up on the back of this transfer mechanism. In summer 2003, *Ultimate Leisure* sought to transfer the licence of a city centre pub called the *Frog and Nightgown* which, for a short period of time, the company had traded as *Mims. Mims* was demolished after Newcastle City Council compulsorily purchased the site as part of an urban redevelopment scheme. *Ultimate* applied for a 'special removal' of the *Mims* licence to one of their other properties, the *Gresham* hotel. The *Gresham* was located on Osbourne Road, a busy night strip in the up-market suburb of Jesmond. *Ultimate* sought to re-open the *Gresham* as *Bar Bacca,* a new 1,000-capacity addition to what had become one of Newcastle's main nightlife areas and the 'hottest' alcohol-related crime hot spot outside the city centre. Interviewed in *The Guardian*, local Labour MP Jim Cousins stated that 'a secondary market has developed for licences, some worth up to £500,000. People with very good insider knowledge can use this market greatly to their personal advantage . . . bringing a process that should be open and above board into disrepute' (Hetherington 2003b: 5).

The High Court granted five Jesmond residents permission to seek a judicial review of the Newcastle justices' decision in the matter. However, the bid to stop the special removal ended in failure. In his judgment,[25] Mr Justice Owen said that the residents' frustration at the situation on Osbourne Road was 'understandable', but that there had been no abuse of process by *Ultimate*. The judge refused the 'Jesmond five' leave to appeal and ordered them to pay £40,000 in interim court costs. The full costs incurred in the case totalled over £500,000 including legal fees on both sides and a claim by *Ultimate* for loss of trade caused by the delay in opening. In an interview with the local newspaper *The Journal, Ultimate's* former managing director, Bob Senior, said: 'We suspect the loss of profits, in what was the hottest summer on record, will be in the range

---

[25] *R (on the application of Bushell & Others) v Newcastle Licensing Justices* [2003] EWHC 1937, [2004] JPL 805, (2003) 153 NJL 1474, *The Times*, September 1 2003, QBD.

of £400,000 to £500,000' (Bolam 2003: 2). Further costs were incurred when the case went back before the magistrates and the licence was granted. The residents' £58,000 legal fees had been underwritten by rival operators *Rindberg Holding Company*, owners of *Osbornes*, the largest existing bar on Osbourne Road.

Playing the system

As noted, prior to the Act, development of the high street was subject to three primary forms of control: planning; public entertainment licensing (PEL) and alcohol licensing. There was, however, often very little co-ordination or consistency of policy and practice between the various regulatory bodies (Delafons 1996, Hadfield et al. 2001). As described, applicants would only apply to the justices for an alcohol licence once the two initial hurdles of planning permission and entertainment licensing had been overcome. It was typically assumed that the justices would look more favourably at applications where the other two pieces of the jigsaw were already in place. Importantly, the previously mentioned, Justices' Clerks' *Good Practice Guide* sought specifically to prohibit licensing magistrates from taking into account matters that had previously been considered by a local authority.[26] As described below, this aspect of the *Guide* created something of a lacuna which could be exploited by operators and their legal advisers. The following case notes describe how particular aspects of the legally distinct—but practically overlapping—planning and licensing systems could be pitched against each other:

In 2003, a leisure chain applied to the justices for a new SHC in order to develop the site of a former cinema. The relevant planning permission and public entertainment licensing had already been obtained. The history of the planning application was, however, somewhat murky. As a long disused cinema, the development site had retained a D2 Use Class. Put simply, this meant that the building had already been designated a broad land use planning classification which incorporated both

---

[26] Paras 1.22 and 3.13. The stated purpose of this recommendation was to 'avoid conflict and confusion and to save applicants having unnecessarily to argue the same points before both the committee and the local authority' (1.22). As the *Guide* states '. . . the committee must be careful not to trespass into areas for which the local authority is statutorily responsible, for example, planning . . . Applicants should not be required to debate issues which have already been addressed and determined' (3.13).

cinemas and nightclubs; it was therefore possible for the applicants to convert the premises into a nightclub without obtaining further planning permission. However, the applicant's aspirations for the premises involved the opening of one of their successful branded bars. This required an application for a change of use from the D2 to the A3 (food and drink) planning category. At the planning hearing, the applicant's lawyers presented the local residents who were objecting with a stark choice: would they prefer to live near to a 'nice sophisticated bar, serving food'—which therefore required achange of use to A3—or next door to a new nightclub, the plans for which could be drawn up immediately without further recourse to the planning process?

In their subsequent submissions to the liquor licensing bench, the same lawyers made much of the fact that the applicant's proposals for the site had been approved by the council's planning department and had therefore been deemed a suitable location for the development. In a report to the court commissioned by the local police, I attempted to challenge this assertion by recounting the methods by which planning permission had been obtained. Counsel for the applicant successfully argued for the removal of these 'offending paragraphs' citing the provisions of the *Good Practice Guide*.

It was by such means that applicants were able to slip the regulatory net, using the complexity of the various processes to their advantage. The ability of specialist lawyers to exploit the system through ad hoc opportunism highlighted a lack of co-ordination within and between regulatory bodies and a more general failure to adopt a coherent strategy for how the NTE should develop.

Deals, concessions, and voluntary 'pollution levies'

Chapter 7 describes how applicants often attempted to establish 'corporate social responsibility' (CSP) credentials by offering a range of proposals to assist crime reduction. Such proposals might be made in the hope of avoiding trial proceedings altogether.[27] For example, in one instance, the owners of a large

---

[27] In such instances, those applying for licences concede a degree of prospective guilt by implicitly accepting the arguments of those objectors who posit a correlation between new licensed development and the exacerbation of crime risk. On being notified of objections, it may be that the applicant is able and willing to accommodate them. The objections might be overcome either by agreement with the objectors or by imposition of conditions on the grant of a licence and, where conciliation results in the withdrawal of objections, the authority may then proceed to issue a licence. In such cases, there is no further contest, 'no testing of

estate of licensed premises in Central London negotiated a deal with the City of Westminster involving the termination or cutting back of activity at certain sites, in return for permission to expand their business elsewhere. The more common scenario was for applicants to seek the removal of objections in exchange for some form of voluntary contribution to the local crime prevention arsenal (typically in the form of situational crime prevention hardware, or security personnel). As the following case notes illustrate, problems could occur when one group of objectors decided to take the bait against the wishes of another:

In 2002, a corporate operator announced plans to develop the site of a former supermarket in Macclesfield, a market town in North West England. The application was for a new 8,000 sq. ft, 700-capacity branded bar with a late licence. The site was awarded planning permission for change of use and also a PEL by the local authority. These permits were granted in the face of opposition from the police and local residents who argued that the area was already 'saturated' with licensed premises. Police were experiencing particular problems, as the town's police station had no cell space and each arrestee had to be processed ten miles away in Wilmslow, taking officers off the street for considerable periods of time. At a meeting of the local council's licensing committee, a Chief Inspector alluded to the problems caused by this personnel shortage, stating that his officers were 'actually scared sometimes because they are vulnerable in the street'. During the PEL hearing, the bar chain offered the police and local authority £15,000 over a three-year period for CCTV and other policing aid. The offer also included installation of additional street lighting and the company's help in setting up a 'pub watch' scheme, wherein licensees assist the police by co-ordinating their own crime prevention activities. The PEL was granted and the company's proposals accepted, pending the grant of an alcohol licence by magistrates.

At this stage, the identities of all the objectors were known and the applicant's lawyers took the unusual step of making personal telephone calls to opponents at their homes. Even more surprisingly, Cheshire Constabulary did likewise, advising objectors that they no longer intended to oppose the application as the assurances given by the applicant at the PEL hearing had met their concerns. The residents decided to stand their ground, fighting the case on their own, without legal representation.

evidence, no calling of witnesses, and no open court trial' (Baldwin 2000: 246), both sides are spared the significant cost of further legal fees, regulators can inform the public that they have 'done something about crime' and the applicant gets his or her licence.

Even though the police had withdrawn their objection, the residents won a minor victory when the local justices refused the licence. The applicants immediately appealed the decision and the case was reheard in Warrington crown court, some forty miles away. In Warrington, the residents made an emotional appeal to the bench, presenting video evidence which showed the aftermath of a night in the town centre. One witness described how she had seen two men and a girl performing 'indecent acts' against the wall of her house and how one of them had left his trousers in her garden. Despite the objectors' protests, the court granted the applicants a 1am SHC, thus allowing the development to proceed.

This example illustrates how the making of concessions and striking of deals may help applicants to divide and conquer their opponents. Given the stance of the police and local authority, many residential objectors would have capitulated in the face of an intimidating, time-consuming, and potentially costly legal battle (see Chapter 6). The applicants would then be in a win-win situation, as any monies contributed to the crime reduction budget would, in all likelihood, be considerably less than the legal costs they might otherwise have incurred. Such approaches share much in common with the notion of 'planning gain' wherein, 'companies can, quite legitimately, give money or benefits in kind to a local authority as a condition of receiving planning permission' (Monbiot 2000: 132). This wheeling and dealing may be understood as a tactic used by the trade to get regulatory agencies 'on side', thus facilitating the procurement of commercially prized locations. Such offers involve the application of a rather skewed logic which may be expressed as: 'we probably will pollute your environment, but don't worry because we'll help you clean up afterwards'.

Many happy hours: the high street as a competitive market-place

Commercialization of recreational activities tends almost invariably, in the competition for patronage, to increase the emphasis upon stimulation (Burgess 1932: xiv).

Whilst on-circuit sites carry a market premium, expansion cannot proceed indefinitely. Over time, areas become commercially saturated and, in order to maintain profitability, competing operators may be forced to compromise their business format in relation to issues such as admission and drinks pricing policies. Discounting is often associated with particular trading periods known as 'happy hours, that might, in fact, last for several hours, or an entire evening. The happy hour concept originated in the United States and was initially introduced as a way of boosting trade during early-evening and mid-week trading periods (BBPA 2002: 5). In some nightlife areas, it is now possible to drink at significantly reduced prices for much of the night—'surfing the happy hour' as it is known. Drinks price wars occur, with two-for-one promotions and other bait being used to get people through the doors and keep the tills ringing.

Criticism of such practices has emerged from within the industry's own ranks. Dave Daley, head of the *National Association of Licensed House Managers*, told *The Observer* how some of his members were put under pressure by 'head office' to draw up business development plans explaining how they might retain customers after 11pm and maximize sales opportunities during extended opening hours introduced under the Act. Daley described how bonus schemes of up to £20,000 per annum were being offered to managers who consistently exceeded their sales targets (Hinsliff and Asthana 2005). This emphasis on profit has, unsurprisingly, been linked to increased levels of alcohol consumption and associated disorder (Hu 2003). The best way for operators to avoid such competitive pressure is to offer a niche product characterized by some form of distinction or exclusivity (typically music and/or design-oriented). However, premium niche markets tend to develop on secondary circuits and can be almost impossible to access once one is positioned within a negatively perceived area (Hobbs et al. 2003: 259–261 for a related discussion).

Summary

This chapter has charted the rise of the contemporary late-night leisure market in Britain's high streets. It has shown how business expansion was facilitated by a number of political and regulatory shifts and also by changes in commercial practice which favoured the development of branded venues within central urban areas. The chapter recounts how exploitation of night's economic potential involved the suppression and desecration of an influential youth movement which rejected alcohol in favour of other drugs, and how specific tactics were developed by the trade and their legal champions to successfully navigate the regulatory terrain, thus securing prized development sites.

De-regulation began incrementally through the exploitation of a variety of legal loopholes long before implementation of the Act. Lack of strategic vision, combined with an absence of will and financial muscle, militated against the type of pro-active regulation necessary to achieve ambitious plans for diversity, social inclusion, and public safety. With competing attractions and regulatory restraints largely removed, the drinks industry was free to pursue its drive for profit; a course which increasingly led to fighting within its own ranks. This intra-trade rivalry involved attempts to gain or retain commercial advantage through selective manipulation of licensing legislation and, latterly, through the waging of price wars to protect market share. The following section explores the social settings that these various processes helped to forge, paying particular attention to the indigenous modes of social control pertaining within them.

Part II

The Contemporary Environment

4

Behind Bars: Social Control in Licensed Premises

The ability to exert control over the behaviour of one's customers is essential to the successful operation of licensed premises. In exploring the constitution and application of control, this chapter highlights a key conceptual deficiency of previous studies; namely, the tendency to focus upon individual elements of the security agenda such as venue design, managerial style, and the application of discretion by door staff when selecting customers for admission. One issue that has been insufficiently explored is the extent to which controls are applied, and applied strategically, and diffusely, to the behaviour of those persons who do gain entry. The chapter identifies a general failure to acknowledge the way in which operators seek to create holistic 'illusions of order' through the purposive orchestration of many different tasks and activities. It discusses how, in some instances, these activities are supported informally by a premises's regular clientele; strong and sustainable informal controls allowing even those businesses located in busy city centres to operate successfully without the need for bouncers. Such premises are then compared with venues frequented by the largely anonymous crowds that populate the high street leisure circuit.

The chapter explains how, in seeking to enhance profitability by achieving a maximal balance in the tension between customer intoxication and control, the high street operator must develop a more sophisticated arsenal of security techniques. The methods used to manipulate customer mood and behaviour are shown to be broadly constituted, comprising an artful mix of various elements. Like a great culinary creation, each ingredient must be applied with fortitude, as getting one element wrong can have deleterious consequences; inappropriate music selection or drinks promotions, for example, serving to sour the mix. A central aim of this chapter is to explore how security roles within such premises become (i) intrinsic to the work of all members of staff who deal directly with the public; (ii) constituted as a 'team effort' involving staff performing a variety of ostensibly unrelated work tasks; and (iii) quite *atypically* require reactive intervention by dedicated security staff and the public police.

The chapter refers exclusively to venues located within British urban centres. Premises were drawn from a broad range of trading formats, from hybrid drinking/dancing/eating establishments within the contemporary bar sector, to public houses and nightclubs of a more traditional aesthetic. The analysis is informed by interviews with managers/licensees, bar and floor staff, disc jockeys (DJs), and others working within licensed premises, together with participant observation— including retrospective insight gleaned by the author in the course of his experiences as a working DJ. The chapter begins by briefly acknowledging the role played by physical constituents of the control agenda, before addressing its more central concerns, the proactive activities applied in order to manipulate the social environment.[1]

Physical aspects of control

It has long been recognized that the physical design, presentation, and maintenance of pubs and bars may influence the behaviour and expectations of their patrons. As a general proposition, it is said that unattractive, poorly designed and inexpensively furnished premises may be more likely to foster acts of aggression and violence (Forsyth et al. 2005, Graham et al. 1980, Graham and Homel 1997, Leather and Lawrence 1995). Informants spoke of the high volume of cleaning and maintenance work involved in operating a venue and the ongoing importance of this work in presenting their businesses to the public. When designing their units, many of the high street chains had attempted to move away from the traditional pub aesthetic associated with male (implicitly

[1] The analysis is unavoidably partial as it attends only sparsely to ways in which the pharmacological effects of alcohol and other intoxicants may contribute to acts of aggression and contested control situations. For reviews of this literature see Graham et al. (2000), Lipsey et al. (1997).

blue collar) drinking culture, both in terms of so-called 'female-friendly design features' such as large windows and light and airy open-plan spaces, and operationally, in terms of pricing policy and food offers (Chatterton and Hollands 2003: 149–157). These changes reflected a transformation in the social function of many urban barroom environments from that of 'poor man's club' (Kingsdale 1973)—a central fixture of working-class life during the nineteenth and most of the twentieth century—toward 'aspirational' consumption in the glittering, bureaucratically-controlled and themed environments of the new night-time high street. These changes are cogently and (now) amusingly captured in Mass Observation's description of the pubs in 1930s Bolton, in which the 'lounge' area was:

... a large comfortable room with decorations such as to be found in any home ... a better home than the ordinary worker's home ... one of cleanliness, ashtrays, no random saliva, few or no spittoons (1943: 106).

On the high street, a premium is placed upon efficient processing of the large crowds that descend during the weekend and at night. Aggressive responses are often associated with customer discomfort in relation to restricted access to the bar, lack of seating, noise levels, temperature, ventilation, air quality and overcrowding (Graham et al. 1980, Graham 1985, Homel and Clark 1994, Homel et al. 1992, Macintyre and Homel 1997). Safety may also be compromised by the inappropriate use of lighting effects (St. John-Brooks 1998) and glass drinking vessels (Plant et al. 1994, Shepherd 1994). These adverse features of the physical environment may variously fuse crime opportunities with a wide variety of environmental stressors which irritate, frustrate or otherwise provoke customers, particularly those who are intoxicated.

Aspects of interior design, furnishing and lighting have been linked to the problem of overcrowding and the creation of 'blind spots' which prevent effective surveillance of the venue. Some premises vary their lighting policies in order to reflect the differential security issues arising during particular trading periods. On 'dance nights', for example, where there is an enhanced risk of surreptitious drug-related activity, the dance floor area may be kept dark, but additional lighting used to illuminate obscure areas of the venue. Similarly, on mainstream 'party' nights, where greater levels of alcohol consumption and aggression are found, rapidly moving and disorientating lighting effects such as strobe and smoke may be avoided. Many larger venues employ a dedicated lighting jockey to manipulate lighting effects with an eye toward both social control and the creation of an interesting and constantly mutating audio-visual experience.

Open-plan space can be a key component of the high street venue's appeal as the clustering of patrons 'increases the likelihood that sociability among the unacquainted will ensue' (Cavan 1966: 97). As Cavan notes of 1960s San Francisco, customers within urban bars have a tendency to converge within 'milling areas' which consist of 'an open-plan space in the general vicinity of the physical bar'. This practice occurs 'regardless of whether there are seats at or away from the bar available to them' (ibid.: 101). Accordingly, many high street venues are only sparsely furnished in order to cater to the preferences of a consumer base described in marketing circles as the Mass Volume Vertical Drinker (MVVD). Informants identified the need to monitor both the total number of people within their premises and occupancy levels within each individual area:

On a Saturday night we will have about 3,500–4,000 people go through the door, so that's 8,000 journeys on one narrow staircase. We always see our stairs as our big flashpoint; it's the one thing that we've got to get right . . . We use the DJ to tell people to move down to the extremities of the building to give new people coming in and people around the bar some more space . . . then it's down to the doormen to limit the people coming in . . . We do that by a simple system of clickers: one doorman clicks in, one doorman clicks out. We don't do one in and one out; we wait 'till twenty have gone, then let twenty in, because you have to give people the chance to come up the stairs and blend in with the crowd' (Ken, independent bar owner).

At the bar, service must be efficient in order to minimize frustration among waiting customers. Bars need to be well staffed and fully stocked in anticipation of the influx of people during peak trading periods. As well as assisting in crowd control, these techniques can have a significant impact upon profitability, as venues will often generate most of their weekly income within a few short hours of night-time trading.

Although often arising in relation to physical aspects of the drinking situation, the environmental stressors discussed interact with, and are partially constitutive of, the social environment one finds within licensed premises. Having indicated a number of ways in which features of the physical environment within licensed premises may be used to exert control over patron behaviour, the following paragraphs will discuss various concordant techniques that may be applied to the social environment.

Social aspects of control

Our understanding of high street licensed premises as contexts for social interaction and control may be usefully informed by contrasting such settings with other public drinking occasions in which incidents of aggression and violence are comparatively rare.

The makings of the 'local'

The traditional English pub has often been characterized as a facility which serves largely static or geographically-confined communities (Mass Observation 1943, Vasey 1990). To this day, such premises may function as what Oldenburg (1997) describes as 'third places' or 'great good places'; environments in which people meet and socialize outside of their homes (first places) or locations of work (second places) (Kingsdale 1973). Within such venues, people enjoy the company of others whom they know, whilst also encountering 'strangers'. Relationships between customers and staff may be intimate (Mass Observation 1943: 133–134, Ritzer 2004: 42–43) and involve active co-operation, with customers being willing to help out in various ways (Cavan 1966: 231–233). For staff, there is often little distinction to be drawn between work and social life and those who no longer work behind the bar may return to socialize with former colleagues and customers (LeMasters 1975, Marshall 1986). Although there will usually be no formal criteria for admission, camaraderie between 'regulars' (Katovich and Reese 1987) may afford some sense of attachment or belonging (LeMasters 1975).

In sociological accounts of the traditional pub, the publican is typically identified as the 'host' of a valued community facility; a well-known authority figure. Privy to local gossip, these men and women were deeply embedded in the social and cultural life of their area (Mass Observation 1943, Vasey 1990). In some close-knit communities, the risk of tarnished reputation could exert a powerful calming influence (LeMasters 1975, Roberts 1971) and intimate understanding of local antagonisms and rivalries and the individual personalities of their customers allowed hosts to be proactive in controlling behaviour within their premises.

Anthropological research indicates that drinking practices are notable for their historical and cultural specificity, with drinking styles and associated behaviours being learnt through processes of socialization and imitation (Heath 2000, MacAndrew and Edgerton 1969). Until quite recently, barroom environments in Britain might typically have been bastions of exclusively *male* sociability, from which women were effectively excluded (Hey 1986, Rogers 1988). These themes have been explored by a number of sociologists, who argue that in working class industrial areas, for example, pubs and bars historically functioned as social institutions in which older men taught their younger male apprentices 'how to handle their drink' (Dorn 1983, Gofton 1990, Kingsdale 1973). Within this masculinist tradition, introductions from regulars and the serving of an apprenticeship in 'drunken comportment' (MacAndrew and Edgerton 1969) allowed consecutive generations of drinkers to be assimilated into the 'insider' group (Katovich and Reese 1987). As Mike told me:

If you're strict at 16, 17, and don't let them in, they're not going to come in when they are of age. We start getting a few when they are a little bit older. They might start comin' in with older people from work and decide that *The Dog* is alright for a few pints. They tell their mates 'why pay three quid a bottle when you can have a few pints here?' So you make money that way and you keep that customer for life (assistant manager, city centre pub).

Remnants of these informal methods of social control may often be found where licensed premises continue to serve the needs of a largely regular and predictable consumer base. Even in urban centres, one can still find premises which operate in this way, being physically and/or culturally and aesthetically removed from the main drinking circuits. Although ostensibly open to all, these more traditional venues are often of little appeal to the (mostly) younger crowds of 'action' seekers (Cloyd 1976). As a barman at one such establishment put it:

We are off the loop. We've had more strangers in since they opened the *Havana* bar up the road, but mostly, it's the same faces. We don't get the youngsters and the big groups and even when we do, they only come in here for one drink anyway 'cos it's not lively enough for 'em. We're not like a bottle bar where they just go in for bottles and shooters, y'know, we're like for pints and we get the older women from thirty onwards. The young lads, they want to go where there's the younger girls; y'know, with the short skirts (Jim).

An Englishman's pub is his castle

It's a local in the town centre. This pub is self-regulating, so we don't really have any trouble (Tony, licensee).

In the following paragraphs, the term 'regulars' venue' will be used when referring to those premises in which control over key aspects of activity, behaviour, and social atmosphere is shared between staff and the businesses' core clientele who exercise 'territoriality' with regard to the venue (Cavan 1963, 1966, Katovich and Reese 1987, LeMasters 1973, Lyman and Scott 1967). Within such venues there may be implicit rules regarding the maintenance of light-hearted conviviality, such as the avoidance of serious and potentially divisive and inflammatory conversational topics like politics and religion (Cavan 1966, Mass Observation 1943, Vasey 1990). Moreover, the relatively 'thick' social bonds between regulars may perform a protective function with regard to unwelcome and challenging intrusions by transient visitors.[2] To this extent, 'habitués treat the bar as though it "belonged" to them, as though it were no longer within the domain of *public* drinking places' (Cavan 1966: 211). As Mass Observation (1943: 106) observed: 'casuals are somewhat resented if they drop into the tap-room. It would be bad form for a stranger to go in there for a drink. And he would probably notice that the regulars were not very pleased to see him.'

Territoriality may be exercised differentially in relation to particular areas of the premises, with distinct groups of regulars claiming ownership over specific spaces (Hobbs 1988, Roebuck and Frese 1976). This spatial differentiation may reflect the

---

[2] For example, as public drinking places, bars are environments in which women may be the subject of unwanted advances from men (Snow et al. 1991), the status of regular or friend of the regulars may allow women to feel more comfortable and relaxed in their interactions with male strangers (Parks et al. 1998).

existence of complex social hierarchies and interrelationships between regulars (Katovich and Reese 1987) contributing to the creation of a 'rigidly stratified institution' (Hobbs, ibid.: 142–143), largely impenetrable to the outsider.

If staff-customer control situations are contested and threaten to get out of hand, staff may call upon and/or involuntarily receive, assistance from regulars. Such venues are therefore, to a large degree, self-policing. In some instances, 'turf defence' (Gottlieb 1957, Lyman and Scott 1967) operates largely through word of mouth, as the premises and its clientele have a sufficiently 'rough' reputation to intimidate and deter the transient visitor, including potential troublemakers:

Kids on the town don't cause us problems, they wouldn't *dare*. A lot of the older people would have no hesitation in telling them to calm down. We have a lot of big regulars, y'know, who have a presence about them, who would have a word . . . because the last thing they want is a ban on somewhere they like to drink Steve (barman, regulars' venue).

These informal social control mechanisms and the general predictability of the environment allow many regulars' venues to eschew formal admissions criteria and the use of door staff. Customers who appear to be of legal drinking age, even those who may be 'rough-looking' are 'given the benefit of the doubt' and 'treated as they are found' within a space which is ostensibly open to all who 'behave themselves'. However, as Cavan (1963: 21) notes:

The home territory character of any bar is dependent upon the indigenous population's ability to control the presence of outsiders. The problem for those who define and utilize a public drinking place as a home territory is the problem of handling outsiders who may attend to the bar in terms of its apparent public character.

Under certain circumstances, the indigenous group's attempts to exercise territoriality may break down due to the 'swamping' of the venue by outsiders whose actions cannot be effectively controlled:

There was a match day last year which attracted a big hooligan element shall we say . . . A group of thirty lads, just going 'round drinking at all the bars and wearing the colours; of course, when the match disgorged, it was them versus the supporters. A chap staggers in and says 'can I get a drink?' and I say 'No way, you're too drunk. Sit in the corner with a glass of water.' I say to his mates, 'you can have a drink 'cos you're all right, but he's not getting any.' Of course, they're trying to give him a drink and the touch paper was lit, they wanted a fight and it just went 'Boof!' They're turning us over. So there's me and one of my barmen getting him out and they turn on us. Course, y'know, black eyes, bruising, shall we say, and we had to defend ourselves to a certain extent. The police were called, but by the time they arrived they'd been and gone. We had four staff and there were thirty of them. Some of the regulars tried to help us but they got hurt too. So my philosophy now is stand well back, we don't really want everyone involved, we don't want our regulars getting hurt (John, manager, regulars' venue).

The potential risk of swamping goes some way to inform the choice of whether or not to employ door staff. In venues located on or near a high street drinking circuit, this threat may be very real.

Enter the high street

I used to work in a bar on Bile Street. If there was a fight, the customers would just turn away, wouldn't lift a finger Esther (bartender, regulars' venue).

Paul Cressey's *The Taxi-Dance Hall: A Sociological Study in Commercialized Recreation and City Life* (1932), an investigation of the Chicago dance halls of the 1920s, can be regarded as a seminal ethnography of the urban NTE. In his concluding chapter, Cressey explains the import of the book's subtitle:

In the last analysis, the problem of the taxi-dance hall[3] can be regarded as the problem of the modern city ... There is, first of all, mobility, impersonality, and anonymity ... The taxi-dance hall also reflects in the extreme, the commercialism and utilitarian considerations which characterize the city. In it even romance is sold on the bargain counter ... Moreover, in the transient contacts of the ballroom one feels no personal responsibility for the conduct of strangers seen there. As a result, any effective control which is exercised must be formally imposed

[3] Taxi-dance halls were ballrooms in which men paid to dance with young women: 'like the taxi driver with his cab, she is for public hire and is paid in proportion to the time spent and the services rendered' (p.3). The proceeds were split between the operators of the premises and the dancers. The dance halls were the source of moral outrage within sections of middle class American society due to anxieties regarding promiscuity and female emancipation (Burgess 1932, Dubin 1983).

from without, either by the manager himself or by others whose interest is in civic welfare. Thus the informal social control arising naturally and without special concern in the village situation must be supplanted in the urban dance hall by formal regulations, by institutionalized methods of supervision, and by systems of control imposed forcefully and externally upon the dance hall patrons (287–289).

Cressey's analysis retains contemporary relevance as it echoes in the comparisons that may be drawn between regulars' venues and premises which occupy the high street drinking circuit. On the high street, the mix of people is dynamic and intoxicated strangers from a variety of areas intermingle. Although high street businesses may establish some form of rapport with their customers—through brand identity, at least (see Chapter 3)—the service of an indigenous population is necessarily supplanted by the manipulation of largely anonymous and transient crowds. High street premises serve a discrete social function to that of the regulars' venue; one in which the sociability of neighbourhood and work gives way to the search for excitement, sexual encounter, and spectacle (Cloyd 1976) within a context of conspicuous and often exaggerated consumption (Brain 2000). These conditions discourage meaningful interaction between customers and staff. Even though the same customers may attend week in, week out, relationships remain superficial and deeper social attachments may never be formed (Katovich and Reese 1987):

PH: Do you get many regulars?

Tim (barman, high street bar): Yes, but I have no personal relationship with them. It'll just be a 'Hi, y'alright?' behind the bar, because you're busy. They'll stop for a couple of drinks and next Friday they are back in again. It's really difficult to know where they come from and where else they go, 'cos you haven't got time to talk to them.

Circuit venues—especially those situated some distance from shopping and business facilities—are often closed during the day-time and the 'quietest' nights of the week. This mono-functionality acts to further sever the link between venues and their host communities by militating against the acquisition of regulars.

The operating practices of high street venues were criticized by off-circuit licensees for creating bad publicity for the licensed trade as a whole. This critique had a number of coherent themes, including the discounting of drinks, the serving of underage or highly intoxicated customers, and a generally irresponsible business ethos skewed towards the maximization of alcohol sales and profit (Asthana 2005, Hinsliff and Asthana 2005). The following comments were typical:

At *Flames* on Brand Street you'd get targets to meet and bonuses on drinks' sales. The area manager would just come in on a Monday morning, never at night, and just say 'What were your takings? Did you make a lot of money?' He'd never say 'Was there any trouble?', or 'What type of punters did you get in?' Down there you just play the loudest music, get as many people in as you can. Just keep your head down, keep selling the bottles, don't talk to people (Becky, manager, regular's pub).

High street venues and the imposition of formal control

Commercial exploitation of the high street leisure market has involved the concurrent development of formal and regularized modes of control. The co-operative and mutually supportive activities required to impose and maintain consistent operational practice allow staff to feel more secure in what can be a frantic working environment. Moreover, these 'rules of the house' play an important commercial role in ensuring that 'unruly elements' are not allowed to encroach in ways that could be bad for business. Yet, high street venues do not always adhere to the dictates of 'company policy' and even when they do, such policies will often sanction hedonistic behaviour, that within a more traditional pub setting, 'your regulars wouldn't stand for'.[4] The formal social controls brought to the fore within high street premises have generally less disciplinary efficacy than the

---

[4] *Yates' Plc*, for example, recently installed steel dancing poles in venues throughout their national estate. These fixtures have been placed in dance floor areas to afford customers the opportunity to engage in impromptu 'pole dancing'. As in many other high street venues, live video images of dancing customers are shown on plasma screens throughout the venue. This footage is interspersed with music videos and details of drinks promotions. These features permit high street operators to use the sexual allure of their own customers as a sales promotion device.

informal social controls exerted by regulars. Paradoxically therefore, the greater behavioural latitude to be found within high street premises requires that the open-door policy of the regulars' venue, in which all customers are 'assumed innocent until proven guilty', is replaced by more strict criteria for admission.

Boundary work

In high street venues, admissions procedures become perhaps the single most important aspect of security; for in such busy and high-spirited environments, 'once customers enter the premises, policing them is far more difficult' (Hobbs et al. 2003: 120). Thus, although security staff may be dispersed throughout the premises, the majority of them are likely to be found guarding the main entrance. The 'front of house' represents a 'checkpoint or filter' through which *potential* customers must pass whilst their 'credentials' are evaluated (Monaghan 2002a: 412). The patron selection process represents the best opportunity to establish a market niche and fulfil long-term business ambitions. As a result, venue managers may also spend much of their time at the door in order to meet and greet customers and ensure that the door team are working in accordance with expectations:

In the queue you are looking for people to stand in a way that is reasonably well-behaved, you are trying to prevent people from joining the queue who are not suitable so you don't get as many knock backs at the front door. When they do get to the door, obviously you are selecting people on age, making sure they are not intoxicated, no signs of drug usage, and the manner in which people dress. It is vital that the people who are working the front door know the type of clientele that we expect inside. We are trying to keep people who are not likely to mix well together, separate. There is no point having, like, a football hooligan-type mentality crowd in an environment which is dance-focused and who would fit in better in a place which plays party music. You need to select people of a similar mindset who have a certain empathy with each other, again, to prevent public order situations. You may have to conduct searches and detain people found with any illegal substances or concealed weapons (Mike, nightclub manager).

Door staff and management regard the retention of discretion as paramount, being intimately connected to personal authority and the protection of property and persons: as the nightlife legend goes, 'management reserve the right to refuse admission'.

Social control and the pleasure professional

I hope I help make people feel happy, get them drunk and giggly, and get them laid (Kevin, owner/operator, independent bar).

Once customers are inside the premises, it is essential that they be entertained. When visiting high street premises, consumers seek to purchase not only alcohol, but more importantly, the shared experience of time-out. Ethnographers have long described the importance of levity and 'social licentiousness' in barroom settings (Cavan 1966: 236, Goffman 1963: 126–127, LeMasters 1973, Roebuck and Frese 1976). 'Behaviour which is permissible or constitutes no more than normal trouble in the bar encompasses a broad range of activities that are often open to sanction in other, more serious, public settings' (Cavan 1966: 67). The security-related activities of the staff team are impositions from the more serious world of daylight and must remain subtle lest the spell of unadulterated abandon be broken. As Neil, the manager of a high street pub explained:

You try not to be too dictatorial and you need to be tolerant of people. People come in for a good time and I want them to have one. You've got to think, 'Well they are away from home, probably been on the drink all day, having a bit of a play-time' and after a while you say, 'Right, enough's enough!' and they'll quite happily accept that. I'm not going to say, 'Well there's no play-time'. Like, if they are up at the bar shoutin' and singin' and it's full that's immaterial; but it's just when they are fightin', or they are shouting and being noisy when the bar is empty, then I would need to say something to them. I just say, 'You've had your five minutes play-time and you're back in class now!'

There are, of course, pleasures to be enjoyed by the controller as well as the controlled. Staff teams within high street venues usually consist of young, sociable, and outgoing people who enjoy interacting with others. The working environment provides a good source of anecdotes and staff may often form friendships and go clubbing together at the end of their shift. For groups of young people such as students who may not have a lot of money to spend, bar work can provide an opportunity to earn a living whilst enjoying the atmosphere of premises they might otherwise choose to visit as customers. In successful premises, staff and customers will feed off each other's energy and enthusiasm. Busy venues can be exciting and many people enjoy being part of a large crowd. The intensity of experience on a 'good night' draws in customers, staff, and management alike:

I enjoy the buzz of here, the adrenalin of a choca bar, five deep at the bar and six staff runnin' around, it's great, it's lush, y'know, with everyone singin' along to *Hi Ho Silver Lining*. You'd like to have a few pints and join in yourself (Lenny, manager, chain bar).

Yet, the ready opportunities for pleasure—intensified in various ways by control over the means of pleasure production—require considerable degrees of self-discipline. Members of staff are part of a *team* charged with the performance of responsible *work* tasks. The working environment is one of heightened risk and there may be considerable personal and financial costs associated with 'getting it wrong', which may increase incrementally according to the physical capacity of the premises. It is a key task of all members of staff (not only management and security) to ensure that both they, and their customers, are able to enjoy themselves, but within limits (Roebuck and Frese 1976: Chapter 7). Exerting control over the pleasure of others requires abstinence, or at least restraint, in relation to one's own consumption of intoxicants; the artful negotiation of sexual opportunities (Monaghan 2002c, Roebuck and Frese 1976); the curbing of creative (Becker 1963), or aggressive urges; the avoidance of overt favouritism; the balancing of familiarity and authority; and the strict management of time. As the following paragraphs explain, this ability to remain 'in control' of oneself and others is regarded as a prerequisite of professional conduct and entails three key constituents: vigilance; manipulation of mood; and the management and diffusion of conflict.

Vigilance

You're just on alert all the time (Peter, assistant manager, high street pub).

Violent incidents within licensed premises usually develop via a process of escalation. Early intervention can serve to minimize conflict and increase the likelihood that matters are resolved peacefully and unobtrusively. The staff team must therefore be vigilant, actively monitoring customer behaviour to ensure that, whenever possible, any problems are detected at an early stage. Experienced staff spoke of the importance of knowing what to look for:

People chatting and laughing and listening to music an' carrin' on is different to people arguing . . . You can see a lot of people lookin' in the same direction, people movin' away from an area (Lynne, bar tender, high street pub).

As Monaghan notes, security staff are 'usually situated individually at various strategic and often highly visible surveillance points . . . the top of stairs, close to bars and on balconies overlooking bars, dance floors and other populated spaces' (2002a: 413). The mere presence of a uniformed staff member was felt to reassure customers and remind potential troublemakers that their activities were being monitored. Furthermore, in what could be a crowded and confusing environment, ease of identification was seen as an aid to customers who might need to request assistance or wished to report any incidents they had witnessed. Door staff and management combined periods of static vigil with patrol of the venue:

On a night, instead of serving behind the bar so much I'm out collecting the glasses. You can go 'round every table and see who's sitting there and just keep an eye on things; any potential drug problems or arguments; who's had too much to drink and just taking things away so they can't be used as weapons; it's just basic things. Anyone watching might think 'What you doing that for?', but it's just a case of years and years of experience. (You need to) just clear things away and know what's going on (Jim, manager, high street pub).

Such unobtrusive attentiveness to the apparently trivial minutiae of social interaction is not merely a characteristic of the managerial or dedicated security role. Bar and floor staff regularly move around the venue in order to collect glasses or take customer orders and are therefore well placed to contribute to monitoring activities. DJs will often work from raised consoles which act as vantage points. As we shall see, this physical location, combined with the highly reflexive nature of their work—which involves the constant scanning, assessment, and manipulation of the mood of the crowd—can place the DJ at the heart of the venue's overall control strategy.

Policing the limits of intoxication

It's always the drunk ones, it's the people who have been on the piss, have a few more in here and then they get aggressive (Les, nightclub bar manager).

As Prus (1983: 462) notes, it is expected that people will drink, but 'not too much'. 'Actual levels of intoxication tolerated at bars vary considerably.' However, 'when people disrupt or threaten other patrons, become incomprehensible or otherwise lose control of their bodies' (ibid.), a line may need to be drawn. The issue becomes one of a duty of care toward the individual drinker, and to other customers and members of staff. It is the role of the staff team, and especially of management, to monitor intoxicated comportment and use their professional discretion to determine and impose 'cut-off points' beyond which further service will be denied and/or a patron asked to leave.

Staff vigilance is also important in relation to drug-related issues. Drugs awareness incorporates the need for staff to be able to recognize illegal substances and signs of their use, together with health and safety issues relating to customers who may be suffering from the effects of drug ingestion (DPAS 2002, Walker 2001). Drugs awareness also involves vigilance in relation to criminal activities such as drug dealing, the spiking of drinks and use of so-called 'date-rape' drugs such as Rohypnol. Informants spoke of a particular need to monitor activities in and around toilet areas:

If there's three or four lads and they're all going to the toilet together (laughs), y'know what I mean? It's very unlikely that they all gonna need a piss at exactly the same time. So you just go and have a look, walk in, just use the toilet, make them feel uncomfortable . . . and it's taking the toilet seats off and things like that; your toilet-roll holders, making sure they're not flat topped, they are tilted, and there's grooves in the toilet roll holder so there's no flat surface. Make sure hand dryers are head height so they can't snort off it, put Vaseline on the surfaces so the powder will stick to it. Check for this, check for that; if it's an easy place to go, they'll use it—so you need to make things difficult (Ken, manager, high street bar).

Some venues seek to enhance guardianship and surveillance by placing attendants in toilet areas.

Communication

Everybody's watching out for everyone else instead of just one person trying to watch over the whole place, 'cos you haven't got eyes in the back of your head (Pete, manager, high street pub).

Informants stressed the need for good communication between members of the staff team. Effective communication was the vital ingredient which transformed proactive monitoring into the maximization of opportunities for early intervention. However, it could be difficult for staff to communicate in large and noisy venues, particularly where sight lines were obscured. For this reason, a wide range of technologies were employed. In order to avoid disruption to the social atmosphere of the premises, it was imperative that staff communications be indecipherable to customers. In nightclubs, coded hand signals, lighting sequences, DJ announcements, or sounds emitted over the sound system were used to call for security and management assistance.

Many venues used some form of 'panic button' system operated from behind the bar and/or DJ booth to alert door staff stationed at the venue's entrance by means of an audible (bell, buzzer, ring tone) or visual (typically red light) signal. Some larger venues used a coded system of lights, for example, a 'traffic light system' where red, amber and green are used to denote different rooms or areas of the building. Members of staff might also use radio communication systems, particularly when requesting urgent assistance. Handheld radio systems often remained susceptible to background noise interference and many operators therefore preferred to use earpiece or cuff microphones. The noisy environment could even influence the way in which incidents were resolved: 'You may have to eject both parties as it's difficult to play judge within a loud club, so you get them to the front door, away from the loud music where you can actually hear what people have got to say' (Steve, nightclub manager).

Venues also nurtured lines of communication (such as radio-links) with other nearby premises, sometimes negotiating reciprocal arrangements whereby each would supply reinforcement door staff in the case of a serious incident that threatened to get 'out of hand'. Such informal private policing solutions were often regarded by operators and police alike as the preferred first line of defence in dealing with incidents occurring *within* licensed premises. Summoning of the police was usually reserved for extreme situations involving violence. Informants spoke of having access to a silent emergency panic button affording direct access to the police station. However, this button was used sparingly, as an action of last resort. [5]

Manipulation of mood

Phat controllers: DJs and the construction of joyful restraint

Although there may sometimes be guest appearances by musicians, television celebrities and pin-ups, in the vast majority of high street venues, DJs are the main generators and controllers of entertainment. DJs have a variety of roles within the NTE. In the 'mainstream' venues that comprise the bulk of the high street, DJs are expected to be highly adaptable. The mainstream DJ is required not only to play popular music, but also, where necessary, to act as compere. Social skills are an important attribute of the mainstream DJ, hence they are sometimes referred to as 'personality DJs'. The DJ provides a focal point for entertainment within the venue and acts as a mouthpiece for venue management, conveying messages to the crowd regarding drinks promotions, future events and last orders at the bar, etc. DJs may also make announcements for customers, including birthday messages and music dedications.

Unpopular, badly presented/performed and excessively loud music and other entertainment, together with poor quality sound, may irritate customers. Poor entertainment can induce boredom and resentment among customers and stimulate heavier drinking, to the detriment of the social atmosphere (Geller and Kalsher 1990, Homel et al. 1992). Conversely, heightened states of arousal may also contribute to aggression. High street chains will therefore attempt to ensure that each of their 'units' strikes an

---

[5] One reason for the reluctance to involve the police related to fears that evidence of crime and disorder might be used against the premises in some way.

appropriate balance between engaging entertainment and provocative over-stimulation. Although regarded as a musical expert, the primary function of the mainstream DJ is to entertain the crowd and create an atmosphere of carefully orchestrated abandon.

DJs, lighting jockeys and other entertainers are very aware of the powerful influence of musical and visual imagery upon mood and behaviour, indeed, the manipulation of mood may be understood as a core component of their craft. DJing is a highly reflexive form of social practice in that it involves constant monitoring of one's own performance in relation to the social atmosphere induced and the ways in which audiences receive particular recordings. Such reflexivity is particularly salient in the context of busy mainstream venues where DJ professionalism becomes intrinsic to social control:

Music policy is a clever form of manipulation that most people do not recognize, even people in the industry. You will find a lot of inexperienced managers, DJs and security staff who don't pick up on these first signs of having discontent within a venue and they are important control measures. It is much more important to control the crowd with music than it is to control the crowd with security staff because if you have to constantly control the crowd with security staff you've lost the plot, basically. You should be creating an environment which keeps people out of that mood where conflict can occur (Jim, manager, high street bar).

DJs working in mainstream venues spoke of being constantly aware of the possibility of being severely reprimanded, or even sacked, for playing the wrong music at the wrong time. In practice, this might involve being somewhat 'over-enthusiastic' in creating an atmosphere that was so frenzied as to render control difficult. Such states were deceptively easy to induce. Whilst novice DJs often interpreted euphoric responses as a confirmation of their skills, hard-nosed managers and door staff would regard such performances as indulgent and unprofessional. 'Problematic' DJing might also involve playing predominately to one's own tastes, or to the tastes of a minority, younger, or predominately male audience. Hence, extended sessions of 'harder' musical styles were ill-advised and certain musical genres, such as Ska, mostly avoided. The main problem with Ska, for example, was that, as one high street DJ put it, 'it encourages big men, who wouldn't ordinarily dance, to start bangin' about and upsetting people' (Ken). There may also be local and regional sensitivities in relation to different musical styles. Entertainers may, for example, need to be advised to avoid performing songs which have particular football affiliations. One DJ explained how his key consideration was to avoid music which appealed to the 'macho' values of customers:

You have to be careful with *Oasis*, because what I can't have is 200 lads just singing at the top of their voices . . . all of a sudden you feel like you are at Maine Road watching a match and it's an intimidating atmosphere (Pete, high street bar).[6]

Hence, high street DJs are expected to 'play safe', tailoring their sets to the perceived tastes of mainstream female, 'light-hearted' (less-discerning), or 'camp' audiences, whilst disregarding the preferences of the venue's 'higher risk' constituencies.

Dealing with requests

Like Becker's (1963) jazz musicians, the contemporary DJ can find the problem of being externally directed by members of the audience particularly problematic (Roebuck and Frese 1976: 240). For the DJ, the fielding of musical requests by customers raises issues not only of professional pride and commercial imperative, but also of social control. As noted, the studious omission of situationally inappropriate music is the most essential component of the DJ's contribution to venue security. DJs must therefore determine the legitimacy of requests in relation to the predicted outcome of their fulfilment. Playing the 'wrong' record in order to appease one persistent, flirtatious, or intimidating

---

[6] Informants also mentioned other forms of entertainment which could give rise to customer over-stimulation. Topless female dancers and strippers, for example, were cited by a number of people as generating a 'wild' and unruly atmosphere amongst customers. Moreover, it was felt that such performances could make the social atmosphere more uncomfortable for female customers, thereby discouraging their (important) patronage:

The premises are party-orientated. It is geared towards the female, y'know, we try an' encourage female-friendly around our premises. Yes, men will follow, but you have to create a happy atmosphere for the average woman (Helen, DJ, high street bar).

customer could be—quite literally in the eyes of an employer—more than your job's worth.

The professional DJ must learn the art of negotiation and emotional management. In directly refusing requests, the DJ may be interpreted as expressing disrespect for the customer's musical tastes, status, or identity. If a customer loses face during such interaction, the DJ runs the risk of receiving an aggressive or even violent response:

> I was in a situation in Dogford where it was the end of the night and I hadn't played this guy's record for him and he threw a bottle of *Pils* and it just missed my head and smashed on the back wall. I've had people in this bar swearing and cursing blind at me because I won't play their record, people tryin' to pull me out of the box (Darren, DJ, high street bar).

Given the frantic pace of their work, DJs have little time to consider their personal safety; yet, they cannot rely solely on receiving physical protection from management and door staff. DJs have therefore developed a repertoire of concise interactional routines which they use to 'soften the humiliation and dampen the prospect of aggressive compensatory behaviour that often follows on the heels of rejection or failure' (Snow et al. 1991: 425). This process of 'cooling out' (Goffman 1952) or managing expectations is similar to that described by Snow et al. (ibid.) in their analysis of women's responses to unwanted sexual overtures.

Although the mainstream DJ will usually have, close at hand, all the software needed to fulfil the vast majority of customer requests, he or she may claim never to have heard of the track, or say something along the lines of: 'Sorry, I haven't got that/got that with me tonight/got that yet/got that anymore'. This type of response forecloses the request, but may elicit ridicule—'I can't believe you haven't got that! Call yourself a DJ!' and leaves the interaction open for the customer to make further (inappropriate) requests. An alternative response might be to promise to play the request later, in the hope that the customer will forget. This response does not work with determined and persistent people who return repeatedly to remind the DJ to fulfil their 'promise'. In such circumstances, DJs may have to fall back on a third form of response—the appeal to higher loyalties: 'Sorry, I'm not allowed to play that because it's a party night/70s and 80s night/ alternative night/dance night tonight', or 'Sorry, the boss won't let me play that, it's against the music policy'. Such responses may be further softened by empathy: 'Yeah, I'd love to play that/I really like that, *but* . . .'. This sentiment may well, in some cases, be honestly expressed.

Many operators issue DJs and other entertainers with sample 'play lists', providing guidance on appropriate and inappropriate musical styles. A number of high street chains have gone further, considering music policy to be an issue of such importance to the atmosphere and concept of their venues that their DJs are no longer afforded professional discretion; fixed play lists are imposed by the company's head office and strictly policed by the managers of each unit. DJ performances are deliberately controlled and deskilled, with the company removing, or at least restricting, any element of 'risk'. Within such venues, departure from music policy may warrant immediate dismissal for DJs.

The fixed play list may be understood as part of the more general process of homogenization described in Chapter 3, through which the night-time high street has been increasingly filled with identikit theme bars. In licensed estates across Britain, crowds are now fed a repetitive diet of tired, safe, and nostalgic party music night-in, night-out. DJs are not permitted to adapt their sets to reflect personal tastes, or the preferences of locally idiosyncratic crowds. There is little space for individuality, creativity, or the establishment of reciprocally appreciative relationships with the consumer.[7] With their bureaucratic top-down prerogatives and 'visions for the brand', many chain operators seek to promote a predictable social atmosphere that is replicated throughout their estate (Ritzer 2004). The night-time high street, far from being a romantic milieu of self-expression or self-discovery through music, is an arena which constrains the creative urges of producer and consumer alike. Risk-averse corporate culture holds both groups in an iron grip in its quest to govern every aspect of the music, mood, and social control nexus.

---

[7] Indigenous 'house anthems' and regionally distinct 'sounds' can generate powerful structures of feeling and association, whilst contributing to the construction of local music scenes (Haslam 1999, Hobbs et al. 2003: Chs 2 and 3). It was, of course, this very reciprocal relationship between the producers and consumers of nightlife which, for previous generations, played a significant role in the constitution of youth sub-cultures.

Different nights, different controls

Notwithstanding the broader shift toward homogenization, in order to maximize the use of their facilities throughout the week, operators may offer niche nights which aim to attract distinct audiences such as students, clubbers and alternative music fans.[8] This approach to business promotion may generate divergent sets of security issues, with the different customer profiles and patterns of drug use on each night requiring an accordingly specialized response from the staff team. Symbiotic relationships between particular styles of popular music and the use of certain illicit drugs have long been observed (Collin 1997, McKenna 1996). Specialist dance music styles, for example, are often associated with the consumption of stimulants such as ecstasy and cocaine, whereas mainstream pop and dance music (the staple diet of the high street) is typically aligned with the consumption of alcohol. These music-drug interrelationships have consequences for the manipulation of mood in contributing to the generation of particular types of conflict situation.

Researchers and other commentators have found that dedicated dance or music venues (as opposed to more drink-oriented venues which feature music) tend to attract generally non-aggressive customers and to experience low levels of disorder. When violence does break out at dance venues this tends to be in relation to control of the door and other security problems concerning the activities of drug dealers.[9] By contrast, it appears that the customers of alcohol-fuelled mainstream premises are likely to be generally more aggressive and prone to involvement in arguments, fights, and criminal damage (Hammersley et al. 2002, Hobbs et al. 2003, South 1999). It should be noted, however, that fashions in music, drug use and entertainment constantly mutate, and that the music-drug nexus may be further complicated by the

---

[8] Mid-week student nights in high street venues rarely adopt a 'students-only' entry policy and admission is often free. The marketing of such nights typically focuses on some form of drinks promotion. Some venues use outside promoters with specialist knowledge, skills or community links to attract customer interest, enthusiasm, and loyalty for niche events.

[9] Gun culture can attach itself to certain types of music. For example, there is a trend for shootings to occur around some 'urban music' nights where firearms may be carried as a fashion accessory and antagonisms between rival gang members may be violently expressed.

increasing popularity of poly-drug use, involving the mixing of illicit drugs and alcohol as 'a matter of routine' (Parker et al. 2002: 947, Deehan and Saville 2003, DPAS 2002, Hammersley et al. 2002, Release 1997).

Having discussed the importance of watchfulness and the manipulation of mood, the following paragraphs will consider the management of conflict through strategic social interaction.

The management and diffusion of conflict

You've got to expect a bit of trouble. If you come into this game and you don't think you'll ever be in a fight or something like that, well, you're stupid aren't yer? (Steve, manager, high street bar).

All of the managerial staff interviewed (male and female, young and middle-aged, and from a wide variety of city centre premises) had been involved in physically violent encounters with customers at some point in their careers. A number still bore the physical scars inflicted during such incidents. Of the violent incidents recounted (often in graphic detail), the majority involved attempts to control the behaviour of customers, against their wishes (Fagan 1993, Felson et al. 1986). This might apply to a very wide range of situations, including the refusal of service at the bar, customers being asked to leave, the attempted confiscation of drugs or weapons, and requests for proof of age.

A number of informants bemoaned the attitude of police, the courts, and their employers, all of whom appeared to regard staff as 'fair game' for assailants, whilst imposing heavy sanctions upon those who acted in self-defence. As Darren, the manager of a high street bar, commented: 'You'd be sent to hell if you did to them what they do to you'. Moreover, although some employers did offer counselling to assault victims, others were not so sympathetic, expecting staff to 'just get on with it as though nothing had happened'. In general, there was an expectation that occasional acts of violence were to be tolerated as part of the job. Inability to cope with what was trivialized as simply the 'rough and tumble' of every-night life was regarded as a sign of weakness, denoting one's basic unsuitability for the licensed trade.

Some of those interviewed pointed to a lack of experience among the management and staff of high street venues. In off-circuit regulars' venues, members of staff were drawn from a broad age range and many had worked within the premises for years. By contrast, informants from the high street venues often mentioned the tender age of their non-managerial staff (often students) who were typically employed on a casual and temporary basis. There was a high turnover of staff in high street premises, reflecting the fact that although the experience of working in such places could be exciting and enjoyable, it was also poorly paid and involved long and unsociable hours. Moreover, workers were de-skilled and often regarded by management as disposable (Leidner 1993).

Although bar and floor staff were selected, in part, by dint of their confidence, attractiveness and effervescence, there was an assumption that they lacked the necessary social skills to cope with aggressive customers. Formal qualifications and training were regarded as a poor substitute for social skills and working knowledge acquired through extended engagement with the public. Many had received basic classroom-based training, but this did not cover all eventualities or fully equip them for the task. They therefore remained vulnerable to predation. For this reason, informants spoke of 'set procedures' being in place. Bar, floor and promotional staff were often encouraged *not* to deal with clients' complaints or other forms of 'trouble', but rather to refer such matters to their supervisor, or a member of the management team, lest they react in a manner which might exacerbate the situation.

Personal authority and rule-setting

My gaff, my rules (Al Murray, 'the pub landlord').

For licensees and managers, the ability to exert control over customer behaviour was regarded as an issue of minimal professional competence. In city centre venues, the 'good manager' was seen as someone with the necessary personal attributes and skills to manage conflict within an environment where there was a great intermingling of people with, often very different, and conflicting, expectations and lifestyles. The greatest risks of violence were associated with premises in which staff had adopted an indulgent approach, allowing patrons to expect that aggressive behaviour would be tolerated (Graham et al. 2000, Graham and Wells 2003, Levinson 1983). It was felt that codes of decorum should always be dictated by management and never by customers. This could only be achieved by establishing consistent standards and creating 'a social atmosphere with clear limits' (Graham and Homel 1997: 177). Personal authority and confidence were regarded as essential to the managerial task. As Jim succinctly noted, 'If you're running a pub, you've got to be able to stand up to people' (manager, high street pub).

A number of informants felt that managers should run the doors during peak admission periods, although it was acknowledged that the use of door staff afforded managers more freedom to talk to customers and monitor activities throughout the venue. The ceding of security issues to door staff was associated with an inability to relate to one's customers. As Patrick, a nightclub manager, told me: 'I see door staff as a last resort, a preventative measure, not as something I just use whenever I snap my fingers, 'cos that's wrong, it sends out the wrong impression.' For some, over-reliance on the door team was seen as a mark of weakness and incompetence, as— particularly, if they were supplied by an external agency—it denoted that the manager had lost control of his or her business. Attempts to shield the youngest, least experienced and most vulnerable members of staff from exposure to danger were tempered by an expectation that everyone should contribute to the defence of a colleague.

Informants spoke of a 'sixth sense', an intuition gained through experience in dealing with people, which allowed staff to spot problematic situations in their earliest stages and pre-empt their escalation. These personal skills were regarded as very difficult, if not impossible, to acquire by formal teaching methods, divorced from direct encounter within the enacted environment. Skills were 'learnt on the job' (Baird 2000a) with the guidance of more experienced mentors. Accordingly, inexperienced managers were thought to threaten venue security. They were regarded as having a comparatively shallow understanding of how the business operated and its typical clientele; more specifically, they were not attuned to local sensibilities and rivalries, and the identities and reputations of local troublemakers. Operating premises in the *absence* of an authority figure was regarded as a potentially risky practice that should be avoided at all cost.

Keeping things sweet

Manners are the lubricant of social relations, the sweetener of personal intercourse, and the softener of conflict (Grayling 2004: 9).

Clearly, non-aggressive responses may help to reduce aggression among persons who have been drinking (Graham 1985, Jeavons and Taylor 1985, Taylor and Gammon 1976). Yet, in comparison to the regulars' venue, it can be particularly difficult for high street operators to act in an *informal* capacity, and their much greater reliance on formal social control techniques (such as rows of menacing door staff) may militate against the creation of a relaxed and friendly atmosphere. As noted, this is a reflection, at least in part, of the diverse and fluid nature of their customer base and the sheer numbers of people who pass through their doors. However, even though opportunities for conviviality with patrons are limited, social skills remain to the fore. Employers select people of a certain 'type' whose personalities render them suited to the task: 'no one should be in "management" if they have a problem with people, especially silly, drunken, or even violent people. Communication skills and confidence are what you're looking for ... ' (Baird 2000b: 80).

When confrontations occur within licensed premises they are likely to be played out in front of an audience. This is important, as customers, particularly young men, often wish to avoid embarrassment or humiliation in front of their peers (Fagan 1993, Gibbs 1986, Graham and Wells 2003, Tomsen 1997). In this context, 'one or usually both protagonists' may attempt to 'establish or save face at the expense of the other' in a sequence of escalating 'moves and counter-moves, each of which increases the probability of violence by reducing the options for a peaceful resolution of the conflict' (Leather and Lawrence 1995: 395, Berkowitz 1978, Felson et al. 1986, Toch 1992). The importance of face-saving goes some way towards explaining why conflict and violence will often occur during the negotiation of control situations. In all such contestations, peaceful resolutions are more likely to be achieved if the controller can draw upon personal resources in the form of experientially rehearsed techniques. For example, as Matt told me:

Never bar anyone when they are drunk: *never*. That's the wrong thing to do, because they don't have anything to lose; they are already barred so they are more likely to react. When people have had a drink they don't want to reason with you, so you refuse them service and you say, 'It's best to come back and we'll talk about it when you are sober'. If you're careful in what you say, they'll just go away with a bit of a whinge (assistant manager, high street pub).

One favoured approach was to remove the 'audience effect' by physically separating the protagonists from each other and from interested bystanders. Staff also employed verbal techniques in an attempt to calm the customer down (Hobbs et al. 2003: 138–142). Although communicating with customers through the fog of their intoxication was never easy, informants suggested that many situations could be defused by allowing customers to unburden themselves to a sympathetic listener. Such approaches to the diffusion of conflict are an extension of the skills learnt through dealing with the more routine scenario of customer service complaints.

Typical sources of customer complaint arise in relation to queries regarding change and the loss of cloakroom tickets. In both scenarios it can be difficult for staff to resolve such issues, whilst at the same time continuing to serve the needs of large numbers of patrons. Complainants may often be asked to wait for considerable periods of time, perhaps until the end of the night when most customers have left, or to return the following day. Such negotiations require particularly sensitive handling in order to prevent theft or loss, whilst, at the same time, seeking to ensure that customers are not conveyed the impression that they are being suspected of dishonesty or condemned as troublemakers. Again, the personal skills of staff, in particular their ability to combine diplomacy and good humour with a calm, confident and assertive manner, were regarded as important contributions to the maintenance of order. However, in busy high street venues, the ratio of staff to customers and general social atmosphere militated against effective use of such skills and differences between regulars' and circuit venues again became apparent in how such disputes were resolved:

We are usually right, but you'd never say to a customer, 'No. You are definitely wrong!' I take the till off, cash it up there and then, and if it's there, it's there, and if it's not, well I can't take it any further. So I say, 'You've had a few beers haven't yer? and I'm sober. I'm not tryin' to rip you off, but I think you've made a mistake haven't yer?' and most of the time people will accept that because you did your best ... Where you have regulars you get to know the people who are tryin' it on (Mike, manager, regulars' venue).

Conversely, the manager of a high street bar described how he:

... resolved it as per company policy. They said they had been short-changed and I said that I would endeavour to check the till at the most convenient and appropriate moment. But we were very busy at the time. You can't be just taking tills off during the course of the night because the place is very very busy and everyone else will get more irritated because you have one less till and they are waiting longer to get served. It wasn't safe to take it off to deal with this one person. I took the person's name, address and telephone number and said that I would, y'know, do my best to resolve it for them as soon as possible; but they weren't interested. They created a situation, got other people involved and that, y'know; it was very disruptive. I didn't have the time to be able to deal with that and deal with the situation with other customers. The thing was getting out of hand, so I got one of the other members of the team to get the doormen while I kept the individual concerned engaged (Paul).

The most socially skilled of managers were proactive in their attempts to soothe interaction with potentially troublesome customers. Cavan (1966: 130–131) notes how bar tenders would present regulars celebrating a special occasion with a gift drink, a practice sometimes employed as a 'means of controlling a variety of situations'. John, the licensee of a city centre regulars' pub, told me how he used this approach to establish bonds of familiarity and reciprocity with strangers. His pub was sometimes visited by 'stag parties'. These were typically large groups of young men from out of town who were very drunk. John (who did not employ bouncers) described how, whenever such groups entered his premises, he would attempt immediately to create a relationship of indebtedness to himself as host, whilst at the same time demonstrating personal authority, ownership and vigilance:

The way I do it is, it's quite simple. I get into them at the early stages, just say: 'Who's the unlucky boy then, getting married? What y'a drinking?' Get them a beer or whatever they want, something just to try an' get friendly with 'em and they're less likely to kick off because you're providing the groom with a free drink, see? Then, if you have to say 'calm it down a bit lads, you're upsetting other customers!', they take it on board.

Other tactics involved a reverse logic, wherein the escalation of aggression arising from a loss of face was actively facilitated, only to be used as justification for the customer's initial identification as a troublemaker:

If they look like they're going to cause trouble, then the staff will say, 'Sorry you can't be served'. But we give them options; maybe they would like a soft drink (laughs) or come back tomorrow night. If they're reasonable, they'll just leave. But if they want to take it a little bit further you go down and say, 'Sorry sir, you can't get served' and by then they have dropped themselves in it by being too aggressive and we just say, 'Well, that's the reason we're not going to serve you' (Tony, assistant manager, high street pub).

When negotiation fails

As Hobbs et al. (2003: 147) note with regard to door staff: 'Once the limits of negotiation have been reached', or violence has already commenced prior to staff intervention, 'then physical force of some kind will be required'. Once the decision has been made to physically remove customers from the premises it is important for the task to be conducted as swiftly and efficiently as possible, with the minimal involvement of bystanders or souring of the social atmosphere. Short of the immediate application of brute force, this can be achieved more easily by monitoring the person's behaviour in order to choose an optimal time for intervention:

If someone's working their ticket, you wait till they are more than half way through their pint before you say ow't and then tell 'em to see off their drink, 'cos you know there's just a mouthful left. If you tell them when they've first got a full pint then they're going to drag it out and they'll just start arguing with you because they've only had a mouthful. Of course, you could take the pint off them and give 'em their money back, but it's easier just to wait till there's a little bit left (Dean, manager, high street pub).

Some sections of the leisure industry have long preferred managers with a 'physical presence' for the running of potentially violent premises (MCM 1990: 17). Accordingly, a high proportion of the (male) managers interviewed for this study possessed an imposing physicality. Many considered themselves sufficiently intimidating to conduct ejections simply by the laying on of hands: 'Just put an arm around their shoulder, lead them to the door' (Tony, high street pub). Some made a point of wearing suits at work to enhance appearances of potency and authority.

If a customer was to be ejected, it was essential to anticipate the course of impending violence and take steps to minimize its effects. If the person was seated, glassware would be swiftly removed from the area and tables and chairs moved aside. In order to make their removal easier, the 'offender' may be encouraged to stand. High-risk customers were approached with caution:

You approach somebody to their stronger side, 'cos if you approach them to their weaker side, then they have a tendency to hit you with their stronger side, but they feel uncomfortable when you stand against the stronger side. If they drink with the left hand, you go beside them by the left-hand side before you throw them out. They can't swing for ya because they've got their hand down like that (demonstrates bent arm) and if they do try to swing a punch with the wrong hand it isn't going to do as much damage is it? (Colin, manager, high street pub).

When negotiation ends, meaning and motive become of little import, as Colin notes: 'It doesn't really matter who is wrong and who is right, you just get 'em out.' Yet, even customers who have had to be physically removed will usually be given further options. Blanket exclusions can create enemies and simmering resentments, not only among the ranks of the excluded, but also among their friends and associates. Licensees and managers would usually attempt to remain fair and reasonable, perhaps telling the ejected to come back another night once they had sobered up, when an apology and a promise of future good conduct may be sufficient to assure re-admission.

Closing time

The last hour of trading has long been a particularly sensitive time in which a disproportionate amount of violence in licensed premises occurs. Although the government anticipate that the extensions of hours permitted by the Act will encourage more graduated customer dispersals, it seems likely that some disparity between the expectations of operators and consumers in relation to closing time will remain and that end of the evening sessions will still require careful management and pre-planning.

Preparation for closing time may involve allowing the atmosphere in the premises to gradually 'wind down' by decreasing the tempo and volume of the music and the intensity of lighting effects. Further admissions to the premises may be prohibited. Ringing bells, flashing room lights, and DJ announcements may be used to call 'last orders' and customers may be requested to terminate any pool playing or other games. Bars are fully staffed in order to cope with any influx of customers wishing to buy drinks. At the terminal hour, bars are closed, bar lights switched off and towels may be draped over pumps and fonts. Music is turned off[10] and the lighting in customer areas intensified. Bar staff will begin to clean up and collect glasses. Whilst clearing up, staff will remind customers that the premises are about to close, a message emphasized by obvious hints, such as chairs being put on tables and the removal of ashtrays. Again, the social skills of staff come to the fore:

It's just a case of shouting 'time', give 'em maybe fifteen to twenty minutes, then you start sayin', 'drink up please, start makin' your way out'. There's people sometimes nurse a little bit of drink in the bottom and you have to coax them, make a bit of a joke of it; 'You got no home to go to?' sort of thing (Ken, bar tender, high street pub).

Any stragglers are encouraged to leave in a more insistent manner. Arguments can be de-personalized by reminding customers that the premises are legally obliged to close at the time specified by their licence. Signs may be displayed, asking people to leave quietly, a message that may be underlined by door staff.

Pricing oneself out of trouble

A dominant shift toward the gentrification of mainstream nightlife has occurred that may be associated with three salient trends: firstly, a 'feminization' of the design and marketing of many venues (Chatterton and Hollands 2003); secondly, the development of new 'aspirational' drinks brands (see Chapter 3);

---

[10] There is a case to be made for not turning the music off immediately, but continuing to wind the night down by playing mellow low-tempo music which may have a calming effect and further stagger departure.

and, thirdly, the increasing provision of food during early-evening trading periods. Food is known to slow the absorption of alcohol into the body, thereby reducing blood alcohol levels (Wedel et al. 1991) and the availability of food (especially substantial meals) has been associated with a reduced risk of aggression (Graham et al. 1980, Homel and Clark 1994).

Gentrification, with its assumed efficacy as a control mechanism, has a long history in the licensed trade. Mass Observation describe in fascinating detail how the pubs of 1930s Bolton were spatially divided into what was, quite literally, a 'spit and sawdust' environment within the workingmen's 'vault', and the somewhat more refined atmosphere of the 'lounge' or parlour (Everitt and Bowler 1996). The lounge had better furnishings and décor, more comfortable seating and fewer (!) spittoons, the aim being to be more 'female-friendly' and to accommodate those in their 'Sunday best'. In an attempt to deter 'undesirables', publicans charged an extra penny on the price of beer to those drinking in the lounge (Mass Observation 1943, 99–100); the idea, in part, being to physically segregate the 'rough' from the 'respectable' clientele, and mixed-sex groups from single-sex (male) drinkers.[11] This attempt to create a two-tier social institution was, however, largely unsuccessful, as patrons would judge a pub in accordance with its general reputation: 'you never got both rooms filled—*you either had a vault crowd or a parlour crowd*' (ibid.: 103). Thus:

At one end of the social scale we find chaps spitting all over the place, often where there is nothing for them to spit into, while in better class pubs and rooms, there are receptacles for spit into which no one does spit (ibid.: 204).

These assumptions regarding the connections between drinks pricing policy, standards of décor, and the behaviour of patrons, remain strong. As Bob Senior, the former managing director of quoted high street operator *Ultimate Leisure* states:

We don't discount on Friday and Saturday nights because we are already full and the right investment gives us the right clientele. It's recognizing that value for money isn't always a pound a pint. It's £2.90 a pint, but

---

[11] Mass Observation (143–145) describe how female drinking in the vault was subject to strict social censure.

having the right clientele in the premises and the wrong kind excluded. Where required and where appropriate we take on other discounters but, as a rule, we go for the value-added end of the market (*Night* 2001a: 18*)*.

As noted in Chapter 3, when supply outstrips demand, standards may be compromised. One high street licensee explained how pricing policy required the drawing of a fine line between optimum competitiveness and the risks associated with going too far 'down-market':

Y'know, if you do your doubles for £2, trebles for £3, your house brand like *Fosters* lager down to £2 a pint, stick a draught beer on for one-and-a-half quid, just keep changin' 'em as well, 'cos people get bored with it. Keep shoppin' around, get cheap alco-pops and stick them on at a competitive price, but don't give it away; don't do that 'cos you'll be full of nuggets and you'll get tarred with that brush of being a rough place (Paul).

Clearly, the practice of serving alcohol at discounted prices can encourage excessive consumption if not employed with caution (BBPA 2002, Nicholson Committee 2003, St. John Brooks 1998). Higher alcohol sales are associated with an increased risk that an establishment's customers will commit an alcohol-related offence (Graves et al. 1981, Markowitz 2000, Stockwell 2001) and experience a range of health and accident-related problems (Casswell et al. 1993, Stockwell et al. 1993). In judging the security implications of drinks promotions, some operators take the long-term view. As Jim, a nightclub manager, explained:

Tequila wanted us to put on a promotions night selling double *Tequila* for a pound. They would do all the promoting, all the radio advertising, have girls walking 'round with shots, that sort of stuff, but we said no. That's a strong bloody drink!—they come in and have two or three double *Tequilas* and they are on their back. Then you need the ambulance and the police get involved.

Goffman's spirit

This chapter has highlighted a key conceptual deficiency of previous studies; namely, the tendency to focus upon individual elements of social control such as venue design, managerial style, and the role of door staff. It points to a general failure to acknowledge the fundamentally purposive, complex, and interconnecting orchestration of such factors. The chapter describes the degree of care that operators may take in designing and operating their premises in order to create the illusion of a safe and controlled environment; an environment one step removed from everyday life in which customers can relax and enjoy themselves among like-minded people. Moreover, it explains why effective controls can only be applied as a team effort.

Erving Goffman (1959: 83–6) notes how impression management in various social settings may be co-produced, individuals being 'bound together formally or informally into an action group in order to further like or collective ends' (p.90). Each team member cooperates in presenting their audience with a particular definition, stance, or version of events, and persons may be allocated various roles within the team: 'whether the members of a team stage similar individual performances or stage dissimilar performances which fit together into a whole, an emergent team impression arises' (ibid.: 85). As Alan, the manager of a high street bar, explained:

It comes down to putting together a team of individual experts . . . Each person understands why they have to do their job in a certain way, the bar staff doing their job, the DJ doing his (*sic*) job, and the cleaners and maintenance people doing their job during the day. We are very proactive, the environment is very tightly controlled and everyone is focused on trying to keep the customer happy; keeping the customer calm.

In some instances, the efforts of staff are supported by the premises' indigenous clientele. Informal social control over behaviour is relatively strong within these regulars' venues, in comparison with those premises which draw their custom from the largely anonymous crowds that populate the high street leisure circuit. Regulars' venues require little overt and formal control by staff. Even in busy city centre locations, they may operate successfully without the need for bouncers.

In high street venues, the maximal balancing of intoxication and control is regarded as a corporate goal which enhances profitability. The manipulation of customer mood and behaviour must comprise an artful mix of various elements. Security measures are applied with fortitude and the creation of a 'safe' and 'controlled' social environment is inevitably a hard-won accomplishment, achieved only through the sustained efforts of strategic and co-operative interactional performance. Such accomplishments require emotional management, careful orchestration, loyalty, and attention to detail. The requisite skills and sensibilities are learned through individual and shared experience, both serving to foster the acquisition of appropriate occupational mores. In order to prove effective, these working practices and expectations must be instilled as second nature; a habitual code implemented by all members of staff who deal directly with the public. Control is then constituted as a 'team effort' involving the performance of a variety of ostensibly unrelated work tasks. Over time, such controls become central to the construction and maintenance of social order within the venue. Yet, the application of control is subtle and opaque, allowing operators to largely eschew the more overt, oppressive, and reactive interventions of bouncers and the public police. Most importantly, the effective application of control helps create a social space in which the majority of customers can relax; an environment which *appears* to be carefree and created with only pleasure in mind.

Rejoinder

The impressions of order recounted above draw upon what are, essentially, informants' 'moral tales' of atrocity and success (Coffey and Atkinson 1996: 63–68). Most high street venues are well-run; however, the possibilities of control are inevitably shaped by market forces and the broader social and cultural environment. All too often, one finds venues attempting to get through the night in a chaotic fashion which involves the taking of risks, whilst minimizing costs and maximizing profits. The following case study offers a detailed description of a night (and lunch-time) spent in and around *Harvey's,* a theme bar in a medium-sized (80,000 population) town in the English Midlands. The events described were observed during the course of one unremarkable weekend (Saturday night and Sunday afternoon). The name of the bar, which is operated by a listed high street chain, has been changed in order to preserve the anonymity of the operator. The case study introduces the notion of a relationship between licensed premises and their surroundings. The import of this relationship will become apparent in the following chapter, in which I explore the theme of social control in night-time public space.

One night in heaven: the high street experience

Harvey's occupies two floors of a glass-fronted building on the High Street. Many of the other national chains are located in close proximity, including *Edwards* (directly next door), *Yates's; Po Na Na; O'Neill's; Bar Med; J.D. Wetherspoon; Chicago Rock Café; Varsity;* and *Toad*. Most of these premises feature 'music and dancing' and are licensed beyond the traditional 11pm watershed. In addition to the brands, the area also has a number of other un-branded nightspots. Although marketed as a 'café bar', *Harvey's* effectively operates as a pub during the day and a nightclub in the evening; the unit trades until 2am, with no admission fee, or apparent dress code.

On the ground floor of *Harvey's*, next to the entrance, there is a small designated 'eating area' consisting of three benches and seating for ten people. There is no cutlery or table dressing, but a sign asks customers to refrain from smoking until 9pm. Sofas and low tables are provided close to this dining area. Most of the furniture in the venue is more primitive, consisting of wooden benches, a line of which stretches along the wall opposite the long ground-floor bar. Each bar has twenty-five pumps for draught beer and lager. During the evening, the floor space in front of the bar is cleared of furniture. At the far end of the ground floor there is a small dance floor, stage, and DJ console. A second bar is located on the first floor, along with more bench tables and a larger dance floor. The DJ works from behind a console on this floor and both dance floor areas are illuminated by disco lights. The walls are painted in neutral, earthy colours, and there are various artefacts and painted motifs pertaining to the theme of the venue around the walls. The slogans 'The liver is evil', 'The liver must die', and 'Punish the liver' are displayed on the ground-floor ceiling beams and are particularly noticeable as one enters the premises. There are a number of large plasma screens around the venue which show footage of football and rugby matches. The kitchens are not visible. Food is advertised as available until one hour before closing. Menus are obtained from the bar during the evening and from the tables at lunch-time. Customers order food at the bar.

Upon my arrival at 7.30pm, the venue is quiet and relaxed with twenty-two customers present, all but one of whom are male. The patrons all appear to be between 25 and 40 years of age. The main activity is drinking and watching sport on the plasma screens. The first floor area is roped off at this time, as is again the case when I return at lunch-time the following day. At 7.40pm I order the most expensive meal, priced at £6.70. Although the venue is not yet busy and my companion and I are the only diners, service is remarkably slow. Our food arrives forty-five minutes after our order, during which time a member of staff comes to check whether we have ordered jacket potatoes or chips with our meal, as she says she cannot remember. When the food arrives it is particularly unappealing. I do not see anyone else eating at *Harvey's* that evening, or the following lunch-time; nor do I see any sign of meals being consumed before my arrival. At 7.55pm, the volume of the music increases considerably and the lighting is turned down low. Additional bar staff and the door staff arrive at 8pm and at about 8.15pm the night-time customers begin to arrive. At 8.30pm, I leave the venue for a few minutes. As I walk a little way up the street, I notice a *Pizza Express* restaurant which is full of diners.

After 9pm, the premises begin to fill. The gender distribution changes as more women arrive. Throughout the busiest periods, about 30 per cent of customers are female. Many customers arrive in large single-sex groups, some of whom are as many as twenty-strong. Some of these groups appear to be stag and hen parties. In one such party, the 'bride' arrives in a nurse's uniform festooned with inflated condoms. Customers and staff have a relaxed attitude towards dress and many wear jeans, trainers, shorts, and sports tops. The most popular attire for men is brightly-coloured shirts with logos such as *Polo* and *Ben Sherman* worn to hang loosely over the tops of jeans or trousers. Women appear, in general, to have made more of an effort to 'dress up' for the evening than have the men. In practice, this means having more flesh on display than clothing. Some men, particularly those with more developed physiques, adopt a similar approach to gendered display, sporting tans, tight-fitting sleeveless t-shirts and a swaggering gait. Both sexes wear clothes in such a way as to reveal bodily adornments such as tattoos and pierced navels. The sexually charged aesthetic is accentuated by images on the plasma screens, which show music videos and customers with bouncing breasts and gyrating torsos downing shots of spirits and bottles of alco-pop. This footage of the '*Harvey's* experience' is interspersed with details of drinks promotions, flashes of the brand logo, and activities within the unit itself. The most popular drinks appear to be pints of strong draught lager, bottled beers and alco-pops. Customers are now predominately aged between 18 and 30, with a small minority appearing older or younger than this. The DJ dedicates a song to a girl celebrating her eighteenth birthday.

At 9.50pm, I notice that a rope barrier has been placed in the street to control entry to the premises. I observe four bouncers, all of whom are male and dressed in a uniform of black trousers and white shirts. The two men positioned at the door provide an imposing physical presence. The other (physically smaller) supervisors seek vantage points: one on the stairs overlooking the ground floor area, and one at the top of the stairs, watching over the first floor. The manager, a man of slight build, who appears to be in his early 20s, also performs a security role. He divides his time between the door, where he scrutinizes customers as they arrive, and patrols of the venue. At 10.15pm I notice that a group of clearly underage girls are refused entry.

The atmosphere is now hectic, with large amounts of alcohol being consumed. Notices behind the bar advertise 'shooters' (mixtures of spirits and fruit juice) called 'Illusion' and 'Sex on the Beach' for £1-a-shot, and bottles of lager at 'two for the price of one'. The music can best be described as mainstream pop and party music from the 1960s through to the present day. There are no flyers or posters advertising forthcoming entertainment, all promotional material relating to cut-price alcohol and special nights promoting a particular brand of drink. The only sources of entertainment are the DJ-generated music and lighting and the images on the plasma screens. Noting the statement on a chalk board that food is available until 1am, I attempt to order some chips. It is now 10.20pm. A barman tells me that I can have the food if I am able to inform him where I will be sitting. This is not possible. All the tables on both floors are occupied by groups of drinkers and eating at the extremely crowded bar is not a viable option. Faced with the prospect of eating chips whilst standing up in a hot and crowded environment, I decide not to place the order.

People are now dancing on both dance floors; although this is a primarily female activity. Women dance with luridly coloured bottles in their hands from which they take the occasional swig. It is noticeable that the female customers who are dancing are 'on display', both to the men who have positioned themselves around the dance floor areas, and to other people in the venue who are watching the plasma screens. At 10.25pm, two girls get up on the tables to dance. This is encouraged by the DJ, who invites everyone to 'dance up on the tables, wherever you want, we don't care!'

At 10.40pm I decide to leave *Harvey's* for a period in order to observe activities in the surrounding area. At this time, customers are entering and leaving the venue in all directions. The constant flow of people around the town centre and the number of people I see in more than one venue is suggestive of a drinking circuit. Movement of customers between *Harvey's* and some of the other branded establishments is particularly evident. When I return to *Harvey's* at 11.30pm I have to queue for ten minutes in order to obtain re-admission. As I queue, I see one male customer roughly ejected by door staff. He continues to curse and remonstrate with police officers who are positioned outside the venue. After a brief struggle with the police, the man is arrested and taken away in a police van.

By midnight, customers are dancing on all available table space on both the ground and first floors. Many of the customers dancing on the tables and chairs continue to hold glasses and bottles in their hands. Glasses are dropped, tipping their contents onto the table, before rolling off and smashing on the floor. Drinks spill onto people who are sitting and standing below, to the obvious annoyance of some. However, most customers seem oblivious to danger, defilement, and dry cleaning bills. Two of the girls who are standing on the tables clutch each other and engage in a session of French kissing and heavy petting.

At 12.15am, the venue appears full to capacity. Despite having five serving staff, the first floor bar is short-staffed. This bar area is now very crowded and it takes each customer around ten minutes to get served. Although the staff make periodic journeys through the crowd in order to collect empties and clear broken glass from the floor, every available surface is now covered in partially or entirely consumed drinks. Two large plastic 'wheelie bins' containing empty bottles are located on the ground floor in prominent public areas near to the staircase and the dance floor. The floor staff drop empties into these open receptacles as they pass; both are overflowing by the end of the evening. The male toilets are newly decorated and well-maintained, but in the course of the evening become flooded and strewn with refuse.

Despite the chaotic and sometimes fraught atmosphere, I encounter no violence or serious conflict within the premises. At 12.27am I notice two male police officers watching the venue from inside their vehicle. They are parked in a side street which has a clear view into the premises. From 1.30am, a police van is positioned directly outside *Harvey's*, this vehicle having earlier been parked outside other venues. I note that a public CCTV camera located on the side of a building further up the street is directed toward the *Harvey's* entrance. When its bars close at 2am, *Harvey's* retains around 90 per cent of the peak occupancy levels observed at midnight. Customers leave *en masse* at around 2.15am, when they are herded out by door staff. I stand on the street and watch as the venue is cleared and its doors locked. It takes some time for the crowd to disperse and gaggles of customers remain outside *Harvey's* for over half an hour.

During the 2–3am period, the pedestrianized High Street remains crowded with groups of excitable people talking loudly and shouting. The street is littered with food and take-away boxes and I notice pools of vomit and a strong smell of urine around some of the shop doorways. Gradually, the crowds move on to a nearby street where there is a taxi office, a taxi rank, and a late-night take away. There is no indication that buses or trains are available. By 2.25am, large numbers of people have congregated in this adjacent street. They spill from the narrow pavements into the path of passing vehicles. Long queues for taxis develop, which remain until around 3.30am.

I join a queue to buy food at the *Charcoal Grill Kebab* and recognize many people I have seen earlier in the night. At 2.40am, I witness fighting among a group of young men (aged approximately 16–19 years) outside the take away. The 'action' occurs within a few feet of me as I eat my 'full donner with everything on'. I see one youth punch another full in the face, prompting others to join in. The victim, who now has blood streaming from his nose and onto his white shirt, appeals to onlookers: 'I don't want any trouble . . . I'm just trying to eat my cheesy chips!' Within seconds, about ten people are involved and the combatants begin chasing each other down the street. One young man is pulled to the ground and kicked. On the pavement outside the take away it is now difficult to discern the difference between spillages of blood and tomato ketchup. The youths involved are people I have seen drinking in *Harvey's*, and also in other venues. The incident, which lasts for about fifteen minutes, creates a feeling of tension in the area and a number of onlookers became visibly distressed and agitated. Some people try to intervene to stop the fighting and one bystander calls the police on her mobile phone. A young girl with long dark hair and a red dress flails her arms and grabs at the shirt of one of the men, 'Leave 'im. Leave 'im alone, you fat fucker!' At 3.10am, two police officers arrive by car and another two on foot. The incident has passed.

5

Contesting Public Space

At night, the city's spaces are transformed in ways which make them anew (Amin and Thrift 2002: 120).

The privatization of night-time public space

Like other urban environments, the night-time high street is characterized by a proliferation of ostensibly 'public' spaces that are 'being redefined as communal spaces with similar features to those that exist on private property' (Shearing and Wood 2003: 411). The negative consequences of the rise of privatized public space have been emphasized in relation to social exclusion, ownership, security, design, homogenization, and the curtailment of political and cultural expression (Christopherson 1994, Davis 1990, Hannigan 1998, Reeve 1995, 1998, von Hirsch and Shearing 2000).[1] Although drawn from a variety of disciplines, these critiques of privatized public space share a common thread in highlighting the social and normative implications of assigning large tracts of urban space to consumers, rather than the citizenry as a whole.

These issues appear especially controversial and ambiguous in relation to those formerly wholly public areas that have been transformed into 'communal spaces . . . that cut across the public–private distinction' (Shearing and Wood, 2003: 419).[2] Perhaps the

[1] Criminological analyses have generally focused more narrowly upon exclusion, expulsion, and social control within 'mass private property' such as shopping malls and recreational theme parks (Shearing and Stenning 1987, Wakefield 2000).

[2] One of the best British examples of this can be found in Liverpool city centre. With the assistance of Liverpool City Council, development company *Grosvenor Estates* has secured a 250-year lease for an area covering thirty-five streets between the Paradise shopping district and the Pierhead on the Mersey. *Grosvenor* has

most important implications of these transformations in ownership and control relate to the social mix of citizens encouraged to populate these hybrid spaces. People's experience of public space is diverse and attains meaning only in the context of personal identity as shaped by dimensions of gender, age, race, sexuality, and class (Day 1999, Green et al. 2000, Moran et al. 2003, Mort 2000, Pain 2001, Valverde and Cirak 2003, Walkowitz 1992, Watt and Stenson 1998). Approached in this way, the critique of (day-time) privatized communal space may be mirrored in relation to the night-time high street only in so far as it can incorporate one fundamental twist.

'Painting the town red' (embracing the night)

Research suggests that in high streets, shopping malls, and similar sites of day-time consumption, 'perceived risk is strongly associated with what has been termed "avoidance behaviour" ' (Beck and Willis 1995: 220, Oc and Trench 1993). Consumers who feel unsafe will often elect to take their custom elsewhere. As the success of privately owned, out-of-town shopping and leisure facilities implies, many day-time consumers are attracted by regimes of safety, accessibility, and predictability enforced by a discreet security presence (Reeve 1995). Beck and Willis go so far as to argue that in shopping environments, consumer perceptions of security are a 'precondition for commercial success' (1995: 227). Such understandings have been influential and go some way to explain the rise of Town Centre Management (TCM) and Business Improvement District (BIDs) schemes (Hobbs et al. 2003: 256–257, Holden and Stafford 1997, Jones et al. 2003) through which the perceived security benefits of 'mass private property' are applied to the British high street. As discussed below, similar security concerns and avoidance behaviours have been noted in relation to the NTE. Yet, among *core consumers* of nightlife, attitudes may be divergent.

allocated £100 million to compulsory purchase of all of the buildings in the zone in order to build 350 flats and houses and a new shopping centre. Controversially, public rights of way and rights to assembly in the area are to be transformed by private ownership, with such activities requiring the express permission of *Grosvenor*. Private security forces or 'quartermasters' patrol the streets and have the power to remove people from the area whom they deem undesirable. There are also plans to provide additional public police patrols at the developer's expense.

Young Britons are socialized into a culture that exhibits a considerable degree of ambivalence toward alcohol. On the one hand, drinking to intoxication is widespread and often regarded as a socially acceptable, legitimate, and pleasurable activity. On the other, young people may often be mindful of the risks associated with heavy drinking and seek to regulate their behaviour in order to avoid various harmful consequences. Certainly, our cultural predilection for drinking to excess and engaging in related violence is nothing new. Yet, as Chapter 3 attests, it is necessary to recognize that significant changes have occurred in relation to both the types of location in which young people drink and the types of product they consume. The new night-time high street is much more than a physical entity, it is a special kind of 'place' or 'behaviour setting' (Barker 1968); a time–space environment (Giddens 1984) in which a standing pattern of behaviour occurs that is largely unique to that setting. In the evenings and at night, particularly at weekends after 10pm, there is a tendency for people predominately aged from 17 to 25 years to visit urban centres. Nightlife in our towns and cities is focused primarily around high street areas which function as destinations for those seeking 'time out', not only from their daily routines, but also from their ordinary states of consciousness.

Although, as discussed in Chapter 2, the search for nocturnal escape is an enduring feature of our cultural history, more research is needed which heeds the voices of contemporary nightlife consumers. Much of the work on young people's drinking practices has focused on adolescents (Brain et al. 2000, Coleman and Cater 2005, Honess et al. 2000, Plant and Plant 1992) and whilst many of these studies' findings may be indicative of broader cultural trends and attitudes, similarly systematic attention has yet to be paid to young adults. For example, comparatively little is known of 18–30-year-olds' motivations for drinking, or the meanings they attach to nightlife participation. Studies conducted by the Home Office, perhaps unsurprisingly, reflect a governmental focus on what are seen as the 'problematic' social norms and influences of so-called 'binge drinkers' and recreational drug-users (Deehan and Saville 2003, Engineer et al. 2003, Richardson and Budd 2003). What is absent from these policy-oriented studies is a more analytically sophisticated and open-ended exploration of young adults' identity construction in relation to the branding and consumption of alcohol and other drugs (Brain 2000, Griffin et al. 2005, Harnett et al. 2000, Measham 2004, Reith 2005). As Newburn and Shiner (2001: 4) note, 'while there is considerable descriptive data on young people's drinking, much less is known about why British young people drink, the place and meaning of alcohol in young people's lives and the social contexts for drinking'. This said, a handful of qualitative studies (Chatterton and Hollands 2003, Malbon 1999, Winlow and Hall 2006) have provided fascinating insight into the type of 'mainstream' British nightlife cultures so long neglected by those social scientists who prefer to wallow in the romance of a good old-fashioned sub-culture. This literature, together with that which points to the 'normalization' and widespread emotional attractions of psychoactive consumption (Parker et al. 1998, 2002, Measham 2004), tells us much about the manner in which some nightlife participants may now approach and use the night-time city. It would seem that, for many, the night represents a temporal 'frontier' (Melbin 1978) beyond which the security conscious values and behaviours of the day give way to an almost converse set of concerns.

Consuming in safety/consuming in danger

As Wilkström notes, 'the downtown area . . . particularly at night, is the most socially unstable public environment in the city' (1995: 437–438). Nightlife areas are often crowded, chaotic, noisy, and dangerous places, populated by 'beautiful people' and characterized by a comparatively lawless atmosphere of low-level disorder: illegal parking, the sounding of horns and sirens, arguments, and speeding emergency vehicles. Some people would describe these scenes as stressful or frightening; others as exciting. It is this very edginess and instability that contributes to the function of the night-time city as a safety valve: a zone of opportunities for 'letting off steam'. NTEs are driven by the realization that not everyone wishes to consume in 'safety' (Ditton 2000) and towns and cities now compete to offer a weekly carnival atmosphere to young people. Yet—although after-dark adventures must not become routine, must not lose that element of spontaneity, uncertainty and risk—most consumers will wish to *regulate* their excess. They will 'dive into the action . . . but not *too* much' (Reith 2005: 234). They will seek to retain an element of control;

the ability to step back. Voluntary risk-taking in negotiating a potentially dangerous environment, whilst managing the psycho-active experiences of self and others, is part of the fun.

Expeditions are rarely conducted alone, as the night-time high street is not hospitable to the 'window shopper' or detached *flâneur*—it is a place of active engagement in collective rituals of mass consumption. For some, the environment becomes a stage for the enactment of fantasy and display, a place where one may 'be oneself'. There is, thus, a tension between the individualistic concerns of self-expression and the enjoyment of a 'high', and the various attractions of shared experience; of being part of 'the crowd'. For regular participants, nightlife may provide some sense of belonging and affiliation to a community of like-minded souls (Roebuck and Frese 1976, Winlow and Hall 2006). Under neon light, people may be drawn together through their shared determination to play as hard as they work, or perhaps, by the wish to escape the suffocating pressures, monotonies and expectations of everyday life (Cohen and Taylor 1992).

These apparent modifications in 'practical consciousness' (Giddens 1979) have far-reaching implications for social interaction. As described in Chapter 4, consumer adoption of the 'night-time attitude' (Gusfield 1987: 78) is intimately understood by leisure operators. Within licensed premises, operators skilfully exploit consumer expectations whilst simultaneously imposing their own 'house rules'. Accordingly, the marketing methods used to attract patrons sometimes belie full commitment to the order maintenance concerns of those policing and regulatory bodies who would seek to impose the restraints of the day-time economy upon the business of the night (Swinden 2000). Mutual understanding between producer and consumer ensures that within the night-time high street, profitability can not only be maintained, but even enhanced, under conditions of danger. This is made possible through a:

... containment of people and their identities within these spaces, the constitution of their choices around agendas of obedience and consumption ... For many, such spaces are not intimidating, but inviting, even seductive; they pull you in, and often do so, ironically, by appropriating, sanitizing, shrink-wrapping for ready resale the very urban culture—local flavour, street cool, excitement—they displace (Ferrell 2001: 226).

One of the key criminogenic departures between day-time and night-time urban consumption may be traced to a consideration of who does, and who does not, populate night-time public space. As Worpole (an influential proponent of the 24-hour city concept during the 1990s) acknowledges:

... at present the bid to extend the economy of the city centre into the small hours is principally coming from the licensing and restaurant trade. We have yet to see the 24-hour library or the 24-hour study centre, let alone the 24-hour railway or bus station. So the project ends up as being targeted at those with money, principally the young and other groups with large amounts of disposable income ... what is being created is a central core of high consumption (Worpole 2003: 1).

Comparative analyses of the uses and meanings of alcohol have revealed the extent to which drinking cultures are both socially constructed and historically contingent (Heath 1995, 2000, MacAndrew and Edgerton 1969). Yet, the comparisons with continental European licensing systems drawn by proponents of the '24-hour city' failed to take account of dramatic differences in drinking culture between the UK and many of its European counterparts (Adams 2005, Room 2004b). Some of the most salient differences have, of course, been 'graphically illustrated by media reports of alcohol-related disorder involving Britons on holiday, and at "stag and hen" events in Europe' (Light 2005a: 270).

One important implication of Britain's 'culture blind' approach to licensing de-regulation has been that, although once deserted streets have indeed been brought to life, the anticipated benefits of a safety in numbers have yet to be secured. As Worpole concedes, the 'enhanced safety through animation' approach (Chapter 3) can only work where city centre space is regarded as 'public space and democratic space', open to all (ibid.). The British experience has shown that, when planning a sustainable NTE, one must consider not only the size, but also the composition, of an area's street life. The following paragraphs provide further insight into the demography of the night-time high street by considering the social profile of offenders and victims.

Offenders

It is sometimes assumed that offences committed in a nightlife context relate almost entirely to the activities of the stereotypical heavy drinking and casually dressed young male. Although alcohol 'misusing' 'weekend warriors' (Marshall 1979) who actively seek out violence as a recreational activity (Burns 1980, Dyck 1980, Tomsen 1997, Graham and Wells 2003)[3] may well inflict a disproportionate amount of harm, they also tend to be few in number. In their summary of empirical evidence from Cardiff—drawn from an unusually comprehensive data-base of alcohol-related crime and disorder—Maguire and Nettleton (2003) found that most of the 'trouble' occurring in and around nightlife areas was spontaneous and unplanned. Although those arrested for violent or disorderly behaviour were mostly young and male, the majority had no previous convictions.[4]

Victims

The most important predictor of victimization is exposure to risk. Exposure is associated with socio-demographic, lifestyle and area factors and is therefore distributed very unevenly between different social groups (Budd 2003, Kershaw et al. 2000, Mattinson 2001). A number of studies have shown that, in comparison with other groups, those who go out at night, especially for entertainment, are more likely to become victims of violent crime (Budd 2003, Felson 1997, Gottfredson 1984, Lasley 1989, Miethe, Stafford and Long 1987). Intoxicated revellers, especially if they find themselves unable to find transport home late at night, are placed at greater risk of accidental injury, robbery, sexual assault, and various forms of street crime (Giesbrecht et al. 1989, Magennis et al. 1998, Shepherd and Brickley 1996, Wechsler et al. 1994). The crowded and chaotic nature of nightlife areas is attractive to a variety of offenders and those seeking to exploit informal economic opportunities, such as street robbers, bogus taxi drivers, unlicensed vendors, rickshaw touts, pickpockets, drug dealers, prostitutes, and pimps. In a nightlife environment, these activities may be pursued in conditions of relative anonymity.

[3] Graham and Wells, for example, found that 'male-to-male aggression in drinking settings reflects a form of social conformity or a rite of passage for at least some subgroups of middle class males'. For their sample, fights were 'considered normative and not necessarily undesirable' (2003: 561–562).

[4] Although some offenders had been arrested for violent or public order offences four or more times in the past, these recidivists constituted only fifteen per cent of the total number of arrestees (Maguire and Nettleton, ibid.: 36).

'Taxi mate?'

The closure of London Underground train services after 12.30am and a shortage of licensed black cabs can create transport difficulties for those enjoying the capital's nightlife. Many revellers end their night with a search for transport and, quite possibly, a journey home in the private car of a total stranger. The following case notes describe events witnessed in the course of two nights spent observing activities outside an 'exclusive' West End nightclub:

It is weekend and activity outside the *Geisha Club* is constant. From 10.30pm onwards, people gather near to the club's entrance. It is unclear whether these people are meeting friends, celebrity spotting, or attempting to negotiate their way onto the guest list. Most customers arrive on foot, others by taxi or private car. Peak activity around the door occurs between 11.00pm and 3.45am, but it is not until approximately 11.30pm that queues began to form. The peak inflow of customers occurs between midnight and 1.30am. After midnight, the street fills with mini cabs, arriving, waiting, and leaving. This activity makes what is already a narrow street, difficult to negotiate. Cars are double-parked and periodically pull up outside the club, their drivers chatting to door staff. At one point, a police van is caught in the ensuing gridlock. From 2am onwards, a few customers begin to leave the premises. After 3.15am, movement intensifies as large groups gather on the pavement.

As customers leave, other people converge, attracted by the rich pickings around the door; homeless men beg for money, and photographers appear. These scavengers penetrate the crowd of high-spirited and inebriated customers. The atmosphere is noisy and frenetic. Minicab drivers and door staff barge through the excitable throng. Dawn is breaking, but only lovers are in a rush to get home. There's plenty of time to sleep when you're dead.

Only a small number of people leave on foot, as an un-licensed minicab business is in operation. This service is organized by a stocky, middle-aged man with a mobile phone, clipboard and pen, who liaises with door staff. Customers are assigned to waiting, or newly arriving vehicles, or told to wait on the pavement until a car becomes available. It's now 3.45am on Sunday morning and I've seen enough. I ask for a 'taxi' to East London, and my friend and I are told to wait until a driver is found. I am offered a price of £22 for the journey, which I haggle down to £20. We are led to an adjacent street. As we walk, the driver informs me that different cars incur different prices. He points out a *Peugeot 205* (£12), a *Mercedes* priced at £50, and his own aged *BMW* at £22. He opens a rear passenger door and tells us to get in. I note that the car has no licence plates, meter, or communication system, and that the driver has no identity badge. Our chauffeur requests that we sit in the car while he goes for a 'piss'. I sit and watch as he empties his bladder onto the pavement, in full view of passers-by. He then takes a plastic bottle out of the boot, lifts the bonnet, and pours water into the radiator, which is giving off steam. He puts the bottle back in the boot and gets into the car. During the journey he tells me that he works for the *Geisha*. When we arrive at our destination I give him £20. He demands a further £2, but is unable to offer change for a £5 note. He has 'run out' of receipts.

Maguire and Nettleton (2003) found that the majority of those arrested for alcohol-related violence were young white males (around half aged between 20 and 30) who were first-time offenders and who lived locally, and that 'assault victims whose details were recorded had fairly similar profiles to offenders in terms of age, sex, and residence' (2003: 36).[5] Clearly, nightlife brings offenders into contact with victims in numerous ways, with victim movement patterns often proving 'as important in determining where and when a crime occurs as offender movement patterns' (Brantingham and Brantingham 1995: 11).

The following paragraphs consider the social constitution of the night-time high street and the contribution of its narrow population profile to the construction of time-space locales notable for their objective crime risk.

From high street to 'street for getting high': the purification of night-time public space

Those familiar with sociological analyses of the urban condition will note the gulf between the type of communal public/private spaces of consumption described above and the characteristics of public space, as commonly understood. Urban public space, and city centre streets in particular, are almost universally celebrated by liberal scholars as a distinctive realm, 'the natural home of difference' (Sennett 1990: 78). Such areas are regarded as accessible spaces of free and spontaneous assembly in which 'different ages, races and classes, ways of life, abilities can all crowd together'

---

[5] British Crime Survey data has shown that the very highest risks of victimization are borne by those who share some combination of the following characteristics: young; male; single; unemployed; frequently visiting nightclubs or pubs; high levels of alcohol consumption (Budd 2003: 11).

(ibid., Berman 1986). They are also seen as democratic spaces which facilitate freedom of action, free speech and the expression of citizenship rights (Carr et al. 1992).

Non-exclusivity is the defining feature of public space, which, as well as being its greatest strength, can also prove its fatal vulnerability. Public space, can, 'over time, be colonized or dominated by particular groups or interests, thereby losing its inclusive status' (Worpole and Greenhalgh 1996: 15–16, Lyman and Scott 1967: 239–240). One of the most effective ways to mould the human ecology of cities is through the ownership or control of property, land use and commerce (Berman 1982, Davis 1990). Writing of the corporate occupation of US cities, Ferrell notes how non-consumers are recast as unwelcome outsiders, whose cultures are 'expurgated, 'disappeared', rendered invisible and inaudible' (2001: 227). Ferrell's concerns are predominately spatial; however, once a temporal dimension is added, this analytical thrust may be adapted in interesting ways to the contemporary British urban condition. As Chapter 3 relates, a wholesale de-regulation of alcohol licensing occurred during the 1990s, facilitating the leisure industry's ever greater colonization of urban space and time. Mono-functionality emerged as a key indicator of the shift towards increasingly privatized night-time public space (Sennett 2000), influencing 'who uses it, who feels welcome to use it, and who knows better than to try and use it' (Hannigan 1998: 192):

In the bars around here you simply can't find a seat or hold a conversation because it's too loud. They were talking about opening a jazz or blues club, but people who want that aren't going to come down here. There used to be some good restaurants but they are either closing, dumbing down, or just turning into bars, because the type of people who come here now just want to drink. The people who used to come won't come these days because they don't want to socialize with people who are heavily drunk or heavily drugged (Les, city centre resident, South West).

The agglomeration of licensed premises forged by market forces has nurtured a form of functional apartheid within which the alcohol-focused bar and club scene dominates. A process of social cleansing has occurred, as areas become appropriated by large crowds of consumers. Competition between the many—basically similar—operations has driven the tendency for cut-price drinks promotions and increased the pressure on operators to fulfil the expectations of their core consumers. *Laissez-faire* has spawned a tyranny of the minority. This mass appropriation of night-time public space now:

... affords opportunities for idiosyncrasy and identity. Central to the manifestation of these opportunities are boundary creation and enclosure. This is so because activities that run counter to expected norms need seclusion or invisibility to permit unsanctioned performance, and because peculiar identities are sometimes impossible to realize in the absence of an appropriate setting (Lyman and Scott 1967: 237).

Yet, sub-minority consumers can find their opportunities for idiosyncrasy thwarted by commercial homogenization and invasion by the wider body, as (arguably) occurred in the case of Manchester's Gay Village (Hobbs et al. 2003: Chapters 2–3, Moran et al. 2003).

Although commercial purification in the night-time high street has become at least as virulent as in its day-time counterpart, symptoms of the process continue to diverge. Both arenas place strong emphasis on consumption, leisure, and spending, and—though ostensibly open to all—both are characterized by inequality of access, intolerance of diversity and minority groups, and the exclusion of non-consumers:

Recently, I looked out of my window and saw a girl kneeling down in some sick, giving this guy a blow-job. She was so drunk, she didn't really know what she was doing. I felt like chucking water over them. Now I'm not a prude, but, y'know, it really was a sorry sight to see. But that just said to me a lot about the way this area's gone (Emma, town centre resident, West Midlands).

Difference is manifested in consumer reactions to danger. In a fundamental departure from the day-time setting, consumer purification of the *night-time* high street has corresponded with an increase, rather than decrease, in danger, conceived here (following Jermier 1982: 198) as 'an objective property of urban time and space grounded in the interpersonal interactions of the inhabitants of that time and space'.

Not for me, thanks! (avoiding the night-time city)

PH: Do you ever go out in West Road?

Tony (local, age 27): 'Nah, it's fulla' scum'.

One of the most significant drivers of high street development has been the 'honey-pot effect' through which areas attain local and regional renown as epicentres of entertainment and release (see Chapter 7). Many of these areas also attain more negative reputations as hot spots of violent crime (see Chapter 1). As a result of the core consumer group's domination of both licensed premises and public space and their often aggressively hedonistic demeanour, other citizens may feel effectively excluded from participation in nightlife. Research conducted in a number of cities including Nottingham (Oc and Tiesdell 1997), Leeds (Spink and Bramham 1999) and Swansea and Cardiff (Thomas and Bromley 2000) has found that many people seek to avoid urban centres at night, perceiving them to be threatening environments dominated by drunken youths. Social incivilities (such as public drunkenness and urination) and physical incivilities (such as litter and vandalism) can generate fear in a large number of people by conveying negative messages about the social conditions in an area (Nasar and Fisher 1993, Skogan and Maxfield 1981, Warr 1990, Wilson and Kelling 1982).

In both Swansea and Cardiff, Thomas and Bromley (2000: 1425) found that, 'the concentrations of public houses and late-night clubs, and the principal transport termini were perceived to be especially problematic.' In contrast to the initial 24-hour city expectations of increased feelings of security through the animation of public space, people expressed their '*highest levels of anxiety* with regard to the areas which were the *most populated* at night' (ibid., my emphasis). Thus, in the NTE, hot spots of both fear and crime are found to converge in areas where social interaction is at its most intense.

One important lesson to be drawn from the fear of crime literature is that some people feel better equipped to confront danger than others[6] and that, in many cases, 'self-imposed precautionary measures limit mobility significantly' (Law 1999: 570). Studies of the occupational culture of persons involved in

---

[6] Thomas and Bromley (2000: 1422–1425) note that whilst the most frequent visitors to the city centre at night (young men) 'consistently recorded the lowest levels of disquiet', the least frequent visitors (older people, especially women) 'displayed the highest levels of anxiety'. Such responses accord with studies that indicate how people's perceptions of an area may be influenced by factors other than direct experience (Girling et al. 2000, Hollway and Jefferson 1997, Sasson 1995).

a variety of dangerous work tasks further illuminate this point. It would appear that those whose identities are strongly linked to their work and to the importance of impression management in front of colleagues may be more likely to find experiences of danger challenging, gratifying, or at least, less threatening, especially when such dangers are confronted in a group setting (Fitzpatrick 1980, Haas 1977, Kinkade and Katovich 1997, Mayer and Rosenblatt 1975). There is evidence to suggest that nightlife participants whose experiences and identities are strongly shaped by co-consumption with friends, associates and peers may similarly develop feelings of confidence and territoriality which permit greater capacity for 'playful' engagement with environmental danger (Carr 1998, Graham and Wells 2003, Green et al. 2000, Malbon 1999, Valentine 1989). As noted, this adventurous collective constitutes nightlife's core consumers.

The generation of fear (or indeed hostility) within local populations is essentially an exclusionary process which can have the effect of further undermining commercial diversity and discouraging wider participation in nightlife. This may be an important issue for public order, as it is widely assumed that the very presence of socially and culturally diverse crowds may serve to 'normalize' the on-street environment, thus enhancing informal controls. Widespread avoidance effectively ghettoizes nightlife areas, setting them aside for the more aggressive forms of youthful hedonism. Thus, the growth of the night-time high street (at least in its present guise) appears to have made our urban centres less accessible to the majority of citizens (Spink and Bramham 1999), with fear of crime now presenting a 'formidable barrier' (Thomas and Bromley 2000: 1425) to the development of more diverse and inclusive nightlife.

Notwithstanding the above, some people may avoid the night-time high street not because they are fearful or annoyed about the activities they find, or assume, go on there, but rather because such activities simply do not (or no longer) appeal to them. Perhaps what the area has to offer in terms of consumer choice, services and accessibility is simply inadequate to meet their needs. Such responses are unlikely to be restricted to older people, family groups, and ethnic and sexual minorities. Many types of people find the alcohol-focused bar and club scene of little appeal, and not all elect to stay home. Some may seek out the remnants of an alternative, peripheral, and/or music-oriented form of nightlife. As Jacobs notes, 'duplication of the most profitable use' serves to undermine 'the base of its own attraction, as disproportionate duplication and exaggeration of some single use always does in cities' (1961: 259).

Removing disorder, introducing danger

Granted that disorder spoils pattern, it also provides the material of pattern (Douglas 1966: 95).

Concern regarding the concentration of public violence in nightlife areas cannot be dismissed as merely symptomatic of moral panic or historical amnesia. As noted in Chapters 3 and 7, over time, crime patterns map closely onto those of commercial development. There is overwhelming evidence to suggest that people's fears and avoidance behaviours correlate quite accurately with the hot spots and hot times for violent crime. It is therefore hardly controversial to regard the night-time high street as an ecological zone of objective danger.

In the above passages, I associated dangerousness with communal spaces shaped by the logic of the market rather than public regulation and the ideals of liberal democracy. Within this time–space environment, forms of comportment and practical consciousness had been nurtured that were essentially antipathetic to those of normative (day-time) sociability. Yet, in relation to the social setting I describe, it is questionable whether the term 'disorderly' can be applied; issues of situated meaning arise when analysing how behaviours that conform to the dominant expectations and orderings of their enacted environment might be so conceived. Within a human ecology devoted almost entirely to the pleasures of intoxication, the drunken, boisterous, and violent consumer can hardly be regarded as 'matter out of place' (Douglas 1966, 1970). Such understandings have a long heritage in ethnographies of place, stretching back to those scholars of the Chicago School who explained crime and delinquency, 'principally by the effects of the isolation of certain natural areas' which fostered 'a kind of surrogate social order, an alternative pattern, which replaced the workings of conventional institutions' (Downes and Rock 2003: 71).

In order to illustrate this point it is necessary to distinguish between zones of danger and zones of disorder. The two categories are not mutually exclusive as areas can be, at once, both disorderly and dangerous. However, the following paragraphs draw upon some classic themes in urban sociology to argue that, in relation to the night-time high street at least, disorderly public spaces are apt to be less dangerous than 'orderly' ones.

The night-time high street—a mono-functional, consumption-oriented zone of objective danger—stands in stark contrast to the type of disorderly environment described within the pages of seminal urban scholarship (Berman 1986, Jacobs 1961, Lofland 1973, 1998, Sennett 1970, 1990). In these various reflections on the urban condition and the uses and meanings of public space, one finds a variety of positive conceptions of urban disorder. Here disorder (understood as chaotic, unpredictable, and 'messy' social interaction) is regarded as intrinsic to a mature and sophisticated urbanity. Whilst purification of the city involves the zoning of activities into discrete functional nodes, disorder is characterized by an unstructured 'jumble of concurrent events and peoples inhabiting common ground' (Sennett 1970: 142).

The relations between persons fostered by this form of disorder are regarded by urbanist scholars as meaningful in so far as those who occupy public space are obliged to encounter and interact with diverse others. This confrontation with diversity serves to challenge individual beliefs and behaviours, including timidity, prejudice and egocentrism. In negotiating diverse public space, one encounters people who are very different from oneself, including those in relation to whom one disagrees, disapproves, or feels at least mild antipathy or fear (Lofland 1998: 243, Sennett 2000). This 'hard edge' to the city is celebrated by dint of its role in the development of a mature *pro-social* attitude. It is only through repeated encounter and negotiation with the Other that one may develop more urbane cosmopolitan sensibilities. As Sennett notes, 'anarchy is being brought into the city as a positive principle' (1970: 171). Schlör, a cultural historian firmly entrenched in the urbanist tradition, describes the archaic pull of big city nights wherein people found: 'pleasure in the discovery of this new world and pride in having taken the decisive step out of the shelter indoors and onto the streets' (1998: 56). For Schlör, this ability to negotiate disorder becomes integral to a 'newly forming urban mentality' in which 'the complete city dweller has to learn to master the night' (ibid.).

Crucially however, in order to teach cosmopolitanism, public spaces must not be regarded as *too dangerous*. If an area is avoided by all but a like-minded minority—who both shun and help to create danger—then 'no lessons can be learned' (Lofland 1998: 243). Urbanists regard uniformed policing and other types of formal social control as of secondary importance in preventing crime. 'Successful streets', characterized by positive disorder, are seen as, to a large extent, 'self-policing' (Berman 1986: 481, Jacobs 1961, Sennett 1970, Worpole 1992) due to the greater efficacy of informal social control.

Such analyses find support among criminologists. Loader, for example, notes that resolutions to the problems associated with young people's colonization of public space in and around residential areas may rely, 'not so much on better policing, as the development of economic and social conditions that enable the police to recede' (1994: 524). It is inescapable to conclude that the processes of commercial agglomeration, consumer colonization, and cultural purification that have accompanied the de-regulation of the night-time high street have generated an array of social and environmental harms. There has often been a lack of strategic vision and a general neglect or failure to regulate in ways which might preserve 'effective public custodianship of shared public spaces and facilities' (Taylor 1999: 123). As Tim Hope argues, effective community crime prevention must be alert to issues of context, attending in particular to the establishment of the 'necessary social pre-conditions through which individual criminal motivation or behaviour can be changed, or crime-related harms reduced through everyday, routine practice' (Hope 2001: 421). The following model suggests how a vicious circle may be set in motion.

Vicious circles in the criminogenic purification of night-time public space

The 'honey-pot' effect generates an increase in alcohol-oriented leisure activity and the formation of a night-time high street. This acts as a crime generator; however, in contrast to the day-time high street, the increased security risk has a negligible effect on the profitability of key businesses, as it fails to deter their core consumers. However, citizens who do not share the social characteristics of the core consumer group, due to their age, ethnicity, religion, sexuality, or lifestyle, begin to avoid the area. The increase in objective danger thereby promotes homogeneity and a decrease in the diversity of local facilities. Widespread avoidance by the majority population fuels this commercial consolidation and cultural purification, as the area comes to be regarded as an environment in which control and functionality has been ceded to the core consumer. This erosion of diversity serves to further sever the links between the area and its host community leading to an atrophy of informal social control. Atrophy of informal control contributes to an increase in objective danger. Businesses in the area further direct their energies toward meeting the preferences of those consumers who are least deterred by, and disproportionately contribute toward, the generation of such danger. The area becomes even less attractive as a destination for other users and those seeking to develop alternative non-alcohol based facilities. The circle is repeated as new licensed premises enter the market.

Policing the night-time high street

Peace and order in the streets of a town have always depended more upon individual standards of right conduct and the state of public opinion, than the size and efficiency of the local police force (Salusbury-Jones 1938: 126).

The above model accords in some ways with popular criminological understandings of an incivility-inspired 'spiral of decline' associated with broken windows theory (Wilson and Kelling 1982). However, my model, which relates solely to the NTE, departs from such perspectives by providing little analytical support for 'quality of life policing'. To illustrate this point, let us consider the following extract from Wilson and Kelling's seminal paper:

The wish to 'decriminalize' disreputable behaviour that 'harms no one'—and thus remove the ultimate sanction the police can employ to maintain neighbourhood order—is we think a mistake. Arresting a single drunk or a single vagrant who has harmed no identifiable person seems unjust, and in a sense it is. But failing to do anything about a score of drunks or a hundred vagrants may destroy an entire community (1982: 35).

This logic does not transfer at all easily to a context in which the street population ('community') that is being policed regards public drunkenness as normative. Nightlife consumers and the police will often hold divergent conceptions of order, 'with tacit knowledge defining night-time public space as a zone of fun on the one hand and a zone of hazards on the other (Philips and Smith

2000: 490). As one police Sergeant, with five years frontline experience of policing a city centre in the North West of England, explained:

It's like on that TV programme, *Ibiza Uncovered,* or at football matches, in certain places it's acceptable to scream and shout and sing at the *top* of your voice. Although that behaviour could be classed as disorderly, if you've got 4,000 people in one area doing it, it's obviously acceptable to them, and nobody's going to make any complaints. Jane

As Whyte noted of street-level policing in 1930s Boston, when confronting a social order 'whose perpetuation depends upon freedom to violate the law . . . the smoothest course for the officer is to conform to the social organization with which he is in direct contact and at the same time to try to give the impression to the outside world that he is enforcing the law' (1943: 138). It is important to note, however, that if such adapted expectations have claim to legitimacy, such claims will derive not only from the preferences of the street population itself, but, more strongly, from the demands of an ascendant political economy. In re-packaging the night-time city as a realm of 'fun and games', it is powerful leisure industry players and their political allies, rather than the policed, who remould dominant conceptions of order.

Resource pressures and the duty of care

My observations of public order policing and interviews with officers of all ranks suggest, without exception, that a very large proportion of night-time incidents are alcohol-related in one way or another. Environments characterized by mass consumption of alcohol and other intoxicants place a disproportionate strain upon the resources of the police and other public services such the Ambulance Service and hospital Accident and Emergency Departments (AEDs).[7] A very wide variety of incidents can and do occur throughout the night and across all areas of the city, however, the greatest concentration of 'emergencies' occurs in nightlife areas,

---

[7] This point is illustrated in a national study of the impact of alcohol misuse on the work of emergency service and emergency health care workers, including police, paramedics, and AED clinical staff. The study found the NTE to be placing a significant and chronic strain on these agencies which impacted upon standards and the availability of services for the public at large (Alcohol Harm Reduction Group 2003).

especially in the period after licensed premises 'throw out'. During such periods, police officers may be forced to prioritize their responses to criminal activity, in the sense of failing to respond to, or deciding to leave, situations they would otherwise have dealt with, because of an urgent call to attend to an even more serious matter. Pressures can be such that resources are routinely diverted from other areas and policing priorities. As Stephen Green, Chief Constable of Nottinghamshire, told the Nottingham Crown Court:[8] 'At the moment, the only way we can cope with the level of policing demand is to leave the outlying districts of the City Division short of police officers on a Friday and Saturday night' (Green 2003: 10). As one PC from a Midlands city explained:

From a public order bus point of view, unless it is something very urgent we won't leave the city centre. You just can't afford to, because you can guarantee that as soon as you start travellin' out, something will start happenin' that requires your attention. It depends how many officers you've got on, but we can be runnin' around all night, some nights. Y'know, you need the presence there just so people can see ya. Jim

PH: Under what circumstances would you leave to attend incidents outside the centre?

Jim: It would have to be a major disturbance for us to go; a violent incident. We wouldn't go for a burglary. We will not leave the city—no way!

A persistent feature of the observation periods was that when officers responded to an incident which resulted in them taking people into custody, the officers were then removed from operational duty to complete paperwork pertaining to those incidents. The time taken in the custody area would vary according to whether a queue of prisoners was waiting. Following procedure correctly might mean that, throughout the night, several hours were taken up without tangible outcome. Persons under the influence of alcohol presented particular challenges for operational policing in that their behaviour was both unpredictable and—as a general rule—not amenable to normal standards of reasoning to defuse conflict:

If you've got a violent prisoner, it will take three of you to deal with one guy and there's no doubt about it, so that's three of us off the streets for

---

[8] In a licensing case involving police and trade objections to the opening of a new nightclub in Nottingham city centre.

however long it takes for it to calm down, get them booked in. It's a long process and if there's already one (prisoner) waiting and you're there with yours as well; there's only three cells here in the town and the nearest space for more is fifteen miles away (Tony, Sergeant, population 150,000 town, Yorkshire).

Dealing with alcohol-related incidents claimed police resources—notably cells—for considerable periods of time. This was particularly true when a Forensic Medical Examiner (FME) declared a detained person unfit to be interviewed due to their degree of intoxication. For officers on public order duty, even the most minor incident involving an arrest would require around one hour of non-operational time whilst in the station, additional to the time spent in dealing with the incident itself. On the streets, resource pressures could be such that officers were unable to act unless and until reinforcements could be mustered:

It can be scary, if there's only two of you and there's 400 people coming out of the clubs and you know that assistance is maybe five or ten minutes away. If a disorder situation does break out and there's not enough of my staff to deal with the situation . . . At the end of the day, you need to protect people, because there's more public out there than there are police, so you need to protect the police (John, Inspector, seaside resort, South Coast).

This sense of vulnerability can inform decisions to arrest. As one male Constable told Nottingham Crown Court, 'I would say that there are occasions when arrests do not take place because of the danger of inflaming a situation' (Brophy 2003: para. 15). When facing both resource constraints and a disjuncture between their own conceptions of order and the expectations of the policed, officers have little option but to apply discretion in responding flexibly and pragmatically according to circumstance (Livingston 1997, Werthman and Piliavin 1967):

When it gets to smashing bottles and kicking over bins or, y'know, just jumping on innocent people who are walking past or queuing for a taxi or a bag of chips, then yes, that's where the line is drawn, because nobody, whether they are having a good time or not, has the right to just attack somebody else. You have to consider how many people are there to assist you and how badly the people are behaving . . . We would normally just go up to them and warn them and then they just walk off; 'Ok then!' and start doing it again (Mike, PC, population 120,000 city, South East).

The inability to adopt a 'hard line' approach due to the size of the crowds, social atmosphere, and resource restrictions, was lamented by some officers who regarded it as a ceding of police authority. As Rubinstein (1973: 166) notes, 'for the patrolman the street is everything; if he loses that, he has surrendered his reason for being what he is':

You do have to turn a blind eye, certainly more recently and that's purely due to the volume of people that are out on the street. It frustrates me and it frustrates other officers, because they know that at the end of the day, if you are going to deal with someone effectively because they are being disorderly and they are committing whatever offences, they may have to be arrested. So they are doing things that in the past they would have been arrested for. But, you know that that officer is going to be taken off the street to deal with that and if we dealt with everyone who was behaving like that we wouldn't have anyone (officers) left on the streets. You do have to turn a blind eye and it gets frustrating (Paul, Sergeant, population 90,000 town, West Midlands).

In most instances, however, the liberal use of discretion by officers was regarded as an unavoidable and situationally appropriate element of the task:

We make a low number of arrests, but the opportunity is there to spend all night locking people up for drunken, loutish behaviour; but you have to decide, is this behaviour normal? Is it actually going to develop into something more serious? Whilst we may not accept people urinating in the street, what is the alternative? If we were to arrest everybody who urinated in the street ... there's thousands of people around, so the people that do find themselves under arrest by my team have *really* pushed their luck. Y'know, they've refused to stop fighting, or they've started to fight with the officer. So I would say it's a low number of arrests, but lots and lots of tolerance and even more advice (Dave, Inspector, Greater London).

Indeed, some officers regarded a tolerant attitude as a prerequisite; a mark of professional competence:

My team are able to talk to people and control situations; they are good at defusing and talking people down. They've been chosen because they've got good experience and they are tolerant. Now with the tolerance you may say, 'well, perhaps you're condoning people's behaviour', but we don't see these people in their normal day-to-day lives, we only ever see them when they are drunk, or perhaps they've had drugs and they are not behaving. We don't know what their normal behaviour will be like, so we have to tolerate a little bit more and that's what we do. We don't know where they come from, or what walk of life they come from, we don't know what they do during the day. As I said before, anybody can find themselves in a situation that they don't want to be in, but they don't know how to get out of, and can end up getting themselves arrested. Most people are fighting for whatever reason that seems significant at the time, but they are such insignificant reasons that when they are sober they think to themselves, 'Just what was I doing?' But that's the side of people that we never see (Mike, Sergeant, Northern city).

This attuned sensitivity to the transformation of identities and standards of conduct extends beyond the management of public order to encompass a paternalistic role in attending to the casualties of the night. The duty of care burden associated with intoxicated persons can be onerous (as well as unpleasant) and falls primarily on the police, whenever—as is often the case—a person refuses medical treatment. In a fraught and emotionally charged environment, this duty can be difficult to discharge:

You try and help people and all they want to do is fight with you because they don't want any help and it's a very difficult thing because police officers are just human beings. It's a very difficult thing to walk away from somebody who's got a broken nose and there's blood everywhere and they must be in pain, but if they are giving you loads of abuse, won't tell you their name, don't want you to get an ambulance, or won't even get in the ambulance, then what can you do for that person? It's very difficult for officers. You think, 'His nose must be killin' him!' but people just don't want your help (Jane, Sergeant, West Midlands).

In addition to the walking wounded, police must also deal with people who are physically incapacitated through intoxication. Such people may be taken into custody, where, if they have visible injuries, they may require the services of an FME. Custody officers are then required to undertake frequent, labour-intensive checks on the welfare of such persons, including 'rousing' to ensure consciousness.

These observations illustrate the scale and difficulty of the crime control, crowd management, prioritization, and duty of care responsibilities vested in the police and other frontline public services. To borrow an economist's term, intoxication, and

primarily alcohol consumption, carries with it 'externalities'—
costs that do not accrue to the leisure and drinks industry, and
which are therefore unlikely to be taken into account when companies make cost/benefit decisions about their business strategies
(Bakan 2004, Coase, 1986). This point is made forcibly by
Stephen Green in relation to Nottingham city centre:

> The people who need us most are being deprived of our service by
> organizations that require our help only to be able to continue to make
> large profits. The fact is that 100,000 sober people in Nottingham city
> centre during the day-time cause the police no great problems. However,
> as soon as you put alcohol into the equation the city becomes a very dif-
> ferent, and much more violent, place (Green 2003: para. 11).

The restless city

In addition to the expropriation of emergency services, the night-
time high street may also have a more direct impact upon residential communities. 'Duplication of the most profitable use', can,
as Jacobs predicted (1961: 259), take its toll on the quality of life
in central urban areas:

> During the day the place is dead and families don't come down anymore.
> Since all the bars sprang up, this area is just geared to beer and the night-
> trade. We don't even have basic facilities. The only other facility we've
> got down here is a newsagent (Sarah, city centre resident, South West).

A comparative study of mixed-use residential and leisure districts
in four Northern European capital cities (Berlin, Copenhagen,
Dublin and London) found that all areas 'had similar problems . . .
especially in relation to noise, crowds, litter, and social disorder.
Each locale had experienced a conflict between business and residential interests' (Central Cities Institute 2002: 7). The authors
state: 'it is striking that in each of the case study areas, problems
were associated with a concentration of licensed premises' (ibid.:
81). Accordingly, residents living in close proximity to the night-
time high street were forthright in describing the degradation of
their surroundings:

> We threatened the city council with getting the press down to photo-
> graph Brass Street residents cleaning the streets themselves, because we're
> so *sick* of the stuff that is left. What they don't do is spray the streets and

these streets are covered in grease because it's food that's chucked down and you can't sweep that, so it gets trodden on and when it rains, you're actually sliding about on the pavement 'cos its so thick. It's just disgusting. You go to walk the dog in the morning, and the glass, and the filth, and the rubbish, even when you're coming back about 10 or 11 o'clock. You think, 'The shoppers coming down here must think this place is a slum' (Louise, city centre resident, South East).

Nigel used dark humour to recount his experiences:

The only good think about vomit is the very next day it's all gone. Y'know, sometimes you have to step over half a dozen vomits to get to my front door. But the next morning it's gone. But that's not the council cleaning it up, that's the rats and the pigeons that finish it off. *It's sickening*. If you come down Bain Street about 5'oclock in the morning, that's when all the rats come out; 'cos, I've been awake at that time and I've looked out of my bedroom window, and I can't believe the size of these rats! They know what time to come out and that's when all the clubbers have gone home (city centre resident, North East).

Noise nuisance is a recurrent theme of residential complaint. From early evening through to the early hours of morning, noise sources may include sounds emanating from venues, and customers drinking outside them; crowds of pedestrians on the street; traffic noise, including car horns, stereos, and sirens; ventilation systems; the sound of glass bottles being dropped into skips; and the purr of street cleansing machines as they converge on an area once revellers have dispersed. These sounds offer little respite for the sleeper before the rumblings of the new day begin.

The *Guidance* recommends that the appropriate way to deal with noise and nuisance in residential areas is to attach various conditions to premises licences (DCMS 2004b: 7.38–46). However, given that many residential concerns relate to activities occurring on the streets (rather than simply in relation to noise emissions from within premises), it is difficult to see how licensing conditions relating to noise might fully address the issue:

It's the people who are causing the noise rather than the venues, just the sheer number of them. It's also the loudness of the music in these bars and so their hearing shuts down, so when they come out they're just shouting and screaming at each other and plus they're not just tipsy, they are *blind* drunk (Scott, city centre resident, North East).

Where due regard is paid to the individual merits of an application, the *Guidance* does allow for limits to be placed upon the opening hours of premises. However, in keeping with the government's general stance on extended hours, there is a presumption in favour of later opening (ibid.: 6.10) and intervention is deemed permissible only in very restricted and legally contestable circumstances. Residents may object only if they live 'within the vicinity of the premises'. The term 'vicinity' is taken to mean that the objector's residence 'is likely to be directly affected by disorder or disturbance occurring ... on those premises or immediately outside the premises' (5.33). The *Guidance* imposes no strict boundaries and it is left to the licensing authority to decide whether, on balance, the objectors' homes or businesses are close enough to be directly affected. Although the Government has claimed that the Act provides 'new levels of protection for local residents and communities' (DCMS 2003, cited in Light 2005b: 109), it should be noted that there were no such limitations on those entitled to object before the licensing justices under the old legislation. Moreover, interpretations of 'vicinity' may be strict. For example, in August 2005, the residents of Berkley Court, an apartment block located only 150 yards away from one of the busiest pubs in Birmingham, were prevented from objecting to its application for a 3am licence. The licensing authority accepted a submission by the operators, *J.D. Wetherspoon*, that Berkley Court was not in the 'immediate vicinity' of the pub and that it would therefore be unlawful to hear the views of residents. Such decisions imply that, in future, local people may well 'have less rather than more of a say in licensing decisions' (Light 2005a: 284).

The artificiality of such restrictions is illustrated in the following case study which explores the neglected topic of vehicular-traffic related crime in a mixed-use leisure/residential area.

Cruising time

Central London's congestion problems are widely known and commented upon. Demands from residents, businesses and visitors create tremendous pressure on the number of on-street parking spaces. From 17 February 2003, a congestion charging scheme came into effect from 7am to 6.30pm during weekdays in an attempt to reduce traffic levels during day-time hours (hence the scheme did not directly affect *night-time* traffic levels). The City of Westminster has a statutory duty to manage on-street parking seven days a week, with enforcement duties contracted out to a company which supplies traffic wardens. 'Normal' street parking controls run from 8.30am to 6.30pm. Pressure to control more areas for more of the time is increasing, however, especially in the West End. West End streets remain noisy and congested with traffic until around 4.30am and anecdotally, many who work in the area say that it is often busier at 3am than it is at 3pm, complete with traffic jams. It is difficult to compare the two time periods with regard to parking, however, because during the day people either pay and/or are time-limited in terms of parking, whereas at night there is no time limit on visitor parking. There may also be seasonal factors.

In the West End, residents' permit zones and double-yellow lines are patrolled twenty-four hours a day, although metered bays and pay and display spaces are not controlled at night. As a result, cars are often present for longer periods of time during night-time hours. The council has begun to investigate the potential for further controls on street parking as a result of complaints from businesses that parking is difficult to find. Parking controls are also seen as one way of reducing the problems associated with illegal minicabs. Joint enforcement operations with police, bailiffs and other agencies are conducted on a regular basis. Around forty parking attendants patrol the West End at night (out of a total of approximately fifty for the whole borough, and around 250 during the day).

The following paragraphs describe the environment in which parking attendants work, providing some insight into the 'feel' of an important aspect of London's nightlife.

In one particular area where a one-way system is in operation, the presence of a number of nightclubs and late-night take-aways acts as a magnet for traffic. Groups of young men cruise the area in glistening drop-top convertibles and other sporty or 'prestige' cars. The cruisers aim to attract as much attention to themselves as possible, both visually and audibly—hence the mandatory 'bored out' exhaust pipes and thumping bass-heavy sound systems. When observing activities in the area for any length of time, one sees the same cars repeatedly circulating. The occupants stare, whistle, and shout at pedestrians; addressing their attention to young females in particular. Sometimes the cruisers will stop to talk to people on the street or simply to hang out and pose next to their cars. These activities can last for half an hour, or more. The cars are parked illegally on double yellow lines, or double- and treble-parked in a manner which partially blocks the thoroughfare and reduces the speed of the traffic flow. Other drivers become frustrated and angry, prompting the sounding of horns and vocal remonstrations.[9]

At the same time, the area attracts a more modest and sober fleet of vehicles: late-night London's illegal minicabs. Private cars driven by solitary males crowd the pavements, whilst their agents approach anyone who looks as though they might be enjoying themselves with the offer of a 'taxi'. Occasionally, deals are struck between the drivers of cruising vehicles and loitering pedestrians, small items are passed surreptitiously from car window to pocket. Those entering or leaving licensed premises are approached by touts, dealers, panhandlers, and other people simply giving out flyers. Some revellers negotiate with the 'taxi drivers' and are driven away. If traffic wardens or police arrive the cruisers and minicabs simply move on, only to complete the circuit again and re-park once the coast is clear. Basic conflicts of interest emerge between those tasked with maintaining highway order and those deriving social and economic gain from unfettered motility.

Even at the heart of a world city, the late-night population is relatively parochial. The wardens and their public occupy a distinct and socially restricted human ecology in which time–space routines converge. Thus, associations between the regulator and the regulated are not always fleeting. Amidst the series of encounters that occur week-in, week-out, ownership of the streets must be negotiated through the fluid and uneasy accomplishment of an indigenous order. In nightly contestations over the appropriation of public space, conflicting concerns of freedom, respect, identity, and commerce find immediacy face to face.

Night-shift traffic wardens are licensed to challenge and disrupt the lifeworld of the streets. This task can have serious personal consequences, as anger and resentment are expressed in personalized grudge matches between patrolling wardens and recidivists. Yet, lacking the training, authority, and resources of a police officer, wardens are susceptible to intimidation, with verbal abuse, including threats from unlicensed minicab drivers and touts being routine. Physical assaults sometimes involve weapons, and even firearms. In one incident, a warden patrolling the area

---

[9] The issue of cruising and traffic congestion in nightlife areas is rarely addressed in UK literature on the NTE, or even in wider discussions of the 24-hour city. This contrasts with debate in other countries such as the US, where cruising is endemic (Berkley and Thayer 2000). This omission may well reflect implicit and culture-relative assumptions of British researchers regarding the central role of alcohol in nightlife and its relationship to urban disorder—issues which tend to obscure other contributory factors in the generation of environmental stress (Elvins and Hadfield 2003).

described above was so badly beaten that he was unable to walk for several months. Because of greater security concerns at night, attendants work their beats in pairs as opposed to singly during the day-time. They record offences via a handheld terminal and give periodic reports of their location. However, police support is rarely forthcoming and even though special operations have been mounted in which the wardens turn out in force, enforcement is failing. The contractors accept that parking restrictions cannot always be enforced late at night, as some areas are considered to be simply too dangerous.

Eyes upon the street

Simply by going about their daily lives, residents act as place managers (Connolly 2003); attachment to their homes and communities encouraging them to perform a territorial function with regard to surrounding public space:

When I hear screams at three o'clock in the morning my instant reaction is to get out of bed and see what's going on. There's a lot of unreported crime goes on round here, especially violent disorder, you'll hear that from everyone you speak to (Mike, city centre resident, South East).

However, 'natural surveillance' (Jacobs 1961) can only be effective if residents receive adequate support from the police and other enforcement agencies. In many cases, the problems become so incessant that residents give up and stop reporting all but the most serious of incidents. This call fatigue can be brought on by frustration at an apparent lack of response. In such circumstances, residents may feel driven to take direct action:

I had a taxi parked underneath my window for about twenty minutes and he was hooting his horn and had the bass turned up on his stereo. In the end I just lost it and threw a bucket of water down on him. He knew he'd been out of order and just moved on (Nigel, city centre resident, North West).

However, those oppressed by the nightly invasion of their area can sometimes be deterred from defending their interests through fear of reprisal:

I'm really scared here in my own home. Last week one of them comes into my garden and starts urinating, so I start chasing him with a floor brush. His mate turns round and starts threatening to beat me up. I won't be doing that again (Lucy, city centre resident, East Midlands).

Residents who take a stand may also face intimidation at the hands of licensed businesses:

When I rang the manager of *Toast* to complain about the noise he just slammed the phone down. Ten minutes later he was kicking and punching on the door of my flat. I saw some of the staff from *Bliss* putting a dead rat on the windscreen of my neighbour's car . . . ' (Elaine, city centre resident, North East).

This open and visceral conflict is fuelled by the ghettoizing and profit-maximizing compulsions of the night-time high street. The corporate occupation of supposedly diverse city spaces permits the responsibilities which accompany the negotiation of difference to be cast aside. The expectations of residents are re-framed as 'problems' emanating from their own 'intolerance', rather than legitimate calls for restraint upon the actions of business and its patrons. Both the trade, and more entrepreneurially-inclined politicians, will often attempt to portray residents as narrow-minded 'yuppies' who choose to live in central urban areas, only to complain about what they find. The message conveyed is stark: those who don't like things the way they are should move out. This view is, of course, highly controversial and contestable (see Chapter 7), not least because failure to protect the interests of residents may serve to compromise the broader urban regeneration agenda (Chapter 3, Central Cities Institute 2002, GLA 2002a, 2002b, LGA 2002).

For many participants, these darker sides to the NTE are, as one 19-year-old male consumer put it, 'just the way things are'. Nightlife in Britain tends to be socially exclusive. For most of the population, the opposing worlds of night and day will rarely meet. Problems for those with a vested political and/or economic interest in the nocturnal status quo begin to occur only when non-indigenous commentators, such as national and local media, councillors, pressure groups, or the families of assault victims, begin to voice concern. As discussed below, this is typically followed by knee-jerk reactions and publicity stunts by the authorities in an attempt to assuage public anxiety.

Anti-social behaviour and the errant consumer

The ethic of consumer sovereignty inherent to neo-liberalism eschews market intervention and promotes an individualized mode of governance in which control of consumption, and any harms relating to it, become a responsibility solely of the consumer (Harvey 2005, Room 1997). Regulatory attention becomes focused upon the identification and punishment of an 'irresponsible minority', with 'highly discriminatory' measures being taken against 'specific groups of people in certain symbolic locations' (Crawford 1998: 155). In contrast to the day-time economy and its criminalization of the non-consumer, the most likely recipients of punitive action in the night-time high street are, of course, 'those most thoroughly seduced of consumers, to the tune of a dozen lagers' (Hobbs et al. 2003: 273). Whenever political disquiet gathers pace (see Chapter 1), the state moves only to reassure an anxious electorate, criminalize errant consumers, and encourage toothless self-regulation.[10]

Industry leaders are sensitive to the flux of public discourse and adept in responding to any change in political climate. In many cases, legislative shifts which appear at first glance to be hostile to their interests, may actually serve to re-direct regulatory attention in convenient ways. As Pearce and Tombs note, 'corporations and their representatives themselves play dominant, often covert, roles in the development of regulations to which they are then subjected; they then play key roles in negotiating the ways in which, and the extent to which, such regulations are actually enforced' (1997: 103). Trade organizations such as the BBPA, *The Portman Group*, and BEDA have been among the most vociferous critics of cut-price drinks promotions; central government's enshrinement of the 'binge drinker' as official folk devil (Strategy Unit 2004) prompting the industry to offer the 'happy hour' as a sacrifice to the regulatory agenda. Trade organizations have rushed to issue 'guidance on best practice' and launch 'public education' campaigns warning consumers of the perils of overindulgence.[11]

---

[10] Such patterns of events, labelling and response have historical precedence, most recently in the 'lager lout' phenomenon of the mid-1980s (see Hope 1985, Tuck 1989).

[11] Measures which have been shown to be particularly ineffectual in reducing levels of alcohol-related harm; the most effective strategies involving legislative controls

Despite their doubtful efficacy, such exercises in 'corporate social responsibility' have succeeded in promoting measures that 'nobody's going to be against, and everybody's going to be for' (Chomsky 2002: 26), allowing the industry to convey the impression that it is determined to clean up its act. Such responses reduce political pressure on the state, permitting it to remain true to its ideological commitments. Interventionist options are rejected and industry is, once again, permitted to elect its own modes of regulation in the form of *voluntary* codes of practice' (DCMS 2004b, Strategy Unit 2004). The hunt for 'bad apples' thereby takes its place alongside the extended hours argument as the most convenient and superficially plausible smokescreen through which to obscure the criminogenic effects of routine business practice (Currie 1997, 1998, Taylor 1990).

In addition to self-regulation, the state–industry nexus seeks to promote 'quality of life policing' as the best way to respond to the issues facing the night-time high street. Attempts are made to introduce a greater uniformed presence tasked with enforcing rules and imposing 'standards of behaviour'; developments closely aligned with the shift toward private sector funding and control of crime reduction.[12] There is an increasing tendency among police forces to conduct short-term, high profile 'zero tolerance' campaigns; a trend encouraged by the introduction of Fixed Penalty Notices (FPNs) and exclusion orders for 'anti-social behaviour'. Such approaches are easily understood, widely publicized, and have a populist appeal in seeming to 'tackle' or 'treat' various symptoms of an 'anti-social society' (Colls 2003) characterized by individual irresponsibility and moral decay. During the summer and Christmas periods of 2004, the Home Office Police Standards Unit instigated high profile policing operations in town and city centres across England and Wales. These campaigns focused upon localized hot spots and were reactive in their emphasis upon individual offenders and unscrupulous venues.

combined with strict enforcement (Academy of Medical Sciences 2004, Babor et al. 2003, Edwards et al. 1994, Room 2004).

[12] This has involved the installation of an extensive array of hardware, including CCTV and bottle banks; personnel in the form of street wardens and community support officers; targeted, private sector funding of the public police; through to transport initiatives, and the introduction of Business Improvement Districts (Hadfield and contributors 2004b).

The twin-pronged self-regulation/high profile policing approach meets the convergent needs of a government anxious to gain political capital from being seen to 'clamp down on drunken yobs' and put more 'bobbies'—or at least, 'uniforms'—on the beat, and an industry keen to demonstrate its social responsibility credentials in ways which have a minimal impact on the bottom line. As one police licensing Sergeant put it:

> The philosophy, of course, behind the government's line is that you can sell as much booze as you want, for as long as you want, and that the police will have more draconian powers to mop up afterwards. Peter

This reactive approach does not find favour with all police officers, some of whom appear particularly well placed to comment. Assistant Chief Constable Rob Taylor of Greater Manchester Police (a former ACPO spokesperson on licensing) stated:

> If you look at the new legislation, there are some pretty strong powers in there, new police powers, enhanced powers. But, our view, as we've said, is we want to *prevent,* we want to *reduce,* we want to be *pro*active; we don't want to have to be reacting after the event. We don't want a weak system that allows the wrong type of premises to be in the wrong area, open for the wrong time, and a load of crime and violence to emerge out the back of it, and for us to have to start using our powers *unduly* to try an' put the wheel back on. That's a point I'd like to make very forcibly.

Taylor's views on the permeability of the thin fluorescent line echo those of the famous urbanist scholar, Jane Jacobs, who noted that 'no number of police can enforce civilization where the normal, casual enforcement of it has broken down' (1961: 41). There seems more than a hint of hypocrisy in focusing the public policy response on a consumer group who have accepted the invitation to transgression offered to them by business, central government (and in many instances, local government) in the name of post-industrial progress. Young adults in Britain (and especially in non-metropolitan areas) may have few viable alternatives other than to partake in alcohol-focused night-time leisure. Within a degraded high street environment, young people, as well as offending, also bear the brunt of victimization. Once situations get out of hand and the corporate 'brandscape' no longer performs its intended function of promoting positive civic imagery, this same group of consumers—who were initially welcomed with open arms—find themselves criminalized. Tabloid newspaper reporting reflects these themes. For example, under the triumphant headline 'Yobs to be Caged', the *Daily Express* reports how police in Blackpool and the Greek resort of Faliraki have sought to introduce 'giant mobile street cages, which can detain up to fifty troublemakers at a time' in order to compensate for a lack of cell space (Pilditch 2003: 27).

In her response to Douglas's work on risk and blame, Lupton notes that: 'people may sometimes be blamed for being "at risk" just as they were once blamed for being "in sin"'(1999: 49). Furthermore, blame may be apportioned to others, including one's adversaries, 'as a means of diverting attention away from oneself' (ibid.). This distinct reluctance of central government and the courts 'to penalize the "suppliers" of crime opportunities contrasts markedly with the enthusiasm with which 'their "consumers" are punished' (Garland 2001: 127). Such approaches also play a role in categorizing those persons as disreputable and dangerous and drawing attention away from other types of offender and offences (Harcourt 2001); as Crawford asks, 'where is the "zero tolerance" of white collar crimes, business fraud, unlawful pollution and breaches of health and safety regulations?' (1998: 155), or, one might add, criminogenic development and trading practices.

The latter point may be illustrated by reference to Cheshire Constabulary's 'Operation Yellow Card' of December 2003, described on the front page of one local newspaper as a 'crackdown' involving 'a tide of fifty officers washing through the town centres of Macclesfield, Wilmslow and Knutsford' (*Macclesfield Express* 2003: 1). This 'cleansing' exercise resulted in forty arrests, 'the highest number ever recorded in a single weekend' (ibid.). Interestingly, the local police had recently withdrawn their objection to the opening of a large new theme bar, which despite contributing monies to the local crime prevention budget and making assurances to a crown court that it would bring 'family entertainment' to Macclesfield town centre (see the description of this case in Chapter 3), had—according to the same newspaper—been the site of 'a glassing, a five-man brawl, three reported assaults and five crimes of theft and criminal damage' within the first five months of trading (ibid.: 8).

In presenting this critique, it is not my intention to deny the importance of personal responsibility and individual agency by suggesting that consumers are blameless, or that their actions are in some way structurally or spatially determined. The aim is simply to offer a rejoinder to official discourse and to suggest why effective long-term responses to the problems of the night-time high street may never be found within its narrow and politicized boundaries. In developing this theme, Part III will explore the workings of the licensing system, a process of adjudication in which such matters are routinely mooted.

Part III

Contemporary Contestations

6

The Combatants

Licensing matters are integral to the contestation of the night. As a method of constraining the criminogenic actions of the leisure industry, their import and efficacy cannot be over-emphasized.[1] This chapter, the first of three concerning licensing litigation, profiles various categories of witness in the licensing trial (the role of advocates and of the bench are discussed in Chapters 7 and 8).[2] In describing participants, I employ 'ideal types' (Gerth and Mills 1946). These are not caricatures, but rather abstractions which accentuate and bring together a number of commonly observable characteristics to form a coherent whole. Ideal types do not correspond exactly with empirical instances and make no claims of exhaustiveness. Rather, they act as sensitizing constructs (Blumer 1969) with which concrete examples of phenomena may be compared (Coser 1977). The analytical value of these typifications will become apparent in Chapter 8, where it is argued that regulatory outcomes are accomplished through strategic interactional performance, as shaped, in part, by the personal identities, skills, and resources of social actors.

---

[1] For general reviews of medical and scientific opinion regarding the importance of direct market intervention in public policies involving alcohol see Academy of Medical Sciences (2004), Barbor et al. (2003), Room (2004).

[2] Trial proceedings are also attended by non-participant observers, including supporters of both sides; students; local journalists, trainee solicitors and legal secretaries recording dialogue in shorthand; and barristers' pupils who come to learn the skills of their mentors. In high profile cases one also finds 'spies', who come to gather information for their own future purposes. Spies may include executives from competitor companies, junior lawyers, and police officers from other areas.

Residents and non-competitor businesses

In recent years, both local and central government have encouraged the mixing of land uses within town and city centres (Chapter 3, DETR 2000, DoE 1996, Urban Task Force 1999). Homes, offices, shops, and other businesses are now often located in close proximity to night-time leisure facilities. Chapter 5 indicted how, in central urban areas, the conflict between night-time leisure operators and other stakeholders may become acute. Often the most impassioned and vocal opposition to new licensed premises will come from individual residents or loose affiliations of residents formed in opposition to a specific proposal.

Residential development in urban centres has involved processes not only of re-population, but also of gentrification (Edwards 2000, Tallon and Bromley 2002, Wynne and O'Connor 1998). Residential objectors principally arose from the ranks of these middle class incomers, or from residual middle class groups wishing to resist the tide of commercial encroachment.[3] Residents' associations and more informal coalitions will typically attempt to mobilize local public opinion and lobby the police, or other agencies, for support in their objections. In objecting to a new licence application, or requesting that an existing licence be reviewed (see Chapter 3), local residents and day-time businesses will often highlight issues such as noise nuisance, disturbance, litter, fouling, criminal damage, and the fear of crime, which, they claim, are related to late-night revelry and the customers of licensed premises:

Linda (32), an advertising executive, lives with her schoolteacher partner, Simon (35), and their 2-year-old daughter, Holly, in a third-storey waterside

---

[3] It is approaching a platitude in licensing circles to observe that the making of representations is a largely middle class pursuit, with the voices of working class residents rarely heard. I found this to hold even in instances where the usual lobbying practices work in reverse, with the police or local authority actively seeking residential support for their own objections. In one case, a block of twenty-seven council flats shared an adjoining wall with a former bank earmarked for conversion into a theme bar. Upon attendance at a case briefing I found to my surprise that the police had made no attempt to mobilize residential opinion within the flats. Upon querying this I was informed that such approaches would be futile as the residents held 'anti-police attitudes' which, it was felt, precluded them from co-operating with the police even in circumstances (presumably) of their own advantage.

apartment. The couple purchased their newly-built home, part of a converted warehouse, from the property developer and have lived there for almost five years. Both enjoy the convenience of living close to work, and particularly before Holly came along, the opportunities for after-work socializing. The couple like life in the city as it allows them to be, and to feel, close to the centre of things: shopping; transport hubs; cultural and sports facilities, etc. Products of a suburban upbringing, they are also drawn to the edginess and anonymity of the city. As young adults it permits them a feeling of escape from the restrictive cocoons of security that family and friends wove for them in early life.

Yet, things are beginning to change. Life in the flat has become more stressful over the last two years as new late-night bars have sprung up along the waterfront. Linda and Simon used to enjoy wining and dining at *Booth's* and some of the other local restaurants, but now the area is swamped with 17–25-year-old drinkers, six nights of the week (only Tuesdays are relatively quiet). The social atmosphere in the area has become more wild and rowdy and the longer-established bars and restaurants have had to adapt their offer, going 'down-market' in order to meet the expectations of the new crowds. Getting Holly to sleep at night is a constant battle as the infant is repeatedly woken by violent nocturnal sounds: shouting and screaming, horn-blowing taxis, pumping car stereos, and the sirens of speeding ambulances. Revellers have taken to running up the metal fire escape at the back of the flats and their favourite trick is to urinate down onto the residents' cars. Linda and Simon still love their flat, but the urban dream is beginning to sour. If this new bar opens it could be the last straw.

Although they have the right to object to licence applications, it can be very difficult for residents and small businesses to maintain their resistance to encroaching development. For those living near to city centre drinking circuits and other popular nightlife areas, the necessity to repeatedly object to new applications and variations can become stressful, frustrating, and time-consuming. Once they embark in correspondence with an applicant's lawyers, issues surrounding the apportionment of blame for environment stress, previously assumed to be self-evident, are immediately rendered ambiguous (see Chapter 7). Of course, the residents may have their own legal representation, but specialist barristers are few in number, costly, and sometimes reluctant to offend potentially lucrative (trade) clients.

Considerable effort is required of residents in preparing and presenting their case. Perhaps the two biggest obstacles are time and money. Residential objectors usually require financial and technical support from third parties, typically police, local authorities or trade protectionists. This form of co-operation can provide access to otherwise prohibitively expensive lawyers and expert opinion. If such backing cannot be found, the battle may be lost before it ever begins, as most objections are dropped.

On rare occasions residents would go it alone, ploughing through voluminous paperwork filled with legal and technical jargon. Sometimes residents would even present their own case. Such actions were risky, as even if they avoided incurring substantial legal expenses of their own, the financial implications of losing, were this to include an order to pay the applicant's costs, could be immense. Courts, and particularly crown courts, were often located far from objectors' homes. Moreover, hearings were invariably conducted during the day-time and on weekdays, requiring many lay objectors to arrange time off work or alternative care arrangements. Proceedings often went more slowly than predicted, with the witness required to wait for several hours to give testimony. Much of this waiting remained unexplained and witnesses could wait in vain, only to be told to return the next day. Pursuit of one's objection therefore required considerable commitment and sacrifice, including a preparedness to be guided by the dictates of the court and its open-ended use of time. For these reasons, many residential objectors were drawn from the ranks of the more affluent retired. As well as being 'time-rich', well-informed, articulate, and committed, objectors needed strong wills, thick skins and an even temperament in the face of hostile and sometimes intimidating cross-examination which might involve attacks on their personal integrity (see Chapter 8). Even if a case was won in the magistrates' court, the applicant could launch an appeal and the expense and trauma would begin again in the crown, and even High Court. Licensing cases were typically fought for several months, but could last for over two years.[4]

Campaigners

Colin (64), a retired university lecturer, has lived in Oldtown since his student days in the 1960s. Well-travelled, articulate and IT literate, he lives the frugal lifestyle of a middle class bohemian. Colin has always been drawn to public life and has been an active supporter and organizer

---

[4] Monbiot (2000: 130–131) raises similar concerns regarding the court-related experiences of lay objectors in planning appeals.

of various left-wing political causes. He devotes considerable time to his role as chair of the local civic trust. The purpose of this organization is to campaign for the preservation of Oldtown's historic centre. Colin has been monitoring trends in licensing over recent years and is concerned about an encroachment of branded bar chains, which he sees as undermining the distinctive and genteel character of the area. At a recent meeting, members of the trust voted to oppose all new licensing applications for the centre of Oldtown.

Campaigners are typically local community representatives, including politicians (MPs and councillors), who testify on behalf of their constituents. The most prominent campaigners are those who represent residents', community and amenity societies. Examples of such groups from across England include the Canterbury Alliance of Residents, Durham Civic Trust, Headingley Network (Leeds), the Redland and Cotham Amenities Society (Bristol) and the Soho Society (Flanagan 2005). Groups will often cast votes in relation to the pursuit of objections. Where a strong oppositional stance can be established, representatives of such groups may make frequent appearances in licensing trials as objection witnesses. These activities are supported by voluntary organizations such the Network of Residents' Associations (NORA) and the *Open All Hours Campaign*, an alliance of amenity groups, charities, and councillors, who lobby central government on licensing matters and exchange information of assistance to objectors.

Police

At one time, the police rarely objected to new licence applications provided they were satisfied that the premises would be competently operated by 'reputable' people. In recent years, some police forces have become more militant. As noted in Chapter 5, the explosion of the high street leisure market has placed a considerable burden on police resources and many people within local communities feel intimidated by activities in night-time public space. The high profile media reporting of city centre violence and the findings of community consultation exercises have often resulted in calls for police action to 'reclaim' urban centres at night (Hobbs et al. 2003: 103–104). Where these conditions pertain, police objectors may urge licensing authorities and the courts to give credence to the view that applications should be denied, as further expansion of the high street can only exacerbate existing problems (see Chapter 7).

Police witnesses may be drawn from all ranks and have a wide range of responsibilities within their organization. In many cases, dedicated police Licensing Officers will give evidence, together with other officers who have night-time operational experience. Where an objection is led by the police, submissions may be organized in such a way that officers from various ranks emphasize different aspects of the case, with even Chief Constables being known to enter the witness box. A Police Constable (PC), for example, might focus upon his or her experiences of operational policing and the processing of intoxicated arrestees, whilst an Inspector might present local crime data and CCTV footage, whilst outlining the impact of the NTE on broader policing strategy, resources and deployment.

Where the application is made by a high street chain, officers may present evidence from covert visits to other premises in the company's estate. Similarly, officers from other forces may be invited to offer their views on the suitability of the application. One force conducted a telephone survey to gather police opinion from around the country. However, as indicated in Chapter 3, police licensing departments are typically accorded low organizational priority and such concerted effort is rare.[5]

Sergeant Bill Stevens is approaching retirement, having spent 30 of his 51 years as a police officer. He started to deal with licensing enforcement issues as a Constable twenty years ago and has been Partytown's Licensing Officer for the past eight years. Bill has a heavy workload. There are over 500 licensed premises in the city centre and his responsibilities include issues as varied as criminal activity and money-laundering by licensees; the supervision of door staff; monitoring of operating standards/enforcement of the licensing laws; the processing of police input in new licence applications and reviews; and intelligence gathering with regard to intimidation, theft, fencing, illicit drug offences, and

---

[5] In only four cases did I see police attempting to survey other forces or invite officers from other areas to share their experiences of a brand. Police witnesses may sometimes be reluctant to come forward to give evidence on behalf of other forces. There are two primary reasons for this. Firstly, they may see admitting that problems have been experienced as an organizational failure on their own part, to which they do not wish to draw attention. Secondly, they may wish to avoid prejudicing their working relationship with the company.

alcohol-related violence. Bill and his secretary work alone from a cramped office in the central police station. He is contemplating retirement amid an avalanche of paperwork.

Despite the pressures, Bill enjoys his work. He performs a set of highly responsible and politicized tasks which belie his lowly rank. His experience and technical knowledge allow him to operate as an influential power broker in shaping governance of the night-time city. Although his stance is informed by general force priorities, he is a key adviser to senior officers in the shaping of licensing strategy. His day-to-day role involves the generation of compliance mostly through regular, personal, and informal contact with licensees and venue managers. He represents the trade's 'first port of call' for all police-related issues and exercises considerable discretion in how and when to apply 'the rules'.[6] Bill's main concern is to impose a set of police-defined minimum standards for the operation of licensed premises in the city and to apply them consistently. Bill knows that business people seek a 'level playing field' when it comes to regulation and feel compelled to respond to situations they perceive to be commercially disadvantageous. He therefore wants to 'keep the lid on' the number of late-licences and the number of new premises in certain areas, as he knows existing operators will react *en masse* to any new threats to their competitiveness. Unbridled competition within the NTE conflicts with police-defined conceptions of order.

As Bill's profile indicates, police Licensing Officers represent the order maintenance interests of the state in every-night regulation of the business community. In contested licensing matters, both sides may attempt to achieve a negotiated settlement (see Chapter 3). As in other spheres, the regulators attempt to 'enforce through persuasion—they advise, educate, bargain, negotiate, and reach compromise with the regulated' (Tombs 2002: 119, Pearce and Tombs 1998), applying both the carrot and the stick.[7]

---

[6] Unsurprisingly, companies will advise their managers to establish a good working relationship with their local Licensing Officer. The combination of lowly rank, relatively high levels of discretion and an often 'sociable' relationship between regulator and regulated, creates ample opportunities for corruption and favouritism. For this reason, many forces choose to change their Licensing Officers on a regular basis.

[7] Police objections and enforcement activity may be restricted by the threat of litigation. As Tony, a Licensing Officer from the West Midlands told me:

An Inspector now has the power to close down any licensed premises for a limited period, just on his say-so. The first Inspector who does it, of course, runs the risk of getting his arse sued off. Ha, ha, ha, . . . we live in that sort of business I'm afraid!

Despite the police preference for informal and locally-constituted modes of regulation, the development strategies of the bar chains remain outside the remit of licensees and regional management. Such decisions are made by senior executives in far-flung head offices. Thus, although a company's local representatives may have nurtured strong links with the police, perhaps through participation in a vibrant Pubwatch scheme (Hadfield and contributors 2004a), hawks at head office may ultimately regard 'business as war' (Punch 1996: 228–229), destroying carefully nurtured goodwill in the ruthless and single-minded pursuit of prized sites.

The resource constraints placed upon police licensing departments are often matched by senior officers' wishes to avoid becoming embroiled in costly legal battles with developers. Decisions to object are not made lightly and occur only where the higher ranks have made a strong commitment to the view that such conflict is a necessary cost of proactive policing. This stance usually emerges only after sustained attempts to work 'in partnership' with business have floundered. The presence of police officers as objection witnesses in court is therefore salient in indicating the breakdown of routine non-litigious communication between the public and private sector.

Leisure industry competitors

Many objections are motivated by trade protectionism. Protectionists (acting either individually or as a consortium) will typically seek to mirror the stance of other objectors in their expression of crime, disorder and nuisance concerns. In many cases, trade objectors choose not to make their own representations, preferring to act as advisers to other parties such as local residents, for whom they may underwrite some, if not all, legal expenses (see Chapter 3). Trade backing can provide substantial assistance to an objector's cause, both financially and through the utilization of established links with elite advocates and specialist legal teams.

Local authorities

During the research period (2000–2005), a number of local authorities, when adjudicating the old PEL system, were seeking to impose 'saturation policies'. This involved applying a presumption against the grant of new licences, and variations to existing licences, which would result in increased capacities or extensions to late-night trading. In attempting to protect what they regarded to be the public interest, such authorities had to be willing and able to engage in incessant, prolonged and robust litigation. The City of Westminster, the UK's largest licensing authority, had to deal with around fifty appeals against its decisions at any one time and incurred legal expenses in excess of £2 million per annum. Whilst the Westminster experience was undoubtedly extreme, it was also instructive in indicating the leisure industry's willingness to challenge market interventions regardless of the considerable time, effort and expense involved.

As the respondents to an appeal, local authorities would call a range of in-house witnesses, notably, the Licensing Department Manager. These officials were responsible for defence of the licensing committee's decisions and general policy stance. Council witnesses might also include members of the licensing inspection and/or noise teams, and, in some cases, Environmental Health Officers. Other objectors such as residents and police officers, together with experts, might also have been called. Under the new system, licences may only be denied if and when a representation is received from an external source (see Chapter 3). Special Saturation Policies may be applied in cases where representations have been made; however, each case must be judged on merit and the *Guidance* places onerous responsibilities on the licensing authority and objectors to provide evidence of a link between new openings and rises in crime, disorder and nuisance. In appeal cases, the new licensing authorities are again named as respondent and trials may proceed as before, with the authority calling witnesses in its defence.

Applicants

Simon Bull is a tall, 39-year-old man of athletic build. He has a tanned complexion and short greying hair. Immaculately groomed and exquisitely dressed in a navy blue suit, pale blue shirt and mauve silk tie, he swears the oath, gives his full name and address and confirms his title as Chief Executive of *Chuck City Bars Plc*. Simon is taken through his statement by counsel, Sir Timothy Davenport QC. He begins by listing his previous experience in a number of senior roles within the leisure industry, including Chief Executive and Operations Director of a high street fast food chain and Deputy Operations Director responsible for new development acquisitions at a pub company. Simon appears immediately to be a confident and impressive witness.

Throughout the history of licensing, regulatory authorities have taken a keen interest in the personal character of the licence holder (Kolvin 2004). All activities occurring in or around licensed premises have been regarded, to a large extent, as the responsibility of those whose names are displayed above the door. The sale of drink, in particular, has been regarded as a responsible task, to be performed only by a 'fit and proper person'.[8]

At trial, applicants will attempt to convince licensing committees, magistrates and the judiciary of their professional experience, competence, and good character. This approach is adopted regardless of the manner in which, in the context of the contemporary high street, an applicant's *personal* responsibilities for the day-to-day running of the business may recede. Those who testify at trial are invariably senior figures such as Chief Executives, Managing Directors, Estates Managers, and Operations Managers—people at the very pinnacle of their organizations—working, primarily, from a desk in head office.[9] This is not to suggest that applicants omit to describe the manner in which premises are to be run. On the contrary (as we shall see in Chapter 7), this theme lies at the very heart of their submissions. Evidence of this type is typically delivered by Operations Managers who are responsible for the general orchestration of day-to-day trading practice across the company's estate. Giving evidence under oath in relation to operational procedure is not a task entrusted to the person actually selected to perform this role; the corporate chains do not present their prospective venue managers for judicial scrutiny. Benches are simply assured that the local manager will be experienced, fully trained and suitably qualified in accordance with company practice.

Possible reasons for the omission of more junior staff as application witnesses may be implied from the analysis of strategic

---

[8] This focus upon individual responsibility is strengthened under the Act by the introduction of 'personal licences' (see Chapter 3).

[9] Of course, venue managers/licensees do appear as application witnesses in trials involving smaller, independent and locally-based businesses.

interaction in Chapter 8. At this juncture, it may suffice to note that, in their courtroom performances, applicants will attempt to convey impressions of honourable, benign, even philanthropic intent. Outside the witness box, more candid views may be expressed. For example, in the course of a pre-trial conference with police objectors, one leisure executive was heard to comment that when his venue opened, people in the town would 'get hurt'. The police voiced their concern about the aggressive tone of this statement. When later asked to explain his comment to the court, the applicant maintained that he had simply meant that local competitors would experience a drop in profits. Regardless of one's favoured interpretation, such exchanges served to frankly expose the cultural dissonance between the police in their role as guardians of civil order and the 'economic mind-frame' (Punch 1996: 240) of a private sector elite.

Supporters of the application

Mike is 22 and is taking a gap year after university. He has returned to his parents' house and is working in a call centre before he starts his 'proper job'. He used to enjoy working behind the bar at a late-night branded venue in his university city. All his friends in the rugby team would come down for cheap drinks and a laugh on the Wednesday 'student nights'. Nightlife in his home town is rather dull by comparison. He has heard that a new *Chucker's Bar* might be opening to replace the old cinema. He thinks the cinema is crap because it's too small and doesn't show a wide enough selection of films. *Chucker's* would be much better; just what the town needs.

In many trials, applicants will present evidence to indicate local community support for their proposals. A popular approach is to commission market research, or, if the application pertains to longer hours or increased capacity within established premises, to conduct a survey of consumer attitudes. These methods may be augmented by the use of lay people as witnesses, where, for example, the witness describes a visit to an existing venue within the chain, which they then go on to favourably differentiate from an area's existing entertainment facilities. Such demonstrations of support are important for three reasons: firstly, to indicate that the development is supported by at least some, if not many, local people; secondly, to offer an alternative perspective to that of the residential objector (at best, a view which appears more balanced, reasonable and representative); and thirdly, to negate the charge that the development is an externally directed imposition.

Supporters of the application are typically drawn from the local residential population and/or from users of the night-time city. Their methods of selection are transparently reactive in that their demographic profile tends to be indicative of some allegedly desirable feature of the proposed venue (for example, its broad age range of customers):

Geraldine, a 42-year-old mother of three, is a nurse. She likes to go dancing with her daughters and nieces and sometimes hires a minibus to go clubbing twenty miles away in Drainville. There's loads of bars in Drainville and they usually end the night in *Marrakesh,* a big nightclub that plays party records from the 1970s and 1980s. Geraldine says she prefers *Marrakesh* to the 'trendy' clubs in her home town of Mossfield, because, even though most of the customers are much younger than her, she enjoys the music and atmosphere. She is delighted to hear that a new *Marrakesh* might be opening next door to *J.D. Wetherspoon* in the old *Kwik Save* building on Mossfield High Street.

This witness selection process forms part of the delicate pre-trial crafting of cases and is closely associated with both the construction of arguments (to be discussed in the next chapter) and subsequent tactics of advocacy, described in Chapter 8. Such instrumentalism is never more apparent than in the commissioning of 'independent' opinion from professional witnesses.

Expert witnesses and licensing consultants

Julie Stevens (54) is self-employed and runs a market research company from a mailbox address in the depths of rural Herefordshire. She has acted as a witness in licensing trials for over twenty years and her list of clients includes most of the major names in the drinks and leisure industries. Her business operates on a national basis and she regularly finds herself in licensed premises, legal briefings and courtrooms, hundreds of miles from home. Julie provides evidence to the courts in the form of market research surveys. Her surveys measure issues such as customers' views of the premises; basic demographic information; modes of transport to and from an area; and customers' experiences of crime and disorder—both as victims and offenders. Of course, the questions explored in her surveys differ from case to case, but they always aim to inform the arguments put forward by the lawyers who commission her. Julie is an established team player who enjoys good ongoing relationships with her clients. Her reports are drafted in such a way as to complement the statements of other consultants typically selected by applicants, such as noise experts, surveyors, traffic consultants, and former police officers.

In many cases, ostensibly independent commentators may be commissioned to 'assist the court' in understanding and weighing opposing arguments and interpretations. Such witnesses are typically professional persons who enjoy some form of current or retrospective experience and/or training, which permits them to proffer opinions on various aspects of a case. They are typically chosen by counsel and commissioned by the parties' solicitors. For such persons, the preparation and delivery of testimony forms part of a range of (usually) self-employed business activity, and competent performance in the witness box constitutes one of a number of services they provide for their clients. These professional participants may be divided into two, to some extent, amorphous groups: 'licensing consultants' and 'experts'.

Licensing consultants rely primarily upon accumulated experience, skills and insight, rather than formal accreditation. Their ranks include ex-police officers (typically Licensing Officers, or those with operational experience of public order policing), private investigators, and retired licensees. Experts, by comparison, make claims to legitimate speech derived from academic qualifications and recognition within some specialized field of knowledge and practice. Expert witnesses may be drawn from a wide range of professions, including market research, acoustics, transport and land surveying, and academia (for example, criminology, psychology and statistics).

For many licensing consultants, and some experts, conducting investigations, writing reports and giving evidence in relation to licensing cases may provide full-time work. Parties will often employ the same counsel and group of professional witnesses in each case, presenting broadly similar evidence regardless of local peculiarity (see Chapter 7). For those selected by counsel to conduct regular work on behalf of corporate clients, the provision of consultancy services can, at least in the short-term, prove to be financially lucrative. Due to their financial muscle and usually superior legal resources, the trade have access to many more professional witnesses than do objectors.[10] Applicants regularly submit legal cost inventories of £50–100,000 much of which is incurred in the procurement of expert opinion. During periods of rapid high street expansion, even consultants brought in on an ad hoc, case-by-case basis may find themselves regular participants in licensing trials across the UK.

As described in the Postscript to this book, the work of consultants and experts will usually involve visiting both the location to which the application refers and other existing premises controlled by the applicant. Consultants with a police, military, or security background may be employed by companies to act as private investigators to observe, and in some instances, covertly film and record, activities in and around the premises of competitors. These tactics were particularly apparent in relation to the thorny issue of compliance with the Licensing Act 1964 s 77 (see Chapter 3) and would sometimes be used to support trade objections. Local authorities might similarly have used consultants' reports in appeal cases to inform and augment the testimonies of their licensing inspection team.

Each party would invariably present largely conflicting expert opinion. If one's opponent had commissioned an expert, it was often deemed necessary to commission counter-opinion in order to avoid being placed at a disadvantage before the court. If professional witnesses were evenly matched in their ability to present credible and persuasive evidence, the impact of such evidence—in relation to each side's case—would be effectively neutralized and balance would be restored. The introduction of expert evidence followed a disease model—one side introduced a virus to which the other side sought an antidote. Ideally, the antidote would prove powerful enough, not only to stem progress of the disease, but also to provide effective immunity and promote the health of one's case.

In many instances, experts were commissioned solely to provide what will be referred to as 'negative' evidence. Negative evidence was derived not from one's own primary investigation of the

---

[10] The commissioning of external opinion is also linked to regulatory shifts. For example, new instructions on the presentation of police evidence pertaining to nuisance and disorder contained in the Justices' Clerks' Society's *Good Practice Guide* (1999) (see Chapter 3) gave rise to increased police demand for expert witnesses.

material facts of a case, but rather from an analysis of secondary sources, chiefly witness statements and other documentation submitted by one's opponents.[11] Where evidence is wholly negative, the role of the expert witness is reduced to its most basic and functional form: the presentation of criticism, counter-argument, and contradictory discourse. The submission of negative testimony could be contrasted with more robust approaches which combined deductive critique of an opponent's position with inductive analysis derived from first-hand experience.

The licensing industry

Many commercial players viewed the licensing process with contempt. For corporate culture, the complexities of 'bureaucratic red tape' and regulatory 'obstruction' were matched only by an irrepressible economic incentive for their circumvention (Punch 1996, Slapper and Tombs 1999). As in other spheres of regulatory practice, such as planning law, a whole legal and extra-legal industry had developed to assist applicants in their navigation of rough regulatory waters (Monbiot 2000: 130–131). The successful anchoring of prized development sites was achieved by commissioning the allied services of law firms, consultancy companies, individual experts, and trade-affiliated public relations organizations. At the helm of this trans-regulatory enterprise there lay a small and elite band of specialist licensing barristers. The following chapter examines the role of these 'generals', recounting how they prepared for battle.

[11] Here the use of time as a weapon was exposed; the preparation and submission of negative evidence depending entirely upon the willingness of one's opponents to disclose documentation in advance. In the interests of procedural fairness, mutual disclosure timetables were arranged as part of the pre-trial shaping of cases. The attempt to present new evidence at trial could therefore give rise to complaint on the grounds of admissibility.

7

Rose-coloured Spectacles Versus the Prophecies of Doom (the Shaping of Trial Discourse)

... there has been, before the trial, a great deal of preliminary preparation, but the judge has not been concerned with it. Each party prepares his own case separately and, so far as he is permitted to do so, conceals his preparations from the other side (Devlin 1979: 56).

The adversary system

An understanding of the role of counsel, and of the magistrates and/or the judge (henceforth referred to as 'the bench'), is a prerequisite to the analysis of social interaction in the courtroom. Licensing trials are shaped by the basic assumptions and commitments of an adversarial system of adjudication that is characteristic of the common law courts. In accordance with this tradition, 'conduct of the litigation up to the point of trial is left entirely in the hands of the parties' with procedure 'designed to concentrate the judicial function into one continuous hearing' (Egglestone 1975: 429). At trial, evidence is presented and elicited by the parties, who question one another in turn. The role of the bench in fact-finding is essentially passive. Benches are 'forbidden to call witnesses or to examine them otherwise than for the purpose of clarifying their evidence where it is unclear' (ibid.). Thus, the bench sit to 'hear and determine the issues raised by the parties, not to conduct an investigation or examination on behalf of society at large' (Lord Denning, cited in Egglestone, ibid.).

The peculiarity of this approach becomes clear when compared with other legal systems, such as the continental European model, where 'adjudication has a more inquisitorial character and where it is not uncommon for the judge to direct the collection of evidence and to stimulate lines of enquiry' (Galligan 1996: 244).

In contrast to the court-directed inquisitorial hearing, the adversarial trial is a 'war of words, a battle between two opposing sides, each of which contends that its interpretation . . . is correct' (Danet and Bogoch 1980: 36). As Devlin explains, the essential differences between the two systems are apparent from their names: 'one is a trial of strength and the other is an inquiry' (1979: 54).

In the adversarial system, the bench act as umpires or arbiters. At the opening of a licensing trial, they are usually naïve as to the substance of the proceedings. Protocol requires that both parties disclose their evidence in advance of the hearing, but the bench are not obliged to read this material before the trial begins. Their first knowledge of a case will often be gleaned from the opening statements of counsel.

Partiality

Above all, if anything was to be achieved, it was necessary to reject from the start any thought of possible guilt. There was no guilt . . . To this end one should . . . concentrate as far as possible on considerations which worked to one's own advantage (Kafka 1994: 99).

Legal scholars have identified fundamental deficiencies of the adversarial process, arising principally from its systematic encouragement of partisanship (Danet and Bogoch 1980, Ellison 2001, Egglestone 1975, Langbein 2003). The system is premised on the assumption that 'truth' is 'best discovered by powerful statements on both sides of the question' (Lord Eldon, cited in Egglestone 1975: 429). Each side is understood to be gathering, selecting and presenting evidence for its own strategic purposes and it is assumed that if each party is allowed to 'dig for the facts that help it . . . between them, they will bring all to light' (Devlin 1979: 60). The bench must decide each case on the basis of this information alone. Clearly, this process contrasts sharply with inquisitorial modes of adjudication in which independent forensic investigators decide the case in the light of information they themselves have collected and analysed. As Devlin (ibid.: 54) puts it, the bench 'do not pose questions and seek answers; they weigh such material as is put before them, but have no responsibility for seeing that it is complete'.

In adversarial trials, it is the parties and their lawyers who define the parameters of the contest. They 'introduce such evidence as they think fit and advance such legal propositions as seem appropriate to them' (Connolly 1975: 439). The system encourages and rewards lawyers for 'using all tactics at their disposal, even those which may seem ethically questionable, such as suppressing evidence, in order to win cases' (Danet and Bogoch 1980: 36, Freedman 1975). With the bench placed 'above the fray' (Langbein 2003: 311), opportunities for the parties to frame and delimit the boundaries of debate are intrinsic to the process. Each battle is orchestrated and controlled by the parties; it is they who select the witnesses, strategically organize the evidence, and ask the questions. The licensing trial is thereby dominated by lawyers and, in particular, by counsel.

Counsel: writers and directors of the script

Charles Britton QC (54) was educated at Eton School and Oxford University and has spent much of his life surrounded by the cloisters and manicured lawns of England's traditional upper class institutions. His chambers overlook a tranquil square bordered by beautiful limestone buildings which shield it from the hustle and bustle of Central London. Charles specializes in licensing work and has become a celebrated advocate, noted for his tact, guile, and fearsome intellect. He represents applicants nationwide and has been instructed in a number of legally significant cases. Charles has a contractual relationship with *Aggro Inns Plc*. He has agreed to supply all *Aggro's* advocacy requirements in exchange for the assurance that he will not represent objectors or competitors in any litigation against the company. Fluent in French and German, in his leisure time Charles attends a gentleman's club in Mayfair, and as often as he can, indulges his passion for sailing. It is now eight years since Charles represented an objector; they can't afford his fees.

Barristers who specialize in licensing are mostly middle-aged, uppermiddle class, and almost invariably male. They often share common educational backgrounds and interests in travel, leisure and the arts. These personal biographies inform and ease their interactions within the insular and exclusive social world of their profession (Pannick 1992). Only a small number operate regularly on the national stage and their work is often associated with particular clients, especially the larger bar and pub chains.

In order to execute each case, counsel must decide what strategy to adopt, what pre-trial negotiations should take place, what sort of evidence should be presented, which consultants and experts should be commissioned, and which lay witnesses should be approached and called. They must advise clients on the best course of action: the empirical and legal strengths of opposing arguments; the balancing of various factors when striking 'out of court' deals; the progress of the case and its likelihood of success; the decision to appeal. Moreover, within the courtroom, it is they who organize and submit the central argument; ask the questions; control the pace, order, and detail of witness evidence (see Chapter 8). Precluded from giving evidence (although, in the cases observed, they often did), counsel's task involved the extraction of testimony, both from their own, and their opponent's witnesses. Counsel would assist their client by forcefully presenting and defending what was ostensibly, 'his' or 'her' point of view. In so doing, as adversarial tradition would have it, they also assisted the court in determining the relative plausibility and import of the evidence.

The occupational morality of counsel

Advocates are, by definition, partial. At trial, their role is to *advocate* a cause, regardless of their personal convictions, opinions, or principles. Thus, although they may not truly believe what they are saying, they will act as though they do. As Pannick opines:

The professional function of the advocate is, essentially, one of supreme, even sublime, indifference to much of what matters in life. He must advance one point of view, irrespective of its inadequacies. He must belittle other interests, whatever their merits . . . It is not for counsel appearing in court to express equivocation, to recognize ambiguity or to doubt instructions. His client is right and his opponent is wrong (Pannick 1992: 1–2).

Unlike witnesses, advocates are at liberty to change emphasis, make contradictory statements, and even to develop and submit completely opposing arguments from one trial to the next. Indeed, a detailed understanding of 'both sides of the question' is essential to counsel, as it enables them to construct their cases more effectively. In everyday social interaction, such inconsistency would be regarded as manipulative, amoral even. Yet, the norms of professional advocacy are quite distinct from those of lay communication. In donning the wig and gown, counsel effectively claim legitimate exemption from the everyday interactional order, assuming the mantle of licensed interrogator and denouncer (Garfinkel 1956). The ethical codes of advocacy both permit and justify the separation of personal values from the execution of one's brief (Du Cann 1964: 34, 39–40, Rock 1993: 39) and the ultimate goal of the trial advocate is persuasion:

The orator, as Socrates emphasized in his criticism of advocacy, does not teach juries and other bodies about right and wrong—he merely persuades them. He seeks to accomplish this task by using whatever arguments are likely to be effective in the tribunal before which he is appearing. He does not confine himself to those points which he thinks are correct. He does not pause to assess whether his submissions have academic respectability . . . the advocate will base his efforts on points which are persuasive, which 'look like the truth, even if they do not correspond with it exactly' (Pannick: 1992: 2, including citation from Cicero 1971).

Trials are won and lost through argumentation and in attempting to persuade the bench, 'words are his tools . . . they must always be to hand' (Du Cann 1964: 46). Effective advocates tend to be highly articulate and sophisticated language users, well versed in the 'art of proving by words multiplied for the purpose, that white is black and black is white, according as they are paid' (Swift 1726, cited in Pannick 1992: 128). Moreover, they need to be single-minded, determined, and creative in pursuing their goals: 'whatever the point to be argued, the resourceful counsel will be able to find some law to support him' (Pannick, ibid.: 51). This persistence must be matched by an ability to focus the attention of the bench on 'anything other than the central weaknesses of a client's case' (Pannick: ibid.: 2).

As McBarnet (1981: 17) notes, 'far from being "the truth", the whole truth, and nothing but the truth' cases are biased constructs which manipulate and edit the 'raw material' of witnesses' accounts. Cases are therefore 'partial in both senses—partisan and incomplete' (ibid.). The routine suppression of ambiguity and doubt and the practice of omitting evidence that is considered 'unhelpful' to one's case is supported by the basic adversarial tenet that the 'truth' will best emerge 'from an orchestrated clash of opposing views' (Ellison 2001: 51). If omission is regarded as a form of lie (Barnes 1994), then, ironically, legal tradition would seem to promote the assumption that 'lies can be a mechanism for producing truth' (Bok 1978: 161). At the same time, adversarial theory provides a ready stock of neutralizations for those lawyers inclined to the opinion that one's ends may justify one's means (Langbein 2003: 306–309).[1]

Preparing for battle

An advocate's professional reputation is measured by trial success, the keys to which lie in successful mastery of each brief. Good preparation requires co-operation from a diligent instructing solicitor. Although sometimes acting as solicitor advocates, licensing solicitors more often play a supporting role to counsel. Solicitors will typically co-ordinate the preparation of cases: contacting and corresponding with their own side's witnesses and their opponent's lawyers; arranging case conferences; obtaining documents and ensuring that important deadlines are met. Expert witnesses may be asked to produce confidential briefing notes in relation to the witness statements of opponents. These are used to assist counsel in the preparation of cross-examination. New arguments and sources of information may be sought such as the latest research, or official crime statistics. Case law is dissected and its legal implications interpreted. Professional witnesses may be sent on last-minute errands in order to clarify some contested fact. These

---

[1] In his defence of advocacy, Pannick (1992) cites the promotion of 'free speech' as a higher duty of the advocate which overrides his or her obligation to the court and to the promotion of just outcomes. Although Pannick candidly admits that acting in the interests of one's client 'does not always promote the interests of society in general' (p.7), from his perspective, the advocate is obligated to promote the cause of each client to the best of his ability, using all means at his disposal that fall within the law. This must include, 'any client, no matter how unmeritorious the case, no matter how great a rascal the man may be . . . no matter how undeserving or unpopular his cause' (p.90), or however unjust or unfair the result. Pannick's view of professional ethics rests upon the 'cab-rank rule' wherein the advocate must, wherever possible, work for any client who requests his or her services. This rule is seen as functional for society in that it ensures that everyone is offered the opportunity to have their case presented forcefully by a legal representative (pp.132–137). Yet, the rank can only function if every customer can afford the fare. Pannick's arguments depend entirely upon the generous provision of legal aid. In licensing, where objectors have no access to public funding, opportunities to commission specialist counsel are stratified in relation to power, wealth and influence. Langbein (2003: 102–103), in his historically informed critique of the adversarial trial, refers to this as the 'wealth effect'.

are 'backstage' activities in which only a trusted inner circle will participate (Goffman 1959: 116–136). As the date of the hearing approaches, counsel will draft a 'skeleton argument' outlining the main legal and evidential bases of their submission. In court, solicitors will closely follow proceedings; often transcribing in shorthand. Following instructions from counsel, they may also co-ordinate the scheduling of witness evidence.

The tactical intuitions and communicative skills of experienced advocates permit a fluidity and spontaneity of performance that can significantly enhance the presentation of each case. Yet, counsel cannot rely solely upon accomplished oratory. The seemingly effortless and polished performances of the courtroom mask considerable preparation, in relation not only to the form in which a case is presented, but also with regard to its *content*. As Ellison (2001: 51) notes, 'in examination-in-chief a barrister does not simply seek to elicit relevant factual information from a witness, but to promote a version of reality in antithesis to the account advanced by the other side'.

The framing of arguments and the writing of scripts

'Witnesses are the fodder of the courts' (Rock 1993: 39) and counsel will take great care in gathering a team of witnesses—preferably, a tried and tested team—for each case. Both professional and lay witnesses have their uses: supporters of the application and residents provide authenticity (accounts of empirical matters and an ostensive link to the sensibilities of the local community); consultants provide detailed description; police officers and experts add analysis and an aura of legitimacy. Counsel work closely with witnesses, briefing each in advance, and editing, shaping, and approving their written submissions. Case construction in licensing requires techniques through which a large body of disparate information can be given coherent form. The strategic organization of evidence is of crucial importance to the presentation of a persuasive case. The key to successful preparation is to develop a basic theory or storyline (Bennett and Feldman 1981) and to identify themes that will provide the bench with a framework for interpretation (Ellison 2001). This involves the fashioning of what will be termed the 'evidential script'.

Script writing is a strategic interpretive process which counsel use to 'frame' evidence and arguments for the purposes of an adversarial trial. The script must have an internal coherence, even though, as an adversarial device, it 'is not by definition about "truth" or "reality" or a quest for them, but about arguing a case' (McBarnet 1981: 17). Thus, 'the good advocate grasps at complex confused reality and constructs a simple, clear-cut account of it . . . an account edited with vested interests in mind' (ibid.). The purpose of the script is to enhance the credibility of one's case, presenting a favourable picture that will gain the respect and sympathy of the bench. It will therefore seek to 'propose and prefer certain meanings over others' (Brown 1991: 17). Script writing involves the art of manipulation and persuasion rather than the ingenuous collection, analysis and reporting of facts. The advocate's concern is to tell a 'good story', not necessarily a wholly truthful or accurate one (McBarnet 1981: 19). Good stories are credible and believable, but not necessarily 'true'. Counsel's opponent will construct a rival viewpoint, an 'antithesis' (Rock 1993: 33). The adversarial ethos ensures that it is left largely to the parties to reveal inconsistencies and errors in each others' scripts, if and when they can. Working from a prepared script allows counsel to control the case, applying their own instrumental order and logic to the evidence. Scripted evidence, 'with its ambiguities and ifs and buts filtered out' is more malleable than the messy welter of social reality and therefore more suited to being moulded into an easily-digestible, consistent and per-suasive case (Bennett and Feldman 1981, McBarnet 1981: 22–23).

The clash of scripts involves the imposition of opposing frames of reference and meaning, and serves to obliterate any semblance of the disinterested pursuit of knowledge. As the scripts are placed before a naïve audience, both sides are able to exaggerate aspects of social reality. The application script offers a construction as viewed through 'rose-coloured spectacles'. According to this view, the application involves routine, benign and non-controversial aspects of general business practice. Issues of controversy and dis-sent are screened out, scaled down, or dissociated from the issues at hand. The applicant's proposals are thereby presented as non-threatening and almost entirely risk-free. By contrast, the objec-tion script may be thought of as a 'prophecy of doom' in which the night-time high street is portrayed as at tipping point, teeter-ing on the brink of anarchy. The applicant's proposed ameliora-tion efforts are largely dismissed as inadequate in the face of an area's pre-existent and seemingly intractable problems. Licensed development is regarded as the generator of an incremental and largely irreversible process of decay.

These opposing frames infuse evidential scripts and can be traced in the minutiae of courtroom interaction. Thus, when the interrogator asks a question, he or she does so from within a particular schema or frame of reference; 'on the other hand, the person who answers a question also has his or her schema . . . which may or may not match that of the questioner' (Shuy 1993: 189). Importantly, the court, and counsel in particular, *expect* witnesses to favour one interpretation over the other, regardless of the weight of evidence, or persuasiveness of an opponent's testimony (Shuy 1993: 188–193). To allude to the messy ambiguities of a situation is simply to *concede*: a point to the opposition.

The following paragraphs will explore the content of opposing scripts. As we shall see, script writing relies upon a variety of stock arguments and concepts which may be moulded into a tried and tested pitch: a discursive formula of persuasion.

The argument pool

The advocate had an inexhaustible supply of speeches like this. They were repeated at every visit (Kafka 1994: 97).

The following typology presents what will be referred to as an 'argument pool', which may be defined as a set of pre-established, yet fluid, and constantly mutating, adversarial devices. The argument pool was developed from the thematic content analysis of field notes, witness statements, and other legal documents relating to oral and written evidence in over fifty licensing cases.

A case is scripted by selecting a set of plausible and interconnected arguments from the pool. These arguments are then rehearsed in the testimonies of each witness in order to convey impressions of consistency, whilst 'hammering one's message home'. Although scripts are frameworks which afford structure to various forms of evidence, they are never adhered to rigidly in their practical application. Arguments drawn from the pool serve as flexibly applied and adaptive resources for legal practitioners, their clients and other witnesses. They address basic themes in licensing around which the particularities of each individual case may be creatively explored. As such, they offer practical weapons of choice for legal duelling.

'Fine food and agreeable company': defensive arguments

Defensive arguments seek to counter or downplay objections.

1. Quality and standards

Quality and standards arguments emphasize the credentials of the applicant and their intentions, and proven abilities, to deliver a quality product. Arguments of this form were used in every one of the cases encountered. This type of evidence has its origins in ancient and morally laden assessments of the 'fit and proper person'. As Brown notes with regard to criminal defendants, it is assumed that the bench will assess applicants against criteria similar to those of control theory (Hirschi 1969)—by looking for 'signs of attachment, commitment, involvement, and belief'—their 'sociological assumptions resting on the premise that weak social bonds are the key causative factors in deviant behaviour' (Brown 1991: 27).

Assessments of personal character remain salient within the licensing court, despite being undercut by commercial changes which have considerably diminished their practical import. As noted in Chapter 6, in the vast majority of trials attended, application witnesses were either head office-based chief executives of national or regional chains, or local independent owners and entrepreneurs. The absence from the witness box of branch managers and other members of the lower orders allowed evidence to focus largely upon sterile accounts of corporate vision and strategy, rather than the rich messiness of local operational particularity. The quality and standards of a company's human resources were demonstrated through an emphasis on general indices and descriptions of professional practice. This involved the outlining of organizational rules and aspirations in relation to staff training and accredited knowledge of the law and 'best practice'. Where the bench introduced questions relating to the personal attributes of frontline staff, these were simply met by assurances of experience, responsibility, trustworthiness, and regular executive-level supervision.

Well prepared quality and standards arguments emphasized professionalism throughout the business plan and proposed schedule of operation. Operational issues typically encompassed by this argument set included: a safe and controlled environment; high quality design and décor; comfortable furnishings; standardized and non-contentious entertainment and drugs policies; high-tech security hardware; professional and council/police approved 'door supervisors'; proactive management techniques; quality food offer; premium drinks pricing; and a strict admissions policy. This adversarial checklist was used to denote the targeting of an older, more affluent, and discerning crowd.[2] A popular approach was to portray one's proposals as invoking a shift up-market that involved clear and welcome dissonance from the visceral and hedonistic mores of binge-drinking culture.

Quality and standards arguments infused the testimonies of trade-commissioned expert witnesses. The following extract was typical:

The availability of three bars in the premises generally ensured that queuing for drinks was minimized and even at the maximum capacity, when people were being politely turned away at the door, it rarely took more than a few minutes to be served. Additional table service was also available. The atmosphere resembled very much that of a party for most of the evening and night. We also encountered groups of businessmen and women who had been attending training courses and awards ceremonies and had chosen the venue for their night out. Many of these people were older than one normally encounters in city centre bars— some in their late 40s and 50s.

In presenting scripted quality and standards arguments, large companies operating a chain of premises appeared to derive some benefit from brand awareness and the ability to demonstrate previous examples of good practice. This issue illuminates

---

[2] Carefully scripted quality and standards arguments often meet with cynicism from professional objectors. As one of Hobbs et al.'s (2003: 259) police informants opined:

Whenever you get an application they never say this pub is going to be for drunken young people who are just out of school, still chewing gum, while drinking from the neck of a bottle and talking about school; they never come to the court and say that. They always say 'well, this is a different pub now; now; it's a different image to all the others which you've granted. This is for the more mature, more discerning drinker and look at our wonderful menu'; and it's a load of bollocks basically and I know that it is at the time. I've been doing this job long enough to know it's the same application done by a different solicitor every time, you know, same keywords, same trigger words, and nothing changes.

186 Contemporary Contestations

interconnections between the homogenization on the night-time high street and the regulatory 'squeezing out' of independent operators, alternative venues, and long-established, more community-based, forms of nightlife. The argument set was used to imply that the 'law is largely respected by the regulated: and that where regulations are flouted, this tends to be on the part of marginal, less responsible, usually "small", companies' (Tombs 2002: 115).[3]

Quality and standards: counter-arguments

The moot point with regard to 'quality and standards' is the degree to which well-managed premises can be said to contribute to problems of on-street crime and disorder. The main rebuttal to the argument involves an acknowledgement of the necessity of good management, paired with a denial of its sufficiency. In countering quality and standards evidence, objectors might well concede that poorly managed premises are likely to account for a disproportionate amount of violence and disorder within their premises and also among their patrons once they have left. However, the objector might also point out that the issue is one of *proportionality*. Perhaps even well-run premises contribute to the problems arising in an area; albeit to a lesser degree? The expectation that licensed premises will be well-run is thus regarded as a necessary, but not in itself sufficient, safeguard with regard to environmental impact.

More specifically, the objector may assert that whilst it is, of course, preferable that licensed premises be well-run, even well-run premises can and do give rise to local problems, particularly when located in close proximity to each other. Strong management and responsible operating practices can help to prevent disorderly behaviour *within* premises, but can do relatively little to influence the behaviour of people as they move between venues or after they have left venues at the end of the night. The clear implication of this is that even applications from operators

---

[3] See also Chatteron and Hollands (2003), Neame (2003). As Chatterton (2002) notes, regulation is often applied differentially to the detriment of small scale local entrepreneurs who are regarded as unknown or risky entities. The 'risky' label can also be applied to alternative music-focused venues, which, despite generating generally lower levels of violence, are sometimes associated with illegal drug use and professional criminal activity (see Chapter 4).

with impeccable credentials need to be considered carefully with due regard to their businesses' potential impact upon a proposed location.

It may be added that the on-street environment in nightlife areas will often be quite different from that to be found within well-run licensed premises it may be crowded, chaotic, and frustrating. Within this context it is also important to note that people of any age or social background, if intoxicated and placed under adverse conditions on the streets late at night, can 'misbehave'. Their misdemeanours may not amount to acts of violence or criminal damage, but might well be expressed as noisy exuberance and emotional, argumentative, or otherwise 'difficult' behaviour. Such problems can be exacerbated in an environment in which people are forced to compete for scarce resources such as late-night transport and fast food.

This set of primary counter-arguments seeks to minimize, and to some degree, side-step, the main thrust of quality and standards arguments. In the majority of cases, advocates regarded it as unnecessary, or even counter-productive, for objection witnesses to challenge the reputation of the applicant. In other cases, quality and standards assertions were met 'head on'.

A number of branded chains are now inextricably linked to the night-time high street (see Chapter 3), which is, in turn, often justifiably associated with alcohol-related crime and disorder (see Chapters 1 and 5). Brand awareness can therefore be something of a double-edged sword. As well as being able to demonstrate examples of 'good practice', national brands are also open to accusations of malpractice. Accusations may be built upon evidence of, for example, staff and/or customer violence; irresponsible drinks promotions; or drug-related activity. Due to the size of their estate, some national brands can face situations where a licence revocation, £1-a-pint-offer, or assault by door staff in Newquay might be brought to the attention of a licensing court in Newcastle.[4] When such evidence is presented, it tends to be taken very seriously by the court, and especially by the applicant's lawyers, who make stringent efforts to refute, deflect, and diffuse.

---

[4] As noted in Chapter 6, competitors and police from other areas may pay close attention to trial proceedings as part of a broader process of intelligence gathering. The fruits of such investigation may sometimes be shared with others.

2. Differentiation

Differentiation arguments are grounded in the tradition of proving 'need' (see Chapter 3) wherein the justices might require applicants to demonstrate that they were offering something new or different to what was already available in an area. In combination with quality and standards arguments, difference from one's competitors might typically be emphasized in relation to the concept and ethos of the business; including pricing, customer care and service, premium food and/or entertainment offer, ambience, management techniques, and investment in security.

Echoing the concerns of the quality and standards set, difference was also expressed in terms of a cultural distancing from the negatively construed mainstream. Advocates often appealed to class-based assumptions and prejudices in distinguishing their client's product from those of competitors, whose customers were constituted as Other: the masses, an undiscerning and largely homogenous 'rabble'. This approach was more sophisticated than it might initially appear. The acknowledgment and elicitation of popular concerns and generalized evidence of crime, was combined—at the same stroke—with their dismissal as unconnected irrelevances, bearing little or no connection to the individual circumstances of the case. In this way, applicants sought to demonstrate to the regulator that they were a distinctive (unique, even) exception to the rule; blameless and 'low risk' operators whose business interests were culturally vaccinated from the problems generated by their neighbouring and inferior competitors.

Differentiation arguments were sometimes used to attack as well as to defend. Competitors' operations might be directly 'named and shamed' for their lack of investment, irresponsibility or incompetence. Existing independent or alternative venues often proved 'easy meat' for corporate applicants who would feed upon stereotypically negative images of their customers. Such approaches often proved effective within a courtroom context in which decision-makers typically had 'little direct experience' or understanding of the activities within their jurisdiction (Chatterton 2002: 31) and the complex relationships between the various 'styles, identities and divisions' to be found within the NTE (ibid.: 43).

Differentiation: counter-arguments

In responding to differentiation evidence, the objector is likely to argue that the distinctions described are largely cosmetic and relate to the exploitation of market niches rather than to any more radical form of functional diversification (Hobbs et al. 2003: 260). The applicant's differentiation frame may be deconstructed and the decision-maker urged not to be swayed by an evidential gloss obscuring more mundane realities. More specifically, the objector might cite evidence to suggest that activities within the proposed operation are likely to be primarily alcohol-focused, especially during later trading hours. Such observations may then be used to suggest that any problems generated would be qualitatively, if not quantitatively, similar to those of other premises. The objector would point out that even the affluent, 'respectable' and otherwise 'well-to-do' can behave anti-socially when in drink, and that even the most exclusive of new bars or nightclubs is likely to generate additional pedestrian and vehicular activity and associated noise in the early hours. It might be added that crime risks in the area are likely to be exacerbated, even if it is assumed that patrons of the premises are more likely to be the victims rather than the perpetrators.

3. Social responsibility arguments

Social responsibility arguments appeal to the concept of public-private partnership and a consensual, self-regulatory and compliance-oriented approach to regulation (Ayers and Braithwaite 1992).

As noted in Chapter 5, the expansion of high street leisure has been accompanied by cumulative and incremental problems generated, in part, by the sheer volume of activity on the streets. Within this context, corresponding shifts in regulatory opinion have occurred (see Chapter 1). Well-prepared applicants now recognize that it may no longer be prudent to rely solely upon tried and tested 'quality and standards' and 'differentiation' arguments. It has become increasingly necessary for them to go one step further in demonstrating active corporate citizenship in relation to issues such as residential quality of life, patron behaviour in public space, and late-night transportation. The wise applicant will now outline their intentions to be a good neighbour and to operate in such a way as to minimize the risks of crime and disorder.

Social responsibility arguments aim to fulfil such criteria; firstly, by identifying specific local problems such as noise, nuisance, and disorder; and secondly, by proposing creative solutions. The applicant is thereby located as standing in partnership with local communities and public sector agencies in their fight against crime and protection of the public interest. To this end, the 'responsible applicant' may swear allegiance to the self-regulatory activities of a local pub and club watch scheme (Hadfield et al. 2005a) and voluntarily commit to a range of undertakings and conditions which might be attached to their licence (see Chapter 3).

Alongside this apparent commitment to partnership there will often be implied or openly expressed criticism of local agencies such as the police or council for failing to apply nationally propagated good practice. It may be suggested that the public sector has 'stood back and done nothing' to improve matters. The applicant's counsel may attempt to turn received notions on their head by recasting his or her client as a philanthropic benefactor bringing experience of national best practice to a backward provincial outpost. 'Innovative solutions' that objectors 'may not have considered', such as the private funding of additional police officers; installation of urinals which pop up from under the pavement at night; sponsorship of late-night bus services; and the provision of a dedicated customer taxi service may be offered. The acceptance of such bait does not necessarily require decision-makers to have faith in the effectiveness of a 'technical fix'. The true potency of social responsibility arguments lies in their ability to impress sympathetic judges and magistrates and to sway doubters. In making such offers, the applicant provides the regulator with additional ammunition with which to respond to the submissions of objectors and justify their decision to grant. A shortage of crime control resources, for example, can no longer be used as an 'excuse' to deny the licence.[5] In sum, social responsibility arguments are used to make an application more robust and defensible. A package of creative measures is offered which aims to neutralize objections and impress the decision-maker. At the same time, the applicant retains

---

[5] The contentious issue of 'paying off' police objections by offering to fund crime reduction initiatives was discussed in Chapter 3.

the ability to steer the regulator toward those initiatives which, although not necessarily most effective in preventing harm, 'look good' and have the minimum impact upon long-term profitability.

Social responsibility: counter-arguments

There are two primary approaches used by objectors to counter social responsibility arguments which may be termed 'the particular' and 'the general'. In submitting particular counter-arguments, the objector will seek to dissect one or more of the specific solutions put forward by the operator. The validity of the proposals will be scrutinized in relation to their feasibility or likely effects. Such challenges are readily combined with objections of a more generalized nature. General objections might begin by asking the following question: at what stage in the development of new licensed premises should social responsibility start? The objector would then point out that it cannot simply be the case that operators commit themselves to the responsibility ethic once their units are fully established and trading profitably. Unfortunately, by this stage it is often too late. The investment has been made and new licensed premises have opened in an inappropriate location and have begun to cause local problems. Although the police have powers under the Act to take action against licensed premises which fail to conduct their business appropriately, in the context of a drinking circuit, it is often extremely difficult to apportion the blame for incidents of street crime to any individual outlet. The police may be faced with an increased level of ongoing problems and it is very difficult to put the 'genie back in the bottle', as the successful revocation of licences is rare (Asthana 2005).

Evidence may be presented to indicate an overstretching of emergency, environmental and transport services (see Chapter 5). As Melbin (1987: 83–84) notes, night-time serves as a window of opportunity for service functions that allow organizations to overhaul and recuperate in readiness for daylight. One symptom of the temporal extension of the leisure economy is that it serves to erode this period of recess and rejuvenation. In the West End of London, for example, London Underground have sought to resist calls for later rail services in order to reserve the hours they need for essential maintenance work. Similarly, street cleaning operations need to be conducted in the brief period between dissolution of the night-time crowds and the start of a new working day.

Against the background of such evidence, the objector might ask how any harm reduction successes might be measured. Blame may be apportioned to the initial regulatory failures which permitted this now chronic set of problems to arise in the first place. Furthermore, adopting the 'polluter pays principle' in order to, for example, fund police over-time payments and arrest more people, may be cast as one of many attempts to 'shut the stable door once the horse has bolted'. The objector may highlight the need to plan strategically the development of nightlife areas in a responsible and holistic manner, thereby preventing the development of degraded urban environments into which additional policing resources must be poured.

The objector might further ask whether a responsible licensed operator, genuinely working in partnership with the police, municipal government and the local community, would choose an existing 'trouble spot' as the only location in which to invest. Surely, if the police can provide good evidence of serious crime risks in a particular location, applicants should heed this and consider locating their ventures elsewhere? Does the very attempt to discredit police evidence in the courts and claim that one's business will have some form of miraculous calming effect belie the true extent of one's commitment to the responsibility ethic? The objector might conclude by arguing that it would be better for polluters not to pollute in the first place rather than to have their licence granted on the condition that they contribute to the clean-up operation. As one local authority witness put it, 'if a bath is overflowing, you turn off the tap.'

Not in my backyard?: attack arguments

Attack arguments seek to directly challenge the case of the objector.

1. Consumer demand arguments

Consumer demand arguments appeal to notions of market freedom associated with political liberalism. This tradition promotes 'material choice and the right to spend one's money' whenever, and however, one wishes (Goodwin 1992: 42). Accordingly, the expansion of the high street is said to be driven by greater levels of disposable income, changing lifestyles and life course transitions, and the emergence of a consumer-driven 24-hour society (Kreitzman 1999,

Moore-Ede 1993). Leisure consumers are said to have increasingly high expectations and to be demanding better standards of service. The applicant might state that their business forms part of an economically important and dynamic industry which is responding to the consumer demand for greater choice and longer trading hours. They might add that their decision to invest in this location simply reflects a wish to provide what their customers want and to exploit wholly legitimate opportunities for growth.

The consumer demand argument may be taken one step further by drawing upon the doctrines of classical economic thought (Smith [1776] 1979) and neo-liberal political economy (Friedman 1982, Hayek 1948). Hallmarks of the liberalist political and economic traditions include a concern with the limits of authority and opposition to interventionist or 'paternalistic' forms of governance (Harvey 2005). Accordingly, licensing may be framed as an unwarranted and 'restrictive' intrusion into the workings of an essentially self-governing market. In the words of one trade consultant: 'The number of licensed premises, like any business, is ultimately decided by the laws of supply and demand'. A corollary of this argument is that any attempt to 'turn off the tap' is not only unjust, but also perverse.

Consumer demand: counter-arguments

Objectors may respond by noting that the *laissez-faire* approach advocated by the applicant appears to have only two primary benefits: firstly, it maximizes freedom of action for the entrepreneur; and secondly, it increases choice for young consumers with relatively high levels of disposable income. The objector might add that these beneficiaries represent only a small minority of the local population; a minority whose needs are already more than adequately met. Similarly, the new consumption choices to be offered are qualitatively limited and remain dominated by the sale of alcohol.

The applicant's interpretation of liberal political thought (if not *laissez-faire* economics) may be challenged by noting that J.S. Mill advocated the curtailment of freedoms in circumstances where their exercise threatened to harm the interests and freedoms of others (Mill 1974). The objector may argue that de-regulation has generated these types of harm by contributing to the atrophy of democratic public space and residential quality of life (see Chapter 5). The objector might point specifically to exacerbated problems of crime and disorder: fear of crime; criminal damage; noise pollution; littering; fouling; and the over-stretching of emergency and environmental services. Moreover, the objector may note that the preservation of 'public goods' is often necessarily illiberal in that it overrides many individuals' interests and often has to be imposed by redistributive or regula-tory measures (Feintuck 2004, Goodwin 1992).

2. Public interest argument

Public interest arguments extend the theme of benefits to the community beyond the issue of valued service and choice for night-time leisure consumers. The applicant may argue that they are willing to invest large sums of money in an area and that this will benefit the local economy, provide new jobs, regenerate an old or disused building, and help to improve the physical appear-ance of the built environment. It may be argued that, as shops, banks and building society offices close down (particularly in secondary retail areas)—due to corporate rationalization, or in the face of competition from out-of-town retail parks—new uses have to be found for town/city centre sites. Leisure investment, it may be argued, offers the only viable opportunity for re-generation and will help bring the area back to life; reversing its economic decline. It may further be argued that the operating plan encompasses not only night-time facilities, but also a range of day-time refreshment offers that appeal to a broad range of customers. More generally, the development will contribute to local taxation via its business rent and encourage visitors into the area who may also spend money with surrounding businesses.

Public interest: counter-arguments

The objector may respond by clarifying that they have no objec-tion to licensed development *per se* and would raise no objection to the application were it to relate to an alternative location in another part of town. They would reiterate that the only reason for the objection is that the site chosen for development is on a pre-established drinking circuit in close proximity to many other licensed premises. The objector may voice their concern that the area is already a crime and disorder hot spot and that the opening of further licensed premises will only add to the problems already experienced in the area. The objector may dispute that the concept will add anything new to the area over and above what is already provided by the other licensed premises. The applicant may be asked to provide a breakdown of 'dry' and 'wet' sales in their existing outlets in order to ascertain the comparative importance of food and alcohol sales. The objector may dispute the assertion that no other use can be found for the building and may cite interest from parties who have expressed an interest in re-developing the site for non-leisure use. The issue of public benefit may be contested in relation to the additional costs to the health, policing and environmental services budget generated by alcohol abuse and the NTE in general. The claim to provide new jobs may be questioned in the context of the closure of many pubs in rural locations, housing estates and the suburbs.

3. Darwinian market arguments

As a general principle, to refuse cases of merit incurs the risk of reducing the quality of premises available to the public and has the effect of artificially keeping poor operators in business through lack of competition. It is submitted that the proper approach should be to weed out the poor operators and encourage good operators. (Extract from the skeleton argument of an applicant in a London magistrates' court 2003)

As described in relation to consumer demand, applicants will often appeal to the tenets of *laissez-faire* economics. The Darwinian market argument extends this theme by describing the market as an evolutionary system in which competition is generally healthy for the aggregate population, but less so for the weaker individuals. Within such a system, it is right and proper that only the fittest of operators will survive (Alchian 1977). Licensing, like other forms of market intervention, has a tendency to lend artificial support to poor operators who would otherwise be 'naturally weeded out by the competitive process' (Barry 1991: 236). From this perspective, improvements can only be driven by investment, rendering the denial of a licence necessarily anti-progressive. In the words of one judge who found this argument persuasive, 'the situation will not be improved by refusing to allow a new entrant of the quality of this applicant into the market—solutions to the area's problems lie elsewhere'.[6] The reference to 'solutions lying elsewhere' relates to the corollary argument that licensing and enforcement activities

---

[6] *Lee-Jones v Chester* Licensing JJ *Licensing Review* 28.

should be focused upon the 'bad' operators who are contributing to existing problems, rather than upon denying new licences to 'good' operators.

Darwinian market arguments rest on two assumptions; firstly, that the operating standards of licensed premises are *the* key predictors of crime and disorder; and secondly, that the introduction of new, well-run, licensed premises will assist *crime reduction* by incrementally forcing competitors either to improve their own standards, lose custom, or (it is implied) eventually close down. Inevitably, Darwinian market devices can only be used in conjunction with 'quality and standards' and 'differentiation' arguments. In order to argue that the good will drive out the bad, the applicant must first establish that they are one of the good. Once quality and standards and differentiation evidence has been submitted, the applicant is then able to argue that to grant the licence would be to improve standards in the area, whilst to deny the licence would be to 'ossify the status quo' and allow it to remain a youth and booze ghetto. In its strongest form, the Darwinian approach submits that the denial of new licences is a 'crude', 'simplistic' and 'counter-productive' response which contaminates the market's delicate ecology.

The Darwinian market: counter-arguments

The objector may respond by claiming that there are, in fact, very few poorly operated premises in the area and that whenever problems do arise, these are acted upon by the appropriate agency. The objector may produce statistics to show that the majority of disorder and nuisance occurs outside licensed premises and on the streets rather than within licensed premises themselves. It may be stated that the key factors contributing to such problems appear to emanate from activity levels in public space associated with high density nightlife; issues which are largely beyond the control of individual licensees or operators. It may be further asserted that the majority of surrounding premises are already operated by well known and respected national chains, many of whom presented similar arguments when seeking to obtain licences. Statistics may be presented to show that crime and disorder in the area increased, or at least failed to decrease, following the opening of such premises. The objector may ask why, if increased competition really does drive standards up, problems in the area have not gradually subsided with each new opening.

The objector may go on to note that the evolutionary model rests upon assumptions of scarcity in relation to a finite consumer base. It is this scarcity which breeds competition. However, when facing a new predator, existing operators will not simply curl up and die: they will fight for survival. Fighting for one's commercial life might involve reducing standards, rather than improving them—alcohol price wars and the dropping of admission standards being obvious examples. Furthermore, is it true that the market has reached its full potential? Can the applicant provide examples of business failure in the area? What if the situation is actually one of plenty rather than scarcity? What if more consumers are drawn into the area following the opening of the premises due to its enhanced reputation as a nightlife destination? In such circumstances, surely the weaker operators will survive and face little pressure to improve their offer.

4. Public safety arguments

Public safety arguments present further corollaries of the quality and standards, social responsibility and Darwinian market themes. The argument set maintains that if licensed premises are well managed and people have a positive experience within them, then this will have a very direct impact on what happens on the streets. Responsible operators are said to preserve and even enhance aspects of the public realm. In the somewhat humorous argot of one 'expert' witness, the area will benefit from 'good behaviour by contagion': the 'well behaved' and 'good natured' customers of well-run licensed premises going out onto the streets to 'spread the good word'. This argument was more technically expressed in a witness statement, as follows:

It is quite clear that the manner in which licensed premises are operated affects the mood and behaviour of the customers, particularly after alcohol has been consumed. The well-established effect of alcohol (ethanol) is to make people more susceptible to cues in their immediate social environment. Where that environment is well controlled and free from aggression and conflict, the effect is one of increased sociability and sense of well-being. Conversely, where the environment contains frustration and cues for disorderly conduct, the consumption of alcohol is likely to lead to much more negative behaviours. These effects can be relatively long-lasting and certainly long enough to influence behaviour among customers on the streets after they have left the premises.

In applications for extended hours, public safety arguments are sometimes used to make the case for physical containment. The provision of additional capacity within well-run licensed premises over a longer time period, is, it is said, preferable to having consumers wandering the streets 'unsupervised' and in search of further entertainment.

Public safety: counter-arguments

In response to public safety arguments, the objector may ask for verification of the claim that the positive effects of drinking within well-managed licensed premises can last long enough to influence the behaviour of customers on the streets after they have left the premises. Two points emerge from this: firstly, how might the applicant explain the effects of the popular ritual of circuit drinking, wherein customers visit a range of, sometimes quite different, licensed premises within the same night. What are the likely effects of this mixing of environmental cues or 'messages'? More fundamentally, what is the nature of the 'message' itself; what powerful social, cultural, or psychological forces are at work to influence customers so profoundly? The witness may be asked to provide clarification of the processes they see at work here. Can research literature be cited in support of such assertions?

Secondly, the objector may point out that, as previously noted, the on-street environment in nightlife areas will often be quite different to that found within well-run licensed premises: it may be crowded, disorderly and frustrating. Noting the applicant's claim that people who have been drinking are more susceptible to cues in their *immediate social environment*, the objector may ask to be told exactly how and why drinking in a 'nice' environment until 2am, for example, will render one less likely to be involved in an incident outside a take-away, or in a taxi queue at 3am.

In further response to the above, and to the corresponding 'patron containment' argument, the objector may reiterate a point previously conceded in relation to 'quality and standards': clearly, some premises will contribute to local problems more than others. The objector may argue that it is those premises which trade into the early hours of the morning which are likely to have the most deleterious impact. Their customers are likely to have consumed more alcohol and many may leave the premises at a time when a greater proportion of residents wish to sleep.

5. The 'mature circuit' argument

A number of applicants made reference to the 'maturity' of the local high street, pointing to the 'relative stability of the area's population'. The concept of a 'mature circuit' was used to argue that a new licensed premise would not attract substantial numbers of additional visitors. A process was described in which, over time, the number of visitors to a nightlife area reached a plateau. Patrons, it was claimed, would be drawn from the area's existing customer base, with business generated at the expense of inferior competitors.

Mature circuit: counter-arguments

Objectors may respond to mature circuit arguments in two ways, one of which involves an acceptance of the basic 'market saturation' premise and another of which seeks to reject such conceptions. Using the former approach, the objector may point out that the concept of maturity implies acceptance of the status quo. If an area can be shown to currently attract a predominately 17–25-year-old clientele and the applicant is also to draw from this customer base, then what does the application have to offer over and above what is currently available? Mature circuit arguments therefore undercut differentiation arguments; the applicants, by their own admission, will do little to generate a more inclusive social mix.

In the second type of response, the concept of maturity is rejected in favour of a contradictory 'honey-pot' effect. Nightlife consumers, it is argued, are similar to day-time ones to the extent that they are attracted 'like bees to the honey', to clusters of outlets conveniently located to fulfil their needs. Such areas offer the exciting ambience of a social gathering in that one can always find 'lots of things going on' and many entertainment venues to 'see and be seen in'. One of the defining features of a honey-pot is its facilitation of customer choice and the promotion of an exciting and vibrant street-life; customers being encouraged to move between premises in order to sample the various styles of entertainment. The objector may claim that nightlife clusters thrive on innovations in design, branding, and operating style, with new and attractive developments acting as the catalyst which draws in additional visitors.

6. The destination venue argument

As noted in Chapter 5, drinking circuits spell activity and excitement for consumers and profitability for the trade. Yet, for the police and other objectors, the term 'circuit' may be loaded with negative connotations associated with binge drinking and crime risk. These understandings may be challenged by the applicant in two ways: firstly, by contesting objector definitions of a circuit; and secondly, by claiming that it is possible to be geographically located within a circuit, whilst not forming *part* of that circuit. For example, when challenged regarding his company's stated preference for developing sites on the high street, the Estates Manager of one PLC argued that the term 'circuit' referred merely to 'a central location, at the heart of things, with good transport links'. Secondly, he claimed that his operations were the perfect antidote to established drinking circuits in that they were 'destination venues' for a whole evening's entertainment. His bars, therefore, functioned as 'circuit breakers': venues which, due to the high quality of their food, drink and entertainment offer, succeeded in stopping circulating revellers in their tracks.

Used in combination with differentiation arguments, the destination venue set seeks to identify the applicant's brand as in some way culturally, if not spatially, distinct from the drinking circuit. As premises used by customers for a full night's entertainment, destination venues are said to stand out from the pack, their strict admissions policies permitting protection against pollution from any unruly elements that may inhabit the area.

Destination venues: counter-arguments

Objector responses to destination venue arguments are illustrated in the following case notes:

As part of his company's application for a new alcohol licence, the Estates Manager for *Lonesome Taverns Plc* described existing *Lonesome Cafés* as 'destination venues' in which customers generally chose to remain for the entire evening. As such, his venues did not 'typically form part of any established drinking circuit'. This statement conflicted with information to be found on the company's website. On a page entitled 'site requirements' which provided details of the company's expansion plans, visitors were invited to submit details of any potential sites suitable for re-development as a *Lonesome Café*. These details included a stated requirement that all new development sites for the brand 'must be on high street circuits, no leisure centres, or retail centres unless city centre'. Why, counsel for the police was prompted to ask, if the concept functioned as a 'destination for a full evening's entertainment', did company policy dictate that new premises would only be developed on existing high street drinking circuits. Surely, a 'destination venue' need not form part of any circuit?

Objectors may pose further questions. For example, from where are customers to be drawn, if not from the existing circuit? If the applicant wishes to attract business from other premises, it will be necessary to adapt to local consumer preferences which may include the desire to visit several premises. If new customers are to be drawn from outside the circuit, will this not add to the cumulative stress being placed upon the area? Might more mature patrons be dissuaded by the venue's location within a youth-dominated crime and disorder hot spot? In sum, *why not* develop the premises in another area of the city?

7. Functional segregation arguments

Even though the role of outlet density as a contributory factor in the generation of alcohol-related crime is increasingly acknowledged (see Chapter 3), views differ as to the appropriate policy responses. Functional segregation arguments assert that the geographical spread of licensed premises should be restricted. The applicant may point to a potential displacement of crime and nuisance to other parts of the city, arguing in favour of containment within easily identifiable 'fuse' areas (Barr and Pease 1992: 207). It may be accepted that these leisure zones will be avoided by the majority community at night, but asserted that their spatial and temporal parameters at least allow for intensive and targeted policing.[7] Functional segregation arguments have received some

---

[7] In its strongest form, this argument has been used to justify calls for the formal designation of 'wild' and 'tame' zones wherein divergent standards of police toleration and enforcement are applied (Ellickson 1996 and the discussion of Alcohol Disorder Zones in Chapter 1).

support from researchers and police officers. Bromley et al. (2000) argue that regulators should encourage the spatial segregation of youth-oriented drinking circuits in order to facilitate the development of alternative nightlife attractions in other areas of the city. The suggestion is that, as some areas already have a tarnished image, the corralling of new developments within them might serve to reduce public anxieties and encourage a wider range of people to participate in night-time activities in other parts of town.

Functional segregation: counter-arguments

Objectors will typically counter the functional segregation argument by noting its echoes of modernist planning and the associated failures of urban zoning. They may go on to recite the tenets of a mixed-use paradigm, emphasizing the assumed benefits of functional diversity. These benefits, as noted in Chapter 5, are said to include the enhanced efficacy of informal social controls, natural surveillance, and territoriality. Objectors may also highlight the importance of a sustainable residential community within the city centre and note the processes through which crime and disorder may be generated by an over-concentration of licensed premises. Displacement concerns may be rejected by noting that other areas of the city would combine fewer crime generating and attracting features with a greater presence of crime 'detractors' (such as residents). The objector may assert that the risk of chronic displacement to other areas is therefore negligible (Maguire and Nettleton 2003). It may be added that enforced containment would only exacerbate existing problems, with harmful consequences for consumers and the image of the city as a whole.

8. Denial of impact argument

In common with functional segregation arguments, the denial of impact set acknowledges the legitimacy of concerns regarding environmental stress and the concept of saturation. Unlike the former, it seeks to 'negate the offence' (Matza 1964), dismissing such concerns as irrelevant to the material facts of the case. Denial of impact arguments seek to meet core objector arguments head-on by challenging their empirical basis. Such challenges usually involve the commissioning of expert witnesses such as planning and transport surveyors, or noise specialists, more usually found in planning tribunals. Such witnesses may give evidence in relation to actual and predicted pedestrian and traffic flows, late-night transport provision, sound measurements, and the land use profile of an area; particularly in relation to the location of residential accommodation and existing licensed property. Such evidence is used to argue that objectors are simply mistaken in their claim that the area is under stress and to deny that the proposed development will have deleterious effects upon residential quality of life, or the safety of night-time visitors.

Denial of impact: counter-arguments

In responding to denial of impact arguments, objectors must carefully dissect the evidence of the applicant's experts. They will also need to submit strong counter-evidence which lends support and justification to the objection. This may be presented by police officers, or local authority personnel, together with their 'own' independent experts.

More generally, objectors may respond by arguing that environmental impacts relate to issues of quality as well as quantity. For example, although night buses or taxis may be 'available', people's actual experiences of using such services might be especially negative. Residents and police officers may be able to offer first-hand accounts which provide some insight into the general 'feel' of an area late at night. Such accounts might address specific concerns such as the fear of crime, overcrowding, frustration, the flashpoint effect at transport termini, the activities of bogus taxi drivers, and the experience of harassment. Similarly, the evidentiary devices used by surveyors, such as pedestrian counting surveys, may be construed as sterile to the extent that they fail to acknowledge that many of those on the streets late at night are likely to be both intoxicated and demonstrative, and to have had their hearing desensitized by loud music. The objector might argue that in such circumstances, even small numbers of people may create menace and nuisance.

9. Dismissal of legitimacy arguments

Dismissal of legitimacy arguments share similarities with the denial of impact approach in that they attempt to portray the objector as in some way mistaken. However, dismissals of legitimacy go further, implying that the objector's views are atypical, or representative only of an intolerant minority. Local residents are the primary target of such accusations. The applicant may argue that town and city centres have long been 'vibrant' areas of night-time entertainment. The residents of such areas therefore knew what to expect when they chose to live there (see Chapter 5). Furthermore, it may be argued that this vibrancy forms part of the attraction of an urban lifestyle and that its side-effects are an inevitable price of convenience. The applicant may go on to suggest that the area's popularity remains undiminished, as reflected in general social and economic trends such as a growing residential population or buoyant property market. The following case notes are illustrative:

As part of a gruelling seven-day hearing, an objector, the chair of the local civic trust, was asked to provide the court with information relating to the personal profile of his organization's membership. This information was then compared with data from the electoral register to show that membership of the trust was highly skewed in favour of older residents. The local population, it was argued, had a high proportion of young people whose views were not represented by the 'conservative' stance of the trust. The applicants then called their own witnesses: a 22-year-old 'supporter' and a market researcher. The market research witness claimed that the local people she had questioned had a very positive attitude toward the opening of the premises, did not suffer unacceptable noise from clubs and bars, and had rarely, if ever, been a victim of crime.

The applicant might also seek to question the legitimacy of local police and licensing authority policy. It may be suggested that such policies were drawn up, not on the basis of good evidence, but rather as a response to lobbying by a particularly vocal and persistent minority. Moreover, the placing of restrictions on extended hours, for example, may be construed as a 'crude' and 'simplistic' measure; out of step with 'best practice' and central government guidance. As discussed in relation to the social responsibility set, 'more effective' solutions may be posited.

Dismissal of legitimacy: counter-arguments

In order to establish and defend the legitimacy of their stance, objectors may seek to rely upon a number of remedial routines.

Residents may admit that they enjoy urban life and do not expect, or want, their local area to be as quiet and peaceful as a suburban street or rural village. They may, however, recount a sorry story of personal experiences during the night-time hours (see Chapters 5 and 6). Residents may claim that the problems have increased in recent years following the opening of more and more licensed premises. They may urge that a line now has to be drawn in order to preserve community life and prevent further deterioration of the public realm.

Objectors may point out that some residents occupy homes or streets which their families have lived in for generations and should not be forced to leave; or that there are poorer residents in social housing who have no option but to stay. They may claim that the re-population of central urban areas is led by childless, upwardly mobile young professionals and students; people who are only likely to remain in the area for a relatively short period of time. Whilst these groups may be avid consumers of nightlife, more residual and static populations also need to be taken into account, including families with young children and the elderly. Many residents may be from ethnic minorities, who for cultural or religious reasons have no wish to consume alcohol or partake in pub and club culture. The objector may argue that, in truth, it is the applicant's customers who are in the minority; is it right that their consumption preferences such take precedence over the competing quality of life requirements of others?

Police and local authority witnesses may respond to dismissal of legitimacy arguments by maintaining that they are simply fulfilling their statutory duties to pursue the objectives of the Act and protect the 'public interest' (Feintuck 2004). Where applicable, both agencies may assert that their stance is informed by robust data collection and community consultation, developed as part of a broader public policy agenda that encompasses local crime and disorder strategy and development planning.

10. Witness integrity arguments

Attacking the integrity of witnesses in order to uncover evidence of perjury, bias, omission, intolerance, aggression, prejudice, or vested interest is a classic method of advocacy. Challenges to witness integrity are therefore included in the pool as a perennial feature of the adversarial tool kit, even though their content cannot be prescribed. In advance of the trial, an opponent's witness statements will be carefully dissected in the hope of identifying integrity issues. In the case of experts, confidential briefing notes may be sought from persons who have the requisite knowledge to provide negative commentary (see Chapter 6). However, integrity themes arise most frequently in response to comments elicited during cross-examination and must therefore be developed by counsel *in situ*. This important aspect of strategic interaction is explored in Chapter 8.

Witness integrity: counter-arguments

There are two primary responses to witness integrity arguments: defence and counter-attack. Unlike many more predictable themes within the argument pool, witness integrity arguments will often involve elements of surprise and the 'ambushing' of witnesses during cross-examination. Opposing counsel then play a key role in the accomplishment of reparation by formulating re-examination questions. These questions provide the witness with opportunities to respond to their accuser. As we shall see in Chapter 8, much rests upon the individual agency of the witness and their capacity to exploit opportunities for remedial action.

11. Reapportionment of blame arguments

The reapportionment of blame set acts as a smokescreen, seeking to shift accusations of liability and contributory negligence away from the operators of pubs and bars. Agencies such as the police and local authorities may be said to have failed in some aspect of their public duties. Blame may be apportioned to inefficiency or lack of vision in relation to policing methods; licensing inspection and enforcement; environmental services; late-night transport; public toilet provision; street lighting; or CCTV, for example. The licensing authority may be accused of creating problems itself though *laissez-faire* policies of the past, when licences were awarded to 'bad' operators. Similarly, the finger may be pointed at off-licences and their customers; street drinkers; fast food outlets; unlicensed vendors; and minicabs, all of whom, so the argument goes, are allowed to 'pollute' the area with impunity.

Further blame may rest with an 'irresponsible' and 'anti-social' minority of consumers (see Chapter 5). These people, it may be argued, would not gain, or even seek, admission to the applicant's premises. They are the customers of inferior premises and off-licences and it is the responsibility of the police to find and arrest them. Whilst these 'flawed consumers' should receive punishment, the law-abiding majority should be allowed to enjoy the urban leisure experience as they see fit.

Reapportionment of blame: counter-arguments

The objector may respond by pointing to inconsistencies in the applicant's argument. Although tight regulation and enforcement is rejected as unwarranted and unnecessarily draconian in relation to the application, such approaches are lauded when applied to other individuals and groups. The objector may argue that although the applicant has sought to criticize the delivery of public services, they have failed to acknowledge that the demand for those services is generated by licensed premises and their patrons. Most people who come into the city centre at night do not do so with the primary intention of buying hot dogs and plastic roses, or for the frisson of riding home in an unlicensed minicab. For the vast majority of visitors, these activities are ancillary to the main purpose of their trip: to visit licensed premises. The objector may go on to note that most of these activities will not involve the sale of intoxicating liquor. Is one to ignore the contribution of those businesses that dominate the night-time high street, spatially, culturally, and economically?

12. Attribution arguments

The adversarial system's insatiable hunger for sources of ambiguity ensures that the forensic dissection of statistical evidence emerges as a salient feature of the licensing trial. The issue typically arises in relation to 'saturation policies' grounded in the notion of an incremental deterioration of the public realm (see Chapter 3). Used in combination with the denial of impact set, attribution arguments seek to question the validity of data underpinning such policies (Harrington and Halstead 2004). In the words of one expert witness:

In order to support their stance, the council would need to present two types of empirical evidence: a) that there has been an increase in the number of pedestrians in the area and this is directly attributable to increases in the total capacity of late-night entertainment premises; b) that the persons committing anti-social acts and crimes are patrons of such premises.

The questioning of police-generated crime statistics is a popular constituent of the attribution set. The applicant may call academic witnesses such as criminologists and statisticians. Such witnesses provide negative commentary which points to various ways in which the recording and analysis of quantitative data may be said to be invalid. High levels or sharp increases in crime are identified as artefacts of the recording process, rather than accurate reflections of 'real' trends. Applicants may also alight upon complexities surrounding the definition and measurement of alcohol-related crime. In so doing, they often cite the findings of industry-funded research, such as that emanating from lobby organization *The Portman Group* (Hadfield 2003).[8]

Attribution: counter-arguments

The issues arising in relation to attribution are complex and regulatory agencies cannot afford to be complacent with regard to issues of quantification (Elvins and Hadfield 2003). Attribution arguments require specific technical responses which will differ from case to case depending upon the type of challenges raised. Notwithstanding, the classic 'dark figure' of crime is likely to loom large. The objector may argue that, in the context of the NTE, even the most robust and comprehensive of databases is likely to underestimate levels of potentially recordable crime and disorder (Lister et al. 2000, Maguire and Nettleton 2003, Tierney and Hobbs 2003).

---

[8] As noted in Chapter 3, *Portman Group*-funded research by the consultant Peter Marsh formed virtually the sole empirical reference for the government's stance on extended hours. Marsh went on to conduct further work for *Portman* in relation to the measurement of alcohol-related crime. His report on the matter concluded that:

We have been unable to discover many extant procedures that can provide anything more than rough indications of the level and pattern of alcohol-related violence and disorder in even the most localized contexts. All existing procedures, in our view, have such serious conceptual and methodological weaknesses that they are unable to provide truly objective and reliable data. (Marsh et al. 2002: 13, BBC 2002, Rogan 2002)

This statement has been critically dissected elsewhere (Hardfield 2003). For present purposes, it is sufficient to note the report's contribution to the argument pool. For interesting discussions of the industry nurturance of compliant 'academics' in other contexts, see Harding (1992), Pearce and Tombs (1997, 1998), Rabin (2001), and Tombs (2002).

13. Extended hours arguments

Extended hours arguments simply rehearse official discourse (see Chapter 3). When applying for a late-licence, applicants will typically begin by espousing 'government policy' which holds that statutory permitted hours have been partly, or even mostly, responsible for the high street's ills. The applicant may present the benefits of extended hours as a received wisdom, supported by influential police opinion, and forming a cornerstone and foundational principle of the Act.

Extended hours: counter-arguments

Again, as discussed in Chapter 3, the objector may point out that the government's position appears to have little empirical support. This stance may be developed by presenting contradictory evidence from the international research literature (Babor et al. 2003, Room 2004a) and from UK cities which have adopted a de-regulatory stance. Thus, the objector may have access to locally-derived evidence. If the area in question already has many extended hours premises, statistics may be available to indicate: a) that crime and disorder has increased or remained constant following the opening of such premises; b) that a temporal shift has occurred, with a greater proportion of offences occurring during the early hours of the morning (Isle of Man Constabulary 2002, Metropolitan Police 2004).

Knowledge wars: policing the boundaries of contestation

To escape the impact of a well-functioning system of propaganda that bars dissent and unwanted fact while fostering lively debate within the permitted bounds is remarkably difficult (Chomsky 1989: 67).

As we saw in Chapter 5, the government/trade coalition places great faith in individual responsibility (of both the consumer and supplier of alcohol), campaigns of health education, and voluntary self-regulation by industry. Room (2004a) has noted how these approaches came to be enshrined in the government's *Alcohol Harm Reduction Strategy for England* (Strategy Unit 2004) despite being shown by the international evaluation literature to be among the *least* effective public policy responses to alcohol-related harm.

This disjuncture between evidence and policy is indicative of central government's attempts to control the agenda of public debate on alcohol. A bounding of debate has occurred which has resulted in an inequality of access to information for objectors, thus compromising their ability to utilize the argument pool. Many of the objector arguments are out of kilter with government policy and are therefore never propagated in official discourse. State power is exercised diffusely in relation to the dissemination of knowledge and the omission of politically inconvenient research evidence from official literature reviews. For example, *Taking Stock* (Deehan 1999), a widely cited Home Office review of literature pertaining to 'alcohol and crime', ignores a voluminous body of work concerning the control of alcohol availability (with the exception of *Portman Group*-derived calls for extended hours). Similarly, the Cabinet Office Strategy Unit's *Interim Analytical Report* (Strategy Unit 2003) which reviewed the evidence base that was to underpin England's *Alcohol Harm Reduction Strategy* (Strategy Unit 2004) has been dogged by controversy. Critics of this review point to the undue emphasis placed upon individuals who 'misuse' alcohol or supply it 'irresponsibly' and the omission of literature relating levels of harm to overall national consumption trends or routine business practice. These are key issues for alcohol policy which have tended to divide the scientific community on one side from the alcohol industry and the government on the other. As the late Sir Richard Doll put it:

Every scientific committee I have ever sat on has concluded that reduction in harm caused by drinking can only be achieved by reducing our overall consumption. It just doesn't work to target a minority. The only people I have seen recommend this is the Strategy Unit (Levy and Scott-Clark 2004: 21–22).

Temperance campaigners, the Institute of Alcohol Studies (IAS) have questioned the degree to which the Strategy Unit was allowed to conduct a genuinely impartial review. IAS report the disbanding of a special sub-group of advisers set up to investigate the impact of alcohol consumption levels across the population as a whole, and mysterious changes to the *Analytical Report's* original text. The author's own access to a leaked draft of this report confirms that the text had originally reviewed research findings from Finland, California and Western Australia. These studies had drawn policy recommendations regarding associations between alcohol availability and alcohol-related harms—principally, in relation to outlet numbers/density and opening hours—that were inconsistent with the assumptions underlying the Act and the preferred approach of trade-affiliated lobby groups.[9]

When questioned by the IAS, the Strategy Unit refused to confirm at whose behest removal of the offending literature had been made. Although the changes radically altered the meaning of the text, none of the seventeen members of the expert advisory group had asked for the changes to be made, nor were they even notified of them (Alcohol Alert 2003: 4). Yet, the suppressed literature addressed themes of key relevance to the practical deliberations of licensing. This 'inconvenient knowledge' was not discussed; it was simply excluded, its potential contribution to the public policy debate silenced within a document which purported to be the most comprehensive review of knowledge on the 'alcohol problem' ever conducted by UK government.

These reflections prompt me to suggest that the official literature reviews pertaining to alcohol-related harm for England and Wales should be regarded as fundamentally political documents rather than neutral channels of information. Their diffuse effects include the ability to steer debate in politically convenient directions (errant consumers; quality and standards of premises) whilst avoiding political icebergs (supply side generators of harm, such as increased availability). The documents referred to, together with other official publications such as the web-based *Alcohol-Related Crime Toolkit*[10] and guidance issued by industry sources such as *The Portman Group* and BBPA, constitute readily available resources for crime reduction practitioners and lay objectors. None provides an objective or comprehensive overview of their subject matter.

The effects of the information disparity

A 'common consequence of social privilege is the ability of a group to convert its perspective on some issues into authoritative knowledge without being challenged by those who have reason to

---

[9] This story was covered in a BBC *Panorama* programme by journalist Andrew Davies screened 6 June 2004.

[10] http://www.crimereduction.gov.uk/toolkits/ar00.htm

see things differently' (Young 2000: 108). Although media and public opinion have periodically turned against the government and the drinks industry on alcohol policy matters (see Chapter 1) it remains difficult for counter-discourses to influence the everyday deliberations of the courts. At trial, *Daily Mail* headlines will always lack the credibility of official literature reviews. Propagation of the official script serves to marginalize dissenting opinion to the extent that 'only specialists would be likely to know things that fall outside it. For the ordinary citizen, one that doesn't have the resources, or the time, or the training, or the education to really dig into things deeply on their own' (Chomsky 1992: 15, 133), opportunities to resist continue to be restricted.

As Chomsky (1989: 8–9) notes, attempting to challenge the interests of a powerful state-corporate nexus 'is costly and difficult; high standards of evidence and argument are imposed, and critical analysis is naturally not welcomed'. The information disparity has served to starve objectors and critics of government policy (particularly those lay audiences who depend most upon official literature reviews) of access to the ammunition needed to fight their corner. Possession of this 'guilty knowledge' underpinned the author's field role and market value as an expert witness.

As discussed in Chapter 3, local authorities have been issued with national *Guidance* in relation to their licensing functions (DCMS 2004b). Any departures from this *Guidance* must be supported by *strong evidential justification*. This requirement conforms to a neo-liberal mode of governance wherein the everyday administration and implementation of governmental activity (the 'rowing') is devolved to a range of local bodies, whilst control of the system is centralized and 'steered' by the state (Osborne and Gaebler 1992). Here one finds the information disparity impacting upon the local governance of crime. Licensing authorities only enjoy the option to depart from the *Guidance* if they have access to the necessary resources and expertise to conduct substantial research and evaluation, or can commission support from outside experts.

As Tombs describes, influence over the distribution of knowledge and research funding allows corporate actors to express ' . . . the generalized power of scientific discourses, within which there is a presumption in favour of official, scientific—technical knowledge over (often superior) 'local knowledges' (2002: 121).[11] Objectors were often thwarted in their attempts to generalize from the particular, falling back on personal experience and observations of local conditions that could all too easily be dismissed as 'anecdotal'. Police officers, in particular, often expressed frustration at being unable to access research evidence which reflected their own professional judgments and tacit occupational knowledge. They certainly could not rely on ready-to-hand information in the form of official publications, such documents being couched in the distinctly unsympathetic language of official discourse. In this context, the thirst for robust sources of local-level data became ever more acute.

Applicants, by contrast, faced no such constraints. Their preferred approaches to harm reduction were widely propagated by government and legitimized by inclusion in official literature reviews. Their arguments were thereby placed at the top of the hierarchy of credibility (Becker 1967, Chomsky 1989), further bolstering the ideological supremacy of a pro-business politico-regulatory agenda.

Summary

This chapter has described the pre-trial shaping of cases within an adversarial system of adjudication. It has identified a number of recurrent arguments and highlighted their importance as strategically organized components of case construction. The chapter also noted inequalities of power and influence between opposing parties in the alcohol policy debate. These disparities were reflected in the attempt by government to selectively restrict the dissemination of research evidence. Such activities were seen as detrimental to licensing objectors in that they served to de-legitimize their arguments and obscure sources of empirical support, whilst correspondingly strengthening the cause of their industry opponents. The following chapter builds upon these insights by exploring ways in which the parties move to promote and defend their interests in court.

---

[11] In the licensing field, this occurs even though much of the most widely propagated knowledge may best be described as 'pseudo' science (Valverde 2003).

8

Notes from the Frontline: Licensing and the Courts

The centrepiece of the adversary system is the oral trial and everything that goes before it is a preparation for the battlefield (Devlin 1979: 54).

The adversarial tradition regards the opportunity to participate in a live oral hearing as fundamental to fair procedure (Galligan 1996). Many previous studies of the courts have focused on the social practices of the criminal law and the experiences of lay people as victims, defendants, and prosecution or defence witnesses within the criminal trial (Carlen 1976, Ellison 2001, Emerson 1969, Linton 1965, McBarnet 1981, Rock 1993). When determining licensing matters, licensing authorities and the courts perform an *administrative* function. This role '... does not involve deciding between the rights or interests of particular persons. It is the exercise of a power delegated by the people as a whole to decide what the public interest requires.'[1] The English administrational trials studied in this book were constituted mainly as gladiatorial struggles between partisan teams of professionals, with relatively limited involvement by lay people. This chapter explores the interactional devices employed by opposing counsel and witnesses in pursuing their goals. Particular attention is paid to the differential experiences of lay and professional witnesses as they attempt to negotiate the regulatory arena, deliver testimony and maintain composure in the face of determined cross-examination.

One seemingly universal feature of trial settings is that proceedings are conducted in accordance with a set of regulations which control the content and form of testimony, thereby delimiting

---

[1] *Regina (Alconbury Developments Ltd and Others)* v *Secretary of State for the Environment, Transport and the Regions* [2003] 2 AC 295, para. 74, per Lord Hoffman.

interaction. In discharging their administrative functions, licensing authorities and the courts are required to act fairly and in accordance with the rules of natural justice. Natural justice maxims provide that decisions should be free from bias, partiality, personal advantage, commitments or interest (Light 2004). The twin pillars of natural justice are the right to have one's case heard by an independent and impartial tribunal and the right of both sides to have their views heard before a decision is reached. More specifically, natural justice affords each side the right to know the case made against them and the opportunity to 'test' and correct such assertions. In order to uphold natural justice, most trials and tribunals are governed by rules of procedures which stipulate the approved means for introducing evidence, ruling on admissibility, examining witnesses, and so on. However, the procedural rules of the administrative tribunals in which I participated departed in many ways from those of the criminal courts explored by previous ethnographers.

English administrative tribunals are required to act quasi-judicially, which involves, at a minimum, deciding each case on its merits, taking into account all relevant considerations, and observing basic tenets of fairness and impartiality (Light 2004a, 2005a, Manchester et al. 2005). In criminal, and some civil trials, rules of evidence are used to control the content of the testimony that may be introduced. In determining licence applications, administrative decision-makers enjoy a broader discretion in governing the conduct of hearings[2] and they do not apply strict rules of evidence.[3] Although an adversarial approach is adopted and each party calls evidence in support of their case, 'hearsay' evidence is admissible[4] and there is no burden of proof. This means

---

[2] Darbyshire (1984) notes the important role of the Justices' Clerk in training the magistracy and advising them on issues of law, practice and procedure. The Clerks' influential role in licensing matters was illustrated in Chapter 3's discussion of the *Good Practice Guide: Licensing* (Justices' Clerks' Society 1999).

[3] There were, for example, no strict rules as to the timetable for disclosure of documentary evidence and witness statements. These matters were often simply agreed between the parties in advance of the trial.

[4] Under the 'hearsay rule', a statement, whether of fact or opinion, is not normally admissible as evidence where it is made otherwise than by a person giving oral testimony in court. Similarly, persons cannot give evidence as to what they heard another person say about an event; they can only give evidence as to their own experience or knowledge. Testimony may be classified as inadmissible

that no party has anything to 'prove'—it is up to the committee/ justices/judge to decide disputed issues on the 'balance of probabilities', according to the persuasiveness of the evidence they have heard.[5] All bodies that exercise administrative functions are required to observe the usual tenets of administrative behaviour[6] and their judgments may be subject to inspection by the Administrative Court (see Chapter 3).

Despite the relaxed rules of evidence in licensing trials, the predilection for oral testimony remains strong and the bench may indicate their intention to accord less weight to documentary and filmic evidence that cannot be 'proved' by the appearance of a supporting witness (Barnes 1994: 37–9). The oral tradition employs cross-examination as its primary technique for assessing the credibility of witnesses and unearthing evidence that might otherwise have been omitted or suppressed (Ellison 2001, Lynch and Bogen 1996, Pannick 1992). The primacy of oral evidence and of its face-to-face testing is, in part, explained by the format of contests 'waged on a day (or several days) in court' (Egglestone 1978: 35) before an un-prepared decision-maker.[7]

hearsay if its purpose is to establish the *truth* of what is contained in the statement. Hearsay statements are often considered to be unreliable because they are a) not submitted on oath; b) not able to be challenged by cross-examination, and c) afford the bench no opportunities to observe the demeanour of the witness at the time the statement is made.

[5] In criminal cases the prosecution bears the burden of proof and the standard of proof is higher, being that of 'beyond reasonable doubt'.

[6] These include the avoidance of bias and perverse actions, adherence to the rules of natural justice, the 'Wednesbury rules', the requirement to take account of material considerations, the maxim of 'legitimate expectation', and the duty to give reasons (Light 2004a, Wade and Forsyth 2004). All of these are principles of administrative law and they form the usual grounds for challenging the decisions of public bodies.

[7] Not all decision-makers in licensing cases are 'unprepared'. Licensing justices and licensing authorities are entitled, and indeed expected, to bring their own local knowledge and experience to bear on the applications brought before them. To this extent, they are akin to tribunals. Similarly, in some areas, district judges hearing PEL cases in the magistrates' courts held some degree of familiarity with the issues, if only through their hearing of previous appeals. In crown court appeal cases the situation was noticeably different, with the bench usually appearing to have no previous experience or knowledge of *local* licensing issues, at least. The rules governing liquor appeal cases actually required that magistrates sitting on the crown court bench were mostly drawn from other areas. Counsel for the applicants often saw advantage in this arrangement in that the involvement of a judge and a non-indigenous bench provided them with greater opportunities to steer trial

The format of hearings

Advocates sought to exploit the wide procedural discretion of the administrative courts, identifying tactical advantage in the strategic manipulation of time. For example, trials would often begin with opposing submissions from counsel regarding who should 'open.' The bench's decision on this point then determined which chain of witnesses would be heard first. Once this initial skirmish had occurred, battle would proceed. Counsel would submit their 'skeleton arguments', summarizing the empirical evidence, relevant legislation and case law. They would then offer guidance to the bench on appropriate reading from large paginated bundles of evidence. The first party would then present their case, calling a usually lengthy list of witnesses. The scheduling of witness evidence would be determined on an ad hoc basis as the trial developed. Each witness would step up to a raised witness box, swear an oath, and then be led through their 'evidence-in-chief'. The witness would then be cross-examined by their opponent's counsel followed by re-examination by their own counsel. Once the first party's evidence had been completed, the other side's witnesses would be called and the process repeated. When both sides had delivered all their evidence, each counsel would summarize their case in a 'closing speech.' Judgments were typically 'handed down' in writing some time later. These documents summarized the facts and arguments put before court and offered reasoned explanation for the bench's decision. The matter would then conclude with further submissions and pronouncements regarding costs.

Staging

Sociological studies have drawn analytical insight from the paraphernalia of trial settings: the physical arrangement of courtrooms; the strategic control of time; and the adaptation of conventional modes of communication (Atkinson and Drew 1979, Carlen 1976, Emerson 1969, Lynch and Bogen 1996, Rock 1993). The organization of space and time has an important impact upon the experience of witnesses. For example, the witness

discourse in the direction of legal theory and away from empirical matters in respect of which the local justices, by dint of their greater familiarity with the area, may have held 'prejudicial' views.

is impelled to 'speak up' by the distance between self and audience, whilst the structural elevation of the witness box displays them for public scrutiny. Time is manipulated through the scheduling of testimony and attempts by counsel to control the style in which questions may be answered.

An important element of trial staging is the production of 'formality' (Atkinson 1982, Atkinson and Drew 1979). Evidential and procedural rules, for example, may assist in resolving such problems as how to conduct trials within finite time limits, organize turn-taking, and assure topic relevance. Other rules govern the oral and bodily activity of participants. The entrance of the bench is both 'staged and heralded' with a call from the usher to 'all stand' (Carlen 1976: 31). Participants and observers are expected to bow in the direction of the bench each time they enter or leave the court, to sit in silence unless called upon to speak, and to remain controlled in their gestures and movements.

Trials are notable for their peculiar speech exchange systems in which the sequential patterns of everyday conversation are eschewed in favour of a rigid question and answer format (Lynch and Bogen 1996: Chapter 4, Matoesian 1993: 107–109). As O'Barr, (1982: 17–18) notes, legal language ('legalese') can be extraordinarily wordy and pompous, unnecessarily repetitive, lacking in clarity and 'above all, simply dull'. Words are given specific legal meanings or replaced by phrases from Latin and French; archaic and obsolete forms abound. In legal documents and oral submissions, lawyers will often use lengthy sentences containing professional jargon and a complex syntax. Legal professionals embellish their roles with deferential courtesies. Titles such as 'your honour', 'your lordship' and 'my learned friend' highlight the self-justificatory assignment of hierarchy and control. In the higher courts, counsel and judges wear flowing gowns and horsehair wigs. In one case, an elderly High Court Judge presiding over a quite unremarkable crown court appeal was flanked by an equally aged, cutlass-bearing 'guard' wearing body armour and a helmet plumed with ostrich feathers. Critical analyses have identified such staging mechanisms as variously strange, absurd, intimidat-ing, and incomprehensible to the uninitiated (Carlen 1976, Emerson 1969, Pannick 1992).

Trial protagonists are involved in what Philip Manning refers to as the 'production of credibility', a process 'integral to both trust and deception' (2000: 283). As Manning notes, 'what is credible may or may not be true' (ibid.: 293); the key concern for those wishing to achieve credibility is that it be *believable*. Credibility—the 'quality of being *believable*' (ibid.: 283)—*is* accomplished through interaction and is a necessary, and hard won, component of persuasiveness. Manning points to Goffman's work as a sustained attempt to analyse the production and reproduction of credibility by means of the various resources and strategies people use to make their actions appear trustworthy and convincing. In *The Presentation of Self in Everyday Life* (1959), for example, Goffman offers a 'dramaturgical' approach to social analysis in which the theatre forms the basis of analogy with routine interaction. According to this analogy, 'man, the role-player, presents himself in different guises and with different masks, he collaborates in staging scenes and dramas, he makes use of props and settings, and he relies on a diversity of scripts' (Rock 1979: 170). Dramaturgical analogies remain apposite when applied to the analysis of interactions within the small-scale, bounded, and formal social setting of a trial.[8] Following Goffman, it is possible to think of courtroom interaction in terms of a number of dramaturgical metaphors, particularly those of actors, scripts,[9] performances, stages and audiences. The notion of a dramatic performance is congruent with the way in which the parties typically organize and frame their interactions, carefully orchestrating the impressions they convey to the court.

In the live conflict situation of a trial, the importance of impression management in the accomplishment of credibility is strongly apparent (Brannigan and Lynch 1987, Lynch and Bogen 1996). Within the courtroom, judges and magistrates are required to 'weigh' the evidence and make far-reaching decisions. In so doing,

[8] The dramaturgical perspective, when understood as its author originally intended, as a comprehensive account of everyday life, is now widely regarded as inadequate (Manning 1992: 51–55). Critical readings of Goffman have dismissed the dramaturgical model as describing a 'two-dimensional world in which there are scenes but no plots' (Manning 2000: 292). Goffman himself chose to eschew the theatrical metaphor when he went on to develop the themes of *The Presentation of Self*...in his later work (Goffman 1974). Yet, if their limitations are acknowledged, dramaturgical metaphors may still provide useful analytical insight in relation to specific social settings.

[9] The concept of 'script' was initially introduced in Chapter 7 in relation to the organization of case construction.

they inevitably act partly on inference from appearances. Opposing parties must therefore convey favourable impressions of themselves through the construction, maintenance and defence of their scripts, and the individual and collective integrity of the actors. Credible and persuasive performances involve the strategic use of written, oral, and bodily modes of communication. These performances must be enacted within a hostile environment in which opponents seek to actively undermine one's interactional accomplishments.

As noted in Chapter 7, witnesses are expected to co-operate with counsel in presenting and defending a largely pre-determined evidential script. The trial setting fosters a 'competitive atmosphere likely to encourage the witness in the view that … if he fails to come up to expectations, or gives away too much in cross-examination, he has let the side down' (Egglestone 1975: 432). The deepest of alliances fosters relationships of 'reciprocal dependence' (Goffman 1959). Each individual actor—be they a noise expert, traffic surveyor, licensing consultant, or market researcher, etc.—will allude to, or seek to rely upon, some aspect of their teammates' evidence. Such a deployment of skills and resources in the presentation of self and strategic management of evidence is crucial to effective engagement with the adversarial system. The following paragraphs explore the *differential capacities* of witnesses in attempting to accomplish individual and team credibility.

Professionals and real people

Important distinctions could be drawn between participants in relation to their degree of familiarity with the courts and legalistic forms of interaction. Differentially successful attempts to meet the perceived expectations of the court were observable in relation to the oral and bodily performance of witnesses; the presentation of self having an important impact upon the manner in which evidence was both delivered and received. Similar issues arose in relation to the professional competencies of counsel: their mastery of the brief; confidence; abilities; tactics in cross-examination and the eloquence and creativity of their submissions.

It was possible to typify two very broad categories of participants in the licensing trial: 'professional witnesses' and 'real people'. The names used to identify these categories are not of the author's own invention, but are rather indigenous terms used by, or familiar to, the lawyers and other courtroom actors with whom he mixed. In more formal terms, they might therefore be described as 'member-identified' (Lofland 1976) or *in vivo* categories (Strauss 1987).

Professional witnesses

Professional witnesses are persons who regularly participate in licensing litigation as part of their work. They have learnt, by a process of acculturation, how to prepare for the courtroom and how to behave once inside it. Professionals pay attention to detail, often for strategic and instrumental purposes. They present themselves 'properly', fulfilling contextual expectations with regard to dress, grooming and comportment. Professionals understand, and make an effort to comply with, courtroom ritual and etiquette. More specifically, they have acquired and nurtured presentation skills, including a range of linguistic and para-linguistic techniques, which can serve to enhance the potency of their communicative performances (Conley et al. 1978, O'Barr 1982). Their ranks encompass lawyers, together with many applicants, police officers, local authority officials, licensing consultants, and experts. The mark of professionalism as a witness is experience, sometimes augmented by formal witness training.

Some professionals spend much of their working lives in court, whilst others are fairly infrequent attendees.[10] Of all professionals, it is the lawyers—barristers, solicitors, and their assistants—together with court staff, such as clerks to the court, and members of the bench (judges and magistrates) who have the deepest insider knowledge and status (Rock 1993). It is this insider group which controls use of time and space within the court, interprets the rules and conventions of procedural fairness, and shapes the delivery of witness testimony.

Real people

Informants sometimes used the term 'real people' to refer to amateurs—persons who did not regularly participate in licensing

---

[10] Some professionals such as Accident and Emergency Department (AED) Consultants will appear as witnesses as part of their work on a very occasional and ad hoc basis. Such persons are not classified as professional witnesses, as their degree of involvement in courtroom culture is strictly limited.

litigation as part of their work and who possessed only limited knowledge of courtroom mores. Real people and their testimonies added a degree of colour and authenticity to proceedings that was often lacking in the more scrupulous submissions of professional witnesses. Their stories were therefore regarded as important, but—all too often absent—constituents of the adversarial script. The characterization of Linda and Simon in Chapter 6 indicated ways in which the content of objections by lay persons has largely shifted in focus from moral entrepreneurship to a concern with 'quality of life' issues. Accordingly, real people were usually local residents and/or the owners of small non-leisure businesses.

Although most real people dressed formally when they came to court, a sizable minority wore more casual clothing and appeared to have paid little attention to their personal grooming. This, of course, was in marked contrast to the presentational style of the professionals. As we shall see, significant differences between the two groups were apparent in relation to their oral and bodily performances. Some real people were better equipped than others to adapt to the expectations of the court. Witnesses of high social status, for example, were more likely to be familiar with public speaking, appropriate forms of self-presentation at formal social occasions, and the use of elaborate and technical language codes. All professionals, even those with formal legal qualifications, begin their courtroom careers as real people. The intricate requirements and expectations of the setting could be learnt only through repeated exposure.[11]

Know thine enemy

Notions of procedural fairness require that evidence be heard in full. As noted in Chapter 6, this means that real people might be forced to sit through hours of stupefying detailed submission and pedantic cross-examination. Most of the delays in court were caused by problems in the scheduling of court time and the length and detail of the arguments. In relation to the latter, real people sometimes felt that their opponents were deliberately using time as a resource and weapon against them.

The adversarial and fateful nature of the trial could make waiting a peculiarly unpleasant experience. Lay witnesses would

---

[11] See the postscript to this book for an account of my own 'moral career'.

often find themselves in close physical proximity to their opponents. They were required to share corridors, restaurants, waiting areas, and toilet facilities with those they were effectively accusing. For men, the spatial arrangement of urinals, for example, could facilitate especially fraught encounters which needed to be negotiated with care within a context in which the usual rules of civil attentiveness were suspended (Williams 1998). Application teams were predominately comprised of high status middle-aged men who often seem comparatively at ease within the courtroom setting. Their confidence, attire, and often bulky, or toned, body shape, afforded them an imposing and sometimes intimidating physical presence.

Many professionals appeared to know one another and during breaks in proceedings the lawyers among them typically engaged in light-hearted banter. These exchanges indicated seemingly genuine feelings of mutual empathy and respect between a set of protagonists who were 'simply doing their job' (see below). Although the more confident of non-lawyers sometimes attempted to dissipate tension by engaging in jocular small talk, the interactions of professional witnesses and parties to the case were usually characterized by a more forced and formal 'politeness'. In the most bitter of struggles, this superficial etiquette broke down, to be replaced by the frosty exchange of grimaces, stares, sarcasm, and wry smiles. Although one applicant quietly informed me that he intended to 'nail me', overtly aggressive behaviour during waiting periods was rare. This said, talk was mostly serious and the atmosphere conspiratorial. Opposing teams would dominate the public spaces of the court as they huddled together in packs around be-wigged and gowned counsel. If briefing rooms were available, these groups would retire to discuss tactics and evaluate proceedings behind closed doors. Inexperienced witnesses might be seen sitting in corridors, red-faced and silent.

Once inside the courtroom, each team would align itself in bench seating behind counsel; one team to the right of the court-room and the other to the left. The objection team—which rarely comprised more than four witnesses—would be flanked by an application team, seated in rows like the ranks of some dark-suited army. In smaller courtrooms, the benches were often shorter and opponents would be forced to sit next to one another. Faces would become stern and solemn now. The applicant's professional soldiers would rise from their trenches one by one to deliver their evidence, bombarding their opponents with argument after argument in an attempt to jettison the full script. As we shall see, the adversarial approach to adjudication sometimes had a profound effect upon the courtroom experience of lay witnesses. In the fog of war, inexperienced combatants became nervous and confused. Although officially 'released' by the bench after giving their evidence, many professionals chose to remain in court as spectators and advisers. Lay witnesses, by contrast, almost invariably left the battlefield as quickly as possible.

'There may be some questions': real people in the witness box

One senior counsel with whom I had previously conversed on friendly terms in an earlier case made the symbol of a cross with his fingers when I entered the court. Although on this occasion he was to be my interrogator, I was perturbed and surprised by this somewhat hostile action. 'I thought you liked me, last time we met?' I asked. '*That* was when we were commissioning you', he replied with a grimace.

As Devlin (1979: 61) notes, 'the theory is that the witness is partisan; an advocate refers to him as "my witness" and "your witness"'. Witnesses were regarded and treated accordingly. When presenting evidence-in-chief, counsel engaged witnesses in a gentle, polite and conversational tone (Rock 1993: 29). The witness would be taken through their proof, with counsel strategically highlighting particular paragraphs that the witness was invited to confirm and/or explicate. As Rock (ibid.) observes, witnesses were then required to face cross-examination, a form of questioning that was 'neither gentle nor conversational'.

Presentation of the objection script would often depend upon the testimony of real people. The objection case might therefore be immediately disadvantaged by a corresponding reliance on the neophyte witness. Public speaking under oath in a highly peculiar and formal social setting could be a disconcerting, even terrifying, experience. Once witnesses took to the stand, they might face a gruelling cross-examination lasting several hours. All eyes would fix upon them. Compelled to reply to every question, their bodily as well as verbal performance would be scrutinized: posture, grooming, accent, and delivery. As their testimony began, the dark rows would begin to whisper, smirk, and sneer, sometimes emitting exasperated sighs. There might be a shuffling of papers as notes were passed forward to counsel; the applicant's foot soldiers being eager to please their general by supplying him with every ounce of available ammunition. Court etiquette required that answers be addressed to the bench rather than towards one's interrogator. To the real person this could appear strange and 'unnatural'. Answers were often stilted and mumbled and the witness would be asked to 'speak up'.

Cross-examination was often uninhibited, its object being to challenge, denounce, undermine, and discredit (Ellison 2001, Garfinkel 1956, Rock 1993). Counsel might use black humour to tease and goad the witness. Witnesses would often be humiliated, their opinions dismissed, integrity questioned, intelligence insulted, and status belittled; they might be mocked and provoked. All of this was conducted in front of an attentive audience. Yet, the role of the bench as decision-makers and impartial arbiters created an expectation of passivity in permitting counsel to proceed in making their case largely as they saw fit. This expectation militated against interventions by the bench to assist a witness in distress (Connolly 1975, Devlin 1979, Ellison 2001, Pannick 1987, 1992).

When facing cross-examination, many witnesses, and especially real people, displayed para-linguistic symptoms such as a shaking of the body; a flushed or pale visage; perspiration; fidgeting; avoidance of eye contact with others; and a tense and hunched posture. Unfortunately for the witness, these recognized signifiers of stress, anxiety and embarrassment are also popularly identified in the legal orthodoxy with deception. This concern with what is sometimes referred to as 'demeanour' evidence is rooted in the highly contestable belief that a dishonest witness will betray themselves by displaying a particular set of readily identifiable behavioural cues. These assumptions conflict with research in forensic psychology which indicates that non-verbal behaviours, in trial settings and elsewhere, may be characterized by a range of cultural, social and individual differences (Ekman 1985, Ellison 2001, Shuy 1993, Wellborn 1991).[12] As Ellison notes, orthodox

[12] Ekman (1985), for example, identifies verbal behaviours such as shifts in speech pattern and vocal pitch as more reliable indicators of veracity.

legal assumptions serve to discount 'the high levels of stress commonly experienced by witnesses testifying in accordance with conventional adversarial methods' (ibid.: 77).

Emotional management

Goffman notes how social actors will usually attempt to project an impression of themselves which has 'positive social value' (1967: 5). This projection is referred to as the *face* he or she presents to the world. During mundane social interaction, people perform 'face-work' as they seek to regulate their behaviour in order to maintain a consistency between their actions and projected selves (1967: 12–13, Manning 1992: 39). In most social situations, people conspire to protect not only their own face, but also that of others. Goffman regards such 'tact' as a vital lubricant of interaction, used to preserve social situations that might otherwise break down. The use of tact protects people from the distress and embarrassment that can occur when others perceive a disjuncture between their projected and actual selves: 'felt lack of judgmental support from the encounter may take him aback, confuse him, and momentarily incapacitate him as an interactant. His manner and bearing may falter, collapse and crumble' (Goffman 1967: 8). Such ruptures of the interactional order are subject to social censure. In order to save face in encounters with others, one is expected to retain control, to 'pull oneself together', to maintain *poise*; that is, one's 'capacity to suppress and conceal' any feelings of shame (ibid.: 9).

Trials are social settings in which this implicit ritual order is disrupted and new, more overt, rules imposed. In court, social actors are formally restricted in their ability to protect the face of others. Witnesses present themselves in order to be 'tested' and to have their weaknesses exposed. Moreover, the adversarial system provides advocates with full justification and motivation to perform the role of interrogator with little thought for the feelings of opposing witnesses (Ellison 2001, Rock 1993). During cross-examination, people's face-work is directly and repeatedly challenged and any perceived inconsistency between one's projected and actual self may be harshly exposed. In order to withstand cross-examination, witnesses have to be 'thick-skinned'. In more formal terms, they must develop the performative capacity to control the expression of their emotions, measuring their responses and maintaining poise to an unusual degree. The witness box is a lonely place, to the extent that witnesses must save face without the interactional support of others.[13] Moreover, although placed in this situation of conflict, witnesses do not have license to launch disparaging counter-attacks against their interrogator. Witnesses are bound by the peculiar communicative rules of the trial, which permit them only to respond to the content of questions. The character of one's accuser is not deemed relevant or challengeable in the way it might during everyday argumentation.

Witnesses may be 'broken down', becoming tearful, or making clearly exaggerated or aggressive outbursts. Such passionate responses are understandable. Real people will often have a significant personal stake in the outcome of a trial. Yet, to rise to anger, or reply with sarcasm, is to take counsel's bait (Schopenhauer 1896). Such exchanges, displayed for critical inspection in open court, permit counsel to engineer unfavourable impressions of the witness as overly emotional, irrational, narrow-minded, or prejudiced. As Goffman notes, 'a competent person is expected to retain composure even under the most trying circumstances; to become flustered and lose poise usually reflects adversely on one's character' (1967: 97–98).

Counsel must choose their victims with care lest they fall out of favour with the bench (see Du Cann 1964: 122). In licensing, this requires 'going softly' with the frail and elderly. Whilst it would be easy, and perhaps tempting, for counsel to bully such witnesses, they will often have gained the respect and sympathy of the court through their presence alone. They may accordingly receive a 'friendly', if patronizing, cross-examination, focusing on mild questioning of consistency and the exposure of knowledge gaps; perhaps in relation to their own experiences of the streets at night.

Counsel will attempt to expose ambiguities and lack of preparation, casting objectors as 'NIMBYs' and portraying their objections as misguided and unreasonable. As noted in Chapter 6, campaigners are particularly susceptible to character assassination

---

[13] In the case of 'procedurally unfair' questioning, a witness's own counsel may seek to disrupt the cross-examination in order to make an appeal to the bench. More direct assistance from counsel may only occur retrospectively in the form of prompts to clarify or temper certain points during re-examination. As noted, adversarial theory militates against protective interventions by the bench.

as their cause may be portrayed as non-representative, elitist, reactionary, or doctrinaire.[14] To admit to holding strong established beliefs on a subject is to admit one's partiality. Far from consigning images of prudery to the dustbin of history, the denial of moral prejudice in contemporary licensing has served to re-emphasize such matters within adversarial discourse. Defending oneself *against the charge* of taking a principled stand is now one of the key challenges facing those objection witnesses who lack the recourse to notions of pseudo-scientific objectivity enjoyed by experts (see below). The legal masquerade demands an outward façade of dispassionate risk assessment. This is not easily understood by real people, particularly the chronically sleep deprived and those required to cleanse their steps of vomit and urine each morning. As both witnesses and observers, real people can be emotional; openly expressing their frustration, resentment, and cynicism regarding the behaviour of licensed operators and their patrons. On occasion, they may perceive indications of bias and openly criticize and heckle the bench. Such behaviour challenges the sanctity of a carefully orchestrated formal occasion and invariably prompts stern chastisement.

Lawyers and other professionals viewed real people as flaky and unpredictable performers whose perceived emotionality and occasional outbursts could compromise the most 'sound' and 'rational' of arguments. Choice of words and manner of delivery were regarded as all important in conveying acceptable and convincing arguments. Residents disposed to rant about the 'young animals tearing up our flower-beds' would give a much more negative account of themselves than the person who calmly, determinedly, and systematically catalogued specific instances of anti-social behaviour, whilst expressing well-informed sympathy for young people with few viable leisure opportunities.

Language games

As well as manipulating a witness's emotions, counsel may also seek to direct their words. Counsel will make every effort to reframe an opponent's script as inconsistent, illogical or incoherent.

---

[14] Correspondingly, counsel for the objector may enquire as to how supporters of the application were recruited; were they paid in money or kind? Do they have any financial interest or personal or professional links with the applicant?

In pursuing this destructive agenda, counsel may find assistance in the institutional rules governing interaction in trial settings. As noted, one important feature of courtroom interaction is that it does not conform to taken-for-granted norms of conversation and argumentation (Linton 1965). Cross-examination, for example, is in many respects a unique form of communicative action, 'since it provides the questioner with immense authority, incorporates legal limitations on how a witness can respond, and is oriented to third-party judgment' (Brannigan and Lynch 1987: 142). An extensive literature on the 'special' use of language within trials has shown, sometimes in painstaking detail, how advocates employ language strategically in order to denounce, coerce, and persuade (Atkinson and Drew 1979, Bennett and Feldman 1981, Garfinkel 1956, Jacquemet 1996, Lynch and Bogen 1996, Matoesian 1993, Molotch and Boden 1985). Guides to courtroom practice written by experienced lawyers often go into great detail in describing the application of tried-and-tested strategies for manipulating the content, form and timing of an opponent's testimony (O'Barr 1982: 31–7).[15] This emphasis on occupational acculturation and the inculcation of practical skills implies that courtroom success can, to a large degree, only be accomplished through purposive interaction.

The exercise of discursive control

One frequently observed tactic of advocacy involves the termination of a particular line of questioning immediately a contrast, admission, or apparent anomaly has been engineered. Cross-examination has a game-like quality. Once a 'goal' has been scored, the scorer will often seek to leave the field of play. The phrase 'I have no further questions your honour', followed by a lengthy pause, is often used to provide the umpire with an opportunity to recognize and ponder some 'incongruity with, and hence damaging puzzle over, the witness's evidence' (Drew 1985: 145–6). As Shuy (1993: 144) notes, in everyday conversation, a person would usually have the opportunity to say: 'Wait a minute.

---

[15] There are many practical guidebooks on the tactics of advocacy aimed at the neophyte barrister, some of which have attained the status of classic texts, retaining their relevancy over several decades and frequently reappearing as reprints and revised editions (Bailey and Rothblatt 1971, Du Cann 1993, Hyam 1999, Munkman 1986, Napley 1970, Wellman 1997, Wrottesley 1930).

I haven't had a chance to tell you what I meant.' The trial is not a setting where such emendations can easily be made: 'witnesses can only answer questions that they have been asked. They cannot volunteer new topics or start new question/answer sequences. Once cut off, they must be quiet. Once misunderstood, they must live with the misunderstanding' (Shuy: ibid.).

Termination devices may therefore leave the witness in a state of frustration, feeling that their answers have been 'edited' by counsel in order to change the meaning or emphasis of their words, or to submit a distorted and incomplete impression of their opinions (Shuy 1993: 137–148). When attempting to control and direct topics to their advantage, counsel may insist that the witness answer questions with a simple 'yes' or 'no'. This technique seriously restricts the witness's freedom to express and explicate matters: 'they may want to tell the whole truth and nothing but the truth but they are prevented from doing so by the very process that demands it' (Shuy 1993: 136). As O'Barr (1982: 119) points out:

One of the most frequent complaints of witnesses, especially first-time witnesses, is that they had little opportunity during the trial to tell their version of the facts. Instead, they typically report, the lawyers asked only *some* of the relevant questions and consequentially they only managed to tell part of their story.

Clearly, counsel will often be very sophisticated language users and the professional skills and resources they bring to bear in cross-examination can place less proficient language users, or indeed almost any inexperienced lay person, at a significant disadvantage (O'Barr 1982, Shuy 1993: 202). Lay witnesses will often perform poorly, presenting an unconvincing case even when their evidence is highly credible in terms of factual content (Conley et al. 1978, Schopenhauer 1896). Shuy (1993: 136), himself an experienced expert witness, notes how 'most witnesses are not skilled enough verbally to match attorneys who are practised in winning their cases. They are not aware that in every question they are asked, a possible trap is lurking.' However, in this game of 'cat and mouse', the interrogated are, of course, not passive: 'The success or failure of denunciation . . . hinges on the nature of the response made by the denounced' (Emerson 1969: 142).

Defensive strategies

Counsel's purposive manipulation of question-answer sequences in order to avoid certain topics whilst emphasizing others 'can also be the basis on which the witness may detect that purpose in the questioning' (Atkinson and Drew 1979: 134). Witnesses who understand the basic nature of the adversarial system are 'generally cautious in the way they answer questions . . . alive to the probability that counsel will try in various ways to upset their evidence' (Drew 1990: 40). Witnesses have to be confident and assertive enough to disrupt the unilateral flow of counsel's questioning by making measured and qualified answers, using responses such as 'yes, but'. Proactive witnesses will frame their answers in such a way as to best exhibit and defend the script that they and their team mates wish to present (Lynch and Bogen 1996), whilst taking care to 'avoid endorsing those aspects of cross-examining counsel's versions that differ from, or are detrimental to, their own version of "the facts" ' (Drew 1990: 62). Witnesses may seek to anticipate and disrupt the course of counsel's questioning; giving qualified answers at every available opportunity, with the aim of denying counsel the materials out of which a convincing case may be built.

When direct responses to an accusation cannot be avoided, the witness may seek to employ defensive devices that counter or dissolve the discrediting implications of counsel's charges. These linguistic forms are not unique to the setting and have been variously described by sociologists as excuses and justifications (Atkinson and Drew 1979, Emerson 1969, Scott and Lyman 1968) and techniques of neutralization (Sykes and Matza 1957). Witnesses use such devices in order to negotiate the preservation of favourable impressions before the court in relation to personal and team identity and the credibility of their script. As we saw in Chapter 7, due to the largely scripted nature of the evidence presented in licensing cases, it is possible for protagonists to anticipate possible challenges and draw upon a pool of well-rehearsed counter-arguments. Crucially however, access to the argument pool is differentially and asymmetrically allocated in accordance with professional knowledge and/or trial experience. Real people will typically have limited awareness of the range of possible responses and can make none of the claims to legitimate opinion available to their 'expert' adversaries: 'A person of lower status has a weaker claim to the right to define what is going on; less trust is placed in her judgments; and less respect is accorded to what she feels' (Hochschild 1983: 173). The defensive options open to the lay witness may often be restricted to 'giving delayed and qualified responses, expressing apparent confusion about the questions, and agreeing with the prosecutor (*sic*) in only a hypothetical and minimized way' (Brannigan and Lynch 1987: 115). Such responses may, of course, be framed by counsel as evasive.

In sum, cross-examination can be characterized as a struggle between advocate and witness over impressions of credibility and persuasiveness. The rules of the game are loaded in favour of the interrogator who controls the selection, sequencing, and juxtaposition of evidence, determines the topics to be raised and their relative emphasis, and seeks to restrict the submission of embellished or narrative testimony (Atkinson and Drew 1979: 187, Ellison 2001, Matoesian 1993: 35, 100).

Pride and prejudice: the examination of experts

Clerk to the Court (preparing for witness to be sworn in): What oath do you swear?

Expert witness (social scientist): Doctors swear the Hippocratic Oath.

The examination of experts and consultants (henceforth referred to as experts) invariably begins with a brief review of their credentials. The listing of title, qualifications and institutional affiliation serves to draw the court's attention to the peculiar identity of the witness; a process that immediately presents him or her in 'the best possible light' (Bennett and Feldman 1981: 138).[16] Invocation of professional status and expertise establishes a *membership category* (Sacks 1972) entitling the witness to exalted claims to knowledge that 'obviate the need to ask how the person

---

[16] In jury trials, the Crown Court Bench Specimen Directions offer guidance to the judge on the adducing of expert evidence. These instructions give a clear sense of how the court proposes to limit the potential influence of expert evidence. No comparable directions are issued in the licensing courts. This permits counsel to build up their own experts or diminish their opponent's, free of any of the guidance used in jury trials. Indeed, in licensing cases, lawyers are able to refer to people as 'experts' who would never qualify to give evidence in criminal trials, for example, ex-police officers acting as 'licensing consultants'.

knows' (Potter 1996: 126, cited in Williams 2000: 126). Moreover, the witness is imbued with authority, constituted as a set of personal and/or institutional resources or 'category entitlements' that can be drawn upon to justify their views and make their opinions count (Williams 2000: 126–129). To paraphrase Lynch (2004: 165), one's classification as an 'expert' is 'more than a label; it is a term of praise and a mark of privilege'. Entitlements to authoritative speech help to legitimize the witness's testimony and to some extent modify the usual expectations that a witness will have detailed empirical knowledge of local particularities (see below). The knowledge claims of experts, when matched by their apparent independence, are important factors in influencing their selection for the team. During the trial, these status-related entitlements effectively translate into a set of practical resources to be deployed both offensively and defensively in interaction by experts as they seek to promote their evidential script.

The realities constructed through the presentation of scripts are validated and brought to life through the testimony of witnesses and remoulded in the exchanges between witness and lawyer. Chapter 7 describes how counsel will seek to shape their team's case in preparation for trial. Counsel will then aim to reproduce this script through strategic interaction during the trial itself, engineering an artificial fit between what was prepared and what is presented. In order to maintain the coherence of the script, counsel must collaborate closely with their team, each individual working hard to process disparate information and present it within the appropriate interpretative frame. The lawyer carefully leads the witness through their testimony, 'offering cues about how broadly to answer the question, what to volunteer and what to anticipate in the next question' (Bennett and Feldman 1981: 121). This is accomplished by phrasing questions to one's own witness in such a way as to elicit tactically 'useful' responses, whilst at the same time, using emphasis to make some pieces of evidence appear more significant than others. Counsel may also use evidence-in-chief as an opportunity to draw out any potential weaknesses in a witness's testimony and assimilate them into the script, thus 'stealing a cross-examiner's "thunder" and neutralizing the effect of detrimental evidence' (Ellison 2001: 52).

As noted, a key tactic of counsel is to ask questions that require very precise and concrete answers. This approach is used to corral debate within the boundaries of a preferred script by narrowing the possibilities for broader or alternative interpretations of the evidence. Bennett and Feldman (1981) refer to a struggle between opponents to expand or contract the range of potential interpretations. Strategic organization of question sequencing is used to elicit 'definitions of evidence consistent with the larger underlying story that is being developed' (Bennett and Feldman 1981: 121). In staging this endeavour:

It goes without saying that the degree of success . . . depends a great deal upon the willingness of the witness to cooperate and his or her ability to respond to the cues in a line of questioning. Some witnesses are more cooperative and more receptive to cues than others. As a rule, expert witnesses . . . are the most effective partner with whom to play out a tactic of co-operation . . . Expert witnesses generally have schooled the lawyer in advance on the terminology that can be applied to their evidence . . . and they deliver a confident line of testimony . . . Expert witnesses get a lot of practice in trial situations. This hones their sensitivity to the tactical moves of their examiners. Not only does this experience make expert witnesses excellent players in a cooperation game, it also enables them to disrupt effectively the efforts of opposing lawyers to orchestrate their testimony (Bennett and Feldman 1981: 124).

With experience, professionals learn to control the outward expression of their emotions (Hochschild 1983). This emotional work involves studied attempts to avoid the sort of 'breakdown' and disruption of testimony described in relation to real people. Rock (1993: 61) identifies counsel as 'performers whose composure and command could contrast quite tellingly with that of the ruffled civilian: they were the managers, not the managed, the cool, not the heated'. Lawyers and professional witnesses were well rehearsed in the art of what Goffman (1959: 211) refers to as 'dramaturgical discipline . . . the crucial test of one's ability as a performer'. Professionals were 'disciplined performers who succeeded in suppressing their spontaneous feelings, in order to give the appearance of sticking to the affective line, the expressive status quo' (ibid.). As Goffman explains, to exercise dramaturgical discipline is to display loyalty to one's team. Like all teams, the licensing team values and rewards its members for acts of self-discipline. Loyalty to team involves a willingness to reflexively monitor one's performance. One must seek not only to perform to the best of one's ability, but also to limit and repair any damage to team credibility sustained in the course of one's performance:

> ... a performer who is disciplined, dramaturgically speaking, is someone who remembers his part and does not commit unmeant gestures or *faux pas* in performing it. He is someone with discretion; he does not give the show away by involuntarily disclosing its secrets. He is someone with 'presence of mind' who can cover up on the spur of the moment for inappropriate behaviour on the part of his team-mates, while all the time maintaining the impression that he is merely playing his part (ibid.: 210–211).

If disruptions to the script cannot be avoided or concealed, perhaps because of the submission of new and destructive information by one's opponents, or because of a *faux pas* committed by oneself or one's team-mates: 'the disciplined performer will be prepared to offer a plausible reason for discounting the disruptive event, a joking manner to remove its importance, or deep apology and self-abasement to reinstate those held responsible for it' (ibid.: 211). The reparatory/defensive devices open to experts and other professionals are generically identical to those referred to above in relation to real people. Many concrete examples of reparation responses in licensing trials were, of course, described in Chapter 7. Yet, 'to establish such defences successfully before an often hostile and suspicious audience requires the skilful use of various techniques of presentation—in short requires a competent performance on the part of the ... actor involved' (Emerson 1969: 144). As the Irish comic, Frank Carson, put it, 'It's the way you tell 'em'.

As Rock (1993: 32) concludes, each side's case is 'a *thesis*' to be defended in a manner that is 'substantially rhetorical'. Some combatants are more accomplished orators than others. Professionals may have benefited from extensive pre-trial training in courtroom presentation skills (Solon 2004). Also, as regular team members, they will simply be more experienced than real people. This means that they may have presented similar evidence on numerous occasions in the past, attended many more pre-trial conferences and have a greater familiarity with the argument pool. In sum, they will have become seasoned team members, playing their own well-rehearsed and finely tuned parts in interdependent cooperation with counsel, their director. These accumulated skills, when combined with claims to exalted knowledge, served to enhance the oral performance of experts.

Expert witnesses were particularly notable for their articulacy; refined elocution; succinctness; and comparatively relaxed, open, and confident demeanour. Many experts were able to maintain a 'sunny disposition' throughout their testimony and were able to smile or crack an inoffensive joke even during periods of intense questioning. Experts would often embellish their testimony with colourful metaphors and anecdotes, making the performance of lay witnesses appear 'wooden' and staid by comparison. As well as using humour and charm to woo the court, experts typically delivered their testimony in a loud, clear, and dispassionate tone. Strategic communicative action can be understood as a pre-requisite of courtroom credibility and persuasiveness (Brannigan and Lynch 1987). By applying their refined skills of impression management, experts were able to portray their client's cause as positive, benign, and reasonable, thereby often winning the sympathy of the bench.

Research in the field of forensic oratory has long indicated associations between styles of speech, previous trial experience, and various indices of social status, class, and educational background (Conley et al. 1978, O'Barr 1982). In transcripts of the testimony of lower status groups and lay persons of all social backgrounds, research has found a greater incidence of language types thought to undermine the credibility of oral evidence in formal legalistic settings.[17] In their co-authored research, Conley and O'Barr associate more confident and 'powerful' testimonial styles with witnesses of high social standing in society at large and/or in those persons accorded high status by the court. In particular, people who testified repeatedly on the basis of their professional expertise displayed few features of a 'powerless' speech style. In general, my findings corroborated this. Expert witnesses were often more assertive than lay people and thus more successful in their attempts to prevent counsel from controlling and misrepresenting their evidence.

These factors have an important impact upon the interactional performance of witnesses within the adversarial system. *Form*

---

[17] These included hesitant forms, hedges, intensifiers, fragmented narratives, and heavily accented or hyper-correct speech (Conley et al. 1978: 1383).

matters as much, if not more than, content (O'Barr 1982). The generally more polished and robust presentational style of professional witnesses, particularly experts, may have a favourable influence on the reception of their testimony quite independently of the validity and truthfulness of what is said. Conversely, of course, the nervous, hesitant, faltering, and disjointed style more often displayed by lay and/or inexperienced witnesses, is likely to be less persuasive. The evidence of such witnesses may appear to be less credible simply by virtue of the manner in which it is presented (Conley et al. 1978: 1392, Egglestone 1975: 432, Ellison 2001: 23, O'Barr 1982: 69–70). In sum, reflexivity, loyalty, and confidence were the marks of a consummate performance by expert witnesses and other professionals. These interactional skills had been honed by repeated exposure to the adversarial system and nurtured through the application of pre-existent resources derived from social status and exalted claims to knowledge.

Attacking the knowledge claims of experts

Counsel (abruptly, with a sneer): So you are a Criminologist? Perhaps you could tell the court what that means? and what it has got to do with my client's application?

During cross-examination counsel may launch a direct attack on the knowledge claims of experts, questioning aspects of their experience, professionalism, and other sources of entitlement. The witness's curriculum vitae may be dissected and any apparently inconsistent views expressed in earlier work 'exposed'. Witnesses assigning themselves the status of an academic or 'scientist' may be asked whether their work has been subject to independent peer review. The witness may be presented with unfavourable reviews, or asked to disclose the sources of their research funding. If a witness is young, or comparatively inexperienced, their biography may be unfavourably contrasted with the maturity and experience of an opposing witness. Conversely, the validity of knowledge claims made by older and/or higher-status witnesses may be challenged by dint of their social identity, which, it is insinuated, effectively debars them from an understanding of the youthful and visceral mores of the night-time city. Counsel may attempt to test the witness by asking a question that might reasonably be expected to fall within their range of expertise: a random technical clarification, or a question which probes their knowledge of the law or current policy debate. If the witness is unable to answer, answers incorrectly, or even hesitantly, then counsel may succeed in casting doubt upon their professional competency.

As Lynch (2004: 167) notes, one of the special privileges of the expert witness is 'the right to give "hearsay" testimony on behalf of members in a relevant profession or field'. Yet, courts are often concerned, not only with the assessment of individual experts, but also with appraising the credibility and relevancy of their respective disciplines. Criminologists, chartered surveyors, psychologists and statisticians, for example, may all proffer opinions on a topic that derive from highly divergent frames of reference and meaning. In cross-examination, counsel may instigate a line of questioning involving 'boundary work' wherein the witness is invited to reflect upon and clearly designate the limits of his or her expertise (Lynch, ibid.: 173–176). The bench are then tasked with the onerous duty of shifting:

> ... between two registers: on the one hand, paying homage to science's transcendence by seeming to honour the categories that set science apart; on the other hand, remaking the distinctions between science and common sense through case-centred decision-making. (Jasanoff 2004: 10)

Trials remain bastions of empiricist thought in which heavy reliance is placed upon fallible human capacities of observation and memory (Rock 1993). Events experienced at first-hand, as described by witnesses, are usually of great interest to the bench, however 'unrepresentative' they may be. Moreover, courts are concerned to avoid 'the production of bullshit' wherein 'a person's obligation or opportunities to speak about some topic exceed his knowledge of the facts that are relevant to that topic' (Frankfurt 2005: 63). For this reason, experts may find that their claims to rarefied insight do not entirely shield them from criticism, particularly if heavy reliance has been placed upon secondary sources and deductive reasoning, presented in the form of negative counter-evidence (see Chapter 6). However grand the expert's reputation or deep their retrospective knowledge of similar events, they will be expected to have 'got their hands dirty' (Lynch 2004: 176) unearthing primary sources of information. Those with cleaner hands may find themselves exposed to quite predictable lines of attack: how, if one has not experienced the brand or the area at first hand, can one possibly be entitled to form a valid opinion? Perhaps the witness has visited the area, but only briefly and at the wrong time, or on the wrong day. The day of the visit may be said to be unusual in some way: a public holiday or the date of a major sporting event or emergency. Perhaps the weather was unusually fine or inclement? This emphasis upon the 'directly experienced' and 'observable' extends to the expectation that a witness will have attended trial proceedings throughout and be aware of any issues raised during the examination of previous witnesses. Experts, in particular, may be criticized for failing to address the arguments and proposed solutions of their opponents.

These epistemological assumptions are compromised by the bench's almost universal lack of experiential knowledge regarding the matters upon which they are tasked to adjudicate. Judges and police officers, for example, usually inhabit very different social and professional worlds, allowing for a divergent interpretation of the facts, anchored in quite different realities. In a setting where almost all 'bad news' emanates from objection witnesses or media reporting, objector testimony can more easily be framed by the applicant's counsel as vexatious rumour, ill-informed anecdote, or exaggeration. As Bennett and Feldman (1981: 175) remark:

Bias can result when an adequate story is told, but the listener lacks the norms, knowledge, or assumptions to draw the inferences intended by the teller. The internal consistency and the significance of stories can be damaged if listeners and tellers live in different social worlds and hold different norms and beliefs about social behaviour.

This issue is illustrated in the following extract from my own cross-examination in a Central London PEL trial:

Counsel: If the premises were to close at 3am, where do you think customers would go?

PH: I don't know.[18]

Judge (intervenes laughing): Well, they'd go home wouldn't they?!

Counsel (with a smirk): Yes, your honour.

---

[18] My reasons for giving this answer will be apparent to readers of Chapters 3 and 5.

The need for lawyers and the bench to understand the meaning and implications of the evidence that is put before them places an onus upon experts to impart technically sophisticated knowledge in a clear and concise manner (Thompson 2004). Experts are expected to be effective communicators who are capable of simplifying esoteric concepts and avoiding the use of their own occupational jargon. As the following extract from the cross-examination of a psychologist indicates, being 'too academic' can create a breakdown in communication which prevents evidence from being properly tested:

Counsel: So do you think there is any relationship between the number of licensed premises in an area and the amount of crime?

Witness: Yes, the relationship is inverse.

C: Inverse? You mean as the number of pubs goes up, crime goes down?

W: Yes, this is generally observable. As competition increases, so standards rise and the crime rate falls. Good management accounts for 45 per cent of the variance of assaults.

C: Where does that figure come from?

W: It comes from my own research.

C: Did you say variance?

W: Yes, variance.

C: Could you explain that word please?

W: Variance is a term used in statistics. It is the mean of the sum of the squared deviations from the mean score divided by the number of scores. The larger the variance, the further the individual cases are from the mean.

C: Oh never mind! Let's move on.

A clash can occur between counsel, who may wish to elicit opinions expressed clearly and authoritatively in 'black and white', and the more conscientious experts who maintain that they can only provide a range of conclusions. Counsel may gain dramaturgical advantage over experts who appear pedantic, unable to communicate their ideas clearly, and unwilling to proffer unambiguous conclusions (Schopenhauer 1896). Benches will often share the legal mind-set and associate equivocation with evasion.

When selecting team members, counsel's choice of experts is, to a large degree, influenced by their reputation or known ability to perform. Counsel therefore shun witnesses whom they find to be 'difficult', 'flaky' and 'inconsistent', or whose input has to be continually monitored and controlled by means of time-consuming and detailed instruction. The experts in greatest demand are loyal co-conspirators who understand the broad script and its parameters. Such witnesses do not need to be groomed as they will, for the most part, already know what is expected of them and how to deliver it. Experts, therefore, have a clear financial incentive to please counsel by providing a loyal, disciplined and partisan service. Generous remuneration ensures a ready supply of alternative 'legal resources', eager to supply whatever a client requires. Thus, the expert's earnings—notwithstanding any other sources of income—become dependent upon a willingness to compromise (Becker 1963). It is by such means that licensing litigation, as an inherently market-driven, adversarial and aggressively instrumental approach to dispute resolution, militates against the principled and conscientious witness.

Relationships of patronage and reciprocal inter-dependence between counsel and experts are an open secret in licensing circles, allowing issues of partiality to emerge as the expert's Achilles heel. As we shall see, questions of objectivity, or its lack, arise as major themes in cross-examination.

Rhetorical piping, subliminal tunes: questioning the objectivity of experts

Applicant (owner of an independent bar chain) protesting to the court about my presence: The council is using this man as a weapon against me.
District Judge (curtly): He is not a weapon; he is a witness who is here to assist the court.

In formal legal orthodoxy, expert witnesses are held to owe an overriding duty to the court rather than to the party that commissions them (Harding 1992, Thompson 2004). Yet conversely, in a live adversarial trial setting it is usually taken for granted by participants that opposing witnesses will hold firmly entrenched allegiances to their team. Conscientious experts may therefore find themselves in an uncomfortable and ethically compromising position. From the moment they accept their commission, they will begin to feel the weight of their client's expectations. As hired hands they will be expected to 'know their place' in the team, deferring authority to counsel. At team meetings and other briefings, counsel may outline confidential strategies for fighting the case; tactics will be devised and the witness's advice may be sought. The expert will receive instructions regarding the type of evidence required. Counsel will, if only tacitly, indicate that such evidence must assist, and in no way prejudice, the case. To remain useful (and therefore employable), experts must be flexible in allowing themselves to be used as weapons of adversarial engagement. Once their report has been prepared it will be submitted to counsel as a *draft*, and any potentially damaging remarks or offending paragraphs will be edited or removed at counsel's behest. Counsel may attempt to influence a witness's interpretation of the facts and request further work on any point he or she wishes to emphasize.

If inexperienced, the expert may produce written work that is considered syntactically inappropriate: too wordy and academic, or loose and naturalistic in style. Counsel may provide detailed instructions for revision of the text in order to 'encourage' the witness to adopt the 'clear and concise' style of a legal proof of evidence report. The standard of the report in terms of both content and presentation may be markedly poor and the witness may produce reports that appear to be hurried adaptations of a generic template submitted in many previous cases. Experience fosters risk-aversion; a reluctance to tamper with tried, tested and finely-tuned arguments that appear both safe and *sufficient*. In deviating from the script, a witness risks setting their client's case adrift; they may find themselves in uncharted and dangerous waters where they may flail, and ultimately perish. If experts play the game as instructed they are less likely to shoulder the blame if things go wrong. An 'unhelpful' report would simply be rejected and could spell the end of the working relationship.

Seasoned experts present a veneer of objectivity in all 'front stage' interactions. As noted, they are also often adroit and persuasive witnesses, allowing cross-examination to become an extended battle of wills. In challenging the testimony of experts, counsel will seek to reveal partiality, vested interest, evasion, and half-truth (Du Cann 1964). In exploring what he refers to as the 'sociology of lying', Barnes (1994) defines lies broadly as 'statements that are intended to deceive'. He then breaks such statements down into two types: 'omissive lies' which involve the withholding of information and the evasion of questions, and 'commissive' lies that involve the *distortion* of information. When taking the oath, the witness swears to tell 'the truth, the whole truth, and nothing but the truth', yet, 'though the injunction presents its three parts as equally important, in practice, lies of omission are widely regarded as less reprehensible than lies of commission; they also provide fewer possibly vulnerable statements for the opposition to latch on to' (Barnes 1994: 37). As noted in Chapter 7, the adversarial system works in such a way as to reward each party for omitting evidence that is unfavourable to its case. Issues of omission must then be unearthed by cross-examination, as the following dialogue illustrates:

Counsel for the applicant: Can you describe the instructions you were given by the council's solicitors before making this video recording?

Witness: I was asked to visit the area late at night and record goings on.

C: How many hours did you spend in the area?

W: About ten hours, over both of the two Saturday nights.

C: But you didn't film for all of that time did you?

W: No.

C: Were you instructed to film anything in particular?

W: Yes. The solicitor told me to look for sources of noise, police activity, and trouble going on, that sort of thing.

C: Well, true to your brief, you found some urination and the like. But would it be true to say that you only pressed 'record' when you saw something of interest, something adverse, or bad going on?

W: I filmed the things I thought were relevant.

C: Yes. And how long is the film you made?

W: Fifty four minutes.

C: So, for nine hours and six minutes you saw nothing worth recording did you?

W: I only filmed when things started to happen.

C: Quite. (pause) I have no further questions.

The rhetorical strengths of the evidential script and its constituent arguments reside as much in omission as in content. The most popular approach to the organization of expert evidence involves the adoption of a narrow frame of reference for debate; one which ignores the broader view and selectively omits issues or details of potential detriment to one's case. Constructing a mask of objectivity requires a sophisticated understanding of the argument pool. This permits an opponent's perspective to be acknowledged, if and only if, it can be assigned low credibility or priority. For such reasons, the cross-examination of experts will often focus more upon what their testimony omits, rather than what it actually contains.[19] These spaces between the truth and the whole truth are counsel's most fertile hunting grounds.

In the testimony of experts, analytical rigour was notable for its absence. There was little recognition of complexity, ambiguity and doubt, with experts selecting only those studies which were supportive of their preordained script. Witnesses would go on to employ this restricted literature uncritically when developing their arguments. There were, of course, dramaturgical advantages to be gained from adopting such a blinkered approach. The forthright witness who states his or her opinions baldly may often prove more convincing than those who temper their evidence with talk of methodological fallibility and the limits of knowledge (Egglestone 1975). In his dialogue with *Gorgias*, Socrates characterized oratory as the art of persuasion and the giving of affective pleasure, rather than the teaching of truths, or the quest for knowledge. For Socrates, the orator did not possess any authentic 'craft', but simply a skill for rhetoric, a knack for entertaining, convincing, and pleasing an audience:

Oratory doesn't need to have any knowledge of the state of their subject matters; it only needs to have discovered a persuasion device in order to make itself appear to those who don't have knowledge that it knows more than those who actually do have it (Plato, *Gorgias*: 459c).

Many experts enthusiastically espouse their cause and have gained reputations for presenting particular sides of the debate. They may even be regarded as aligned with individual parties.[20] Some become embroiled in the politics of trade protection, obliging them to request advice from regular employers whenever they receive enquiries from a new client (for example, the solicitors

---

[19] As noted, in an adversarial and partisan system, the omissions of one party's script are likely to constitute the content of their opponent's.

[20] In cases of serious disagreement between experts, the courts have the power to order opposing witnesses to meet in order to clarify areas of agreement and disagreement. This did not occur in any of the trials observed.

representing a competitor and/or objector (Charity 2002).) As one classic commentator notes, dogmatism, in its strongest form, involves the expert becoming 'so warped in their judgment by regarding the subject in one point of view, that, even when conscientiously disposed, they are incapable of expressing a candid opinion' (Wellman 1997: 76).

Lists of previous clients provided by some experts read like a 'who's who' of the drinks industry. In one trial, counsel told the court that one member of his team had completed 'over 150 previous reports for pub companies' (noise expert); whilst another had the benefit of 'twenty-three years' experience in giving evidence in planning and licensing cases' (surveyor/licensing consultant); a third expert was described as being 'very familiar to everyone in licensing' (market surveyor). Such descriptions can be used to enhance the credibility of a witness only within a context in which it is assumed that the decision-makers hold 'a formalistic legal view of impartiality and expertise' and 'are prone to accept this ideology and appeal to its authority as a basis of establishing fact and drawing inferences' (Harding 1992: 135).

Undue bias can be insinuated by the probing of a witness's financial interests or business practices. One consultant openly admitted that the purpose of his business was to 'help operators obtain their licences'. Counsel also discovered that the man's wife held substantial shares in the applicant's company. Witnesses may be asked how many times they have given evidence on behalf of their client; how often they have given evidence in total; and how often they have worked for the 'other side' (for an applicant or objector generically). The witness's choice of words may be found to indicate bias. One crown court judgment criticized an expert for answering questions in an evasive manner and expressing his 'faith' in the applicant's brand. Experts are expected to strongly refute suggestions of bias by '*dramatizing* their innocence'; that is, by charging their responses with indignation and hurt (Brannigan and Lynch 1987: 136). Defence of personal integrity was one of the rare circumstances in which professionals would employ readily observable emotional cues, as on these occasions it was assumed to *enhance*, rather than detract from, the persuasiveness of their words.

Other issues arise in relation to the submission of negative evidence by experts; that is, as discussed, evidence purposely commissioned as a critique of an opponent's position. As well as the open submission of verbal and written critiques, negative evidence may take the form of confidential briefing notes for counsel. The presentation of evidential critique can be played out repeatedly in the courts in a series of moves and counter-moves which develop incrementally, case by case. These tactics can spell danger for the experts concerned. Counsel may seek to expose or construct antagonistic rivalries between the witnesses. The notion of a feud or personal grudge can be used to discredit one or more of the witnesses involved. If seen to 'touch a nerve', this line of questioning can be used to undermine testimony by implying malevolence. Such events can stall, or even put an end to once lucrative careers as a legal resource.

Although enacted in courtrooms across the land, licensing trials provide a window onto a small, highly specialized and incestuous professional world in which all the key players know one another, at least by reputation. In this world, 'dirt' is dug and gossip traded; professional performances appraised and reputations moulded. Experts inhabit the periphery of this world. For them, the maintenance of good working relationships with counsel and the main commissioning legal firms is crucial. Work is episodic, shifting from periods of overwhelming intensity to the quiet times, when commissions are sporadic or virtually non-existent. A popular witness in high demand one year may be castigated and regarded as unemployable by the next.

It is rare for an expert who usually appears on behalf of an applicant to change sides and appear for an objector (and vice versa). It may be assumed that those who do, might better protect themselves against accusations of bias. However, unlike advocates, witnesses do not enjoy immunity from the charge of inconsistency. There may be other dangers involved in attempting to 'swap scripts', which, under cross-examination by an effective counsel, can be exposed to devastating effect:

In one trial involving an appeal by *High Life Inns PLC* against the decision of a magistrates' court, the police commissioned a private investigator regularly employed by one of the company's main competitors, *Massive Leisure PLC*. The findings of a hostile cross-examination, which focused upon the witness's role within a trade protection feud between *Massive* and *High Life*, were reflected in the crown court's judgment. *High Life's* counsel implied that the witness bore grudges against both his client's company and an opposing witness, and suggested that *Massive* may even have sought to unduly influence the police's case by offering the services of 'their' witness. The bench's acceptance of this criticism severely damaged the witness's reputation, spelling ruin for a once lucrative consultancy business.

Thus, experts must proceed with caution, ever mindful of the transience of their utility. Loyalty, obedience and courtroom success are rewarded by amenable and remunerative working relationships. Yet, these links are tenuous. Licensing litigation is a hard-nosed business in which everyone is expendable. The systematic pressures and professional mores of a market-driven adversarial system militate against the submission of impartial testimony. For this reason, the careers of the system's foot soldiers can be unpredictable and short-lived, as each individual eventually succumbs to discredit under hostile cross-examination and adverse judgment. The performance of witnesses is ruthlessly monitored: 'experts who do well stay in the little black book and those that do not are summarily removed' (Solon 2004: 17).

Handbags at dawn: the duelling of gentlemen

Solicitors . . . like to please their clients and for that purpose . . . pick a good fighter (Devlin 1979: 59).

Trials are 'suspenseful' and 'fateful' (Danet and Bogoch 1980: 38) for participants and especially for the opposing parties in whose names they are fought. The trial is inherently dramatic in that it involves conflict—'conflict between two versions of reality' (ibid.). Yet, for counsel (those actors who perform the leading role), the events of court may be experienced as 'merely a show' (ibid.); a somewhat sterile demonstration of professional competence involving little connection with personal values. As a barrister interviewed by Rock (1993: 83) opined, 'counsel are only putting a case. You don't believe in your case. You suspend belief. You are simply a vehicle for putting a case.'

As indicated in Chapter 3, disputes are often resolved through mutual agreement between the parties. These negotiations occur in 'backstage' social settings, characterized by the absence of clients and the bench. On such occasions, counsel may shed the dramaturgical mask of righteous indignation: playful banter, knowing smiles, puns, and in-jokes serving to frame the conflict as ironic. Backstage bartering involves a subtle power play of pitches, trade-offs and compromises, making it more consensual than 'front-stage' advocacy. Its aim is to avoid lengthy trial proceedings and achieve rapid results, free from the formal impediments of legal theory and procedure. Counsel will assess the relative strengths and weaknesses of their case were the issues to be fought in open court.[21] This process allows each protagonist to focus upon identification of the 'bottom line'—an outcome that would be at least minimally acceptable to their respective clients. Counsel cannot decide for themselves where this line is to be drawn. A series of offers and counter-offers may be made, but at each stage of negotiation counsel are compelled to seek instruction from their client. Counsel will, of course, make their own opinions known and are likely to exert significant pressure upon clients to accept deals they think provide low risk and cost-effective resolution.

To highlight this preference for efficient and 'rational' disposal is not, however, to imply that counsel make no emotional investment in the outcome of their trials. In 1996, a trade team defeated their police rivals in a crown court appeal case concerning the opening of *Liberty's* nightclub in Nottingham. *Liberty's* proved to be a landmark case which opened the floodgates for the development of Nottingham city centre; an area which now contains over 350 licensed premises within one square mile (Green 2004). In an interview with BBC journalist Andy Davies, the specialist solicitor advocate Jeremy Allen, who acted for the applicants, recalled his feelings:

That was a *huge* moment. I mean, it was just fantastic. It was like Nottingham Forest winning the European Cup. We kept a reasonably straight face in *court*, but I can remember coming out and just punching the air, we were so thrilled (*Panorama*, 6 June 2004).

Many advocates appear to live for the court. The trial provides them with opportunities to pit their wits against respected opponents and to display flair, intellect, humour, and charm in front of an attentive and appreciative audience. Cross-examination—the peculiarly legalistic form of social interaction that can be such a terrifying and degrading experience for the lay witness—may often

---

[21] As explained below, the reputed attributes and prejudices of the adjudicator/s may form an important element of this assessment.

be regarded by counsel as exciting and creative work; a sport, or art form, even (Wellman 1997). In their attempts to orchestrate the trial, counsel must continually assess the mood of the bench,[22] reflexively adapting their own performances accordingly. The arguments of an opposing team and explicit prejudices of the bench are obstacles to be negotiated. Counsel must be thick-skinned and persistent, taking every opportunity to make 'mountains out of molehills' (Pannick 1992: 5).

These challenges have a game-like quality which can serve to make trial interaction more exciting for the professional. Despite the existence of various structural and systematic skews, outcomes remain unpredictable and successes hard-won. Convoluted exchanges between counsel that may seem dry and boring to the uninitiated, can, for the actors themselves, represent a form of self-affirming 'edgework' which tests the boundaries of professional competence: 'what they seek is the chance to exercise skill in negotiating a challenge, rather than turn their fate over to the roll of the dice' (Lyng 1990: 863). In open court battles—where 'back-stage' negotiation has failed—opponents 'tend to be fiercely competitive, anxious (sometimes obsessed) to win' (Pannick 1992: 6).

In the socio-legal literature one finds frequent use of metaphors which liken the trial to physical violence and warfare (Danet and Bogoch 1980: 42, Pannick ibid: 89). As Danet and Bogoch (1980: 41) argue, 'the adversary model of justice requires the attorneys representing each side to be highly combative, and, moreover, to be evenly matched in combativeness . . . to be combative is to be ready or inclined to fight; pugnacious'. Similarly, for Devlin, 'it is

---

[22] The parties do, of course, face something of a judicial lottery. Benches are not always impartial and individual members may acquire a reputation among lawyers for displaying particular prejudices. Some may be openly critical or dismissive of one side's witnesses and adopt a harsh tone with one counsel, whilst displaying warmth to his or her opponent. Bench members may display such biases through facial expression and bodily stance and also linguistically via expressions of exasperation such as sighs or 'tuts'. Questions from the bench may be worded in particular ways and from a certain perspective which serves to indicate that they have already accepted the assumptions or propositions of one side in preference to those of the other. These 'warning signals' are closely monitored by legal professionals in order to monitor the 'feel' of how a case is progressing and its likely outcome. Actions of the bench are carefully scrutinized for any signs of bias which may be construed as grounds for appeal.

in cross-examination that the British trial comes closest to fisticuffs' (1979: 58).

The gladiatorial cut and thrust of advocacy is approached with gravitas. It is considered a matter of professional courtesy to remain on civil terms with one's opponent. Protocols of formal address such as 'my learned friend' reveal more than a 'euphemistic legal amity' (Pannick 1987: 154). As noted, during breaks in proceedings, counsel will usually converse with one another in a friendly and sociable manner. Fraternization is important to the occupation subculture of trial lawyers as it allows the 'impression of opposition' to be 'dramaturgically speaking . . . shown up for what it partly is—the purchased performance of a routine task' (Goffman 1959: 193–194). In even the most embittered battles, counsel will usually attempt to sprinkle their linguistic blows with puns or self-depreciatory comments. These lighter moments are mixed with requisite expressions of deference and sycophancy, as counsel attempt to establish a rapport with all but the most hidebound of benches.

As discussed, such courtesies are rarely extended to opposing witnesses. Advocates are conditioned to regard themselves as having an overriding duty to their client (see Chapter 7). Professional efficacy therefore demands an indifference to the welfare of one's opponents. To empathize is to betray one's client, an action that may amount to professional suicide. As Rock (1993: 174) found, 'those who dwelt too much on the pain of the lay witness would not last long as effective advocates'.[23]

Of course, witnesses often *are* evasive. Some will try to avoid giving straight answers or seek to sidestep or ignore fundamental points. The challenge for counsel is to remain dogged in their pursuit of answers, exposing unsubstantiated rhetoric and material omission, question by question. The raw testimonial style of the layperson can sometimes be framed as honest and unadulterated; accomplished advocacy exposing the gulf between the professional witness's cautious, scripted, and politicized

---

[23] Counsel enjoy 'a blissful immunity' from the legal consequences of defamation and cannot be sued for words spoken in the course of a trial, even where 'malice and misconduct' can be shown (Pannick 1992: 94–95); counsel are licensed to denounce (Emerson 1969, Garfinkel 1956), possessing 'a standing invitation to be clever at someone else's expense' (C.P. Harvey, cited in Pannick 1992: 95).

approach and the more open and natural answering style of the
naïve real person.

When questioning their own witnesses, counsel will 'seek to
elicit testimony ... in a manner that enhances its persuasive
impact', using 'deliberate juxtaposition, repetition, and duration
to emphasize or disguise the significance of certain information'
(Ellison 2001: 52–53). These devices are notably theatrical;
'brilliant advocacy focuses on the strengths of the case and tugs at
the emotions of the audience' (Pannick 1992: 7).

The loser standing small

For every winner there must also be a loser. Those performances
and interpretations judged to be most compelling will prevail. The
differential competencies of counsel often prove significant in
contributing to the eventual outcome of trials and correlate with
both the inequitable financial resources of opponents and the
verdict of cases (Langbein 2003). These asymmetries of power,
which serve to challenge and skew notions of natural justice and
due process, were fully acknowledged in licensing circles. Such
inequities have long been individualized by liberal commentators
who regard them as no more than inevitable quirks of a healthily
functioning legal system:

Although all advocates are equal before the law, in court they continuously flaunt their own inequalities. The lawyer regards this with indifference, even when the result is reflected in a verdict, since it is to some
extent inevitable ... If the system were to be changed merely in order to
guard against disparities in skill in advocacy it would lose more than it
would gain. For to curb the natural abilities of the advocate would (be
to) rob him of his independence and freedom ... Du Cann (1964: 9–10).

Yet, solicitors and their clients were far from 'indifferent' in their
selection of counsel. Barristers who performed well were held in
high esteem by the trade, with some companies negotiating
retaining contracts which guaranteed preferential access to their
services and protection from 'poaching' by their enemies. Elite
specialists were feared opponents whose victories were the stuff
of occupational legend. Some had forged reputations as 'licence machines', on the basis that, as an applicant, you approach them, 'press
the right buttons and your licence emerges' (Collins 2002: 46).

Pressing buttons was an expensive pursuit. One barrister, frequently representing applicants in the toughest cases nationwide, could reputedly command fees of up to £30,000 for a two-day trial. It is a platitude to note that access to such representation was assigned by wealth, power and connections.

A plague of suits: trade teams on tour

Licensing hearings are dominated by the testimony of expert witnesses and it is application teams who rely most upon their services, some calling as many as twelve to fifteen in each trial. Trade interests therefore not only benefit from the most accomplished and vociferous counsel, but can also call upon the largest army of loyal and experienced mercenaries. When a nightlife brand is being rolled out across the country, the captains of industry—together with their carefully selected legal entourage—go on tour, descending on any town where resistance to their applications is met. The repeated rehearsal of evidence in courts nationwide allows these 'away teams' to present an especially consummate performance: witness statements and legal arguments are refined; presentation skills polished.

When the corporations come to town, effective opposition is rare. For many lay objectors it will be their first time in court. Home teams are comparatively under-funded, ramshackle and amateur; intimidated by the pinstriped swarms they see moving effortlessly from swish hotel to crumbling court. In one case, in which an industry conglomerate joined forces with the police to oppose a new nightclub application, the author was commissioned by the trade group in order to save police costs. The following case notes describe this introduction to the world of the 'away team':

The first day of the trial has drawn to a close and I am asked to attend an out-of-hours conference at the trade team's hotel. It is anticipated that I will be called to give evidence the following morning. I enter a stylish and expensively furnished lounge where I am introduced to the advocate, Jeremy Forbes-Hamilton, and a gaggle of solicitors, legal secretaries and licensing consultants. The group order generous quantities of tea, coffee and handmade biscuits, as they discuss the day's events: the pronouncements and mannerisms of the bench; the performance of witnesses and their opponent's counsel. After about half an hour of chit-chat, counsel takes me to one side to discuss my report and the briefing notes I have been asked to prepare. He seeks to test my knowledge and attitudes and to tease out any information I may be able to offer regarding Dr Dray—an expert due to give evidence on behalf of our opponents.

I am placed in an uncomfortable situation, as I know that in another case, in only two weeks' time, these roles are to be reversed. On this forthcoming occasion, Forbes-Hamilton will be cross-examining me. Furthermore, he will be commissioning Dr Dray, and there will—in all likelihood—be another meeting such as this, in which *my* reputation and evidence becomes the target! I am, therefore, mindful not to say anything which might damage my next client's case, or render me vulnerable to attack. In the world of licensing, time is money, and conversations with counsel are always conversations with a purpose. The advocate is a skilled communicator and seeks to put me at ease. I am asked about a colleague's reluctance to appear in licensing cases; the number of times I have given evidence; who else I am working for; how many times I have been matched against Dr Dray? He pumps me for personal information about Dray: what do I think of him? How well regarded is his work? Who funds it? Counsel admits that he has commissioned Dray before and alludes to the man's well-known drink problem; a topic upon which he refuses to elaborate.

We play a strange game of cat and mouse in which he does all the purring and I squeak. We both know it's not just about this case. He mentions, quite casually, that this will probably be the only time we are both on the 'same side', so it's 'a unique chance to get to know one another'. In other words, I'm a one-off hired hand. I answer questions accordingly. The conversation is generally friendly and occasionally entertaining, if somewhat stilted. I am anxious to appear helpful and excited to be placed in a new and intriguing situation. I want to help him win the case, but I'm cautious not to be easy with my opinions or say anything too controversial.

It was with such focused determination that trade teams prepared for battle. Applicants won around 80 per cent of the cases observed. To pursue a sporting analogy, although home teams scored the occasional 'giant killing' victory, away teams enjoyed certain fundamental advantages. Chiefly, they had greater financial resources and better, more expensive, players. When reflecting on his team's past glories, the ruthless logic of the adversary system permitted one lawyer to be candid:

PH: When you turn up in court with the best barristers and a team of experts, do you think it is an equal contest?

Licensing solicitor: No, not an equal contest at all. I am there to get the best result for my client and usually we do just that.

Conclusion: the power to persuade

'Microsociological' analyses have long been criticized for failing to acknowledge structural inequities of power,[24] yet from an interactionist perspective such admonishments are misguided (Dennis and Martin 2005). The pragmatist orientations of interactionist thought eschew theoretical dualism (Rock 1979, Rorty 1999) allowing patterns of inequality and differential relations of power to be understood in an alternative way to those traditions which regard 'structure' and 'agency' as separate entities, each with its own distinct ontology. For interactionists, the concept of 'structure'—if used at all—is employed metaphorically to denote dynamic 'conditions of action'. As Schwalbe et al. (2000: 439) explain:

To speak of linking action to structure implies the need to build a theoretical bridge between different orders of social reality. But from an interactionist standpoint, there is no need for such a bridge, one end of which would rest on a reification—'structure' being a metaphor for recurrent patterns of action involving large numbers of people.

As these authors go on to clarify:

It is equally mystifying to think of a distribution of wealth, status, power, education, or other resources as a 'structure' to which action must be linked. A distribution of resources, be it equal or unequal, is not a structure, it is a *condition* under which action occurs . . . What is it then that exists *beyond a setting* and constrains action within it? It can only be the actual or anticipated action of people elsewhere, enabled (or constrained) by the resources available to them (Schwalbe et al. 2000: 439–440).

According to this view, exclusively 'macro-level' level analyses rely upon dubious metaphysical categories and concepts. Moreover, they are distinctly uninformative, providing little insight into the constitution of social hierarchies and the ways in which power, influence and control may be manifested, resisted, and reproduced in everyday life (Anderson and Snow 2001, Branaman 1997, 2003, Dennis and Martin 2005, Rogers 1980).

[24] See, for example, Gouldner's (1970: 378–390) criticisms of Goffman.

When analysing conditions of action within concrete social settings, interactionists see actors as possessing a range of skills, resources and capacities. Crucially, the differential power of actors rests in their ability to intentionally direct the course and outcome of their encounters with others.[25] In conflict situations such as a trial, the asymmetrical allocation of skills, resources and capacities will influence one's ability to present oneself effectively and control the impressions one projects. Those actors who have the least access to resources are likely to face the greatest number of interactional constraints,[26] including a more limited capacity to defend themselves against an opponent's denunciations. However, '. . . the reproduction of inequality, even when it appears thoroughly institutionalized, ultimately depends on face-to-face interaction' (Schwalbe et al. 2000: 420–1). Thus, the dynamics of power can only be explored in retrospect. In order to explain inequality, rather than merely document it, one must attend to the processes that produce and perpetuate it. This requires the engagement of sociological imaginings alert to ways in which 'symbols and meanings are created and used to sustain the patterns of interaction that lead to inequality' and the manner in which 'inequality itself is perceived, experienced, and reacted to, such that it is either reproduced or resisted' (ibid.).

This chapter has explored the contestation of the night within the administrative courts. It has described the trial experience of combatants and their use of various interactional devices. Trade teams typically possess superior resources; however, as we have seen, their desires cannot be met simply by command. Their opponents also possess varying degrees of social and economic capital, which they deploy to resist imposition of the corporate will. Each team applies its resources to the pursuit of particular interactional goals, such as 'information control, impression management, and remedial results' (Rogers 1980: 103).

Going to court is a gamble for both parties, as trial success— like all interactional accomplishments—is precarious (Goffman 1959). Yet, those actors who find themselves ill-equipped to effectively

---

[25] For further discussion of this distinctly interactionist approach to the study of power, social stratification and its various precepts, see the journal *Symbolic Interaction* (2001 24/4).

[26] See Goffman's analysis of the 'territories of the self' in *Relations in Public* (1971: 28–41).

engage resource-rich adversaries, and whose testimonies can be construed as obscure, may find that their opinions are afforded little credibility. The power to persuade through 'strategic interaction' (Goffman 1969) is enhanced not only by form, but also by *content*. Credibility can be accomplished more easily if one's 'message' conforms with, and makes direct appeal to, dominant ideology (Giddens 1976: 112–113). As noted in Chapter 7, ideological factors impact upon trial discourse by serving to artificially enhance the persuasive power and credibility of trade arguments.

Inequities in verbal and non-verbal communicative performance between applicants and objectors, and correspondingly between lay people and professionals, reflect existing relationships of power and play a key role in the construction, legitimization and perpetuation of such relations. Differential and asymmetrical interactional constraints thereby shape trial proceedings, favouring the establishment and maintenance of hierarchies (Branaman 2003, Matoesian 1993). The industry's success in the licensing courts is a product, not only of pre-existent material and ideological advantage, but also of continued interactional accomplishment. Favourable judgments are medals which the victors wear with pride; the claim to have earned one's success serving to further legitimize the position of privilege. Yet, winning battles is made easier when one has powerful weapons at one's disposal and the biggest and best trained army. 'Just . . . as settlements depending on physical means favour the physically strong . . . settlements depending on verbal means similarly favour people who are either on their own, or through their advocates, most able to manipulate words' (O'Barr 1982: 11). However, as Bennett and Feldman (1981: 150) note:

> . . . if rhetoric, style, legal moves, diversionary behaviours, and the like, matter, their impact lies in their connections to key structural elements of the stories in a case. In other words, it is simplistic to explain the effectiveness of lawyers in narrow terms of oratory, charismatic presence, or legal knowledge. Effectiveness is more a function of whether these and other resources can be employed selectively at critical junctures in the development of the overall story.

Courtroom success relies not only upon the effective deployment of powerful oratory and other linguistic strategies, but also upon the 'backstage' preparation of scripts and the enhanced ability of expert witnesses to work with counsel in promoting them. Deep understanding of the argument pool, combined with fluid, but at the same time, strategically-focused interaction, forms the essence of consummate professional performance. These performances distinguish the professional from the real person.

Trade teams are therefore systematically advantaged by the adversarial mode of adjudication. Many facets of courtroom dramaturgy, from the physical staging and procedural strictures of the trial, through to the establishment of knowledge claims, management of emotions, and the para-linguistic presentation of the self, assist trade teams (more so than objectors) in their attempts to skilfully promote the evidential script, whilst denouncing the cause of their adversaries. All of these factors help explain the practical success of trade teams: their success at persuasion within the confines of a specific mode of adversarial adjudication. The implications of these recurrent successes are explored in the following (and concluding) chapter.

9

Contesting the Night

Commercialism, in its freedom to follow unrestrainedly wherever the profit motive seems to lead, appears to have the advantage over other city forces and institutions (Cressey 1932: 288).

After a long process of expanding individual freedom and relaxing social and cultural restraints, control is now being re-emphasized in every area of social life—with the singular and startling exception of the economy, from whose deregulated domain most of today's major risks routinely emerge (Garland 2001: 195).

The city

This book has explored the contestation of the night in British cities. The narrative began with an account of night's cultural history and the influence that cultural representations of the night have exerted upon the governance of urban communities. The two chapters that comprised Part I documented the deviant associations of nocturnal activity and long-standing tensions regarding its propensity to appropriate formerly residual tracts of time and space. The nightlife of cities has long provided an arena for resistance and release, emerging as an appendage and driver of progressive lifestyles and culture. For much of the nineteenth and twentieth centuries it encouraged the growth of a cosmopolitan ethic through facilitation of increasing intermingling of the sexes, classes, ethnic and racial groups, and latterly sexualities. Accordingly, nightlife presented one of the perennial challenges of urban governance in relation to recurrent struggles over the usage and meanings of public space.

The influence of broader cultural cross-currents ensured that the tension between upholders of a strict nocturnal order and those who wished to exploit the night's economic potential became closely associated with the regulation of alcohol. Management of the night-time city has thus had long associations with the dictates of police, magistracy and municipal government via their administration of the licensing laws. Yet, the cultural history of nightlife is not a mere shadow of our shifting relationship with alcohol. Nightlife cultures have sometimes evolved in ways that are quite distinct from prevailing attitudes to drink. Moreover, the regulation of drinking has historically done little to impede—indeed, may even have assisted—the democratization of the night through the dissolution, however partial, of associated patriarchal, racial, and age-related modes of oppression.

Part II suggested that the rise of the contemporary night-time high street may have begun to place this historical process of democratization into reverse. Chapter 5 described how high street expansion occurred contemporaneously with the regulatory suppression and commercial appropriation of alternative nightlife cultures such as 'rave'—an influential youth movement which rejected alcohol in favour of other recreational drugs. This process was assisted by neo-liberal modes of governance characteristic of a post-industrial economy. Regulatory constraints which had once held the alcohol-based leisure market in check were gradually either removed or rendered impotent. The drinks industry used its newly-won freedoms to maximize the night's economic potential. Its strategies focused upon the development of branded and homogenized leisure enclaves within central urban areas.

Whilst in the day-time economy, consumer perceptions of safety were considered a prerequisite of commercial success, in the night-time high street, suppliers and consumers nurtured an atmosphere of excitement and release. Market forces shaped communal spaces accordingly, corporate leisure effectively creating a bounded and purified social setting; a nocturnal playground for the exclusive use of its own consumers. Moreover, the proliferation of licensed premises encouraged litigious jousting between corporate aristocrats through selective manipulation of the regulatory system and the waging of alcohol price wars to protect market share. As the sites of engagement in rituals of mass hedonistic consumption, these 'streets for getting high' became zones of objective danger, effectively removed from the public realm and foreclosed to the wider community. On a conceptual note, Chapter 5 questioned whether social settings devoted almost entirely to the pleasures of intoxication could be conceived as 'disorderly'; drunken, boisterous, and even violent behaviour being contextually commonplace and unremarkable. Such environments thereby conformed to an identifiable and, to some extent, predictable pattern. These homogenous consumption zones stood in contrast to more inclusive public spaces of the city, which although 'disorderly', and often dangerous, conformed more closely to the liberal democratic ideal.

The theme of commercially-imposed, rather than democratically-constituted, social order was brought to the fore in a discussion of social control in pubs, bars and nightclubs. Chapter 4 highlighted a tendency in the research literature to focus upon individual or limited combinations of factors in the strategic management of crime risk and a consequent failure to acknowledge the purposive, complex and interconnected orchestration of security-related activity. Key differences between venues in their approach to the social control problematic were acknowledged. These disparities reflected the premises' physical and social location within a differentiated leisure market.

Chapter 5, by contrast, described how public policing of the *streets* was more often reactive, and increasingly reactionary. Although frontline police officers regarded maximal tolerance as a prerequisite of the policing task and a mark of professional competence, this 'soft' mode of control did not fit the political expediencies of central government. The concern of the executive was to assuage the fears of an anxious electorate, whilst at the same time maintaining its intimate and supportive relationship with the drinks industry. Licensing de-regulation, combined with corporate technologies of profit maximization, had been accompanied by a number of harmful externalities, including the re-establishment of an almost Medieval sense of exclusion and fear of the night that effectively placed much of the central urban residential population under curfew. Yet, there continued to be 'a real reluctance to penalize the "suppliers" of crime opportunities' that contrasted 'markedly with the enthusiasm with which their "consumers" were punished' (Garland 2001: 127). The ethics of free trade and doctrine of consumer sovereignty inherent to neo-liberal governance eschewed direct market intervention and promoted alcohol policies which regarded consumption levels and any related harms as the sole responsibility of individual consumers and suppliers. As political disquiet about levels of violence on the high street gathered pace, the state–industry nexus concerned itself with criminalizing errant consumers, vilifying industry 'bad apples', conducting sporadic high-profile 'quality of life policing' campaigns, and promoting toothless voluntary self-regulation.

Custodianship of night-time public space—which, for a brief historical period, had been principally governed by administrative bodies in accordance with a vision of social democracy—was returned to the holders of economic power. The state's failure to attend to the criminogenic externalities of *routine* business practice on the high street had begun to compromise its ancient and basic function as the guardian of public order. Fiefdom and monarchic regimes had been replaced; but, like their predecessors, the new corporate overlords employed armies of lawyers, sycophants and bruisers to wrestle and retain control of the night.

The trial

The basic mechanism in the resolution of conflicts is not an equally shared, communitarian allocation of truth, but rather an allocation of truth based on dominance over communicative processes (Jacquemet 1996: 11).

Noting the persistence of corporations in their drive to secure commercially-prized developments, Chapter 3 highlighted a number of specific tactics developed by the industry's legal representatives to successfully mould and navigate the regulatory terrain. Part III developed this theme by identifying the licensing trial as a key arena of contestation; exhortations to work in 'partnership' emanating from an image-sensitive political and economic elite serving only to disguise the many vitally opposing interests that rendered opportunities for compromise tenuous and relationships of trust contingent. A whole legal and extra-legal industry had developed, primarily to assist applicants in their pursuit of commercially-directed goals. Specialist licensing barristers were identified as the linchpins of this enterprise. It was they who orchestrated the preparation of cases and the presentation and testing of evidence at trial.

Chapter 7 highlighted the relationship between central government and the drinks industry in attempting to control the agenda of debate concerning alcohol-related harm. Much of the suppressed information concerned the findings of empirical research of key relevance to the deliberations of licensing authorities and the courts. In particular, official literature reviews (and industry-derived research/guidance notes) were identified as fundamentally political documents, rather than neutral channels of information, from which 'inconvenient' knowledge had been omitted. Thus, an inequality of access to information was identified which exclusively disadvantaged objectors, whose views were typically out-of-step with government policy. These state-sponsored attempts to bound debate had important consequences within an adversarial setting where it was left to the parties to reveal the deficiencies of each others' scripts, if, and when, they could. Cross-examination—the principal theatre of adversarial duelling—involved a struggle between advocate and witness over impressions of credibility and persuasiveness. Free market ideals were threaded through the arguments-in-chief of applicants and their counsel's cross-examination of objectors. Application scripts espoused simple, individualized explanations of alcohol-related crime that were legitimized by their correspondence with the foundational assumptions of central government policy and popular media representations of binge drinking. This cluster of sentiments, beliefs, capacities, and resources served to shape trial discourse, enhancing the persuasive power of trade arguments to the detriment of objectors.

The occupational culture of legal professionals fostered an indifference to the welfare of their opponents, encouraging advocates to employ language strategically in order to denounce and coerce. Witnesses and counsel had differential skills, resources and capacities which enabled and constrained their attempts to accomplish individual and team credibility. These factors served to impact upon oral and bodily performance and the manner in which evidence was both delivered and received. Licensing trials were conducted, principally, as gladiatorial struggles between partisan teams of professionals. The asymmetrical distribution of performative skills correlated with both the inequitable financial resources of the parties and, more often than not, with the verdict of cases. Representation by elite specialist counsel was assigned by wealth and connections; advantages which almost invariably favoured the applicant. Trade teams benefited, not only from inclusion of the most accomplished and vociferous lawyers, but also from their capacity to muster a platoon of loyal and experienced experts. These ostensibly independent commentators could be relied upon to act as team players; mercenaries to the cause. Thus, the ability to persuade operated quite independently of the justifiability of what was said. At trial, the presentation of objection scripts was therefore compromised by extrinsic conditions of action. This occurred in three ways: firstly, at the level of experience and social membership status, the exalted knowledge claims and polished performances of the expert serving to corrode 'anecdotal' evidence and underline the performative naivety of the lay person/practitioner; secondly, through the application of unequal financial resources—the holders of economic power being able to secure the services of specialist legal teams who had developed fine-tuned techniques for strategically manipulating features of the adversarial system—including the preparation of scripts and the organization of talk in trial settings; and thirdly, at the level of content; credibility being accomplished more easily where one's script conformed with, or directly appealed to, dominant ideology. As Chomsky tells us, 'if you're critical of received opinion, you have to document every phrase' (1992: 77).

Regulatory capture and the local governance of crime

There is, to be sure, no neat way to draw the line between persuasion and force (Rorty 1989: 48).

When summarizing the Act in Chapter 3, it was noted that licensing authorities were required to grant all premises licence applications where no objection had been received. In introducing this rule, central government sought to restrict the power of local administrative bodies at the very time when many had intended to adopt a more cautious approach to licensing. When drawing up their licensing policies, around 40 per cent of councils had identified certain areas as 'saturated' with licensed premises (Harrington and Halstead 2004). In these locations, local authorities were seeking to impose a 'policy presumption' against the granting of new licences, where it was felt that additional premises might threaten the crime preventative objectives of the Act. However, with the 'must grant' requirement in place, the licensing authority could not implement such policies, unless, and until, objections were received from an external source. By imposing this rule, the Act duly removed the ability of licensing authorities to engage in the strategic governance of crime. The onus was placed upon 'interested parties' such as local residents and 'responsible authorities' such as the police to carefully scrutinize every licence application.

Although the *Guidance* is not binding and a licensing authority may depart from it where local circumstances permit, there must be evidence to justify departure. In the case of saturation policies, or attempts to restrict the closing time of premises, this will inevitably require the detailed measurement of local patterns of complaint, disturbances and crime. The opaque wording of the *Guidance* increases the risk that, in seeking to uphold their Statements of Licensing Policy, licensing authorities may become embroiled in protracted litigation, culminating in judicial review. Judicial review provides the trade with a means by which to directly attack licensing policies. This may involve challenging the authority's interpretation of the *Guidance* and its judgement in formulating and implementing its policy statement. In order to protect their policies from legal destruction, authorities must ensure that statements are very carefully drafted and applied (Light 2004a). The High Court will expect to find clear empirical justification in the form of well-researched evidence of the special circumstances pertaining in the area or areas to which the policy relates. Of course, judicial review also provides a mechanism through which the authority might seek to refine the drafting of its policy in order to render it more legally robust. With the official mandates that govern licensing in the post-reform era framed in such a way as to allow for variations and different interpretations, local licensing policies have become the fodder of the higher courts. In the struggle between regulator and regulated, judicial review thus emerges as the ultimate sanction: the most potent weapon in the contest for the night.

As noted in Chapter 6, the *threat* of court action casts a long shadow, with the financial, personal, and organizational implications of litigation acting as a spur to concession and capitulation that is felt most sharply by objectors. The spectre of the courtroom may even constrain the actions of licensing authorities. In Bath, for example, councillors cited the fear of judicial review as a primary reason for rejecting the introduction of a saturation policy, despite receiving robust submissions regarding its necessity from the police, residents' groups, and even local licensees. Licensing committee members argued that their policy, and the policies of other smaller city authorities, would be seen as soft targets by the industry's legal teams, with the ensuing victories then employed as precedents with which to attack 'bigger fish' such as the City of Westminster.

The trials in which the author participated were not about truth or falsity, but rather, about winning or losing. More specifically, they concerned whose subjectivity—the applicant's or the objector's—was judged to be the objectivity of the matter. Chapter 8 discussed how trials were something of a gamble for both parties as they involved the intentional deployment of a range of skills, resources and capacities in interaction. The practical successes of trade teams arose by dint of their success at persuasion and a seasoned ability to denounce the arguments of their opponents. These patterned interactional accomplishments combined with the threat of litigation and ideological affinities with central government to create a situation of 'regulatory capture' (Bakan 2004: 152) wherein trade interests became enmeshed in a multiplex institutionalization of power. When the corporations came to town, effective opposition was rare. To pursue a sporting analogy, although home teams scored the occasional 'giant killing' victory, away teams dominated the game by dint of their greater financial resources, better and more expensive players, and the power and influence of their support structures. These asymmetries—individualized by liberal commentators as no more than inevitable quirks of a healthily functioning legal system—served to skew notions of natural justice.

Classic studies of the criminal courts (Blumberg 1967, Carlen 1976, Emerson 1969, Sudnow 1965) spoke to the way in which courtroom interactions exposed the fiction that defendants and state prosecutors stood as equal adversaries before the law. So, in the licensing trial, one now finds a similarly 'institutionalized technology of semiotic and verbal coercion' (Carlen ibid.: 98) directed at local public sector agencies and their constituencies in attempting to resist imposition of the corporate will. The non-interventionist ethos of neo-liberal governance militates against the restriction of business development in all but the most dire of circumstances. Whilst the state seeks to punish, in the name of public order, those individuals who exploit criminal opportunities, it continues to actively serve and protect the interests of those corporations whose modes of operation generate such opportunities.

The democratic deficit

In a way, they seemed to be conducting the case independently of me. Things were happening without me even intervening. My fate was being decided without anyone asking my opinion (Meursault in Camus 1982: 95).

It is worth recalling that the research for this book was conducted in 2000–2005, a period in which the old licensing system was still in force. As Light (2005a: 283) notes, in citation of a government press release (DCMS 2003), 'chief among the claims for the new system is that it will provide a greater say for the public—licences will be granted by electorally accountable licensing authorities, instead of magistrates, and local residents can make representations and have them taken into account in deciding applications'. The Act also bestows the right to call for a licence to be reviewed if premises are considered to be causing a nuisance. However, it should be remembered that the licensing authority now has no power to deny or review a licence unless, and until, a relevant repres-entation is made. Objections from local residents and the police therefore perform a crucial function in instigating regulatory action and without them the licensing authority remains largely impotent. Central government's curious decision to tie the hands of licensing authorities with regard to implementation of their own crime prevention policies is but one manifestation of the various ways in which the interests of the regulated have come to dominate a system of regulation which exists, ostensibly, to serve the public good.

So will applicants and objectors compete as equals in appeal cases? Will lay objectors get their day in court in any meaningful sense? Or will the future development of our urban centres continue to be determined by the leisure industry's lawyers, rather than by democratically accountable public bodies? It seems inevitable that applicants, especially if they are large companies, will continue to muster substantial resources in presenting their case. Corporations will once again utilize specialist barristers and commission the services of expert mercenaries. Moreover, public sector agencies, and the citizens in whose name they act, will still be required to defend their views in the face of strident opposition. As the right of appeal from a licensing authority is to the magistrates' courts, the justices will retain ultimate jurisdiction. Little will have changed if the appeal mechanism continues to provide the industry with a forum for pursuing its interests through capture of the regulatory process.

If weight is truly to be attached to the views of residents (in particular), their case will need to be robustly presented and defended before the licensing authority and the courts. Chapters 5 and 6 described how lay objectors faced a number of practical and legislative barriers to their participation in the regulatory process. These included the initial hurdle of convincing the licensing authority that they live in the 'vicinity' of the applicant's premises; the day-time and weekday scheduling of hearings; the complexities of the process; the expense of legal representation; the sheer volume of applications in some areas; and the need to provide a robust evidentiary basis for their views.

The intimidating nature of the trial—as discussed in Chapter 8—may continue to deter many objectors, even those who have expressed their views very clearly in correspondence with licensing authorities or the police. Those who do attend court may be discouraged from returning as a result of the treatment they receive from lawyers. Cross-examination, in particular, may be experienced as a 'form of punishment' (Danet and Bogoch 1980: 59), 'ordeal' (Rock 1993: 86), 'or 'degradation' (Garfinkel 1956) that many potential witnesses, both lay persons and uninitiated experts, will understandably seek to avoid. Chapter 8 also indicated how lay witnesses can find themselves largely outside the realm of critical evidence-giving. The testimony of experts and other professionals is often given precedence, as the court concerns itself with detailed exposition of 'scientific' evidence, most of which is actually partisan, and—due to the financial disparities which influence the calling of expert witnesses—pitched in favour of the applicant (Goff 1995).

Unless and until such issues are addressed, licensing trials will remain highly unequal contests. The effects of embroilment in protracted litigation will penalize lay people for attempting to participate in decision-making processes of direct import to their own quality of life. In all likelihood, many residents will feel that they are effectively excluded from the process altogether. For as long as such circumstances pertain, there will continue to be a democratic deficit at the heart of the contestation of the night.

If the government is serious in its avowed attempts to facilitate sustainable social and community life in central urban areas it must address the urgent need to create conditions of choice, participation, and self-direction for objectors. Such conditions can only be achieved by making the licensing process more democratic, wherein democracy is conceived of 'as a process that connects "the people" and the powerful, and through which people are able significantly to influence their actions' (Young 2000: 173). Democratic governance of the night would require the adoption of a procedural conception of justice in which 'maximum public participation can be viewed as a necessary component of the democratic legitimacy of decision-making processes' (Loader 1994: 531).

These reflections raise the question of what might be done to promote opportunity of access. Why must an 'interested party' be defined as someone who is directly affected by 'disorder and disturbance' *on or immediately outside* the premises? (DCMS 2004: 5.33). As Light (2005a: 284) points out, would it not be fairer to allow objections to be made by any person who lives or operates a business in the local area? Adoption of this broader definition of 'vicinity' would do little more than to reinstate the rights held by urban communities under the previous licensing system. Moreover, the formal right to make representations may be of little use to residents if they are unable to obtain technical assistance and financial support. At the very least, this suggests the need for some form of free and independent advisory service,[1] together with a 'legal aid' scheme which might be administered by councils and financed from the licence fees. Of course, even this type of assistance would do little to assuage the ordeal of delivering live oral testimony; the adversarial nature of the appeal mechanism itself serving to perpetuate many asymmetries of power. The following paragraphs highlight basic flaws of the adversarial system, which, it is argued, render it unsuited to the determination of licensing matters and ripe for replacement by alternative methods of adjudication.

[1] Guidance for objectors has been developed by pressure groups such as the Open All Hours Campaign (www.licensingaid.org.uk) and the Network of Residents' Associations (www.nora-uk.co.uk).

Towards an alternative system of adjudication

In *The Origins of Adversary Criminal Trial*, the legal historian, John Langbein, demonstrates how the adversarial system was never 'premised on a coherent theory of truth-seeking' (2003: 333), but rather, promoted 'the deeply problematic assumption that combat promotes truth, or put differently, that truth will emerge even though the court takes no steps to seek it' (ibid.: 338). This point is not lost on more conservative scholars such as Devlin (1979: 62) who, whilst supporting the orthodox view that the search for evidence by two opposing parties will 'discover all that is relevant for and against', candidly admits that 'this is not the same as saying that it will all be presented at trial'.

Supporters of the adversarial system offer a romantic appraisal of combative advocacy as vital to democracy, the rule of law, protection of liberty, and freedom of expression. These ideals are regarded as 'an essential morality' that justifies adversarial practice and 'excuses its excesses' (Pannick 1992: 10, 148–149). The advocate is portrayed as a valiant defender of the 'principle that there is always another point of view, a different perspective, a contrary argument, of which account should be taken before judgment is delivered' (ibid.: 10). This principle is regarded as inviolable, providing lawyers with a justifiable incentive 'to suppress and distort unfavourable evidence, however truthful it may be' (Langbein 2003: 103–104). As discussed in Chapter 7, in licensing trials each party presents what is essentially a body of half-truths reconstituted in such a way as to appear credible and persuasive. In exerting tight control over the information available to the courts, editing and moulding the evidence as they see fit, lawyers obliterate all semblance of the disinterested pursuit of knowledge. Trials are 'conceived not as an inquiry into the final truth of a matter, but as a struggle, quite literally, a "trial of strength", between two competing, partial, and incomplete cases' (Rock 1993: 31, with citation from Devlin 1979: 54). In preparing their case, counsel are not obliged to reveal the confidences of a client, or indeed any information that might assist the cause of an opponent. As Langbein (2003: 332) notes, 'adversary procedure entrusts the responsibility for gathering and presenting the evidence upon which accurate adjudication depends to partisans whose interest is in winning, not in truth'. In laying their 'tales and tale-bearers' before the court, advocates merely offer 'a choice of different constructions' (Rock 1993: 35). Similarly, the bench themselves have no fact-finding role and play no part in investigating the issues they are tasked to decide. As Egglestone (1978: 2) notes: 'the judge does not ascertain the truth in any real sense. What he does is to give a decision on the evidence presented to him.'

The Act identifies crime prevention as a primary objective of the licensing system. A central tenet of contemporary crime prevention policy is that decision-making should be *evidence-based*, that is, that it should reflect and respond to empirical knowledge of its subject matter (Hough and Tilley 1998, Pease 2002). Empirical evidence is clearly preferable to partisan rhetoric as a basis for what are, essentially, strategic public policy decisions. Yet, one of the central failings of the adversarial system—at least, as it is applied to licensing—is that the bench assume no responsibility for fact-finding, acting rather as mere arbiters of conflict and assessors of persuasiveness.

How might appeals be conducted in such a way as to more fairly balance the demands of the community and the rights of private parties? Clearly, licensing appeals must be determined efficiently in accordance with basic maxims of administrative procedure. This requires that some degree of rule-bound formality will always be necessary (Atkinson and Drew 1979). Yet, cross-cultural comparison offers some insight into alternative methods of adjudication. Legal scholars (Devlin 1979, Egglestone 1975, Ellison 2001, Langbein 2003) have long noted how the civil law jurisdictions of continental Europe produce more sound findings of fact than our own common law system. As Egglestone (1975: 430) notes:

Some countries take the view that it is morally necessary that the state should concern itself not only with the decision of a case according to the evidence, but with arriving at a right decision even if the parties themselves do not choose to place the relevant material before the court . . . the court is considered to have a responsibility to see that the case is thoroughly investigated . . . can order the hearing of witnesses, or the production of documents by a party or third party, can direct a report by experts or an on-the-spot investigation.

In this 'inquisitorial' mode, therefore, the court is involved in proactive fact-finding and vested with the authority and necessary resources to perform the task of investigation. Unlike the adversarial bench, who, at the point of trial, remain largely ignorant of the substance of each case, the bench might be comprised of specialist magistrates working from a dossier which encapsulates the findings of their own pre-trial investigations. This determination of regulatory appeals by state-appointed experts has clear precedent in the role of the Planning Inspectorate. Proceedings would be regarded as an attempt by the court to get at the truth, with the lawyers on each side required to assist the investigator in obtaining the best available evidence. Robust local-level data would, of course, need to be gathered by stakeholder agencies, from which the investigators might draw their own inferences.

In discussing issues of procedural fairness, Light (2004a: 59) cites the principle of 'equality of arms' which holds that 'each party must be afforded a reasonable opportunity to present his case—including his evidence—under conditions that do not place him at a substantial disadvantage vis-à-vis his opponent'.[2] At an inquisitorial trial, witnesses would be called and questioned by decision-makers acting in accordance with a fact-finding agenda, rather than by advocates seeking to promote a particular cause. As impartial adjudicators, the examining magistrates would have little incentive to browbeat, humiliate, or intimidate witnesses, misrepresent the meaning of their words, or steer questioning for partisan reasons—suppressing certain matters whilst emphasizing others. Under the inquisitorial system, witnesses would be afforded greater opportunity to communicate their own concerns in a narrative form more akin to natural conversation. This form of hearing would aim to prevent the domination of proceedings by lawyers and other partisan professionals and encourage greater participation by lay people. More generally, the adoption of an inquisitorial approach may help to remove some of the systematic skews which advantage corporate interests in the contestation of the night. In an era in which neo-liberalism has come to shape many facets of our culture and community life, it can easily be forgotten that the effective restraint of commercial ambitions remains a vital component of urban governance.

---

[2] *Dombo Beheer v Netherlands* (1998) 18 EHRR 213, para. 32.

10

Shadowing the Night People: A Methodological Postscript

This postscript explains the methodology and theoretical assumptions that have informed the research for this book. These concerns cannot be detached from the discussion of the book's origins in Chapter 1. Readers of that chapter may recall that the author's personal life history, the access opportunities afforded to him, and the emergent nature of the research topic, encouraged the adoption of an ethnographic methodology. This approach involved the use of participant observation, wherein the sociologist places his or her self at the heart of the research setting and seeks to experience and record events as they unfold.

Participant observation is informed by a pragmatist epistemology, wherein the analytical spotlight is directed toward interpretation of the meanings and understandings of social actors as revealed through social interaction (Atkinson and Housley 2003, Rock 1979). Formal deductive reasoning and *a priori* speculations are largely eschewed in favour of generative processes of empirical investigation. Inferences remain tentative and fluid, being posited only as they emerge *from the data*, to be repeatedly adapted and refined via an evolving process of analytic induction (Becker 1958, Humphreys 1970, Znaniecki 1934). With knowledge regarded as grounded primarily in one's personal engagement with the enacted environment, ontological claims are necessarily modest, cautious, and context-bound. Although attention may be drawn to broader conditions of action that are considered to, in some way, shape interaction, generalizations are typically eschewed in favour of the detailed analysis of process and action within distinct social settings.

The research settings

Fieldwork for this book focused upon three primary social settings: licensed premises located in central urban areas; public space in and around the night-time high street; and licensing trials. These settings were, by nature, open to the public and therefore presented no formal barriers to access. Access to the private domain of pre-trial meetings and correspondence, barristers' chambers, police stations, and the offices of local authorities and business executives, arose in accordance with the requirements of my sponsors. Sampling of research sites was, for the most part, externally task-oriented and informants were accessed by the snowballing of personal introductions, with no pretence to statistical representation. In licensed premises, I conducted interviews with managers, bar staff, DJs, lighting jockeys, door staff, and promoters. I accompanied police officers on public order patrol (in vehicles and on foot) in seven towns and cities: Hereford, Liverpool, London, Macclesfield, Newcastle, Preston, Southport, and Worthing, and accompanied local authority licensing inspectors in London. Interviews, focus group discussions, and more informal 'conversations with a purpose' were conducted with front-line police officers, city centre residents and consumers in towns and cities throughout the UK. High status stakeholders engaged in contestation at a strategic level were also approached, including leisure industry executives; police managers; representatives from alcohol pressure groups; trade organizations; local counsellors; and local authority officers.

Interviews were conducted around a series of emergent themes with open-ended questions phrased in such a way as to encourage narrative testimony. Formally arranged interviews were recorded by Dictaphone, although, in many instances, contemporaneous recording proved impractical or inappropriate. In some field situations—particularly working environments—interviews were frequently disrupted and recording devices tended to disrupt the flow of conversation and/or elicit more guarded responses. In such circumstances, I had to rely upon memory. My method was to make notes at the earliest opportunity. On visits to licensed premises, for example, this might involve retiring to toilet cubicles. I found that recording events and snippets of conversation when fresh in my mind helped retain accuracy and nuance.

Courting controversy

I appeared as an expert witness in licensing trials on twenty-six occasions and attended a further ten trials simply to observe. The trials were conducted in magistrates' courts and crown courts throughout England and Wales.[1] As explained below, my participation in trial-related activities involved three main tasks: pre-trial briefing; the preparation of witness statements; and the presentation of oral testimony.

The process would begin following an approach by a client's solicitor. Once commissioned, I would begin to correspond with counsel and other legal professionals in relation to the preparation of each case. My first task would be to examine bundles of documents containing witness statements and other relevant information, such as previous judgments, architectural plans, promotional material, radius maps, crime statistics, and letters of correspondence. I would be required to dissect these documents and provide counsel with my response in the form of confidential briefing notes. This task involved the critique of arguments constructed by our opponents, the aim being to inform the preparation of witness cross-examination. On many occasions, I would be called to meetings attended by other witnesses. At these events, team strategies for the fighting of each case would be devised.

My main contribution was to prepare and present a written statement (described by lawyers as a 'proof of evidence report'). Very little of this trial-related work was conducted in the region in which I lived (North East England), therefore the research for each case would typically involve one or two weekends away from home in the town or city in question. It would be necessary for me to visit the relevant site and its surrounding area on a Thursday, Friday or Saturday night, in order to observe activities during apposite periods of time. In the case of new licence applications from branded chain operators, I was also required to spend one or more evenings in an existing 'unit'. This would require the planning of further weekends in other areas. Where applications had been made simply to *vary* the licence of an existing premises (typically, by extending its trading hours, or increasing its physical capacity), I would simply visit the venue and its environs.

---

[1] I did not participate in High Court appeal proceedings as they rarely involved a re-hearing of the evidence.

In the course of my visits to over fifty high street premises over a four-year period, I developed a systematic observation schedule to assist in the recording of detailed field notes. I became attuned to those aspects of the social and physical environment indicated by the research literature and by my own experience, to be associated with alcohol-related crime and other forms of 'stress'. In relation to licensed premises this would include issues such as the concept of the business; the availability of food; levels of comfort; customer occupancy levels; age, social profile, and intoxication level of patrons; behaviour of bar and door staff; and drinks pricing policies. Issues recorded in surrounding public space included number, density, size, and terminal hours of premises; availability of transport; location of taxi ranks and fast food outlets; direction and density of traffic and pedestrian flows; noise levels; general profile and demeanour of the crowds; policing strategies; incidents of littering and street fouling; and an assessment of street lighting and CCTV coverage.

Events were recorded in chronological order as each night progressed. To appear unobtrusive, for personal safety reasons, and most importantly, simply to make the task less onerous, I employed friends to assist me. The evenings would begin at around 7–8pm, usually with attempts to buy a meal, and run through until around 3.30am the following morning (or as late as 5am in Central London) when the streets began to clear. In a few cases, where an area was new to me, I was accompanied by police officers or local authority personnel. Officers would sometimes be in uniform and on other occasions would wear plain clothes. These 'authority figures' would answer my questions and impart local knowledge, whilst showing me the 'circuit', the key hot spots, and all the major venues.

Time on the streets and in licensed premises undoubtedly exceeded that spent within the licensing courts, permitting considerable opportunity for observation in a wide variety of settings. Yet, unlike Hobbs (1988), who was able to combine research in the pub with pleasurable socializing, I often found fieldwork in licensed premises and night-time public space to be hard, tiring and frustrating. I was away from home, among strangers and tasked with the detailed recording of almost everything I witnessed; accounts that might later be tested in a court of law. Drinking (very much) was therefore not an option

I could realistically explore. Indeed, spending almost every weekend evening in this environment impacted adversely on my social life and was a source of worry for my family. Despite such drawbacks, my nocturnal movements remained something of an adventure. They provided an exciting element of regress to my pre-academic self, a 'holiday from academic rituals ... an opportunity to get away from books, papers, essays, seminars, and sedentary pontificating on the ills of the world' (Punch 1978: 325).

In court, my primary roles were to submit testimony under oath and present myself for cross-examination. As I was often the only objection witness to have direct experience of the premises and its surroundings, my evidence was usually of central importance to a client's case. It was essential that I pay close attention to the evidence and cross-examination of other witnesses, particularly those of our opponents. On occasion, I would be asked to sit next to, or directly behind, counsel in order to avail myself for whispered questioning and the passing of hastily written notes in relation to unfolding events.

As a fully fledged participant, my experience of the courtroom was quite different to that of non-participant observers such as Bottoms and McLean, who recall their experiences of the criminal trial as 'dull, commonplace, ordinary, and after a while downright tedious' (Bottoms and McLean 1976: 226 cited in Baldwin 2000: 245). By contrast, my experience developed into one of excitement, nervous trepidation, intense concentration and personal challenge (see below). Periods of tedium did occur, but these involved time spent in court corridors and canteens waiting for postponed hearings to begin. The majority of cases proceeded slowly and at a pace determined only by court insiders and other legal professionals (Rock 1993). In their concern to appear fair, magistrates and judges were often loath to assert much influence over the pace of events. Laborious and repetitive submissions were used tactically in order to restrict opportunities for participation by time-pressured witnesses. When scheduling the presentation of their party's evidence, counsel would give precedence to the needs of busy professional witnesses such as police officers and hospital consultants. Such witnesses had to arrange time away from work in order to attend and their co-operation and good will had to be preserved. Control over my own use of time had to be subordinated to the dictates of the court and the strategies adopted by counsel. I fulfilled counsel's expectations with good humour as they enabled me to 'earn as I learned' (Saunders 1997), observing every twist and turn of events.

My field roles were strategically adapted to the requirements of each setting. In some instances—for example, when observing licensed premises for the purposes of a pre-trial report—my role had to be covert in order to avoid provoking actions by the researched that would have disrupted the naturalism of the setting. It was especially important, for my purposes, to prevent the possibility of compensatory behaviour that might have obscured more routine and deviant social practices. I therefore attempted to participate as a legitimate and unobtrusive observer (Humphreys 1970). On other occasions, for example, when requesting interviews, my role was overt and my purposes explicit. In my role as an expert witness, I told clients I was conducting a study of the regulation of nightlife and made no secret of my interest in the social practices of litigation and courtroom interaction. However, to have sought express permission to observe from every participant, in every trial, would have unduly compromised the research. Trials were public spectacles and those present would, in all likelihood, have inferred that, like others engaged in copious note-taking (including legal professionals and journalists), I intended to relate matters to a broader audience.

My analyses of the licensing trial are undoubtedly partial as I have sought to rely upon note-taking and informal interview methods, employed in the course of my own participation. My evolving and inductive approach to analysis involved the coding of data into categories based upon my interpretations of social interaction *in situ* and may paint a different picture from that elicited by other methods, such as formal retrospective interviewing. More fundamentally, the validity of my data must, like all sociological research, remain open to question. I cannot know what impact my presence had upon the settings, or how typical, or atypical, the views and behaviours of my (opportunity) sample may have been. I will never know if, or to what extent, informants sought to purposely adapt their actions and interactions in my presence. In conducting field research, ethnographers (and social scientists in general) have always trod an epistemological minefield; I was no exception.

My personal attributes exerted a major influence over the character of fieldwork relationships. I am a white male who grew up in the North West of England, my social class of origin is the 'petite bourgeoisie'[2] and my age during the research period was early–mid 30s. Of course, researchers are not merely passive observers or scribes, but active participants in the research process (Van Maanen, Manning and Miller 1989), rendering issues of social identity and reflexivity of central epistemological concern (Miller and Glassner 1997). In the interview context, for example, 'the story is being told to a particular person; it might take a different form if someone else were the listener' (Riessman 1993: 11). My DJ and promotions experiences assisted me in establishing rapport with workers in licensed premises, as it allowed me to empathize with their stories and respond appropriately. I found my age to be an asset, as I was still young enough to mingle fairly unobtrusively with the late-night crowds, yet also had sufficient experience and credentials to be taken seriously as an expert witness. My value to the court stemmed, in part, from my ability to get 'close to the action'. I often felt like a colonial anthropologist, tasked with interpreting and reporting upon the mores and rituals of the (ignoble) savage. Licensing trials were dominated by white, male, upper middle class legal professionals. For me, issues of reflexivity therefore revolved around 'class work' much more so than ethnicity or gender. This was because, with few exceptions, black and ethnic minorities were simply absent from the courtroom, whilst women tended to play supporting, rather than key, roles.[3]

[2] Petite bourgeoisie: a group of ambivalent status, who tend to share the economic privileges of the middle classes, but are culturally and socially more akin to the respectable working classes than to middle class professionals, bureaucrats, or administrators (Savage et al. 1992).

[3] I did not encounter any female applicants, nor did I encounter applicants from black and ethnic minorities. Only four female expert witnesses were observed, although women comprised around a third of all police witnesses and approximately half of all lay witnesses—the vast majority being residents, together with a small number of supporters of the application (see Chapter 6). In the magistrates' courts, a significant minority of district judges and magistrates were female; however, in crown courts, the proportion of female judges was much lower, although some benches did include female magistrates. Only twice did I encounter a female advocate and only once a black male advocate.

Learning the craft

The first time I gave evidence was at the crown court in Leeds in 2001. I had rarely set foot in a court of law and my naïvety made me easy meat for counsel, who took some delight in misconstruing my words and exposing my 'incompetence'. My experiences matched those described by Shuy (1993: 201) who warns that:

Expert witnesses who submit to examination and cross-examination should expect to be treated in ways quite unfamiliar to what they are used to in an academic setting. For example, they can expect ridicule of various types. They can expect to be submitted to the temptation to get angry. They can expect loaded questions . . . The expert witness is in a language game and must be alert at all times for traps . . .

As requests for court work began to mount, I resolved to 'get my act together' in order that such humiliations might be avoided. In attending trial and spending time with lawyers, business executives and crime prevention practitioners, I found it necessary to adapt my usual comportment in order to construct a more appropriate professional persona. In the absence of formal training, I learned how a witness was expected to behave through 'the more indirect means of observation and imitation' (Becker 1963: 48). I listened attentively to the cross-examination of other witnesses and the way in which testimony was received. I overheard the conversations of lawyers as they passed judgement on witnesses' performances and asked each counsel I worked with for an assessment of my strengths and weaknesses. In becoming accustomed to courtroom convention, I learned to manage my fear and adopt the necessary emotional fortitude.

Competent performance involved, at a minimum, the ability to translate verbal and written testimony into 'evidence'—a mode of discourse understandable and useful to courtroom actors. As is often the case with the dissemination of social research to lay audiences, submitting evidence required 'simplification that renders a complex world in blacks and whites' (D. Walker 2001: 1, Shuy 1993: 201). My accounts had to be stated clearly, in a form that was largely stripped of academic jargon. I also had to acquire presentational skills. First of all, I learned to dress appropriately. My normal casual and somewhat creased attire was replaced by a black or navy blue suit, shiny shoes, a crisp and well-pressed shirt, and a bright, but sober, silk tie. I learned the formal decorum of the courts and how to interact in an appropriate manner. As with my fieldwork in licensed premises and on the streets, much of my courtroom activity was conducted many miles from home. In the South East of England I found myself attempting to neutralize my Northern accent by adopting my own mutant variety of 'received pronunciation'. As well as learning how to talk, I also had to learn when to keep my mouth shut. In court, conversation among observers was strictly prohibited and even in the 'backstage' arena of the corridor, restaurant or briefing room, unnecessary chat was often unwelcome. Lawyers had to concentrate and continually re-organize their case; nervous witnesses had to be briefed.

Most importantly, I had to learn how to present and defend my report. With experience I became more cautious, robust, even tempered, and assertive. Once confident enough to resist counsels' attempts to cut short or misconstrue my words, I began to use my new speech opportunities to display the breadth and depth of my knowledge, draw upon supportive evidence from other witnesses, and to launch my own 'counter-attacks'. Like Becker's (1963) marijuana users, I found that once these basic lessons of performance had been learnt, my affective responses to the task were dramatically transformed. Trials acquired a new and more positive meaning, becoming exciting and challenging struggles rather than humiliating ordeals: 'what was once frightening and distasteful becomes, after a taste for it is built up, pleasant, desired and sought after' (Becker, ibid.: 56). Of course, the experience of delivering oral testimony remained stressful, but I now had a feeling of preparedness, a fine-tuned sense of danger and the ability to take appropriate remedial action. The scales of interaction were no longer so lopsided; I had learned to play the game.

Having published work which firmly apportioned much of the blame for alcohol-related violence to central government and the leisure industry, I was, and was known to be, sympathetic to objection arguments. It could be argued that these preconceptions prevented me from conducting objective and therefore 'good' social science.[4] However, in recent decades there has been a growing recognition of the inescapably normative and

---

[4] This view is commonly associated with positivism and also with Weber (1949), who argued that social research should and could be value-free.

political dimensions of the research process.[5] It would have been difficult, if not impossible, for me to accept a commission from an industry client in the face of well-researched police opposition. Although, in cross-examination, opposing counsel continually sought to question my integrity, it would have only been in accepting such a commission that more forceful issues of professional ethics may have arisen. In actuality, the adversarial system encouraged both sides to somewhat overstate their case (see Chapter 7). Yet, the evidence presented by applicants often did offend my own interpretations of the matter. In such circumstances, it was not possible to remain dispassionate. As a fully integrated team member, I had invested time and effort into each case and successful outcomes gave rise to considerable personal satisfaction. My reluctantly accepted access opportunity had become a sought after game of strategy; a battle of wills.

[5] Influential proponents of this view have included Becker (1967), Bell and Newby (1977), Gouldner (1962) and, from a feminist perspective, Finch (1984) and Mies (1983).

Glossary

ACPO	Association of Chief Police Officers
ACTM	Association of Town Centre Managers
AED	Accident and Emergency Department
Act	Licensing Act 2003
BBPA	British Beer and Pub Association
BEDA	Bar Entertainment and Dance Association
DJ	Disc Jockey
GMP	Greater Manchester Police
Guidance	Guidance Issued under Section 182 of the Act
IAS	Institute of Alcohol Studies
LGA	Local Government Association
NHS	National Health Service
NTE	Night-time Economy
PEL	Public Entertainment Licence
S 77	s 77 Licensing Act 1964
SHC	Special Hours Certificate

References

Academy of Medical Sciences (2004) *Calling Time: The Nation's Drinking as a Major Health Issue,* London: Academy of Medical Sciences, http://www.acmedsci.ac.uk/p_callingtime.pdf

Adams, T. (2005) 'A Tale of Two Cities', *The Observer: Review* 22 May: 1–2.

Alchian, A. (1977) 'Uncertainty, Evolution and Economic Theory' in A. Alchian (ed.), *Economic Forces at Work*, Indianapolis, IN: Liberty Press.

Alcohol Alert (2002) *Licensing Bill: Government Betrays Local Communities*, London: IAS.

Alcohol Alert (2003) *Alcohol Strategy Questioned*, Issue 3, London: IAS.

Alcohol Harm Reduction Group (2003) *No Half-Measures*, London: Alcohol Harm Reduction Group.

Allen, J. (2003a) 'On the Case: The Licensing Landscape', *Night*, October: 12.

Allen, J. (2003b) 'On the Case: The Licensing Bill . . . Continued', *Night*, May: 14.

Allen, J. (2004) 'On the Case: Court of Appeal Rules OK!', *Night*, May: 11.

Alvarez, A. (1995) *Night: An Exploration of Nightlife, Night Language, Sleep and Dreams*, London: Jonathan Cape.

Amin, A. and Thrift, N. (2002) *Cities: Re-imagining the Urban*, Cambridge: Polity.

Anderson, L. and Snow, D. (2001) 'Inequality and the Self: Exploring Connections from an Interactionist Perspective', *Symbolic Interaction* 24/4: 395–406.

Armstrong, G. (1993) 'Like that Desmond Morris?' in D. Hobbs and T. May (eds.), *Interpreting the Field: Accounts of Ethnography*, Oxford: Clarendon Press.

Asthana, A. (2005) 'One Bar, Three Hours—I was Sold Enough Drink to Kill Me', *The Observer* 23 October, 8–9.

Atkinson, J. (1982) 'Understanding Formality: The Categorization and Production of "Formal" Interaction', *British Journal of Sociology*, 33/1: 86–117.

Atkinson, J. and Drew, P. (1979) *Order in Court: The Organization of Verbal Interaction in Judicial Settings*, London: Macmillan.

Atkinson, P. and Housley, W. (2003) *Interactionism: An Essay in Sociological Amnesia*, London: Sage.

Aubert, V. and White, H. (1959) 'Sleep: A Sociological Interpretation II', *Acta Sociologica* IV/3: 1–16.

Augé, M. (1995) *Non-Places: Introduction to an Anthropology of Supermodernity*, London: Verso.

Ayres, I. and Braithwaite, J. (1992) *Responsive Regulation: Transcending the Deregulation Debate*, Oxford: Oxford University Press.

Babor, T. (2004) 'Alcohol Policy Research: A Quoi Bon?', *Addiction*, 99: 1091–1092.

Babor, T. et al. (2003) *Alcohol: No Ordinary Commodity: Research and Public Policy*, Oxford: Oxford University Press.

Bailey, F. and Rothblatt, H. (1971) *Successful Techniques for Criminal Trials*, Rochester, NY: The Lawyer's Co-operative Publishing Co.

Baird, M. (2000a) 'Management Quality and Training', *Night*, February: 80–81.

Baird, M. (2000b) 'Cost Effective Management and Training', *Night*, March: 80.

Bakan, J. (2004) *The Corporation: The Pathological Pursuit of Profit and Power*, London: Constable.

Baker Associates (2001) *Review of the Use Classes Order and Part 4 of the GPDO (Temporary Uses)*, London: DTLR (Department for Transport, Local Government and the Regions).

Baldwin, J. (2000) 'Research on the Criminal Courts' in R. King and E. Wincup (eds.), *Doing Research on Crime and Justice*, Oxford: Oxford University Press.

Baldwin, J. and McConville, M. (1977) *Negotiated Justice*, London: Martin Robertson.

Barker, R. (1968) *Ecological Psychology*, Stanford, CA: Stanford University Press.

Barnes, J. (1994) *A Pack of Lies: Towards a Sociology of Lying*, Cambridge: Cambridge University Press.

Barr, R. and Pease, K. (1992) 'A Place for Every Crime and Every Crime in its Place' in D. Evans, N. Fyfe and D. Herbert (eds.), *Crime, Policing and Place: Essays in Environmental Criminology*: 196–216, London: Routledge.

Barry, N. (1991) 'Understanding the Market' in M. Loney et al. (eds.), *The State or the Market: Politics and Welfare in Contemporary Britain*, London: Sage.

BBC News (2002) 'Drink Crime Data "Meaningless"', 4 March, wysiwyg://31/http://news.bbc.co.uk/hi/English/uk/newsid_1852000/1852276.sti

BBPA (British Beer and Pub Association) (2002) *Point of Sale Promotions: A Good Practice Guide for Pub Owners and Licensees*, London: BBPA.

Beck, A. and Willis, A. (1995) *Crime and Security: Managing the Risk to Safe Shopping*, Leicester: Perpetuity Press.

Becker, H. (1958) 'Problems of Inference and Proof in Participant Observation', *American Sociological Review*, 23: 652–660.

Becker, H. (1963) *Outsiders: Studies in the Sociology of Deviance*, New York: The Free Press.

Becker, H. (1967) 'Whose Side Are We On?', *Social Problems* 14: 239–247.

Bell, C. and Newby, H. (1977) 'Introduction: The Rise of Methodological Pluralism' in C. Bell and H. Newby (eds.), *Doing Sociological Research*, London: Allen and Unwin.

Bellan, R. (1971) *The Evolving City*, New York: Pitman.

Bennett, M. (1999) 'The Naming and Shaming Game', *Alcohol Concern Magazine*, 14/2: 10–11.

Bennett, W. and Feldman, M. (1981) *Reconstructing Reality in the Courtroom*, New Brunswick: Rutgers University Press.

Berkley, B. and Thayer, J. (2000) 'Policing Entertainment Districts', *Policing: An International Journal of Police Strategies and Management*, 23/4: 466–491.

Berkowitz, L. (1978) 'Is Criminal Violence Normative Behaviour?: Hostile and Instrumental Aggression in Violent Incidents', *Journal of Research in Crime and Delinquency*, 15: 148–161.

Berman, M. (1982) *All That Is Solid Melts Into Air*, London: Verso.

Berman, M. (1986) 'Taking it to the Streets', *Dissent*, Fall: 476–485.

Better Regulation Task Force (1998) *Review of Licensing Legislation*, London: Central Office of Information.

Bianchini, F. (1995) 'Night Cultures, Night Economies', *Planning Practice and Research* 10/2: 121–126.

Bianchini, F. and Schwengel, H. (1991) 'Re-imaging the City' in J. Corner and S. Harvey (eds.), *Enterprise and Heritage*, London: Routledge.

Blumberg, A. (1967) 'The Practice of Law as a Confidence Game', *Law and Society Review* 1: 25–47.

Blumer, H. (1969) 'What's Wrong with Social Theory?' in H. Blumer, *Symbolic Interactionism*, Englewood Cliffs, NJ: Prentice-Hall.

Bok, S. (1978) *Lying: Moral Choice in Public and Private Life*, New York: Pantheon Books.

Bolam, M. (2003) 'Another Blow for Pub Battle Losers', *The Journal*, 3 December: 2.

Bottoms, A. and McLean, J. (1976) *Defendants in the Criminal Process*, London: Routledge and Kegan Paul.

Bottoms, A. and Wiles, P. (2002) 'Environmental Criminology' in M. Maguire, R. Morgan and R. Reiner (eds.), *The Oxford Handbook of Criminology*, 3rd ed., Oxford: Oxford University Press.

Bourdieu, P. (1977) *Outline of a Theory of Practice*, Cambridge: Cambridge University Press.

Boyd, G. (2001) 'Legitimizing the Illicit—Dublin's Temple Bar and the Monto' paper presented at *Night and the City Conference*, Montreal, March.

Brain, K. (2000) *Youth, Alcohol and the Emergence of the Post-Modern Alcohol Order*, Occasional Paper No. 1, London: IAS.

Brain, K., Parker, H. and Carnwrath, T. (2000) 'Drinking with Design: Young Drinkers as Psychoactive Consumers', *Drugs: Education, Prevention and Policy*, 7/1: 5–20.

Branaman, A. (1997) 'Goffman's Social Theory' in C. Lemert and A. Branaman (eds.), *The Goffman Reader*, Oxford: Blackwell.

Branaman, A. (2003) 'Interaction and Hierarchy in Everyday Life: Goffman and Beyond' in A. Treviño (ed.), *Goffman's Legacy*, Oxford: Rowman and Littlefield.

Brannigan, A. and Lynch, M. (1987) 'On Bearing False Witness: Credibility as an Interactional Accomplishment', *Journal of Contemporary Ethnography* 16/2: 115–146.

Brantingham, P.L. and Brantingham, P.J. (1993) 'Nodes, Paths and Edges: Considerations of the Complexity of Crime and the Physical Environment', *Journal of Environmental Psychology*, 13: 3–28.

Brantingham, P.L. and Brantingham, P.J. (1995) 'Criminality of Place: Crime Generators and Crime Attractors', *European Journal of Criminal Policy and Research*, 3: 5–26.

Bromley, R. and Nelson, A. (2002) 'Alcohol-Related Crime and Disorder Across Urban Space and Time: Evidence from a British City', *Geoforum*, 33: 239–254.

Bromley, R., Thomas, C. and Millie, A. (2000) 'Exploring Safety Concerns in the Night-time City', *Town Planning Review*, 71: 71–96.

Brophy, I. (2003) 'Witness Statement of PC Ian Brophy' in *Chief Constable of Nottinghamshire v Clegg (Springwood Leisure Plc)* Nottingham Crown Court, February.

Brown, S. (1991) *Magistrates at Work: Sentencing and Social Structure*, Milton Keynes: Open University Press.

Budd, T. (2003) *Alcohol-Related Assault: Findings from the British Crime Survey*, Home Office Online Report, 35/03.

Burgess, E. (1932) 'Introduction' in P. Cressey *The Taxi-Dance Hall: A Sociological Study in Commercialized Recreation and City Life*, Chicago, IL: University of Chicago Press.

Burke, T. (1915) *Nights in Town: A London Autobiography*, London: George Allen and Unwin.

Burke, T. (1941) *English Night-Life: From Norman Curfew to .Present Black-Out*, London: Batsford.

Burns, T. (1980) 'Getting Rowdy with the Boys', *Journal of Drug Issues*, 10: 273–286.

Calvey, D. (2000) 'Getting on the Door and Staying There' in G. Lee-Treweek and S. Linkogle (eds.), *Danger in the Field: Risk and Ethics in Social Research*, London: Routledge.

Campbell, D. (2005) 'Alcohol-related Disorder and the Nature of the Problem of Social Cost', *Public Law*, 4: 749–763.

Camus, A. (1982) [1942] *The Outsider*, trans. J. Laredo, London: Penguin.

Carey, J. (1997) 'Recreational Drug Wars, Alcohol versus Ecstasy' in N. Saunders (ed.), *Ecstasy Reconsidered*, London: Saunders.

Carlen, P. (1976) *Magistrates' Justice*, London: Martin Robertson.

Carr, N. (1998) 'Gendered Differences in Young Tourist's Leisure Spaces and Times', *Journal of Youth Studies*, 1/3: 279–293.

Carr, S., Francis, M., Rivlin, L. and Stone, A. (1992) *Public Space*, Cambridge: Cambridge University Press.

Carvel, J. (2005) 'Sophisticated Young Drinkers Dump Alco-pops for Cocktails', *The Guardian* 9 November: 5.

Casswell, S., Fang Zhang, J. and Wyllie, A. (1993) 'The Importance of Amount and Location of Drinking for the Experience of Alcohol-related Problems', *Addiction*, 88, 1527–1534.

Cavan, S. (1963) 'Interaction in Home Territories' *Berkeley Journal of Sociology*, 5, 17–32.

Cavan, S. (1966) *Liquor License*, Chicago, IL: Aldine.

Central Cities Institute (2002) *Licensing Reform: A Cross-cultural Comparison of Rights, Responsibilities and Regulation*, London: University of Westminster.

Central Westminster Police/Community Consultative Group (1998) *A Good Night Out! Licensing Working Party Report*, London: Westminster City Council.

Charity, P. (2002) 'Martin v Thomas: The Gloves are Off', *Morning Advertiser* 10 December 121: 2.

Charity, P. (2004) 'MA Opinion: Hours not to Reason Why', *Morning Advertiser* 15 April 190: 13.

Chatterton, P. (2002) 'Governing Nightlife: Profit, Fun and Dis(Order) in the Contemporary City', *Entertainment Law*, 1/2: 23–49.

Chatterton, P. and Hollands, R. (2002) 'Theorising Urban Playscapes: Producing, Regulating and Consuming Youthful Nightlife City Spaces', *Urban Studies*, 39/1: 95–116.

Chatterton, P. and Hollands, R. (2003) *Urban Nightscapes: Youth Cultures, Pleasure Spaces and Corporate Power*, London: Routledge.

Chikritzhs, T. and Stockwell, T. (2002) 'The Impact of Later Trading Hours for Australian Public Houses (Hotels) on Levels of Violence', *Journal of Studies on Alcohol*, 63/5: 591–599.

Chomsky, N. (1989) *Necessary Illusions: Thought Control in Democratic Societies*, London: Pluto.

Chomsky, N. (1992) *Chronicles of Dissent/Noam Chomsky; Interviews with David Barsamian*, Stirling: AK Press.

Chomsky, N. (2002) *Media Control: The Spectacular Achievements of Propaganda*, 2nd ed., New York: Seven Stories.

Choo, A. (1996) *Hearsay and Confrontation in Criminal Trials*, Oxford: Clarendon Press.

Christopherson, S. (1994) 'The Fortress City: Privatized Spaces, Consumer Citizenship' in A. Amin (ed.), *Post-Fordism: A Reader*, London: Blackwell.

Cicero (1971) 'On Duties (II)' in *On the Good Life*, trans. and introduced by M. Grant, London: Penguin.

City of Westminster (2002) *City of Westminster Unitary Development Plan (Revised Second Deposit)*, London: City of Westminster.

Clarke, R. and Findlay, J. (2004) 'Closure Orders' in P. Kolvin (ed.), *Licensed Premises: Law and Practice*, Haywards Heath: Tottel.

Clifton, D. (2004) 'Special Attention: A Special Hours Certificate does not give a Licensed Premises the Same Status as a Late-night Venue', *The Publican*, 905, 3 May: 36.

Clowes, J. (1998) 'Transferring the Burden of Proof on "Need"', *Licensing Review*, 35, October: 18–20.

Cloyd, J. (1976) 'The Market-Place Bar', *Urban Life*, 5/3: 293–312.

Coase, R. (1986) *The Firm, the Market and the Law*, Chicago, IL: University of Chicago Press.

Coffey, A. and Atkinson, P. (1996) *Making Sense of Qualitative Data*, London: Sage.

Cohen, S. and Taylor, L. (1992) *Escape Attempts: The Theory and Practice of Resistance to Everyday Life*, 2nd ed., London: Routledge.

Coleman, L. and Cater, S. (2005) *Underage 'Risky' Drinking: Motivations and Outcomes*, York: Joseph Rowntree Foundation.

Collin, M. with contributions by Godfrey, J. (1997) *Altered State: The Story of Ecstasy Culture and Acid House*, London: Serpent's Tail.

Collins, J. (2002) 'Sounds from the Ministries', *Night*, August: 46.

Colls, R. (2003) 'Same Old Problem . . . Only Worse', *Guardian Society*, 3 December: 3.

Comedia (1991) *Out of Hours: A Study of Economic, Social and Cultural Life in Twelve Town Centres in the UK*, London: Comedia.

Conley, J., O'Barr, W. and Lind, E. (1978) 'The Power of Language: Presentational Style in the Courtroom', *Duke Law Journal*, 78/6: 1375–1399.

Connolly, P. (1975) 'The Adversary System—Is it Any Longer Appropriate?', *Australian Law Journal*, 49: 439–442.

Connolly, P. (2003) 'Analysis: Streets that Police Themselves', *The Guardian* 17 July: 32.

Coser, L. (1977) *Masters of Sociological Thought: Ideas in Historical and Social Context*, 2nd ed., NY: Harcourt Brace Jovanovich.

Coulson, P. (2003) 'Short Shrift for Lords' Amendments', 53, *Licensing Review*, April: 8.

Coupland, A. (ed.) (1997) *Mixed Use Development: Reclaiming the City*, London: Spon.

Crawford, A. (1998) *Crime Prevention and Community Safety, Politics, Policies and Practices*, London: Longmans.

Cressey, P. (1932) *The Taxi-Dance Hall: A Sociological Study in Commercialized Recreation and City Life*, Chicago, IL: University of Chicago Press.

Cresswell, T. (1999) 'Night Discourse: Producing/Consuming Meaning on the Street' in N. Fyfe (ed.), *Images of the Street: Planning, Identity and Control in Public Space*, London: Routledge.

Currie, E. (1997) 'Market, Crime and Community: Toward a Mid-Range Theory of Post-Industrial Violence', *Theoretical Criminology*, 1/2: 147–172.

Currie, E. (1998) 'Crime and Market Society: Lessons from the United States' in P. Walton and J. Young (eds.), *The New Criminology Revisited*, London: Macmillan.

Danet, B. and Bogoch, B. (1980) 'Fixed Fight or Free for All?—An Empirical Study of Combativeness in the Adversary System of Justice', *British Journal of Law and Society*, 7/1: 36–60.

Darbyshire, P. (1984) *The Magistrates' Clerk*, Chichester: Barry Rose.

Davis, M. (1990) *City of Quartz*, London: Verso.

Day, K. (1999) 'Introducing Gender to the Critique of Privatised Public Space', *Journal of Urban Design*, 4/2: 155–178.

DCMS (Department for Culture, Media and Sport) (2002) *Framework for Guidance to be Issued under Clause 177 of the Licensing Bill*, (15 November), London: DCMS.

DCMS (Department for Culture, Media and Sport) (2003) 'Major Reform of the Licensing Laws Completed', Press Release, 9 July.

DCMS (Department for Culture, Media and Sport) (2004a) *Licensing Countdown*, September, London: DCMS.

DCMS (Department for Culture, Media and Sport) (2004b) *Guidance Issued under Section 182 of the Licensing Act 2003*, London: DCMS.

DCMS (Department for Culture, Media and Sport), Home Office and ODPM (Office of the Deputy Prime Minister) (2005) *Drinking Responsibly: The Government's Proposals*, London: DCMS, Home Office and ODPM.

Deehan, A. (1999) *Alcohol and Crime: Taking Stock*, Policing and Reducing Crime Unit, Crime Reduction Research Series Paper 3, London: Home Office.

Deehan, A. and Saville, E. (2003) *Calculating the Risk: Recreational Drug Use Among Clubbers in the South East of England*, Home Office Online Report 43/03, London: Home Office Research, Development and Statistics Directorate.

Delafons, J. (1996) 'Too Many Pubs?', *Town and Country Planning*, 65: 346–347.

DeLamotte E. (1990) *Perils of the Night: A Feminist Study of Nineteenth-Century Gothic*, Oxford: Oxford University Press.

Dennis, A. and Martin, P. (2005) 'Symbolic Interactionism and the Concept of Power', *British Journal of Sociology*: 191–213.

DETR (Department of the Environment, Transport and the Regions) (2000) *Our Towns and Cities: The Future. Delivering an Urban Renaissance*, Cm 4911, Urban White Paper, November, London: DETR, The Stationery Office.

Devlin, P. (1979) *The Judge*, Oxford: Oxford University Press.

Dickens, C. (1934) *The Uncommercial Traveller*, London: Chapman and Hall.

Dickens, C. (1977) *Bleak House*, G. Ford and S. Monod (eds.), London: Norton.

Dickens, C. (1996) *Dickens' Journalism: Sketches by Boz and Other Early Papers 1833–1839*, M. Slater (ed.), London: Pheonix Giant.

Ditton, J. (2000) 'Crime and the City: Public Attitudes towards Open-street CCTV in Glasgow', *British Journal of Criminology*, 40: 692–709.

DoE (Department of the Environment) (1987) *Changes of Use of Buildings and other Land: Town and Country Planning (Use Classes) Order*, Circular 13/87.

DoE (Department of the Environment) and Welsh Office, (1994) *Planning Out Crime*, Circular 1994/5, London: HMSO.

DoE (Department of the Environment) (1996) *Town Centres and Retail Development: Revised Planning Policy Guidance 6*, London: HMSO.

Dorn, N. (1983) *Alcohol, Youth and the State*, London: Croom Helm.

Douglas, M. (1966) *Purity and Danger*, London: Routledge.

Downes, D. and Rock, P. (2003) *Understanding Deviance*, 4th ed., Oxford: Oxford University Press.

DPAS (Drugs Prevention Advisory Service) (2002) *Safer Clubbing: Guidance for Licensing Authorities, Club Managers and Promoters*, London: Home Office DPAS.

Drew, P. (1985) 'Analysing the Use of Language in Courtroom Interaction', in T. Van Dijk (ed.), *Handbook of Discourse Analysis—Volume 3: Discourse and Dialogue*, London: Academic Press.

Drew, P. (1990) 'Strategies in the Contest between Lawyer and Witness in Cross-Examination' in J. Levi and A. Walker (eds.), *Language in the Judicial Process*, London: Plenum.

Dubin, S. (1983) 'The Moral Continuum of Deviancy Research: Chicago Sociologists and the Dance Hall', *Urban Life*, 12/1: 75–94.

Du Cann, R. (1964) *The Art of the Advocate*, London: Penguin.

Dyck, N. (1980) 'Booze, Barrooms and Scrapping: Masculinity and Violence in a Western Canadian Town', *Canadian Journal of Anthropology* 1: 191–198.

Edwards, G., Anderson, P. and Babor, T. (1994) *Alcohol Policy and the Public Good*, Oxford: Oxford University Press.

Edwards, M. (2000) 'Property Markets and the Production of Inequality' in G. Bridge and S. Watson (eds.), *A Companion to the City*, Oxford: Blackwell.

Egglestone, R. (1975) 'What is Wrong with the Adversary System?', *Australian Law Journal*, 49: 428–442.

Egglestone, R. (1978) *Evidence, Proof and Probability*, London: Weidenfeld and Nicolson.

Ekblom, P. (2001) *The Conjunction of Criminal Opportunity: A Framework for Crime Reduction*, London: Home Office Policing and Reducing Crime Unit, http://www.crimereduction.gov.uk/learningzone/cco.htm.

Ekirch, A. Roger (2001) 'Sleep We Have Lost: Pre-industrial Slumber in the British Isles', *American Historical Review*, 106/2: 343–386.

Ekirch, A. Roger (2005) *At Day's Close: A History of Night-time*, London: Weidenfeld and Nicholson.

Ekman, P. (1985) *Telling Lies: Clues to Deceit in the Marketplace, Politics and Marriage*, London: Norton.

Ellickson, R. (1996) 'Controlling Chronic Misconduct in City Spaces: Of Panhandlers, Skid Rows, and Public Space Zoning', *The Yale Law Journal*, 105: 1165–1248.

Elliott, R. and Wattanasuwan, K. (1998) 'Brands as Symbolic Resources for the Construction of Identity', *International Journal of Advertising*, 17: 131–144.

Ellison, L. (2001) *The Adversarial Process and the Vulnerable Witness*, Oxford: Oxford University Press.

Elvins, M. and Hadfield, P. (2003) *West End 'Stress Area' Night-Time Economy Profiling: A Demonstration Project: Final Report to the City of Westminster*, London: City of Westminster, http://www.westminster.gov.uk/planningandlicensing/licensing/forms.cfm

Emerson, R. (1969) *Judging Delinquents: Context and Process in Juvenile Court*, Chicago, IL: Aldine.

Emsley, C. (1996) 'The Origins and Development of the Police' in E. McLaughlin and J. Muncie (eds.), *Controlling Crime*, London: Sage.

Engineer, R., Phillips, A., Thompson, J. and Nicholls, J. (2003) *Drunk and Disorderly: A Qualitative Study of Binge Drinking Among 18–24-Year-Olds*, Home Office Research Study 262, London: Home Office.

Erenberg, L. (1981) *Steppin' Out: New York Nightlife and the Transformation of American Culture 1890–1930*, Chicago, IL: University of Chicago Press.

Everitt, J. and Bowler, I. (1996) 'Bitter Sweet Conversions: Changing Times for the British Pub', *Journal of Popular Culture*, 30/2: 101–122.

Fagan, J. (1993) 'Set and Setting Revisited: Influences of Alcohol and Illicit Drugs on the Social Context of Violent Events' in S. Martin (ed.), *Alcohol and Interpersonal Violence: Fostering Multidisciplinary Perspectives*: 24, Rockville, MD: NIH.

Feintuck, M. (2004) *'The Public Interest' in Regulation*, Oxford: Oxford University Press.

Felson, M., Berends, R., Richardson, B. and Veno, A. (1997) 'Reducing Pub Hopping and Related Crime' in R. Homel (ed.), *Policing for Prevention: Reducing Crime, Public Intoxication and Injury*, Crime Prevention Studies, Volume 7, Monsey, NY: Criminal Justice Press.

Felson, M. and Clarke, R. (1998) *Opportunity Makes the Thief: Practical Theory for Crime Prevention*, Police Research Series, 98, London: HMSO.

Felson, R. (1997) 'Routine Activities and Involvement in Violence as Actor, Witness, or Target', *Violence and Victims*, 12/3: 209–221.

Felson, R., Baccaglini, W. and Gmelch, G. (1986) 'Bar-room Brawl: Aggression and Violence in Irish and American Bars' in A. Campbell and J. Gibbs (eds.), *Violent Transactions*, Oxford: Blackwell.

Ferrell, J. (2001) *Tearing Down the Streets: Adventures in Urban Anarchy*, Houndmills: Palgrave.

Finch, J. (1984) 'It's Great to Have Someone to Talk to: the Ethics and Politics of Interviewing Women' in C. Bell and H. Roberts (eds.), *Social Researching: Politics, Problems and Practice*, London: Routledge.

Fitzpatrick, J. (1980) 'Adapting to Danger: A Participant Observation Study of an Underground Mine', *Sociology of Work and Occupations*, 7/2: 131–158.

Flanagan, B. (2005) 'Does Anyone Get to Sleep around Here?', *The Observer*, 8 May, *Cash*: 16.

Forsyth, A., Cloonan, M. and Barr, J. (2005) *Factors Associated with Alcohol-Related Problems within Licensed Premises*, Report to the Greater Glasgow NHS Board, Glasgow: Greater Glasgow NHS Board.

Frankfurt, H. (2005) *On Bullshit*, Woodstock, NJ: Princeton University Press.

Freedman, M. (1975), *Lawyer's Ethics in an Adversary System*, New Brunswick: Oxford.

Friedman, M. (1982) [1962] *Capitalism and Freedom*, Chicago, IL: University of Chicago Press.

Galligan, D. (1996) *Due Process and Fair Procedures*, Oxford: Oxford University Press.

Garfinkel, H. (1956) 'Conditions of Successful Degradation Ceremonies', *American Journal of Sociology*, 61: 420–424.

Garland, D. (2001) *The Culture of Control: Crime and Social Order in Contemporary Society*, Oxford: Oxford University Press.

Geertz, C. (1973) *The Interpretation of Cultures*, New York: Basic Books.

Geller, E. and Kalsher, M. (1990) 'Environmental Determinants of Party Drinking', *Environment and Behavior*, 22: 74–90.

Gerth, H. and Wright Mills, C. (1946) [1958] (transls. and eds.), *From Max Weber: Essays in Sociology*, New York: Galaxy Books.

Gibbs, J. (1986) 'Alcohol Consumption, Cognition and Context, Examining Tavern Violence' in A. Campbell and J. Gibbs (eds.), *Violent Transactions: The Limits of Personality*, Oxford: Blackwell.

Giddens, A. (1976) *New Rules of Sociological Method: A Positive Critique of Interpretive Sociologies*, London: Hutchinson.

Giddens, A. (1979) *Central Problems in Social Theory*, London: Macmillan.

Giddens, A. (1984) *The Constitution of Society*, Cambridge: Polity.

Giesbrecht, N., Gonzales, R. and Grant, M. (1989) *Drinking and Casualties: Accidents, Poisonings and Violence in an International Perspective*, London: Tavistock/Routledge.

Girling, E., Loader, I. and Sparks, R. (2000) *Crime and Social Change in Middle England: Questions of Order in an English Town*, London: Routledge.

GLA (Greater London Authority) (2002a) *Late-Night London: Planning and Managing the Late-Night Economy*, Urbed in association with CASA and Dr Andy Lovatt, commissioned by the Greater London Authority, the London Development Agency and Transport for London. SDS Technical Report Six, June, London: GLA.

GLA (Greater London Authority) (2002b) *Whatever Gets You Through the Night: 24-Hour Licensing in London*, London: GLA.

Glen, J. (2000), *Licensing Law Liberalisation: The Scottish Experience*, Cranfield: Cranfield University School of Management.

Goff, C. (1995) 'Due Process and the Nova Scotia Herbicide Trial' in F. Pearce and L. Snider (eds.), *Corporate Crime: Contemporary Debates*, Toronto: University of Toronto Press.

Goffman, E. (1952) 'On Cooling the Mark Out: Some Aspects of Adaptation to Failure', *Psychiatry*, 15: 451–463.

Goffman, E. (1959) *The Presentation of Self in Everyday Life*, Harmondsworth: Penguin.

Goffman, E. (1963) *Behaviour in Public Places*, New York: Free Press.

Goffman, E. (1967) *Interaction Ritual: Essays on Face-to-Face Behaviour*, Harmondsworth: Penguin.

Goffman, E. (1969) *Strategic Interaction*, Oxford: Basil Blackwell.

Goffman, E. (1971) *Relations in Public: Microstudies of the Public Order*, London: Allen Lane, Penguin.

Goffman, E. (1974) *Frame Analysis: An Essay on the Organization of Experience*, Harmondsworth: Penguin.

Gofton, L. (1990) 'On the Town: Drink and the "New Lawlessness"', *Youth and Policy*, 29: 33–39.

Goodwin, B. (1992) *Using Political Ideas*, 3rd ed. Chichester: John Wiley and Sons.

Gottfredson, M. (1984) *Victims of Crime: The Dimensions of Risk*, Home Office Research Study, No. 81, London: HMSO.

Gottlieb, D. (1957) 'The Neighbourhood Tavern and the Cocktail Lounge' *American Journal of Sociology*, 62: 559–562.

Gouldner, A. (1962) 'Anti-Minotaur: The Myth of a Value-Free Sociology', *Social Problems*, 9/3: 199–213.

Gouldner, A. (1970) *The Coming Crisis of Western Sociology*, New York: Avon Books.

Graham, K. (1985) 'Determinants of Heavy Drinking and Drinking Problems: The Contribution of the Bar Environment' in E. Single and T. Storm (eds.), *Public Drinking and Public Policy*, Toronto: Addiction Research Foundation.

Graham, K. and Homel, R. (1997) 'Creating Safer Bars' in M. Plant, E. Single and T. Stockwell (eds.), *Alcohol: Minimizing the Harm— What Works?*, London: Free Association Books.

Graham, K., LaRocque, L., Yetman, R., Ross, T.J. and Guistra, E. (1980) 'Aggression and Bar Room Environments', *Journal of Studies on Alcohol*, 41: 277–292.

Graham, K. and Wells, S. (2003) 'Somebody's Gonna Get Their Head Kicked in Tonight!: Aggression Among Young Males in Bars—A Question of Values?', *British Journal of Criminology*, 43: 546–566.

Graham, K., West, P. and Wells, S. (2000) 'Evaluating Theories of Alcohol-related Aggression Using Observations of Young Adults in Bars', *Addiction*, 95/6: 847–863.

Graves, T., Graves, N., Semu, V. and Sam, I. (1981) 'The Social Context of Drinking and Violence in New Zealand's Multi-ethnic Pub

Settings' in T. Harford and L. Gaines (eds.), *Research Monograph No. 7 Social Drinking Contexts*, Rockville, MD: NIAAA.

Grayling, A. (2004) 'The Reason of Things: On Manners', *The Times*, Review, 6 March: 9.

Green, E., Mitchell, W. and Bunton, R. (2000) 'Contextualizing Risk and Danger: An Analysis of Young People's Perceptions of Risk', *Journal of Youth Studies*, 3/2: 109–126.

Green, S. (2003) 'Witness Statement of Stephen Green, Chief Constable of Nottinghamshire' in *Chief Constable of Nottinghamshire v Clegg (Springwood Leisure Plc)*, Nottingham Crown Court, February.

Green, S. (2004) 'The Mop-and-Bucket of a Sick Culture', *Alcohol Alert*, 3: 2–3.

Griffin, C., Hackley, C., Szmigin, I. and Mistral, W. (2005) *Branded Consumption and Social Identification: Young People and Alcohol*, proposal to the Economic and Social Research Council, Department of Psychology: University of Bath.

Gusfield, J. (1987) 'A Passage to Play: Rituals of Drinking Time in American Society' in M. Douglas (ed.), *Constructive Drinking: Perspectives on Drink from Anthropology*, New York: Cambridge University Press.

Haas, J. (1977) 'Learning Real Feelings: A Study of High Steel Ironworkers' Reactions to Fear and Danger', *Sociology of Work and Occupations*, 4/2: 147–170.

Hadfield, P. (2003) 'Review Article: Counting the Cost: The Measurement and Recording of Alcohol-Related Violence and Disorder by Marsh, P. et al., London: The Portman Group', *British Journal of Criminology*, 43/2: 449–451.

Hadfield, P. (2004) 'Invited to Binge?: Licensing and the 24-Hour City', *Town and Country Planning*, 73/7–8: 235–236.

Hadfield, P. with contributions from J. Collins, P. Doyle, R. Flynn and P. Kolvin (2004a) 'The Operation of Licensed Premises' in P. Kolvin (ed.), *Licensed Premises: Law and Practice*, Haywards Heath: Tottel.

Hadfield, P. with contributions by J. Collins, P. Doyle and K. Mackie (2004b) 'The Prevention of Public Disorder' in P. Kolvin (ed.), *Licensed Premises: Law and Practice*, Haywards Heath: Tottel.

Hadfield, P., Lister, S., Hobbs, D. and Winlow, S. (2001) 'The "24-Hour City"—Condition Critical?', *Town and Country Planning*, 70/11: 300–302.

Hammersley, R., Khan, F. and Ditton, J. (2002) *Ecstasy and the Rise of the Chemical Generation*, London: Routledge.

Hannigan, J. (1998) *Fantasy City: Pleasure and Profit in the Post-modern Metropolis*, London: Routledge.

Harcourt, B. (2001) *Illusion of Order: The False Promise of Broken Windows Policing*, London: Harvard University Press.

Harding, J. (1992) 'Due Process in Saskatchewan's Uranium Inquiries' in D. Currie and B. MacLean (eds.), *Re-Thinking the Administration of Justice,* Halifax, Nova Scotia: Fernwood Publishing.

Harnett, R., Thom, B., Herring, R. and Kelly, M. (2000) 'Alcohol in Transition: Towards a Model of Young Men's Drinking Styles', *Journal of Youth Studies,* 3/1: 61–77.

Harrington, J. and Halstead, T. (2004) 'Saturation: Councils "Face Rude Awakening"', *The Morning Advertiser* 2 December 223: 1.

Harrison, B. (1967) 'Religion and Recreation in Nineteenth-century England', *Past and Present,* 38: 98–125.

Harrison, B. (1973) 'Pubs' in H. Dyos and M. Wolff (eds.), *Victorian City: Images and Realities,* Volume 1, London: Routledge and Kegan Paul.

Harrison, B. (1994) *Drink and the Victorians: The Temperance Question in England 1815–72,* Keele: Keele University Press.

Harvey, D. (2005) *A Brief History of Neoliberalism,* Oxford: Oxford University Press.

Haskins, C. (1998) 'The Magistrate Debate: Licensing Powers', *The Magistrate,* October: 216.

Haslam, D. (1999) *Manchester England: The Story of the Pop Cult City,* London: Fourth Estate.

Hayek, F. (1948) *Individualism and Economic Order,* London: Routledge and Kegan Paul.

Heath, D. (ed.) (1995) *International Handbook on Alcohol and Culture,* Westport, CN: Greenwood.

Heath, D. (2000) *Drinking Occasions: Comparative Perspectives on Alcohol and Culture,* Hove: Brunner/Mazel.

Heath, T. (1997) 'The Twenty-Four Hour City Concept—A Review of Initiatives in British Cities', *Journal of Urban Design,* 2/2: 193–204.

Heath, T. and Stickland, R. (1997) 'The Twenty-Four Hour City Concept' in T. Oc and S. Tiesdell (eds.), *Safer City Centres: Reviving the Public Realm,* London: Paul Chapman Publishing.

Hetherington, P. (2003a) 'Battle of the Binge: Is Britain's Drinking Culture Out of Control?' *Guardian Society,* 3 December: 1–4.

Hetherington, P. (2003b) 'Resident Anger as Bars Exploit Licence to Booze', *The Guardian* 24 May: 18.

Hey, V. (1986) *Patriarchy and Pub Culture,* London: Tavistock.

Hinsliff, G. and Asthana, A. (2005) 'Drink Giants' Plans to Fuel Binge Britain', *The Observer* 23 October: 1–2.

Hirschi, T. (1969) *Causes of Delinquency,* Los Angeles, CA: University of California Press.

Hobbs, D. (1988) *Doing the Business: Entrepreneurship, Detectives and the Working Class in the East End of London,* Oxford: Clarendon.

Hobbs, D., Hadfield, P., Lister, S. and Winlow, S. (2002) 'Door Lore: The Art and Economics of Intimidation', *British Journal of Criminology*, 42/2: 352–370.

Hobbs, D., Hadfield, P., Lister, S. and Winlow, S. (2003) *Bouncers: Violence and Governance in the Night-time Economy*, Oxford: Oxford University Press.

Hobbs, D., Lister, S., Hadfield. P., Winlow, S. and Hall, S. (2000) 'Receiving Shadows: Governance and Liminality in the Night-time Economy', *British Journal of Sociology*, 51/4: 701–717.

Hobbs, D., Winlow, S., Hadfield, P. and Lister, S. (2005) 'Violent Hypocrisy: Governance and the Night-time Economy', *European Journal of Criminology*, 2/2: 154–176.

Hochschild, A. (1983) *The Managed Heart: Commercialization of Human Feeling*, Berkeley, CA: University of California Press.

Hogarth, W. (1973) [1738] 'The Four Times of the Day: Plate IV' in *Engravings by Hogarth*, New York: Dover.

Holden, T. and Stafford, J. (1997) *Safe and Secure Town Centres: A Good Practice Guide*, London: Association of Town Centre Management and Marks and Spencer Plc.

Hollands, R. (2000) 'Lager Louts, Tarts and Hooligans: the Criminalisation of Young Adults in a Study of Newcastle Nightlife' in V. Jupp, P. Davies and P. Francis (eds.), *Doing Criminological Research*, London: Sage.

Hollands, R. (2002) 'Divisions in the Dark: Youth Cultures, Transitions and Segmented Consumption Spaces in the Night-time Economy', *Journal of Youth Studies*, 5/2: 153–171.

Hollway, W. and Jefferson, T. (1997) 'The Risk Society in an Age of Anxiety: Situating Fear of Crime', *British Journal of Sociology*, 48/2: 255–266.

Home Office, (2000a) *Time For Reform: Proposals for the Modernisation of Our Licensing Laws*, London: HMSO.

Home Office (2000b) *Tackling Alcohol-related Crime, Disorder and Nuisance: Action Plan*, London: HMSO.

Home Office (2003a) *Respect and Responsibility—Taking a Stand Against Anti-Social Behaviour*, London: Stationery Office.

Home Office (2003b) *Guidance for Local Partnerships on Alcohol-Related Crime and Disorder Data*, London: Home Office Development and Practice Report 6 (Drugs and Alcohol).

Homel, R. and Clark, J. (1994) 'The Prediction and Prevention of Violence in Pubs and Clubs', *Crime Prevention Studies*, 3: 1–46.

Homel, R., Tomsen, S. and Thommeny, J. (1992) 'Public Drinking and Violence: Not Just an Alcohol Problem', *Journal of Drug Issues*, 22/3: 679–697.

Honess, T., Seymour, L. and Webster, R. (2000) *The Social Contexts of Underage Drinking*, London: Home Office.

Hope, T. (1985) 'Drinking and Disorder in the City Centre: A Policy Analysis' in *Implementing Crime Prevention Measures*, Home Office Research Study No. 86, London: HMSO.

Hope, T. (2001) 'Community Crime Prevention in Britain: A Strategic Overview', *Criminal Justice*, 1/4: 421–439.

Hough, M. and Tilley, N. (1998) *Auditing Crime and Disorder: Guidance for Local Partnerships*, Crime Detection and Prevention Series, Paper 91, London: Home Office Police Research Group.

Hu, C. (2003) 'Price Discounts "Out of Control" in Birmingham', *The Morning Advertiser* 11 September, 161: 2.

Humphreys, L. (1970) *Tearoom Trade*, London: Gerald Duckworth and Co. Ltd.

Hyam, M. (1999) *Advocacy Skills*, London: Blackstone.

IAS (Institute of Alcohol Studies) (2005) *Drinking Responsibly: The Government's Proposals: Response from the Institute of Alcohol Studies*, London: IAS.

Isle of Man Constabulary, (2002) *Chief Constable's Annual Report 2001–2002*, Douglas: Isle of Man Constabulary.

Jackson, P. (2004) *Inside Clubbing: Sensual Experiments in the Art of Being Human*, Oxford: Berg.

Jacobs, J. (1961) *The Death and Life of Great American Cities*, Harmondsworth: Penguin.

Jacobs, K. (1992) 'Night Discourse' in S. Heller and K. Jacobs (eds.), *Angry Graphics*, Layton UT: Gibbs Smith.

Jacquemet, M. (1996) *Credibility in Court: Communicative Practices in the Camorra Trials*, Cambridge: Cambridge University Press.

Jasanoff, S. (2004) 'The Idiom of Co-Production' in S. Jasanoff (ed.), *States of Knowledge: The Co-production of Science and Social Order*, London: Routledge.

Jeavons, C. and Taylor, S. (1985) 'The Control of Alcohol-related Aggression: Redirecting the Inebriate's Attention to Socially Appropriate Conduct', *Aggressive Behavior*, 11: 93–101.

Jeffries, S. (2004) 'Give up the Ghosts', *The Guardian* G2 29 October: 2–3.

Jermier, J. (1982) 'Ecological Hazards and Organizational Behaviour: A Study of Dangerous Urban Space–Time Zones', *Human Organization*, 41/3: 198–207.

Jones, P., Hillier, D. and Comfort, D. (2003) 'Business Improvement Districts—Another Piece in the UK Regeneration Jigsaw?', *Town & Country Planning*, 72: 158–161.

Jones, P., Hillier, D. and Turner, D. (1999) 'Towards the '24-Hour City', *Town & Country Planning*, 68: 164–165.

Justices' Clerks' Society, (1999) *Good Practice Guide: Licensing*, London: Justices' Clerks' Society.

Kafka, F. (1994) [1925] *The Trial*, trans. I. Parry, London: Penguin.

Katovich, M. and Reese, W. (1987) 'The Regular: Full Time Identities and Memberships in an Urban Bar', *Journal of Contemporary Ethnography*, 16/3: 308–343.

Kershaw, C., Budd, T., Kinshott, G., Mattinson, J., Mayhew, P. and Myhill, A. (2000) *The 2000 British Crime Survey*, Home Office Statistical Bulletin, London: HMSO.

Kettle, M. (2003) 'Alcoholic Britain should not be Offered another Drink', *Guardian Society*, 2 January: 2–3.

Kingsdale, J. (1973) 'The "Poor Man's Club": Social Functions of the Urban Working Class Saloon', *American Quarterly*, 24/4: 472–489.

Kinkade, P. and Katovich, M. (1997) 'The Driver: Adaptations and Identities in the Urban Worlds of Pizza Delivery Employees', *Journal of Contemporary Ethnography*, 25/4: 421–448.

Klein, N. (2001) *No Logo*, London: Flamingo.

Kolvin, P. (ed.) (2004) *Licensed Premises: Law and Practice*, Haywards Heath: Tottel.

Kreitzman, L. (1999) *The 24-Hour Society*, London: Profile.

Langbein, J. (2003) *The Origins of Adversary Criminal Trial*, Oxford: Oxford University Press.

Lasley, J. (1989) 'Drinking Routines/Lifestyles and Predatory Victimisation: A Causal Analysis', *Justice Quarterly*, 6: 529–542.

Law, R. (1999) 'Beyond "Women and Transport": Towards New Geographies of Gender and Daily Mobility', *Progress in Human Geography*, 23/4: 567–588.

Leather, P. and Lawrence, C. (1995) 'Perceiving Pub Violence: The Symbolic Influence of Social and Environmental Factors', *British Journal of Social Psychology*, 34: 395–407.

Leeds City Council, (1995) *Leeds: 24-Hour City Licensing*, Leeds: LCC Legal Services Department.

Leidner, R. (1993) *Fast Food, Fast Talk: Service Work and the Routinization of Everyday Life*, London: University of California Press.

Leigh, B. (1999) 'Peril, Chance, Adventure: Concepts of Risk, Alcohol Use and Risky Behaviour in Young Adults', *Addiction*, 94/3: 371–383.

LeMasters, E. (1973) 'Social Life in a Working Class Tavern', *Urban Life and Culture*, 2/1: 27–52.

LeMasters, E. (1975) *Blue Collar Aristocrats: Lifestyles at a Working Class Tavern*, London: University of Wisconsin Press.

Levinson, D. (1983) 'Social Setting, Cultural Factors and Alcohol-related Aggression' in E. Gottheil, K., Druley, T., Skoloda and H. Waxman (eds.), *Alcohol, Drug Abuse and Aggression,* Springfield, IL: Charles C. Thomas.

Levy, A. and Scott-Clark, C. (2004) 'Under the Influence', *Guardian Weekend* 20 November: 14–30.

LGA (Local Government Association) (2002) *All Day and All of the Night?: An LGA Discussion Paper,* London: LGA.

Light, R. (2000) 'Liberalising Liquor Licensing Law: Order Into Chaos?', *New Law Journal,* 150/6941: 926–929.

Light, R. (2004a) 'Local Authority Decision-Making and the Licensing Act 2003', *Local Governance,* 30/2: 55–66.

Light, R. (2004b) 'Licensing Update', *Solicitors' Journal,* 148/44: 1341.

Light, R. (2005a) 'The Licensing Act 2003: Liberal Constraint?', *Modern Law Review,* 68/2: 268–285.

Light, R. (2005b) 'On Appealing', *Solicitors' Journal,* 149: 109–110.

Light, R. and Heenan, S. (1999) *Controlling Supply: The Concept of 'Need' in Liquor Licensing,* Bristol: University of the West of England.

Lindner, R. (1996) *The Reportage of Urban Culture: Robert Park and the Chicago School,* Cambridge: Cambridge University Press.

Link, L. (1995) *The Devil: A Mask Without a Face,* London: Reaktion Books.

Linton, N. (1965) 'The Witness and Cross-Examination', *Berkeley Journal of Sociology,* 1–12.

Lipsey, M., Wilson, D., Cohen, M. and Derzon, J. (1997) 'Is there a Causal Relationship between Alcohol and Violence?' in M. Galanter (ed.), *Recent Developments in Alcoholism,* 13: 245–82, New York: Plenum Press.

Lister, S., Hobbs, D., Hadfield, P. and Winlow, S. (2001) *Policing the Night-time Economy in Eastville,* University of Durham Working Paper.

Lister, S., Hobbs, D., Hall, S. and Winlow, S. (2000) 'Violence in the Night-time Economy; Bouncers: The Reporting, Recording and Prosecution of Assaults', *Policing and Society* 10: 383–402.

Livingston, D. (1997) 'Police Discretion and the Quality of Life in Public Places: Courts, Communities and the New Policing', *Columbia Law Review,* 97/3: 551–672.

Loader, I. (1994) 'Democracy, Justice and the Limits of Policing: Rethinking Police Accountability', *Social & Legal Studies,* 3: 521–544.

Lofland, J. (1976) *Doing Social Life: The Qualitative Study of Human Interaction in Natural Settings,* New York: Wiley.

Lofland, L. (1973) *A World of Strangers: Order and Action in Urban Public Space,* Prospect Heights, IL: Waveland.

Lofland, L. (1998) *The Public Realm: Exploring the City's Quintessential Social Territory,* Hawthorne, NY: Aldine De Gruyter.

Lovatt, A. (1996) 'The Ecstasy of Urban Regeneration: Regulation of the Night-time Economy in the Transition to a Post-Fordist City' in J. O'Connor and D. Wynne (eds.), *From the Margins to the Centre: Cultural Production and Consumption in the Post-Industrial City,* Aldershot: Arena.

Lovatt, A., O'Connor, J., Montgomery, J. and Owens, P. (eds.) (1994) *The 24-Hour City: Selected Papers from the First National Conference on the Night-time Economy,* Manchester: Manchester Metropolitan University.

Lupton, D. (1999) *Risk,* London: Routledge.

Lyman, S. and Scott, M. (1967) 'Territoriality: A Neglected Sociological Dimension', *Social Problems*: 236–249.

Lynch, M. (2004) 'Circumscribing Expertise: Membership Categories in Courtroom Testimony' in S. Jasanoff (ed.), *States of Knowledge: The Co-production of Science and Social Order,* London: Routledge.

Lynch, M. and Bogen, D. (1996) *The Spectacle of History: Speech, Text and Memory at the Iran-Contra Hearings,* Durham, NC: Duke University Press.

Lyng, S. (1990) 'Edgework: A Social Psychological Analysis of Voluntary Risk Taking', *American Journal of Sociology,* 95/4: 851–886.

McBarnet, D. (1981) *Conviction: Law, the State and the Construction of Justice,* London: Macmillan.

McCurry, P. (2003) 'Last Orders', *The Guardian* 9 April: 5–6.

McKenna, P. (1996) *Nightshift,* Argyll: S. T. Publishing.

McVeigh, A. (1997) 'Screening for Straights: Aspects of Entrance Policy at a Gay Disco', *Irish Journal of Sociology,* 7: 77–98.

Macalister, T. (2001) 'Wetherspoon Tops Growth Poll', *The Guardian* 6 June: 15.

MacAndrew, C. and Edgerton, R. (1969) *Drunken Comportment: A Social Explanation,* London: Thomas Nelson and Sons Ltd.

Macclesfield Express (2003) 'Crackdown', 31 December: 1–2.

Macintyre, S. and Homel, R. (1997) 'Danger on the Dance Floor: A Study of Interior Design, Crowding and Aggression in Nightclubs' in R. Homel (ed.), *Policing for Prevention: Reducing Crime, Public Intoxication and Injury,* Crime Prevention Studies, Volume 7, Monsey, NY: Criminal Justice Press.

Magennis, P., Shepherd, J., Hutchinson, H. and Brown, A. (1998) 'Trends in Facial Injury', *British Medical Journal,* 316: 325–326.

Magistrates' Association (2000) *Response to White Paper—Time for Reform,* London: Magistrates' Association.

Maguire, M. and Nettleton, H. (2003) *Reducing Alcohol-related Violence and Disorder: An Evaluation of the 'TASC' Project*, London: Home Office.

Malbon, B. (1999) *Clubbing: Dancing, Ecstasy and Vitality*, London: Routledge.

Manchester, C. (1999) *Entertainment Licensing: Law and Practice*, 2nd ed., London: Butterworths.

Manchester, C., Popplestone, S. and Allen, J. (2005) *Alcohol and Entertainment Licensing Law*, London: Cavendish Publishing.

Manning, P. (1992) *Erving Goffman and Modern Sociology*, Cambridge: Polity.

Manning, P. (2000) 'Credibility, Agency, and the Interaction Order', *Symbolic Interaction*, 23/3: 283–297.

Markowitz, S. (2000) *Criminal Violence and Alcohol Beverage Control: Evidence from an International Study*, NBER Working Paper 7481, Cambridge, MA: National Bureau of Economic Research.

Marsh, P., Bradley, S., Peck, F. and Carnibella, A. (2002) *Counting the Cost: The Measurement and Recording of Alcohol-Related Violence and Disorder*, London: The Portman Group.

Marsh, P. and Fox Kibby, K. (1992) *Drinking and Public Disorder*, London: The Portman Group.

Marshall, G. (1986) 'The Workplace Culture of a Licensed Restaurant', *Theory, Culture and Society*, 3/1: 33–47.

Marshall, M. (1979) *'Weekend Warriors': Alcohol in a Micronesian Culture*, Palo Alto, CA: Mayfield.

Marx, K. (1976) [1867] *Capital: A Critique of Political Economy*, Volume 1, London: Penguin.

Mass Observation (1943) [1970] *The Pub and the People: A Worktown Study*, Welwyn Garden City: Seven Dials Press.

Matoesian, G. (1993) *Reproducing Rape: Domination through Talk in the Courtroom*, Cambridge: Polity.

Mattinson, J. (2001) *Stranger and Acquaintance Violence: Practice Messages from the British Crime Survey*, Home Office Briefing Note 7/01, London: Home Office.

Matza, D. (1964) *Delinquency and Drift*, London: John Wiley and Sons, Inc.

Mayer, J. and Rosenblatt, A. (1975) 'Encounters with Danger: Social Workers in the Ghetto', *Sociology of Work and Occupations*, 2/3: 227–245.

Mayhew, H. (1950) *London's Underworld*, P. Quennell (ed.), London: Spring Books.

MCM Research, (1990) *Conflict and Violence in Pubs*, Oxford: MCM Research Ltd.

Measham, F. (2004) 'Drug and Alcohol Research: The Case for Cultural Criminology' in J. Ferrell, K. Hayward, W. Morrison and M. Presdee (eds.), *Cultural Criminology Unleashed*, London: Glasshouse Press.

Mehigan, S. and Phillips, J. with contributions from Barker, K. and Collins, D. (2003) *Paterson's Licensing Acts 2003*, 111th ed., London: Butterworths.

Mehigan, S., Phillips, J. and Saunders, J. (2004) *Paterson's Licensing Acts 2004: Volume 1: Liquor and Entertainment Licensing*, 112th ed., London: Butterworths.

Melbin, M. (1978) 'Night as Frontier', *American Sociological Review*, 43/1: 3–22.

Melbin, M. (1987) *Night as Frontier: Colonizing the World After Dark*, London: The Free Press.

Metropolitan Police (2004) *Preliminary Assessment of the Impact of the Licensing Act 2003 on the Metropolitan Police Service*, London: Metropolitan Police Clubs and Vice Operational Command Unit.

Mies, M. (1983) 'Towards a Methodology for Feminist Research' in G. Bowles and R. Duelli Klein (eds.), *Theories of Women's Studies*, London: Routledge.

Miethe, T., Stafford, M. and Long, J. (1987) 'Social Differentiation in Criminal Victimization: A Test of Routine Activities/Lifestyle Theories', *American Sociological Review*, 52: 184–194.

Mill, J.S. (1974) *On Liberty*, G. Himmelfarb (ed.), Harmondsworth: Penguin.

Miller, J. and Glassner, B. (1997) 'The "Inside" and "Outside": Finding Realities in Interviews' in D. Silverman (ed.), *Qualitative Research: Theory, Method and Practice*, London: Sage.

Milne, L. and Milne, M. (1956) *The World of Night*, New York: Harper and Brothers.

Mirauer, W. (2001) 'A Small Town in England', *Night*, August: 106.

Moir, E. (1969) *The Justices of the Peace*, Harmondsworth: Penguin.

Molotch, H. and Boden, D. (1985) 'Talking Social Structure: Discourse, Domination and the Watergate Hearings', *American Sociological Review*, 50: 273–288.

Monaghan, L. (2002a) 'Regulating 'Unruly' Bodies: Work Tasks, Conflict and Violence in Britain's Night-Time Economy', *The British Journal of Sociology*, 53/3: 403–429.

Monaghan, L. (2002b) 'Hard Men, Shop Boys and Others: Embodying Competence in a Masculinist Occupation', *The Sociological Review*, 50/3: 334–355.

Monaghan, L. (2002c) 'Opportunity, Pleasure and Risk: An Ethnography of Urban Male Heterosexualities', *Journal of Contemporary Ethnography*, 31/4: 440–477.

Monbiot, G. (2000) *Captive State: The Corporate Takeover of Britain*, London: Pan Macmillan.

Montgomery, J. (1995) 'Urban Vitality and the Culture of Cities', *Planning Practice and Research*, 10/2: 101–109.

Montgomery, J. (1997) 'Café; Culture and the City: The Role of Pavement Cafés in Urban Public Social Life', *Journal of Urban Design*, 2/1: 83–102.

Montgomery, J. and Owens, P. (1997) 'The Evening Economy of Cities', *Regenerating Cities*, 7: 32–39.

Moore-Ede, M. (1993) *The 24-Hour Society: The Risks, Costs and Challenges of a World that Never Stops*, London: Piatkus.

Moran, L., Skeggs, B., Tyrer, P. and Corteen, K. (2003) 'The Constitution of Fear in Gay Space' in E. Stanko (ed.), *The Meanings of Violence*, London: Routledge.

Morning Advertiser (2003a) 'Weekly Takings Soar at *Lloyds No. 1* Venues', 11 September: 11.

Morning Advertiser (2003b) '*Luminar* Seeks Equality in Law', 28 August: 15.

Mort, F. (2000) 'The Sexual Geography of the City' in G. Bridge and S. Watson (eds.), *A Companion to the City*, London: Blackwell.

Muchembled, R. (1985) *Popular Culture and Elite Culture in France 1400–1750*, Baton Rouge, LA: Louisiana State University Press.

Munkman, J. (1986) *The Techniques of Advocacy*, London: Sweet and Maxwell.

Napley, D. (1970) *The Technique of Persuasion*, London: Sweet and Maxwell.

Nasar, J. and Fisher, B. (1993) 'Hot Spots of Fear and Crime: A Multi-Method Investigation', *Journal of Environmental Psychology*, 13: 29–49.

Neame, S. (2003) 'The New Licensing Bill: Over-Regulating the British Pub?', *Institute of Economic Affairs Bulletin*, June: 28–33.

Nelson, A., Bromley, R. and Thomas, C. (2001) 'Identifying Micro-spatial and Temporal Patterns of Violent Crime and Disorder in a British City Centre', *Applied Geography*, 21: 249–274.

Newburn, T. and Shiner, M. (2001) *Teenage Kicks?—Young People and Alcohol: a Review of the Literature*, York: Joseph Rowntree Foundation.

Nicholson Committee (2003) *Review of Liquor Licensing Law in Scotland*, Edinburgh: Scottish Executive.

Night, (2000) 'Pride of the North', September: 12–16.

Night, (2001a) 'Ultimate in Leisure', December: 18–20.

Night, (2001b) 'Going Global', September: 36–37.

O'Barr, W. (1982) *Linguistic Evidence: Language, Power and Strategy in the Courtroom*, London: Academic Press.

Oc, T. and Tiesdell, S. (1997) 'Towards Safer City Centres' in T. Oc and S. Tiesdell (eds.), *Safer City Centres: Reviving the Public Realm*, London: Paul Chapman Publishing Ltd.

Oc, T. and Trench, S. (1993) 'Planning and Shopper Security', in R. Bromley and C. Thomas (eds.), *Retail Change: Contemporary Issues*, London: UCL Press.

O'Connor, J. and Wynne, D. (1996) 'Introduction' in J. O'Connor and D. Wynne (eds.), *From the Margins to the Centre: Cultural Production and Consumption in the Post-Industrial City*, Aldershot: Arena.

O'Dea, W. (1958) *The Social History of Lighting*, London: Routledge and Kegan Paul.

ODPM (Office of the Deputy Prime Minister) (2002) *Consultation on Possible Changes to the Use Classes Order and Temporary Uses Provisions*, London: OPDM.

Oldenburg, R. (1997) *The Great Good Place*, New York: Marlowe.

Osborne, D. and Gaebler, T. (1992) *Reinventing Government*, Reading, MA: Addison-Wesley.

Pain, R. (2001) 'Gender, Race, Age and Fear in the City', *Urban Studies*, 38/5–6: 899–913.

Palmer, B. (2000) *Cultures of Darkness: Night Travels in the Histories of Transgression from Medieval to Modern*, New York: Monthly Review Press.

Pannick, D. (1987) *Judges*, Oxford: Oxford University Press.

Pannick, D. (1992) *Advocates*, Oxford: Oxford University Press.

Parker, H., Aldridge, J. and Measham, F. (1998) *Illegal Leisure: The Normalization of Adolescent Recreational Drug Use*, London: Routledge.

Parker, H., Williams, L. and Aldridge, J. (2002) 'The Normalization of "Sensible" Recreational Drug Use: Further Evidence from the North West England Longitudinal Study', *Sociology*, 36/4: 941–964.

Parker, S. (2003) 'Drink and be Merry', *The Guardian* 8 April: 4.

Parks, K., Miller, B. Collins, R. and Zetes-Zanatta, L. (1998) 'Women's Descriptions of Drinking in Bars: Reasons and Risks', *Sex Roles,* 38/9–10: 701–717.

Pearce, F. and Tombs, S. (1997) 'Hazards, Law and Class: Contextualizing the Regulation of Corporate Crime', *Social & Legal Studies*, 6/1: 79–107.

Pearce, F. and Tombs, S. (1998) *Toxic Capitalism: Corporate Crime and the Chemical Industry*, Aldershot: Dartmouth.

Pease, K. (2002) 'Crime Reduction' in M. Maguire, R. Morgan and R. Reiner (eds.), *The Oxford Handbook of Criminology*, 3rd ed., Oxford: Oxford University Press.

Penny, M. (1993) *Nightlife: The Secret World of Nocturnal Creatures*, London: Boxtree.

Phillips, J. (2002) *Licensing Law Guide*, 3rd ed., London: Butterworths.

Phillips, T. and Smith, P. (2000) 'Police Violence Occasioning Citizen Complaint: An Empirical Analysis of Time–Space Dynamics', *British Journal of Criminology*, 40: 480–496.

Pilditch, D. (2003) 'Yobs to be Caged', *Daily Express* 23 August: 27.

Plant, M., Miller, P., Plant, M. and Nichol, P. (1994) 'No Such Thing as Safe Glass', *British Medical Journal*, 308: 6–7.

Plant, M. and Plant, M. (1992) *Risk Takers: Alcohol, Drugs, Sex and Youth*, London: Routledge.

Plato, (1987) *Gorgias*, trans. D. Zeyl, Indianapolis, IN: Hackett.

Potter, J. (1996) *Representing Reality: Discourse, Rhetoric and Social Construction*, London: Sage.

Press, S. (2001) 'The Best Bar None', *Manchester Evening News* 21 July: 30.

Prus, R. (1983) 'Drinking as Activity: An Interactionist Analysis', *Journal of Studies on Alcohol*, 44/3: 460–475.

Punch, M. (1978) 'Backstage: Observing Police Work in Amsterdam', *Urban Life*, 7/3: 309–335.

Punch, M. (1996) *Dirty Business: Exploring Corporate Misconduct*, London: Sage.

Rabin, R. (2001) 'The Third Wave of Tobacco Tort Litigation' in R. Rabin and S. Sugarman (eds.), *Regulating Tobacco*, Oxford: Oxford University Press.

Ragnarsdottir, T. (2002) 'Effect of Extended Alcohol Serving Hours in Reykjavik' in R. Room (ed.), *The Effects of Nordic Alcohol Policies: What Happens to Drinking and Harm When Control Systems Change?*, publication no. 42, 145–154, Helsinki: Nordic Council for Alcohol and Drug Research.

Raistrick, D., Hodgson, R. and Ritson, B. (eds.) (1999) *Tackling Alcohol Together: The Evidence Base for a UK Alcohol Policy*, London: Free Association Books.

Ranatunga, A. (2004) 'Appeals and Judicial Review' in P. Kolvin (eds.), *Licensed Premises: Law and Practice*, Haywards Heath: Tottel.

Ravenscroft, N. (2000) 'The Vitality and Viability of Town Centres', *Urban Studies*, 37: 2533–2549.

Redhead, S., Wynne, D. and O'Connor, J. (eds.) (1998) *The Clubcultures Reader*, London: Blackwell.

Reeve, A. (1995) 'The Private Realm of the Managed Town Centre', *Urban Design International*, 1/1: 61–80.

Reeve, A. (1998) 'Risk and the New Urban Space of Managed Town Centres', *International Journal of Risk, Security and Crime Prevention*, 3/1: 43–54.

Reith, G. (2005) 'On the Edge: Drugs and the Consumption of Risk in Late Modernity' in S. Lyng (ed.), *Edgework: The Sociology of Risk-Taking*, Abingdon: Routledge.

Republic of Ireland Commission on Liquor Licensing, (2003) *Final Report, April 2003*, Dublin: Commission on Liquor Licensing.

Release (1997) *Release Drugs and Dance Survey*, London: Release.

Richardson, A. and Budd, T. (2003) *Alcohol, Crime and Disorder: A Study of Young Adults*, Home Office Research Study 263, London: Home Office.

Riddell, P. and Ford, R. (2005) 'Voters Reject Late-Night Drink Laws', *The Times* 6 September: 2–3.

Ridout (2003) 'High Noon on the High Street', *The Morning Advertiser* 17 July: 38.

Ries, A. and Ries, L. (1999) *The 22 Immutable Laws of Branding*, London: Harper Collins.

Riessman, C. (1993) *Narrative Analysis*, Newbury Park, CA: Sage Publications.

Rietveld, H. (1993) 'Living the Dream' in S. Redhead (ed.), *Rave Off: Politics and Deviance in Contemporary Youth Culture*, Aldershot: Avebury Press.

Ritzer, G. (2004) *The Globalization of Nothing*, London: Pine Forge.

Roberts, R. (1971) *The Classic Slum*, Harmondsworth: Penguin.

Rock, P. (1979) *The Making of Symbolic Interactionism*, London: Macmillan.

Rock, P. (1993) *The Social World of an English Crown Court*, Oxford: Clarendon Press.

Rodaway, P. (1994) *Sensuous Geographies: Body, Sense and Place*, London: Routledge.

Roebuck, J. and Frese, W. (1976) *The Rendezvous: A Case Study of an After-Hours Club*, New York: The Free Press.

Rogan, K. (2002) 'Just the Facts?', *The Publican*, 14 March, http:// www. thepublican.com/cgibin/item.cgi?id=633&d=28&h=30&f=29.

Rogers, B. (1988) *Men Only: An Investigation into Men's Organizations*, London: Pandora.

Rogers, M. (1980) 'Goffman on Power, Hierarchy, and Status', in J. Ditton (ed.), *The View from Goffman*, London: Macmillan.

Rogers, R. edited by Gumuchdjian, P. (1997) *Cities for a Small Planet*, London: Faber and Faber Limited.

Room, R. (1997) 'Alcohol, the Individual and Society: What History Teaches Us', *Addiction*, 92, Supplement 1: 7–11.

Room, R. (2004a) 'Disabling the Public Interest: Alcohol Strategies and Policies for England', *Addiction*, 99: 1083–1089.

Room, R. (2004b) 'Alcohol Control and the Public Interest: International Perspectives' in P. Kolvin (ed.), *Licensed Premises: Law and Practice*, Haywards Heath: Tottel.

Rorty, R. (1989) *Contingency, Irony and Solidarity*, Cambridge: Cambridge University Press.

Rorty, R. (1999) *Philosophy and Social Hope*, London: Penguin.

Rosenzweig, R. (1983) *Eight Hours for What We Will: Workers and Leisure in an Industrial City 1870–1920*, Cambridge: Cambridge University Press.

Rowley, M. and Ravenscroft, N. (1999) 'Leisure Property as an Indicator of the Changing Vitality and Viability of Town Centres: A Case Study' in P. Bramham and W. Murphy (eds.), *Policy and Publics: Leisure, Culture and Commerce*, Eastbourne: Leisure Studies Association.

Rubinstein, W. (1973) *City Police*, New York: Ballantine.

Sacks, H. (1972) 'An Initial Investigation of the Usability of Conversational Data for Doing Sociology' in Sudnow, D. (ed.), *Studies in Social Interaction*, New York: Free Press.

Salusbury-Jones, G. (1938) *Street Life in Medieval England*, Oxford: Pen-in-Hand Publishing.

Sasson, T. (1995) *Crime Talk: How Citizens Construct a Social Problem*, New York: Aldine de Gruyter.

Saunders, C. (1997) 'Earn as You Learn: Connections Between Doing Qualitative Work and Living Daily Life', *Qualitative Sociology*, 20/4: 457–464.

Savage, M., Barlow, J., Dickens, P. and Fielding, A. (1992) *Property, Bureaucracy and Culture*, London: Routledge.

Schivelbusch, W. (1995) *Disenchanted Night: The Industrialization of Light in the Nineteenth Century*, London: University of California Press.

Schlör, J. (1998) *Nights in the Big City: Paris; Berlin; London 1840–1930*, London: Reaktion Books.

Schopenhauer, A. (1896) *The Art of Controversy*, (trans. by T. Bailey Saunders), London: Macmillan.

Schwalbe, M., Godwin, S., Holden, D., Schrock, D., Thompson, S. and Wolkomir, M. (2000) 'Generic Processes in the Reproduction of Inequality: An Interactionist Analysis', *Social Forces*, 79/2: 419–452.

Scott, M. and Lyman, S. (1968) 'Accounts', *American Sociological Review*, 33/1: 46–62.

Sennett, R. (1970) *The Uses of Disorder: Personal Identity and City Life*, New York: Norton.

Sennett, R. (1990) *The Conscience of the Eye: The Design and Social Life of Cities*, London: Norton.

Sennett, R. (2000) 'Reflections on the Public Realm' in G. Bridge and S. Watson (eds.), *A Companion to the City*, Oxford: Blackwell.

Shadwell, A. (1923) *Drink in 1914–1922: A Lesson in Control*, London: Longmans, Green and Co.

Shearing, C. and Stenning, P. (1987) 'Say Cheese! The Disney Order that's not so Mickey Mouse' in C. Shearing and P. Stenning (eds.), *Private Policing*, Newbury Park, CA: Sage.

Shearing, C. and Wood, J. (2003) 'Nodal Governance, Democracy and the New "Denizens"', *Journal of Law and Society*, 30/3: 400–419.

Shepherd, J. (1990) 'Violent Crime in Bristol: An Accident and Emergency Department Perspective', *British Journal of Criminology*, 30: 289–305.

Shepherd, J. (1994) 'Violent Crime: the Role of Alcohol and New Approaches to the Prevention of Injury', *Alcohol and Alcoholism*, 29: 5–10.

Shepherd, J. and Brickley, M. (1996) 'The Relationship between Alcohol Intoxication, Stressors and Injury in Urban Violence', *British Journal of Criminology*, 36/4: 546–564.

Shuy, R. (1993) *Language Crimes: The Use and Abuse of Language Evidence in the Courtroom*, Oxford: Blackwell.

Sime, S. (2004) *A Practical Approach to Civil Procedure*, 7th ed., Oxford: Oxford University Press.

Skogan, W. and Maxfield, M. (1981) *Coping with Crime: Individual and Neighborhood Reactions*, Beverly Hills, CA: Sage.

Slapper, G. and Tombs, S. (1999) *Corporate Crime*, Harlow: Longman.

Smith, A. ([1776] 1979) *An Enquiry into the Nature and Causes of the Wealth of Nations*, R. Campbell and A. Skinner (eds.), Oxford: Clarendon Press.

Smith, I. (1989) 'Effectiveness of Legislative and Fiscal Restrictions in Reducing Alcohol-Related Crime and Traffic Accidents' in J. Vernon (ed.), *Alcohol and Crime*, Canberra: Australian Institute of Criminology.

Snow, D., Robinson, C. and McCall, P. (1991) '"Cooling Out" Men in Singles Bars and Nightclubs: Observations on the Interpersonal Survival Strategies of Women in Public Places', *Journal of Contemporary Ethnography*, 19/4: 423–449.

Solon, M. (2004) 'Experts: Take Your Pick, or Independently Assessed', *The Barrister*, 20, 14 April: 17.

South, N. (1999) *Drugs: Cultures, Controls and Everyday Life*, London: Sage.

Spink, J. and Bramham, P. (1999) 'The Myth of the 24-hour City' in P. Bramham and W. Murphy (eds.), *Policy and Publics: Leisure, Culture and Commerce*, Eastbourne: Leisure Studies Association.

Stanko, E. (1997) 'Safety Talk: Conceptualizing Women's Risk Assessment as a "Technology of the Soul"', *Theoretical Criminology*, 1/4: 479–499.

Stedman Jones, G. (1983) *Languages of Class: Studies in English Working Class History 1832–1982*, Cambridge: Cambridge University Press.

Steele, C. and Josephs, R. (1990) 'Alcohol Myopia: Its Prized and Dangerous Effects', *American Psychologist*, 45: 921–933.

St. John-Brooks, K. with assistance from Winstanley, K. (1998) *Keeping The Peace: A Guide to the Prevention of Alcohol-Related Disorder*, 2nd ed., London: The Portman Group.

Stockwell, T. (2001) 'Responsible Alcohol Service: Lessons from Evaluations of Server Training and Policing Initiatives', *Drug and Alcohol Review*, 20: 257–265.

Stockwell, T., Lang, E. and Rydon, P. (1993) 'High Risk Drinking Settings: The Association of Serving and Promotional Practices with Harmful Drinking', *Addiction*, 88: 1519–1526.

Strategy Unit (2003) *Strategy Unit Alcohol Harm Reduction Project: Interim Analytical Report*, London: Cabinet Office Strategy Unit, www.pm.gov.uk/output/Page 4498.asp.

Strategy Unit (2004) *Alcohol Harm Reduction Strategy for England*, London: Cabinet Office Strategy Unit, www.strategy.gov.uk/output/Page3669.asp.

Strauss, A. (1987) *Qualitative Analysis for Social Scientists*, New York: Cambridge University Press.

Sudnow, D. (1965) 'Normal Crimes: Sociological Features of the Penal Code in a Public Defender Office', *Sociological Problems*, 12/3: 255–276.

Swift, J. (1965) [1726] 'A Voyage to the Houyhnhnms' in *Gulliver's Travels*, London: Methuen.

Swinden, E. (2000) 'Not a Pretty Sight: Poster Campaign that "Promoted Drunken Behaviour" Withdrawn', *Manchester Evening News* 6 October: 3.

Sykes, G. and Matza, D. (1957) 'Techniques of Neutralization: A Theory of Delinquency', *American Sociological Review*, 22: 664–670.

Tallon, A. and Bromley, R. (2002) 'Living in the 24-Hour City', *Town and Country Planning*, November: 282–285.

Taylor, I. (1990) 'The Concept of "Social Cost" in Free Market Theory and the Social Effects of Free Market Policies' in I. Taylor (ed.),

The Social Effects of Free Market Policies: An International Text, London: Harvester Wheatsheaf.

Taylor, I. (1999) *Crime in Context*, Cambridge: Polity.

Taylor, S. and Gammon, C. (1976) 'Aggressive Behaviour of Intoxicated Subjects: The Effect of Third-party Intervention', *Journal of Studies on Alcohol*, 37: 917–930.

Thomas, C. and Bromley, R. (2000) 'City-centre Revitalisation: Problems of Fragmentation and Fear in the Evening and Night-time Economy', *Urban Studies*, 37: 1403–1429.

Thompson, B. (2004) 'Expert Witnesses in the Dock', *The Barrister*, 20, 14 April: 8–9.

Thornton, S. (1995) *Club Cultures: Music, Media and Sub-cultural Capital*, Cambridge: Polity.

Tierney, J. and Hobbs, D. (2003) *Alcohol-Related Crime and Disorder Data: Guidance for Local Partnerships*, London: Home Office.

Toch, H. (1992) *Violent Men: An Inquiry into the Psychology of Violence*, 4th ed., Washington, DC: American Psychological Association.

Tombs, S. (2002) 'Review Article: Understanding Regulation?', *Social & Legal Studies*, 11/1: 113–133.

Tomsen, S. (1997) 'A Top Night: Social Protest, Masculinity and the Culture of Drinking Violence', *British Journal of Criminology*, 37/1: 90–102.

Town Centres Limited (2001) *West End Entertainment Impact Study: Final Report, 2001*, London: City of Westminster.

Travis, A. (2005) 'Public Opposes Licensing Change', *The Guardian* 26 January: 10.

Tuck, M. (1989) *Drinking and Disorder: A Study of Non-Metropolitan Violence*, Home Office Research Study No. 108, London: HMSO.

Turney, E. (2005) 'Trade Says No to ADZs, but Yes to Binge Plans', *Morning Advertiser* 18 August, 258: 1.

Turvil, A. (2003) 'Introduction' in A. Turvil (ed.), *The Which? Pub Guide 2004*, London: Which? Books.

Urban Task Force (1999) *Towards an Urban Renaissance*, London: E&FN Spon.

Urry, J. (2000) 'City Life and the Senses' in G. Bridge and S. Watson (eds.), *A Companion to the City*, Oxford: Blackwell.

Valentine, G. (1989) 'The Geography of Women's Fear', *Area*, 21/4: 385–390.

Valverde, M. (2003) 'Police Science, British Style: Pub Licensing and Knowledges of Urban Disorder', *Economy and Society*, 32/2: 234–252.

Valverde, M. and Cirak, M. (2003) 'Governing Bodies, Creating Gay Spaces: Policing and Security Issues in "Gay" Downtown Toronto', *British Journal of Criminology*, 43/1: 102–121.

Van Maanen, J., Manning, P. and Miller, M. (1989) 'Series Editors Introduction' in J. Hunt, *Psychoanalytic Aspects of Fieldwork*, Qualitative Research Methods, series no. 18, Beverley Hills, CA: Sage.

Vasey, D. (1990) *The Pub and English Social Change*, New York: AMS Press.

Vogler, R. (1991) *Reading the Riot Act: The Magistracy, the Police and the Army in Civil Disorder*, Milton Keynes: Open University Press.

Von Hirsch, A. and Shearing, C. (2000) 'Exclusion from Public Space' in A. von Hirsch, D. Garland and A. Wakefield (eds.), *Ethical and Social Perspectives on Situational Crime Prevention*, Oxford: Hart Publishing.

Wade, W. and Forsyth, C. (2004) *Administrative Law*, 9th ed., Oxford: Oxford University Press.

Wakefield, A. (2000) 'Situational Crime Prevention in Mass Private Property' in A. von Hirsch, D. Garland and A. Wakefield (eds.), *Ethical and Social Perspectives on Situational Crime Prevention*, Oxford: Hart Publishing.

Walker, A. (2001) *Safer Doors: A Training Guide for Professional Door Supervisors*, Geddes and Grossett: New Lanark.

Walker, D. (2001) *Heroes of Dissemination*, Swindon: ESRC.

Walkowitz, J. (1992) *City of Dreadful Delight: Narratives of Sexual Danger in Late-Victorian London*, London: Virago Press.

Warburton, A. and Shepherd, J. (2004) *An Evaluation of the Effectiveness of New Policies Designed to Prevent and Manage Violence through an Interagency Approach (a Final Report for WORD)*, Cardiff: Cardiff Violence Research Group.

Warr, M. (1990) 'Dangerous Situations: Social Context and Victimization', *Social Forces*, 68: 891–907.

Watt, P. and Stenson, K. (1998) 'The Street: "It's A Bit Dodgy Around There": Safety, Danger, Ethnicity and Young People's Use of Public Space' in T. Skelton and G. Valentine (eds.), *Cool Places: Geographies of Youth Cultures*, London: Routledge.

Webb, S. and Webb, B. (1903) *The History of Liquor Licensing in England Principally from 1700 to 1830*, London: Longmans, Green and Co.

Weber, M. (1949) *The Methodology of the Social Sciences*, Glencoe, IL: The Free Press.

Wechsler, H., Davenport, A., Dowdall, G., Moeykens, B. and Castillo, S. (1994) 'Health and Behavioral Consequences of Binge Drinking in College: A National Survey of Students at 140 Campuses', *Journal of the American Medical Association*, 272: 1672–1677.

Wedel, M., Pieters, J., Pikaar, N. and Ockhuizen, T. (1991) 'Application of a Three-Compartment Model to a Study of the Effects of Sex,

Alcohol Dose and Concentration, Exercise and Food Consumption on the Pharmacokinetics of Ethanol in Healthy Volunteers', *Alcohol and Alcoholism*, 26: 329–336.

Weightman, G. (1992) *Bright Lights, Big City: London Entertained 1830–1950*, London: Collins and Brown.

Weir, A. (1984) 'Obsessed with Moderation: The Drinks Trade and the Drink Question (1870–1930)', *British Journal of Addiction*, 79: 93–107.

Wellborn III. O. (1991) 'Demeanour', *Cornell Law Review*, 76: 1075–1105.

Wellman, F. (1997) *The Art of Cross-Examination*, 4th ed., New York: Simon and Shuster.

Wells, S., Graham, K. and West, P. (1998) ' "The Good, the Bad, and the Ugly": Responses by Security Staff to Aggressive Incidents in Public Drinking Settings', *Journal of Drug Issues*, 28/4: 817–836.

Werthman, C. and Piliavin, I. (1967) 'Gang Members and the Police' in D. Bordua (ed.), *The Police: Six Sociological Essays*, New York: John Wiley and Sons, Inc.

Whyte, W. F. (1943) *Street Corner Society: The Social Structure of an Italian Slum*, Chicago, IL: University of Chicago Press.

Wikström, P.O. (1995) 'Preventing City Centre Street Crimes' in M. Tonry and D. Farrington (eds.), *Building a Safer Society: Strategic Approaches to Crime Prevention, Crime and Justice: A Review of Research*, Volume 19, London: University of Chicago Press.

Williams, R. (1998) 'Erving Goffman' in R. Stones (ed.), *Key Sociological Thinkers*, Houndmills: Palgrave.

Williams, R. (2000) *Making Identity Matter*, Durham: Sociology Press.

Williams, S. and Bendelow, G. (1998) *The Lived Body: Sociological Themes, Embodied Issues*, London: Routledge.

Wilson, G. (1940) *Alcohol and the Nation*, London: Nicholson and Watson.

Wilson, J. and Kelling, G. (1982) 'Broken Windows', *Atlantic Monthly*, March: 29–38.

Winlow, S. (2001) *Badfellas: Crime, Tradition and New Masculinities*, Oxford: Berg.

Winlow, S. and Hall, S. (2006) *Violent Night: Urban Leisure and Contemporary Culture*, Oxford: Berg.

Wolkomir, J. and Wolkomir, R. (2001) 'When Bandogs Howle and Spirits Walk', *Smithsonian*, January: 38–44.

Worpole, K. (1992) *Towns for People: Transforming Urban Life*, Buckingham: Open University Press.

Worpole, K. (2003) 'Second Thoughts on the 24-Hour City: Memorandum by Ken Worpole', *Office of the Deputy Prime Minister: Housing, Planning, Local Government and the Regions Committee—The Evening*

Economy and the Urban Renaissance, EVE 33, London: The Stationery Office.

Worpole, K. and Greenhalgh, L. (1996) *The Freedom of the City*, London: Demos.

Wright Mills, C. (1970) *The Sociological Imagination*, Harmondsworth: Penguin.

Wrottesley, F. (1930) *Letters to a Young Barrister*, London: Sweet and Maxwell.

Wynne, D. and O'Connor, J. (with statistical analysis by D. Phillips) (1998) 'Consumption and the Post-modern City', *Urban Studies*, 35/5–6: 841–864.

Young, I. (2000) *Inclusion and Democracy*, Oxford: Oxford University Press.

Znaniecki, F. (1934) *The Method of Sociology*, New York: Farrar and Rinehart.

Index

Administrative tribunals
quasi-judicially, acting 216
Agency
structure, and 255
Alco-pops
development of 59
Alcohol
ambivalent attitude to 125
binge drinking 7
collective rituals of mass
consumption 127
consuming in safety/danger 126–128
consumption, externalities 145
consumption levels, impact of
210–211
discounting 113–114
disorder related to 4
drinking practices, historical and
cultural specificity 86
harm related to
evidence and policy 210
government and industry,
relationship of 262–263
information disparity 211–213
licensing applicants, approach of
213
literature reviews 211
reduction strategy 209–210
research evidence, inability to
access 213
individual responsibility 209
night-time incidents related to 140
permitted hours for sale of,
former 41
public debate agenda 210
related crime, literature on 210
social harms associated with 5
socially acceptable approach to 5
trade organizations, guidance
from 152

UK and European drinking cultures,
differences in 128
uses and meanings, comparative
analyses of 128
young people, attitudes of 125–126
Alcohol Disorder Zones
designation, proposal for 8
Anti-social behaviour
errant consumers 152–156
government policy 6
Avoidance behaviour
night-time economy, concerns
of 124
perceived risk associated with 124

Brands
awareness as double-edged
sword 187
building 47
consumer loyalty, development
of 48
development 47–48
high street 48–50
national awareness 187
outlets, branded 48

Cities
land uses, mixing 160
medieval, night in 25–29
mixed-use residential and leisure
districts 145
night, at, public safety 45–47
nightlife of 259
noise nuisance 146–147, 161
parking, lack of 147–150
politico-regulatory change in 14
public nightlife, development
of 29–30
rats 146
restless 145–147

Cities (*Cont.*)
 traffic congestion 147–150
 24-hour, creation of 45
 urban night, view of 44–45
Consumers
 brand loyalty, development of 48
 criminalized 155
 errant 152–156
 licensed premises, expectations of 127
 personal responsibility 155–156
Corporate social responsibility
 credentials, attempts to establish 74–78
Counsel
 advocates, partiality of 178
 argument pool 183
 arguments, framing 181–183
 bartering between 248–249
 clashes between 241
 client, duty to 251
 cross-examination, view of 249–250
 defensive strategies 232–233
 differential competencies 252
 differential skills 263
 evidence, understanding 241
 fees 253
 language games, playing 229–233
 licensing, specializing in 177
 occupational morality 178–180
 outcome of trial, emotional investment in 249
 precise answers, questions requiring 234
 preparation for battle 180–183
 scripts, writing 181–183
 selection of 252
 testimony, extraction of 178
 tour, on 253–255
 trial, running 176–178
 witnesses, dealing with 228
 words as tool of 179
Courts
 administrative function 215
 criminal, classic studies of 266
 fairly, requirement to act 216
 night, contestation of 256

Crime
 alcohol-related, literature on 210
 local governance 264–267
 prevention, objective of licensing system 271
Crime reduction
 proposals to assist, applicants offering 74–78
Criminal procedure
 ethnographies 16–17
Curfew
 enforcement 27
 medieval Europe, in 26–27

Dance culture
 death of 59
Dangerous work
 persons involved with, occupational culture 134–135
Darkness
 fear of 21–22
 forces of 22
 pranks and hauntings at 24–25
 uses of 23–25
Department for Culture, Media and Sport
 Drinking Responsibly, consultation document 8
 licensing jurisdiction 3
 licensing policy aims 3
 ministry of fun, as 3
Disc jockeys
 joyful restraint, construction of 98–100
 music policy, manipulation by 99
 musical styles to avoid 99–100
 negotiation and emotional management by 101
 night-time economy, roles in 98
 personal safety 101
 play lists 102
 requests, dealing with 100–102
 social practice, reflexive form of 99
 wrong music, playing 99

Entertainment
 public, licensing 31; *see also* Public Entertainment Licence

Expert witness
analytical rigour, absence of 245
attributes of 237
author as 275
boundary work 239
choice of 241–242
client's expectations on 242
competent performance, elements of
    280
conflicting opinions 172
court
    duty to 242
    role in 277
courtroom experience 277
craft, learning 280–282
credentials, review of 233
differential skills 263
discrediting 248
dress 280
emotions, control of 234
examination of 233–242
hearings dominated by 253
hearsay testimony by 239
instructions to 243
knowledge claims, attacking
    238–242
language of 237
licensing trials, in 170–173
negative evidence of 246–247
negative evidence, providing
    172–173
number used 253
objectivity 243
omissions by 244
organization of evidence 244–245
persons being 171
pre-trial briefing 275
presenting and defending
    report 281
previous clients, lists of 246
primary sources of information,
    uncovering 239
professional world of 247
script 234–236
tour, on 253–255
undue bias 246
visits by 275–276
work of 172

written statement 275
written work by 243

Halloween 24
Happy hour
origin of 77
Health education
campaigns 209
High street
honey-pot effect 134, 138
licensed premises on, *see* **Licensed
    premises**
night, at, *see* **Night-time high street**
Human ecology
market forces 2

Interactionism
pragmatic orientations 255
skills, resources and capacities,
    of actors 256
strategic 257

Judicial review
fear of 265
redrafting of policy through 265

Land uses
mixture of 160
Licence holder
personal character of 168, 184
Licensed premises
admissions procedures 92
behaviour of customers, control
    over 81
    bar service 84
    blind spots 83
    conflict, management and
        diffusion of 104–111
    design and operation of premises
        115
    design, presentation and
        maintenance of premises,
        relevance of 82
    door staff, use of 106,
        110, 118–119
    ejection 110–111
    gift drinks, use of 109
    individual elements of 114

Licensed premises (*Cont.*)
  informal 115
  licensees and managers,
    by 105–106
  lighting 83–84
  manners 107–110
  negotiations, failure of 110–111
  non-aggressive responses 107
  physical aspects of 82–85
  regulars, assistance from 88, 115
  self-regulation 87
  separation of protagonists 108
  social aspects 85–89
  staff, violent encounters with
    customers 104
  team effort, as 116
closing time 111–114
corporate estates
  business development
    plans 77
  location, importance of 60–62
  methods used by 63–64
  site, securing 62–76
crowds, efficient processing of 83
cumulative impact 5, 53–58
description in 1930s 83
development of 39
discounting drinks 113–114
disorderly conduct within 186
door staff
  selection of customers for
    admission 81
  use of 106, 110, 118–119
extra policing, levy for 8
falling attendance 58
female-friendly design features 83
feminization 112
food, provision of 113
functional apartheid 132
gentrification 113
growth in number of 5
high street
  admissions procedures 92
  chaotic running of 116
  circuit 90
  closing time 111–114
  communication in 97–98
  concentration of 134

conflict, management and
  diffusion of 104–111
consumer expectations,
  exploiting 127
dancing in 119–120
description of night- and
  lunchtime in 116–121
disc jockeys, role of, *see* **Disc jockeys**
dress 118
drug-related issues 96
entertainment in 93
entry, control of 118
feminization 112
formal control, imposition
  of 91–93
house rules 91, 127
intoxication and control,
  balancing 115
joyful restraint, construction of
  98–100
limits of intoxication, policing 96
marketing methods 127
mood manipulation in 98–104
niche nights in 103
non-managerial staff 105
operating practices 90
over-stimulation of
  customers 98–99
panic button systems 97
personal authority in 105–106
poor entertainment in 98
regulars 90–91
rule-setting in 105–106
security staff in 95
selection of staff 105
short-changing, accusations of
  108–109
social control 93–94
staff teams 93–94
staff, violent encounters with
  customers 104
theft or loss in 108
toilet areas, surveillance in 96–97
vigilance 94–98
impression management 115
introduction to 86
limits of intoxication, policing 96
local problems, giving rise to 186

local pubs 85–89
location, importance of 60–62
Mass Volume Vertical Drinkers
    in 84
municipal control 39
on-licences, transfer of 71–73
on-street environment differing
    from 187
open-plan space 84
operating schedules 42
overcrowding 83
permitted hours for sale of
    alcohol 41
planning permission for 40
proposals to assist crime reduction,
    applicants offering 74–78
protectionism 64–65, 70
Public Entertainment Licence, *see*
    Public Entertainment Licence
public safety issues 55
purchase and stock-piling 71
regular base, serving 86–87
regulars venue 87
security roles within 82
security techniques 81
simplified system for 42
site, securing 62–76
social environment 85
spatial agglomeration 56
special occasions licence 41
special removals 71–73
surroundings, relationship with 116
swamping 88–89
territoriality within 87–89
traditional English pub 85
violent incidents within 94–95
Licensing
appeals 271
applications, *see* **Licensing
    applications**
contestation of night, central to 159
crime prevention, objective of 271
cumulative impact 53–58
de-regulation, externalities
    accompanying 261
democratic deficit 267–269
Department for Culture, Media and
    Sport, jurisdiction of 3

extended hours
    back door de-regulation 52
    case for, scepticism concerning 6
    conflict as to 10
    crime reduction by 4
    effect of 52
    endorsement, lack of 4
    growth of 69
    licensing application, arguments
        in 209
    mitigation of effect 9
    police objections to 51
    policy of 3
    political mood swing 6
    Portman Group, report of 51
    story of 50–53
    strict criteria, former 51
litigation 10, 16
need, concept of 53–54
new positions, public opposition
    to 7–8
new system 42–44
objectors 55
old system 39–41
planning, lack of co-ordination with
    73–74
policy
    aims 3
    development of 3
    Home Office and DCMS, rift
        between 7
    licensing authorities, statement
        from 42
    public debate 6–7
protectionism 64–65, 70
residents, views of 268
restrictive, effect of 4
social actors 16
social mores and regulatory
    concerns 11
urban governance, as tool of 31–32
Licensing applications
advisory service, need for 269
alcohol-related harm, approach
    to 213
applicants 167–169
attack arguments
    attribution 207–208

Licensing applications (*Cont.*)
    consumer demand 192–194
    Darwinian market 195–197
    denial of impact 202–203
    destination venue 200–201
    dismissal of legitimacy 203–205
    extended hours 209
    functional segregation 201–202
    mature circuit 199
    public interest 194–195
    public safety 197–199
    reapportionment of
      blame 206–207
    witness integrity 205–206
  conflicting expert opinion 172
  crime control responses, lack
    of 190
  defensive arguments
    competitors' operations, naming
      and shaming 188
    differentiation 188–189
    experts, evidence of 185
    operational issues 184–185
    quality and standards 184–187
    social responsibility 189–192
  evidence
    oral 217
    rules of 216–217
  hearings, format 218–221
  high street chain, by 164
  interested persons 269
  licensing industry, attitude
    of 173
  local community support
    169–170
  objections to
    campaigners 162–163
    issues 160
    leisure industry competitors, by
      166
    local authorities, by 166–167
    noise nuisance 161
    police, from 163–166
    residents' case, preparing
      161–162
  pre-trial shaping of cases 213
  supporters of 169–170
  trial, *see* Trial

  witnesses
    categories of 159
    expert 170–173; *see also* **Expert
      witness**
    integrity, attacking 205–206
    junior staff, omission of 168–169
    licensing consultants 170–173
    local authority 167
    police 164
  see also **Trial**
Licensing authorities
  administrative function 215
  appeal against decision of 44
  discretionary powers, removal of 57
  effectiveness 58
  fairly, requirement to act 216
  grant of premises applications
    by 43
  licensing objectives 42
  magistrates, transfer of powers from
    42
  National Guidance to 212
    departure from 265
  policy
    implementation 264
    legitimacy, questioning 204
    presumption 264
    Statement of 265
  powers of 5
  problems, accused of creating
    206–207
  restrictions, removing 51
  restrictive stance, taking 57
  Special Saturation Policy 43
  Statement of Licensing
    Policy 42
  transfer of control to 54
  uniformity of practice 54
Local authorities
  licence applications, objections to
    166–167

Market forces
  criminogenic environments,
    creating 2

Natural justice
  maxims 216

Night
    creatures of 21–22
    crimes committed at 27
    cultural aspects of 37
    emblems of 30–31
    medieval city, in 25–29
    organization of hours of 33
    regulation, components of 50
    retreat, time of 31
    revelry and celebration at 24
    scores settled at 23–24
    sexual harassment 32
    social life, studies of 23
    space, control of 50
    street lighting, introduction
        of 28–29
    time, control of 50
Night-time economy
    avoidance behaviour 124
    changes shaping 9–10
    consuming in safety/danger
        126–128
    contemporary consumers 125
    disc jockeys, role of 98
    existing literature 12–13
    exploration of 14
    growth of 69
    new directions 13–17
    policy debate 3
    public order, threat to 1
    regeneration of areas 3
    security concerns 124
    urban, ethnography of 89–90
    work-related risk 9
    working in 9
Night-time high street
    attitude on 127
    bar brands on 67
    branded chains linked with 187
    brands, march of 47–50
    collective rituals of mass
        consumption on 127
    competitive market-place, as 76–77
    contemporary, evolution of 14
    creeping licences 70–71
    cultural mores 65
    cumulative impact 53–58
    danger on 260

    dedicated dance or music venues on
        103
    demarcation 15
    democratization, reversal of 260
    de-regulation 78
    disorder and danger on 136–138
    disorder on 15
    expansion 260
    late-night drinking as part of 68
    leisure market, commercial
        exploitation of 91
    licensed premises, see Licensed
        premises
    mass invasion of space,
        encouragement of 60
    meaning 1–2
    mix of people on 90
    night-time economy, salient and
        criminogenic component of 1
    policing
        blind eye, turning 143–144
        duty of care 140–145
        high profile 153
        order, conceptions of 139–140
        persons physically incapacitated 144
        presence, maintaining 141
        problems of 139–140
        resource pressures 140–145
    post-11pm trading 65
    premises 15
    proceeds of 60
    public drunkenness, normative 139
    public spaces 123
    quality of life policing 153
    residential communities, impact on
        145
    rise of 39, 78
    self-regulation 152–154
    special removals 71–73
    spiral of decline 139
    themed and branded venues on 2
    violence on 261–262
Night-workers
    study of 9
Nightclub
    brands 67
Nightfall
    forces of 22

Nightlife
areas, concentration of violence in
136
cities, of 259
cultural history of 260
democratization 36
Leicester Square, in 35–36
local populations, hostility within
135
location, importance of 60–62
music halls 35
offenders 128–129
on-street environment 187
open-air dancing 33–34
opposition to 32
public, development of 29–30
round-the-clock activity,
contestation as to 33
social exclusive 151
Soho, in 34
theatres 35
transport problems 130–131
urban culture, formation of 36
urban government, challenge of 259
variety theatres 35
victims 129–131
Noise nuisance
cities, in 146–147, 161

Parking
lack of 147–150
Personal licence
individuals holding 42
Planning
change of use 73–74
D2 Use Class, premises designated as
74
licensing, lack of co-ordination with
73–74
Police
licence applications, objections to
163–166
research evidence, inability to access
213
Police licensing officers
work of 64, 164–165
Policing
enhanced powers 154

night-time high street, of
blind eye, turning 143–144
high profile 153
persons physically incapacitated
144
presence, maintaining 141
Operation Yellow Card 155
quality of life 153
streets, of 261
Premises licence
conditions 43
grant of 43
noise nuisance, dealing
with 146–147
objectors 55
requirement to grant 264
review 43
venue, for 42
Public Entertainment Licence
application for 40–41
creeping licences 70–71
planning and alcohol licensing, lack
of co-ordination with 73–74
saturation policies 166–167
time limits, removal of 51
West End venues holding 52
Public lighting
effect of 28–29
Public order
night-time economy, threat posed
by 1
Public services
pressure on, alcohol-related
140–145
Public space
avoidance behaviour 124
communal spaces, turned into 123
danger in 136–138
disorder, removing 136–138
inclusive 261
night-time
avoiding 133–136
behaviour setting, as 125
criminogenic purification
138–139
custodianship of 262
fun, zone of 139
negative public perceptions of 15

offenders 128–129
policing 139–145
population of 128
purification 131–133
social instability 126
victims 129–131
night-time high street, on 123
non-exclusivity 132
privatized, critiques of 123
residential areas, around 138
residential, invasion of 150–151
residents as place managers
150–151
social mix in 124
surveillance 150–151
urban 131

Rave culture
drugs, use of 59
political suppression 59
spontaneous partying 58
story of 58–60
suppression of 58–59
Recreational activities
commercialization 76–77
Research
field work 276, 278
interviews 274
methodology 273–282
normative and political dimensions
281–282
settings 274
Risk
exposure to 129

Security
night-time economy, concerns of
124
shopping areas, in 124
Sexual harassment
night, at 32
Social control
leisure environment, in 2
Social order
commercially-imposed 261
conceptions of 2–3
Social responsibility
corporate 152–153

criteria 190
licensing applications, arguments in
185
countering 191–192
Special Hours Certificate
application for 66–67
denial, appeal against 67–69
drinking, for purpose of 68
facilities, provision of 66–69
food and entertainment, applicants
providing 66
planning, and 73–74
revocation, power to seek 65–66
typical holders of 65
Streets
contestation, arena for 14
living, creation of 46
new dynamism brought to 45
public safety 45–47
Structure
agency, and 255

Traffic wardens
night-time 148–150
Trial
administrative 17
adversarial effect 225
adversarial system 175–177, 258,
270
advocacy, cut and thrust of 251
alternative system of adjudication
270–272
applicants and objectors, positions
of 267
arguments, framing 181–183
away teams 253–255
backstage activities 180–181
backstage bartering 248–249
bench
evidence, understanding 241
experiential knowledge, lack
of 240
meaning 175
role of 175–176
conduct of 263–264
conflict, involving 248
counsel, *see* **Counsel**
eventual outcomes 252

Trial (*Cont.*)
  evidence
    hearing in full 223
    hearsay 216
    presentation of 175
    rules of 216
  formality of 219
  hearings, format 218–221
  impression management 220–221
  inequality of contest 268
  inquisitorial 175–176,
    271–272
  interaction, excitement
    of 250
  intimidating nature of 268
  legal process, as 16–17
  licensing
    oral testimony in 217
    rules of evidence in 216–217
    witnesses, *see* witnesses *below*
  objection case, presentation
    of 225
  opportunity to participate in, right
    of 215
  oral and bodily activity of
    participants 219
  parameters of contest 176–177
  partial analysis of 278
  partiality 176–177
  physical violence and warfare,
    likened to 250
  preparation for battle 180–183
  procedural fairness 271–272
  production of credibility 219–220
  professional participants 221–224
  regulations controlling 215–216
  ritual order 227
  scripts, writing 181–183
  seating in 224
  settings for 218–219
  social class dominating 279
  speech exchange systems 219
  success, precarious 256–258
  tactics 262

  winning or losing, about 266
  witnesses
    categories of 159
    character assassination 228–229
    cross-examination 226, 230, 233
    dealing with 228
    defensive strategies 232–233
    discursive control of 230–231
    emotional management 227–229
    evasive 251
  expert, *see* **Expert witness**
    integrity, attacking 205–206
    interactional performance
      237–238
    junior staff, omission
      of 168–169
    language of 237
    lay and professional, differential
      experiences of 215
    licensing consultants 170–173
    local authority 167
    opponents, proximity to 224
    para-linguistic symptoms 226
    partisan 225
    police 164
    professional 221–222
    questioning 225–229
    real people as 222–223
    scripts 181–183, 221, 234
    termination devices 231
    testimony elicited from 252
    uses of 181
    words, counsel directing 229–230

Urban centres
  encroaching development, resistance
    to 161
  land uses, mixing 160
  residential development 160

Witness
  licensing application, in, *see*
    Licensing applications
  trial, at, *see* **Trial**